KISHI
AND JAPAN

The Search for the Sun

BY

DAN KURZMAN

Foreword by James A. Michener

IVAN OBOLENSKY, INC., NEW YORK

© 1960 by Dan Kurzman

Library of Congress Catalog Card Number: 60-9041

First Printing

Manufactured in the United States of America
by American Book–Stratford Press, New York

Designed by Sidney Feinberg

For Mother, Dad and Fritzi

PREFACE

I FIRST MET Prime Minister Nobusuke Kishi in early 1955 when he agreed to let me interview him in connection with a magazine assignment. Mr. Kishi, then Secretary-General of the Democratic Party, was reputed at the time as a rather shadowy behind-the-scenes politician. Thus, I had expected the interview to be even less rewarding than the usual one granted by Japanese leaders, who are traditionally reluctant to speak frankly to the press, particularly to foreign correspondents. But Mr. Kishi, I was rather startled to discover, spoke as openly and unhesitatingly as any politician I had ever questioned anywhere.

It was clear from his answers that he knew what he wanted. He wanted to be Prime Minister. Nor did he make a secret of his conviction that he was without doubt the most suitable man for the job. I was deeply impressed by Mr. Kishi's frankness and his obviously sincere belief in himself and his destiny. He was, I realized, no ordinary politician.

But even more remarkable than his political personality, it seemed to me, was his apparent political transformation. One of General Hideki Tojo's right-hand men only a few years before, he now claimed to be a democrat, in fact, the man who could best further the cause of democracy in Japan. When Mr. Kishi eventually achieved his goal—the premiership —his story, I was convinced, had become as significant as it was fascinating. He had climbed in less than a decade from a prison cell to the top political post in the land. To understand him, it was clear, would be to understand a great deal about the character of Japan, which had made an equally spectacular comeback.

I contacted Michio Kawabe, Public Relations Consultant to the Prime Minister, and told him that I would like to write the biography of Mr. Kishi. I said that I would appreciate his—and the Prime Minister's—co-operation, but promised only to present an objective picture of Mr. Kishi as I saw him. Mr. Kawabe, who possesses a flare for public relations rare among Japanese, replied that such a portrait would do more to help the world comprehend Japan than a "whitewash" treatment. And the Prime Minister agreed. I was thus granted every co-operation. Mr. Kishi devoted many hours of his valuable time to interviews, and, with Mr. Kawabe's help, cleared the way for me to speak with his relatives, friends, and associates. (I found no trouble getting, on my own, comments from his personal and political foes.) Many of the Prime Minister's private papers were also made available to me.

I am extremely grateful to the Prime Minister and Mr. Kawabe for making this book possible. At the same time, I would like to thank the scores of other persons who contributed to its realization. I am especially indebted to my former assistant, Miss Toshiko Matsumura (now Mrs. John Toland), who interviewed, interpreted, translated, searched newspaper files, and helped to edit the book for me. Special acknowledgment is also due Edward Holten-Schmidt, whose counsel on the handling of the book proved invaluable. Editors Charles Criswell and Warren Eyster, and my agent, Ruth Aley, spent many additional hours working with me.

Background information and helpful advice was furnished me by many of my colleagues in Tokyo, in particular Igor Oganesoff of the *Wall Street Journal,* Minako Shimizu Kusaka of the *Pan-Asia News Agency,* Keyes Beech of the *Chicago Daily News,* and Rowland Gould of the *National Broadcasting Company.* My brother Cal, librarian at San Francisco State College, also deserves mention for his suggestions and aid.

My warmest thanks are extended to members of Prime Minister Kishi's family for their contributions to this book: his wife Yoshiko, his son Nobukazu, his daughter Mrs. Yoko Abe, his elder brother Admiral Ichiro Sato, his younger brother Finance Minister Eisaku Sato, and his younger sister Mrs. Toshiko Tsunemitsu.

I am equally grateful to the many friends and associates of Mr. Kishi's who added their recollections to his story: Foreign Minister Aiichiro Fujiyama, Chief Cabinet Secretary Etsusaburo Shiina, Foreign Ministry Press Information Director Shinichi Kondo, Takeshi Akimoto, Marquis

Koichi Kido, Naoki Hoshino, Shinji Yoshino, Gisuke Aikawa, Kan'ichi Nakayasu, Okinori Kaya, Sakai Wagatsuma, Ryoichi Sasakawa (who provided me with his diary of life in Sugamo Prison), General Tadashi Katakura, Yuki Takechi, Dr. Fujii, and Dr. Hiaruzumi.

Others who supplied me with information and facilitated my research were Ambassador Douglas MacArthur II and members of his staff in Tokyo, and officials of the State Department's Far East bureau in Washington; Saburo Okita, Director of the General Planning Bureau of the Economic Planning Agency, Fukuitsu Aoki of the Ministry of Agriculture, members of the Research Section of the Ministry of Education, and many other Japanese government officials in Tokyo and Washington; Ko Yoon Chong and Choo Kee Kang of the Korean Residents' Union in Japan; Munetada Horiuchi and Tetsuya Tanaka of Hitachi, Ltd.; Frederick C. Taylor, President of the American Trading Company in Tokyo, Walter E. Morgan, American educator in that city, Dr. Felix Moos of the department of anthropology at the University of Washington, and Dr. Hirotatsu Fujiwara of the political and economic department at Tokyo's Meiji University.

To the many others not listed here who assisted me, I offer no less appreciatively my sincerest thanks.

DAN KURZMAN

Tokyo, Japan
March 1960

FOREWORD

IN RECENT YEARS there have lived in Tokyo many American journalists who have applied themselves diligently to the study of Japanese life, and the work of these distinguished writers has done much to improve the world's understanding of what goes on in Japan. Rarely has a foreign country had better friends than the American writers who have worked in Tokyo.

Among this able corps of students, one has enjoyed a rather special privilege. Dan Kurzman is a tall, intense, good-looking, intelligent young man. He has what is known in the trade as "The eye of the Ancient Mariner," that is, he fixes his gaze unalterably upon anyone he is talking to, and stays with his probing questions until he gets a satisfactory answer. I rather think that the special privilege which he came to enjoy grew out of this unusual trait of staring down the opposition.

For when I first met Dan Kurzman he told me the unlikely yarn that he had become friends with Japan's Prime Minister, Nobusuke Kishi, and that he was determined to write a biography of this extraordinary leader. I remember replying, with my customary keen insight into world politics, "Kishi can't last another month. By the time you get a book done, he'll be forgotten."

Kurzman fixed me with his unyielding eye and replied, "Nobusuke Kishi is going to be in office for three more years at least, because he is the only man that can hold Japan's wild and weird political life together."

This assurance staggered me, so I blurted out what was really on my mind: "Dan, I don't believe that Prime Minister Kishi will ever take you into his confidence. Why should he choose you and not the men from the *New York Times* or *Time?*"

My attack did not embarrass Kurzman, and he replied, "Because I like to talk with the man. I like to listen to his stories. And I think I have convinced him that I think he is a great man."

The next week a great scandal broke over the Kishi administration. A smart newspaper photographer hid himself among the shrubbery at a leading geisha house and took shot after shot of the cabinet's long black Cadillacs lined up night after night while their owners were inside playing around with the girls.

"This finishes Kishi," I announced confidently to Kurzman. "When these photographs get into the Japanese homes, your boy is bound to be a dead duck."

"Oh, no!" Dan protested. "You watch. This incident is going to back-fire on the newspapers and Kishi will come out stronger than ever before."

What actually happened is history. Every Japanese scrambled for the damning photographs, studied them carefully and concluded, "Well, if *that's* the way our cabinet is spending its spare time, it must be a pretty good cabinet after all." Precisely as Kurzman had predicted, the people of Japan rallied around Kishi and returned him to power with increased majorities.

When there were riotous fist fights in the Diet, surpassing any that had occurred before, most of the Americans whispered and wrote, "This finishes Kishi." Dan Kurzman explained to me: "Kishi is only letting them blow off steam. The worse they look, the better he looks." And again he was right.

A few months later, when student rioters prevented the scheduled visit of President Eisenhower to Japan, I expressed apprehension that leftist pressure might block final ratification of the United States-Japan Mutual Security Treaty.

"Not a chance," Kurzman assured me. "Kishi will push through the treaty even though he may have to sacrifice his political future to do it. Kishi just doesn't give in on matters involving Japan's best interests."

The treaty went into effect a few days afterward.

After about a dozen of these lessons I became interested in how Kurzman got his understanding of Japan, and particularly of Japan's contro-versial leader, Nobusuke Kishi. One night I discovered what the base of operations was. I accompanied him to one of Tokyo's famous night clubs, where the girls are so pretty that you can hardly believe they are real. Dan's entrance was spectacular. It seemed that every girl knew him, wanted to sit with him, wanted to tell him what was going on. When he was called to the phone, five extremely lovely young ladies crowded about me to tell me that Kurzman-san was their hero. They particularly wanted to know if he was married (he wasn't), and if he had ever spoken to me about any of them (he had), and if I thought there was any chance that he might settle down in Japan (on this I was doubtful). Before he returned to my table, the girls said, "Kurzman-san understands and loves Japan. Has he ever shown you the present-o that Prime Minister Kishi gave him?"

I replied that he hadn't, so when Dan came back to the table I asked to see it, and with some pride he produced it, and a thought came to me then which has persisted until this day: "If a man is respected both by the Prime Minister of a nation and by its prettiest night-club hostesses, he knows something about that nation that the rest of us ought to know."

I am proud to have the opportunity of presenting Dan Kurzman's book on Japan to the American reader. For Kurzman-san is a good example of the kind of young men who have spent the last dozen years working diligently to understand parts of the world which were once called foreign. Today Japan is only a few hours away from Hawaii or Alaska. The problems of Japan are so intimately our problems that we can never again call this island nation foreign.

And in choosing Nobusuke Kishi for the subject of this biography of recent Japanese events, Kurzman-san has selected an enigmatic, powerful, delightful man, once the sworn enemy of the United States, once a common jailbird sentenced by United States authorities, and today one of the most thoughtful and persuasive friends we have in the world. I am glad that Kurzman-san did not choose to write about some Japanese who had worked with us in the days immediately after the capitulation of 1945. Such a Japanese, no matter how fine a man he might be, would always be suspected of having yielded to American pressure.

Kishi has finally resigned from the premiership, but in matters of policy he has yielded to nobody. He is a true Japanese, a product of a militaristic state who has progressed into radically new understandings. I have always admired Kishi because he has been so conspicuously able to grow. I am happy that other Americans can now know more about him.

JAMES A. MICHENER

Bucks County
Pennsylvania
July 1960

CONTENTS

AUTHOR'S NOTE

Nobusuke Kishi resigned the premiership of Japan on July 15, 1960—
"a casualty of the strength of his own convictions," as Ambassador
Douglas MacArthur explained it. Kishi's central conviction has been that
Japan can only remain free and prosperous as a close friend and ally of
the United States. Thus, the revised United States–Japan Mutual Security
Treaty that went into effect on June 23, 1960, after months of rioting and
demonstrating by Japanese leftist-led minority groups, is his monument,
living and vital. The demonstrators forced the cancellation of President
Dwight D. Eisenhower's visit to Japan, dealing Kishi a politically fatal
blow. But his monument, it may be hoped, shall long outlive his personal
defeat.

If Kishi had not pressed so forcefully for the pact, his term in office
might well have been prolonged. But ambitious though he has always
been, he would not sacrifice what he considered the best interests of his
country for his own benefit. True to his character, he courageously condemned himself to political death for the sake of Japan, just as he risked
assassination in 1944 when, as a member of General Hideki Tojo's war
cabinet, he precipitated Tojo's fall in order to pave the way to peace.
Now, as then, Japan has come first.

Kishi, in a sense, is a tragic figure. One of his most cherished dreams
was to win the affection of the public. But as a party colleague said,
"Kishi has become a scapegoat. He has taken on his own shoulders the
hate against conservatives, the hate against America, the hate against
everything." At the same time, many people, with Hiroshima seared into
their minds, have never forgiven him for his ultra-rightist past.

Yet Kishi, who was stabbed in the thigh by a rightist fanatic the day
before his resignation in final ironic tribute to his reformation, has amply
repaid his compatriots for the disaster he helped loose upon them less
than a score of years ago. In the three-and-a-half years he was in office,
Japan, under a democratic system, took giant strides toward the goals he

xvii

had set for it, however obscured this progress may have been by the violence of extremist mobs representing only themselves. In addition to reinforcing its long-range security through conclusion of the Mutual Security Treaty, the country achieved unprecedented prosperity and a highly respected position in the community of nations that was once its mortal enemy. Kishi, in successfully converting himself from a fascist leader and war-minded samurai into a democratic premier, has proved indeed one of the most remarkable men of his time.

The termination of his regime in no way reduces the significance or poignancy of his story. For one thing, as an Elder Statesman, he is likely to continue playing an influential role in government, particularly in view of the succession to the premiership of the candidate of his choice, Hayato Ikeda. Ikeda, a man of considerable character and ability, was once a staunch political foe of Kishi, but, as Minister of Trade and Industry in the Kishi cabinet, developed a deep respect for his chief and has indicated he will carry out his policies.

But even more important, Kishi's story is the story of Japan. And it shall become ever more meaningful as Japan, despite all obstacles, gradually makes its way to the sun along the new and challenging democratic path it has chosen.

KISHI AND JAPAN

The Search for the Sun

PROLOGUE

THE SENATORS ROSE from their brown leather chairs and, turning toward the door, burst into thunderous applause as their guest entered. From the packed galleries rimming the Senate chamber came added thunder. A short, slightly built man strode swiftly down the aisle, flanked by Senators Lyndon Johnson, William Fulbright, Alexander Wiley, and William Knowland. Though he tried to restrain his smile by pressing his thick, sensuous lips together, he finally broke into a broad, uninhibited grin.

The ovation continued as the guest and his escorts took their places at the speaker's table at the foot of the dais. Behind the dais, the Vice-President, outlined against a large American flag that hung between two brown-marble columns, picked up his gavel, and the flat, insistent noise of wood striking wood sounded over the din, which gradually tapered off into silence. The Vice-President said: ". . . Our honored guest is not only a great leader of his own people, one of the greatest leaders of the free world, but also a loyal and great friend of the people of the United States. . . ."

Prime Minister Nobusuke Kishi of Japan, neatly dressed in a black suit and gray tie, rose amidst renewed applause and moved to the rostrum that stood at the center of the marble-surfaced table. He laid his notes down and removed from his inner coat pocket a pair of black tortoise-shell glasses, which he slowly put on. He stood for a moment

1

and waited for the applause to end, fingering his tie, almost too nervous to contemplate the scene that stretched before him like a great trembling Japanese fan. His half-moon eyes seemed to reflect the irony of the occasion. Only a few years before this same chamber had declared war on Japan. Now, on this hot June day in 1957, some of the very men who had participated in that act were honoring him.

When quiet was once again restored, Kishi, his long, thin face outwardly calm except for slightly quivering jowls, began his address, pausing now and then so that an interpreter could translate his Japanese into English.

"Mr. President and honorable members of the Senate: I am deeply grateful for your warm reception and cordial welcome. You have accorded me a great honor today—the honor of speaking in this living citadel of democracy. It has been a thrilling experience for me to drive up Capitol Hill to this time-honored hall. It is an inspiration to me to stand on this rostrum which has witnessed the evolution of the modern democratic process of government, thus providing the pattern for new democracies, including my own country. Today, Japan is endeavoring with pride and resolution to consolidate the foundations of a truly democratic government. The whole effort of our nation is dedicated to this task, for we believe in the lofty principles of democracy—in the liberty and dignity of the individual.

"It is because of our strong belief in democratic principles and ideals that Japan associates herself with the free nations of the world. We are ranged on the side of liberty, justice, and equality because there can be no true peace, no true security, no true progress, nor true human happiness unless men and nations live by these principles. In all our Free World relations, our association with the United States is to us the most important. We are grateful to your country for the generous aid we have received since the war in restoring our shattered economy. We believe that our friendship, our mutual respect and trust, and our bonds of cooperation must ever be strong, especially in these times when tensions persist in many parts of the world. . . . We firmly believe . . . that the democratic method is the only way to serve the happiness of mankind. We must prove that we are right. . . ."

When Kishi finished his speech, he bowed stiffly, and the audience gave him a long final standing ovation. He took off his glasses, put them back in his pocket, and gathered up his papers. Then, with his escorts clearing a path for him, he made his way up the aisle, to be engulfed by a crowd of newspapermen waiting for him outside the chamber. Pausing for a moment, he told them, "I was all wound up while I was making my speech. . . . But as I ended, there was a great applause, and I felt overwhelmed. I am deeply moved at the friendly and cordial reception I received."

Sixteen years earlier, on December 1, 1941, Nobusuke Kishi, clad in morning coat and striped trousers, had been present at another political gathering. This one took place in the Palace in Tokyo—an Imperial Conference attended by members of the Japanese government in the presence of Emperor Hirohito. The group waited in almost total silence for the Emperor's arrival, sitting at a table which extended lengthwise from the Imperial dais at one end of the red-carpeted room.

The chamber was somehow stifling even though cool, wintry air sifted in through a window. A look of almost unbearable anticipation was imprinted on every face, however anticlimactic any discussion might now be, as each man read and re-read the few words of inked writing on the paper that lay on the table before him: "Agenda—(1) The negotiations with the United States have finally failed of consummation; (2) Japan will commence hostilities against Great Britain, the United States, and The Netherlands."

Only Prime Minister General Hideki Tojo, a shaven-headed man with a thick black mustache and round glasses, who sat at the end of one of the two rows of men in the seat nearest the dais, seemed to display no interest in the document. He had issued it. Kishi, seated in the opposite row toward the other end of the table, observed him with admiration —this haughtily erect figure in high-collared khaki uniform, his eyes alternately reflecting restless impatience and deep, fervent thought. The General had the air of a man supremely sure of himself and acutely conscious of the historical importance of the moment. He seemed oblivious of the presence of his colleagues, who included members of the Cabinet, the Chiefs and Vice-Chiefs of the Army and Navy General Staffs, the Chief Secretary of the Cabinet, the Directors of the Military and Naval Affairs Bureaus, and the President of the Privy Council.

Finally, the door opened, and the Emperor, wearing the beribboned uniform of the Grand Marshal of the Army, entered. His subjects stood up and bowed toward him in unison. He nodded, then hurried to the dais and sat down, the signal for the others to follow suit. Tojo rose, and, facing the Sovereign, whose eyes were unfathomable behind a pair of thick black-rimmed spectacles too large for his pale, drawn countenance, started speaking, calmly, confidently, occasionally stealing a look at the notes piled on his desk:

"With His Majesty's permission, I shall manage today's proceedings. On the basis of the Imperial Conference decision of November 5th, our Army and Navy have devoted themselves to the completion of preparations for their operations, while the government has made all possible efforts to readjust diplomatic relations with the United States. The United States, however, not only does not recede a step from its former contentions, but has now begun to demand unilateral concessions by us, adding such new requirements as unconditional and wholesale military evacuation from China, withdrawal of recognition of the Nanking government, and abrogation of the Japan-Germany-Italy Tripartite Pact.

"If we submit to these demands, not only will the honor of the Empire be lost, and any prospect for successful conclusion of the China Affair vanish, but our very existence will be threatened. It is, therefore, clear that we cannot gain our contentions by diplomatic means.

"On the other hand, the United States, Great Britain, The Netherlands, and China have recently increased their economic and military pressure on us; this, in consideration of the state of our national strength, as well as of our strategy, has resulted in a condition in which we cannot passively watch developments. Things having reached this point, we have no recourse but to go to war against the United States, Great Britain, and The Netherlands in order to surmount the present crisis and to preserve our existence. . . ."

Though all the men present had expected to hear what Tojo had just said, the actual pronouncement somehow produced a sense of shock. A glow of exhilaration brightened every face. All lingering doubts were, at least for the moment, dispelled. This wasn't a time for reason or logic, but for faith in the gods. One official after another took the floor to confirm what Tojo had said.

Foreign Minister Shigenori Togo, the muscles in his angular, mustached face twitching slightly, said in reference to the note received a few days before from Secretary of State Cordell Hull, presenting America's terms for a peaceful settlement of the Far East question, that, "all things considered, the proposal is utterly intolerable for Japan, and we must recognize that unless the United States withdraws it almost in its entirety, there is no possibility of realizing our claims by negotiation. Upon the basis of the present proposal negotiation is impossible."

The Ministers of Agriculture and Forestry and of Finance, the Chief of the Navy General Staff, and Tojo again, in his capacity as Home Minister, expanded on this theme. The President of the Privy Council, Yashimichi Hara, representing the Emperor, finally concluded that "it having come to this, I think that there is no alternative to resorting to arms."

Within an hour after the meeting started, an aide went from seat to seat with a neatly inked resolution that read: "Our negotiations with the United States regarding the execution of our national policy adopted on November 5th have finally failed. Japan will open hostilities with the United States, Great Britain and The Netherlands."*

When this resolution of war was handed to him, Nobusuke Kishi, Minister of Commerce and Industry, dipped a brush into a bottle of ink and, in delicate Chinese calligraphy, appended his signature to it.

* The Japanese government decided to designate only the United States and Great Britain as enemies in the final Imperial Rescript of War issued right after Pearl Harbor.

CHAPTER I

❧§❧

THE BROKEN CAGE

NOBUSUKE KISHI is a man who has lived twice—once in a world of sword-bearing ghosts that was more dream than reality, and a second time in a world of humble mortals shocked awake from their dream when it exploded into a nightmare. Kishi has been a guiding influence in both worlds. He is also a product of both, reflecting, in all its delicate tones, the complex character of Japan. Like his country, he has experienced a conversion from totalitarianism to democracy almost as incredible as the conversion of St. Paul.

Kishi was born (as Nobusuke Sato) in Yamaguchi Prefecture in southwestern Japan, an area bristling with the chauvinistic samurai tradition, when Japan was just beginning to flex its modern military muscles. Yamaguchi is the home of the great Choshu clan, which, in samurai days, constantly rebelled against the national authority, and in the years of Westernization following the visit of U. S. Commodore Matthew C. Perry in the middle nineteenth century, directed the miraculous transformation of feudal Japan into a major world power.

Kishi's unusual face, high-lighted by pixy-like oversized ears, a weak chin, and large lips that struggle to conceal a protruding upper set of teeth, deceptively offers little hint that he is a man of stubborn, dynamic nature. And yet he has many of the characteristics of his strong-willed, rebellious, sometimes ruthless Choshu forefathers. Like them, he tends to be coldly pragmatic in pursuing what are often idealistic

7

ends. Before and during the Second World War, the compulsive ideal of Japan's "divine" destiny temporarily overcame his powers of reason. But with Japan's loss of Saipan, Kishi, facing the cruel reality of defeat, courageously sparked Tojo's overthrow at the risk of his life; and when he emerged from a war criminal's prison cell in 1948, Kishi set out to realize a new ideal that had crystallized during his three years' confinement—a strong, democratic Japan. Today, hardly a dozen years later, he is regarded as "one of the greatest leaders of the Free World" by the nation he once vowed to destroy. The Japan Society of Washington nominated him for the 1959 Nobel Peace Prize, and the International American Institute has awarded him a Silver Academy medal "in recognition of (his) efforts to promote world peace."

But if Kishi is representative of the new Japan, he has by no means abandoned the old, at least in a cultural sense. He is a strange, almost freakish hybrid, partly traditional, partly modern, a confused mélange of East and West. He is seldom seen without a scotch and soda at Western cocktail parties, but he still likes to sip sake poured by giggling geishas kneeling beside him on the *tatami,* or matted, floor. He loves nothing more than a filet mignon smothered in mushrooms, but he will go out of his way to visit a restaurant that serves *nasu no karashi-zuke,* or pickled eggplant, a specialty of his native Yamaguchi. He enjoys watching a baseball game, but not any more than a *sumo* wrestling match between two crouching giants with topknot hairdos. As my guest at a party held at the Tokyo Foreign Correspondents' Club one night, he appeared to enjoy the modern entertainment, which featured several bare-bosomed young women, but he is also an ardent enthusiast of the classical *Kabuki* dance, performed with modesty and sensitivity.

Kishi's home, located on a narrow, nameless street in the Shibuya district of Tokyo, is a concrete embodiment of the contradictions that constitute his life. It is a modest eight-room, two-story yellow stucco structure with a tile roof that, from the outside, resembles a Western house, just as many aspects of culture in postwar Japan appear deceptively alien from an exterior angle. But in Japanese fashion, a stone wall conceals the house from view, guaranteeing privacy and preserving the intimate, unworldly atmosphere necessary for communion with nature in the front garden, a painstakingly arranged composition of azalea and camellia bushes, slender pines, dwarfed fir trees, and stone lanterns.

Once inside the wooden front gate, the visitor follows a gravel road skirting the garden and leading to the house. He exchanges his shoes for a pair of slippers in the cement-surfaced entranceway and, taking one step up into the house proper, is ushered by a maid wearing a kimono into a small Western-style reception room. Here can be found several brown leather chairs and a matching sofa, a black bear rug stretched on a red carpet, a large cellular-shaped *hibachi,* or charcoal burner, filled with sand, a portable gas heater (there is no central heating in the house), a tea table on which rests a silver cigarette and cigar box (Kishi chain-smokes inexpensive Japanese Ikoi cigarettes and Havana-Corona cigars) inscribed by Australian Prime Minister Menzies, a corner table decorated with a pair of glittering crystal candlesticks, two glass cabinets containing ivory, porcelain, and wood-carved figures, and on the wall, a huge Japanese black-ink landscape painting and autographed photos of Prime Minister Nehru of India, President Sukarno of Indonesia, Pope John XXIII, and President Eisenhower.

Kishi's small study is also a Western-style room, with desk, easy chairs and sofa, a large reproduction of a *Time* magazine cover, featuring himself, on the wall, and a bookcase that includes such English-language books as *Winston Churchill* by Robert Lewis Taylor, *Modern Democracies* by James Bryce, *American Democracy and Military Power* by Louis Smith, *Principles of Political Economy* by John Stuart Mill, and *USA—the Permanent Revolution* by the editors of *Fortune* magazine. Many Japanese books also fill the shelves, notably several volumes on the life of Yukio Ozaki, a famous Japanese politician who had courageously preached democracy before and even during the war. There is also a book in German—*Seventy-Six Years of My Life* by Hjalmar Schacht, who, as Minister of Economy in the Hitler government, was Kishi's wartime German counterpart.

But the rest of the house is entirely in the Japanese tradition, with smooth-grained polished hall floors, sliding door panels, virtually no furniture, and three-inch-thick yellow blocks of *tatami* which stretch in each room from wall to paper wall. Upstairs in his bedroom, Kishi sleeps on two heavy quilts, called *futon,* spread on the springy matting, with a third quilt used as a cover. After bathing in a deep, sunken, gas-heated tile tub in his tiny bathroom, he retires at about eleven P.M., usually reading for an hour by the light of a little lantern-shaped lamp on the floor next to him.

In another room, in an alcove, is located the *butsudan,* a lacquered shelf on which rests the image of a Buddhist deity, representing family unity, and also several thin white-wood ancestral tablets inscribed with the names of the family dead. Kishi, a Buddhist but not strongly religious, prays here only on special occasions, such as his birthday, but his wife, Yoshiko, a slender, retiring woman with a gentle, motherly face, kneels before the *butsudan* altar daily, lighting a candle on it each time. A *kamidana,* or Shinto god shelf, can be found in an alcove in still another room. A plain, unpainted wooden structure, it serves simply as a decoration now, and as a reminder of a once cherished dream, the Shinto dream of glory and empire as symbolized by the sacred paper talismans from local and national shrines contained in it.

When at home, Kishi, dressed in kimono, spends most of his time in the combined living and dining room, where he sits on a cushion before a square foot-high sandalwood table, his legs, covered by heavy embroidered material that hangs from the edge of the table, dangling in a *kotatsu* pit over a charcoal heater. Beside him is a rectangular *hibachi* with a grating on which a tea kettle of water perpetually simmers. In back of him is a little alcove, called the *tokonoma,* in which hangs a *kakemono,* a wall scroll, portraying in subdued water-color the print-like figure of an ancient Japanese sage.

Kishi is likely to have a breakfast here of milk, soybean soup, rice, and fruit, and a dinner (preceded by a scotch and soda, either Johnny Walker Black Label or Old Paar) that might consist of Japanese smoked salmon, caviar, boiled fish, a filet mignon, and coffee. A maid prepares his meals—with the help and advice of Mrs. Kishi—in a large modern linoleum-floored kitchen equipped with a four-burner gas range, a big refrigerator, an electric toaster, and an electric mixer, all produced in Japan. The cabinet space available for pots, pans, dishes, and supplies would delight the American housewife. When Prime Minister, Kishi normally had lunch out, Western food in his office in downtown Tokyo (where prime ministers work but do not live), or a quick meal of rice and noodles in his Diet Building office when the Diet is in session.

Sitting at the dinner table, in addition to his wife, will be his son and private secretary, Nobukazu, his daughter-in-law, Nakako, and their one-year-old little boy, Nobuo, who live next door in the same compound in a house separated from Kishi's by a tiny rear garden. Nobuo is actually the third son of Kishi's daughter, Yoko, and her husband, Shintaro Abe, the Prime Minister's former secretary and now a Diet member. But the child was adopted by Nobukazu, who had had no son of his own to carry on the Kishi family name.

Political discussion is never permitted to sully the relaxed atmosphere of home. Table conversation is strictly confined to family affairs, the latest *sumo* wrestling sensation, and other small talk. After dinner, Kishi, if he doesn't have work to do in his study, plays with his beautiful brown-spotted Russian wolfhound or bounces his infant grandson in his lap while watching television—usually news or sports programs. A seventeen-inch set is situated just across the room from the dinner table, a convenience which is not entirely appreciated when the Abe boys, Hironobu, seven, and Shinzo, five, insist on watching American cowboys swear vengeance on each other in perfect dubbed-in Japanese.

The intimacy of such homely scenes is seldom diluted by the presence of visitors, except perhaps for relatives like Finance Minister Eisaku Sato, who is Kishi's younger brother. (Kishi is one of ten children—seven girls and three boys.) There is a larger adjoining room for the entertainment of close friends. And when very important people pay a call, particularly foreign leaders on state visits to Japan, they are treated to tea in an exotic teahouse nestled in the greenery of the front garden. The visitors are led along a path of steppingstones, past several stone lanterns, to a fence of long, thick bamboo stalks held together by wisteria vine. They pass through a gate composed of slender bamboo stems arranged in diagonal crisscross fashion, with wisteria wound around each joining, then through a second bamboo gate over which arches a wooden shrine-like structure, and finally into the heart of Kishi's isolated little inner world, where one can experience a few moments of spiritual peace and perspective.

The teahouse, which exquisitely expresses the intricately contrived simplicity of traditional Japanese architecture, is made of unpainted cedar and has a sharply slanting roof of pressed thatch partially covered with tiles. Bamboo is used for benches along the outside walls and for decorative purposes. A wooden sign above the entrance says in white-painted characters, *Kizankyo,* meaning Mount Ki House, after a mountain in Manchuria, where Kishi first made a name for himself as one of the men who built up the industry of that region in prewar days. (It is also the name he uses to sign poems he writes for his family and friends.) Inside the teahouse, the guests sit cross-legged on cushions on the matted floor while Kishi and his wife, both highly trained in their respective roles, perform the Japanese tea ceremony in an atmosphere of meditative silence and contentment.

Most visitors, however, are ushered into another, larger yellow stucco house next door, used for official purposes, where they wait and sip tea in Japanese and Western-style rooms while the Prime Minister dashes from one to the other, keeping his appointments. In the main reception room, there is a bronze bust of Kishi, and a baseball, mounted on a silver holder, signed by the Milwaukee Braves team when Kishi visited the United States in 1957. In another room is stored parchment paper and large brushes which Kishi, who is an expert in Chinese calligraphy, uses to paint characters, usually expressing a poem, for friends or for his own enjoyment. The Prime Minister, when he had this "official" house built shortly after his release from Sugamo Prison, made sure that it was large enough to accommodate many guests, for, in Japan, politicians conduct their business in their homes, and the more people who call on them, the greater is their social prestige and political standing.

Kishi reflects the double cultural standard of his country. Japan, like him, is a peculiar mixture of two worlds. It is a nation in restless ferment, seeking new directions and outlets for its great spiritual and physical energies, yet not quite certain how far or how fast to go. The new Japan is great concrete apartment houses fitted out with special sliding doors one inch higher than the traditional standard for the accommodation of taller Japanese youth, and small, doll-like homes composed entirely of wood, paper, and bamboo; futuristic office buildings, supermarkets, and department stores, some with almost solid fronts of glass, and tiny shops with removable wooden walls that permit wares to be displayed on the street; block-square manufacturing plants equipped with the latest machinery that turn out everything from ships to pocket-size transistor radios, and primitive home factories where parts for these products are made by hand in the glare of a naked light bulb; one-acre rice-paddy farms and gigantic hydroelectric schemes feeding them the lakes of water they need.

Kishi's Japan is also diaper services, such as the International Mothers & Babies, Inc., founded by a geisha, and babies held by a sash on their mothers' backs; the craze for bigger busts, which are accentuated by tight sweaters, immodestly cut Western gowns, and sometimes by paraffin injections, and the age-old practice of binding the chest to emphasize the vertical lines of the kimono (which is often cut low in back to expose the nape of the neck, the traditional focal point of Japanese sex appeal); luxurious restaurants offering the finest Russian, Mexican, Hungarian, French, German, American, Italian, Swedish, and Chinese food, and minuscule *tempura* establishments where the customer sits at a counter on a bamboo stool while the proprietor plops morsels of fried fish on his plate as fast as they are consumed; kimono-clad department store mannequins with blonde hair and blue eyes, and billboard advertisements showing black-haired, brown-eyed Japanese girls blissfully sipping Coca-Cola; broad tree-lined boulevards clogged with traffic directed, in the evening, by dancing goblins—paper lanterns swung by invisible policemen—and winding, gravel alleys where the rich live; Western operas with Japanese singers awkwardly dressed in period costumes and powdered wigs, and ancient *Noh* dramas performed with flowing robes and grotesque masks; theater-size night clubs where stunning hostesses in evening gowns play the role of the modern geisha, and shoebox sake bars with Western names like *Tennessee* and *Ma Chérie;* Christmas lavishly celebrated with all the trimmings—except Christianity—and irreverent strip-teasers tauntingly shedding nun's clothing.

If Japan since the war has changed drastically in an outward, physical sense, this change is only the reflection of a deeper one that has taken place under the surface. Western blood today, with Kishi at the pumping station, flows through its social, economic, and political veins, gradually washing away the ancient roots of a rigidly hierarchal society. These roots began withering with the arrival of the first Occupation troops, as Japan converted itself overnight from an arrogant, aggressive nation into a humble country only too willing to co-operate with the conqueror. There is no simple explanation for this sudden transformation. But one might be found in the traditional respect with which most Japanese, conditioned by history, regard constituted authority, from whatever source it may emanate. This respect had been reinforced by the Emperor's command that his people obey the victors, as well as by the sense of shock and awe born of the realization that the Sovereign would have to take orders from a power greater than himself. With this realization, the people suddenly found themselves left with obsolete moral values and little ethical perspective.

Thus, they used their old values, the only ones they knew, as a basis for establishing new ones. Tradition dictated that any policies and methods that served the interests of Japan were moral, while, conversely, any that failed were immoral. The Japanese considered it only logical to accept defeat and adopt the standards of the nation that, by winning the war, had proved their worth. And this decision hardened as America exerted its authority, not to exploit or humiliate Japan, but to rebuild it, if according to unfamiliar concepts.

Still, it will not be easy eliminating all of the feudal customs that for so many centuries have constituted the foundation of Japanese society. This traditional social structure is as intricate as it is deeply rooted, with every individual fixed in his place on the basis of class, occupation, family position, age, and sex. Like tiny springs or screws fitted into a wrist watch, the human parts are held in place by a complicated network of interlocking obligations called *on*.* The Japanese has traditionally received his most important *on* from the Emperor, his parents, and his ancestors, with whom tight bonds of indebtedness are woven at birth. His repayment for their goodness, called *chu* in the case of the Emperor and *ko* in that of the parents, is required constantly and throughout life in the form of absolute obedience and devotion. In addition, repayment of *giri,* which is of less importance, and for that reason usually more difficult to bear, is due his in-laws, relatives, teachers, and all acquaintances who have ever bestowed upon him the slightest favor or gift. Further, he owes it to his family, his ancestors, and himself to repay his debts to everybody else, and to clear his name when it has been besmirched, however insignificantly, by proving his detractor wrong, taking revenge on him, or sometimes by committing suicide. He is also required to maintain strict self-discipline. He must never outwardly express "human feeling," or *ninjo,* particularly in the presence of strangers, though the Japanese are among the most emotional and sentimental people in the world. *Ninjo* is channeled into a separate compartment of life, quite separate from the sphere of obligations, and manifested through such forms of expression as poetry, art, and love-making with a mistress, prostitute, or occasionally with one's wife.

The obligation that ties the Japanese to his benefactor has little in common with that which Westerners may feel toward each other. A Japanese obeys his parents not necessarily out of love, or even respect or fear, but because of the unwritten contract into which he enters at birth. Though his in-laws may willfully jeopardize his interests, he still owes them *giri* simply by virtue of the fact that they are his in-laws. He may despise someone who has done him some minor favor in the past, but he must repay this favor in full. Moreover, each *giri* repaid must be the exact equivalent of the *on* incurred, for if the debtor underpays he remains in debt, and if he overpays he becomes the creditor. He cannot pay too soon after incurring the debt, either, for this will give the impression that he wants to end the relationship quickly, and will be taken as an insult. Since it is the nature of life that one debt usually leads to another, the Japanese is never really free of an *on*. At the same time, new obligations constantly accumulate.

So ponderous is the Japanese burden of indebtedness that a person will

* The Japanese system of obligations is fully described in *The Chrysanthemum and the Sword* by Ruth Benedict.

often go to great lengths to avoid debt-binding relationships, a tendency that is sharply reflected in the reluctance of most Japanese to give gifts and grant favors, or to accept them, except on special occasions such as the New Year or a wedding.

Once the Japanese acquires an obligation, shirking it is out of the question, for this would result in loss of "face," and bring down upon him the wrath and ridicule of the community. If the violation is important enough, his friends and acquaintances would not even associate with him, and his own family, whose name he has tainted, would all but disown him. The dread of social ostracism is great indeed, for in Japan the recognition and respect of the community is the very sustenance of a man's soul. It may be an ordeal for Kishi and his compatriots to live in the cage of debt in which they are trapped, but it is far harder for them to live outside it. Not many years ago, the daring few who did were called *hinin,* meaning "not men," and were doomed to the fringe life of beggars, prostitutes, wandering musicians or actors.

The powerful influence of the community on each of its members is aptly symbolized by a ceremony that takes place on festival days in every town and village in Japan. A small portable shrine attached to long wooden rods is carried on the shoulders of a great mass of youths who run wild in the streets, pushing, shoving, yelling, as if each were engaged in a personal tug of war with the others, moving in one direction and then in another, threatening to trample anybody foolish enough to be in their way.

In theory, the participants do not determine the direction they take. The god hidden behind the draperies of the miniature shrine does. Before the war, in many villages, if the god directed his supporters into any particular house along the way, they would literally wreck it, stamping upon and breaking up everything in sight. For the wild, irascible movements of the young men represented a heavenly search by the god for those who defied the will of the community, a defiance that could take the form of a dishonest act, or even a marriage involving a woman considered unsuitable for the husband. The residents of any house into which the young men bearing the shrine entered had to pay for their "crime" with the destruction of their furnishings and belongings. Few of the victims would dare add to the anger of the god—and the community—by seeking legal recompense.

Today, instances of village ostracism, or *murahachibu,* are still fairly common. In one case involving a dispute over mushroom-gathering rights, five families who fought against the majority were subjected to the traditional form of rural justice, with even the children forbidden to have anything to do with the dissidents. However, the latter rebelled, as they probably would never have done in prewar days, and took the issue to court. In 1958, the Supreme Court ruled that *murahachibu* constitutes a collective act of blackmail, a criminal offense. But though the guilty parties were given prison sentences, it isn't likely that the principle of ostracism will disappear overnight.

The blight of community disapproval or ridicule, even if not carried to the point of ostracism, is so great that the community itself sometimes tries to save the violator from such a fate by pretending to ignore that a violation has taken place. A clerk who worked for a Tokyo concern was caught stealing company funds, thereby facing the prospect, not only of a jail term, but of bringing disgrace to his family. He had ignored *giri* to his family name. His superiors, however, considered such a punishment too severe, and instead, promoted him to a higher position that did not require him to handle money. As long as the crime was not acknowledged by the company, he would be able to maintain "face" and an unblemished family name.

The stress on group conformity in Japan illuminates the difference between the traditional Japanese and the Western concepts of honor. Whereas honor means to the Westerner proper behavior as dictated by his conscience, regardless of what the community advises, it means to the Japanese proper behavior as dictated by the community, which *is*—though less so today than before the war—his conscience. Honor is thus mainly a matter of reputation, or of *giri* to one's family name.

This is why Kishi's samurai ancestors did not hesitate to slay their families or themselves whenever this was the only way to assuage the anger of their lord. This is also why few Japanese soldiers permitted themselves to be taken prisoner during the war. Capture meant disgrace, the cutting of all bonds with society. Paradoxically, those who were captured suddenly found themselves free men, released from all the pressures and obligations that had previously held them. By suffering the disgrace of capture, they had taken themselves beyond the realm in which moral law, as they had learned it, operated. As a result, many of these once fanatical fighters, to the astonishment of their captors, overnight turned informer on their military units and unhesitatingly offered statistics on troop concentrations, tank strength and other vital matters, seeing no moral stigma attached to such conduct.

On the international plane, Japan's craving for recognition by the world community was no small factor in the molding of its aggressive military past. In going to war against a materially more powerful foe, Japan, under such men as Kishi, was determined to demonstrate the invincibility of the Japanese spirit, and therefore its "right" to dominate Asia, and eventually, perhaps, the whole world. Japan was proud to attack the combined might of the United States and the British Empire. But when it brought upon itself the dishonor of losing a war to these "inferior" nations, it no longer felt tied to the society of ghosts in whose name it had fought and offered its conquerors, after the war, without any moral qualms, complete and sincere co-operation, much as did the captured soldiers during the war.

The crushing weight of *on* has by no means been lifted since the war, but it has been considerably lightened, with people beginning to look at their social debts in less absolute terms.

Fissures in the tightly assembled Japanese social structure have perhaps been least conspicuous on the industrial level. Until the Occupation, a few octopus-like family-owned combines, called *Zaibatsu*, controlled Japan's economy. Under Commerce and Industry Minister Kishi, these *Zaibatsu* (the two largest, Mitsui and Mitsubishi, produced more than forty per cent of all Japanese goods) had played a vital role in financing and fueling the war. They were not only economic giants, but great social organizations within themselves, modern industrial versions of the old but unforgotten feudal clans. The head of the *Zaibatsu* ruling family was, to all intents and purposes, the lord; the executives were the samurai retainers, and the workers were the serfs. Each group was indebted in various ways to the others, which virtually eliminated, for one thing, a labor turnover. The *Zaibatsu* was a twentieth century industrial plant superimposed on a nineteenth century feudal society, and the result was chaotic inefficiency, with mass production possible only because of the sheer weight of the labor force and profits possible only because of the cheapness of this labor.

After the war, General Douglas MacArthur broke these gigantic combines, as part of his democratization program, into smaller independent industrial units. Many of these units have, in recent years, with Kishi's help, reassociated with each other; but such co-operation is along far looser lines. There is today nothing comparable to the lordly family which in prewar Japan had owned ninety per cent of the combine's stock. At the same time, while archaic production methods, exaggerated paternalism and company loyalty, and sheer waste still exist in modern Japan, considerable improvement is being made.

A far more important breach in Japan's feudal structure has already been achieved on the family level. The marriage in April, 1959, of Crown Prince Akihito and Michiko Shoda, a commoner, shows that young people today have much greater freedom to make their own decisions—especially in the choice of a mate. Akihito met his future Empress on a tennis court and took the initiative in getting her accepted as his bride by the royal household after having coaxed her to agree to the marriage. This represented a complete break in Imperial tradition, as well as in Japanese tradition in general. For a Japanese youth to pick his own wife, and for the girl to feel free to accept or reject him, was considered before the war an unpardonable disregard of *ko* to one's parents. Kishi, for example, was engaged to his future bride when both were still children, and had nothing to say about it. In the rare cases of elopement that did occur, the couples found themselves isolated from their families and society. Japanese volcanoes were the traditional burial pits for forlorn lovers.

Even today such tragic endings are not entirely a thing of the past. But the situation is rapidly changing, particularly in the major cities. A system of municipal matrimonial bureaus reflects, in microcosm, the new attitude toward marriage. Though by no means the usual method of matchmaking, these bureaus, run by bureaucrats who are as sentimental in the sphere of family relations as the central government is tough in the field of foreign relations, have, since the war, brought together thousands of mateless men and women. Anyone can apply for a husband or wife. The applicant fills out a form indicating the type of mate he or she wants— physical characteristics, education, family background—and then waits for a letter indicating what is available along the specified lines. Men are usually more particular than women. They can afford to be, for war casualties have left Japan with a preponderance of the weaker sex. Highly significant of the new view on marriage, most men request women with high school educations, although before the war few thought their mates should be educated in anything but housework. Today, many Japanese men prefer woman who have had experience working, feeling that a wage-earning background could come in handy in an economic crisis. In prewar days working girls were considered undesirable as wives.

The principle of *ko* has by no means been forgotten in this governmental scheme for helping young people find each other. The parents of the applicants must sanction a match before the principals involved, if they should approve of each other, can contract a marriage. Indeed, no one can even apply for a marriage partner without parental permission, and it is generally the parents who make out the applications for their young. In the initial meetings that take place between two prospective mates in the bureau offices, the parents are usually present to ease the embarrassment and to make appraisals. The families sit on opposite sides of the room, smiling at each other over cups of tea and occasionally commenting on the weather, as if the meeting were entirely without significance. After about fifteen minutes, the couple and their parents rise, bow to each other, and go on their ways. Later, the parents announce to the young man or the young woman their opinion of the other family. But while they can veto a match, they cannot force their offspring to continue a relationship.

The fact that the Japanese woman today has more than a little to say about the choice of a husband indicates the tremendous advance they have made toward social liberation. In prewar Japan, women were brought up to live either in a world of rice-pots and diapers, or of flowered fans and white-powdered faces: the docile, hard-working housewife, or the coquettish mistress, geisha or prostitute.

The wife cooked for her husband, washed his clothes, brought up his children, stayed out of the way when his men friends came over for a talk, never complained about her sexual frustration, never asked her husband where he had been the night before. On the other hand, the husband had not only the privilege, but also the added prestige of having a second woman. Her duties were to satisfy his quest for pleasure and for beauty, to make erotic love with him, give him baths in deep sunken tubs designed for two, to walk with him in the garden amidst majestically miniature trees, and pluck for him the strings of a *koto* or *samisen*.*

The Japanese man, a heavy creditor in his relations with women, thus satisfied his appetite for both domesticity and sensual excitement by having highly trained specialists in each of these spheres. This dual role of Japanese women reflected the divided personality which the Japanese considered the male as having. The Japanese woman could be a fine wife or a fine instrument of pleasure, but not both. The Japanese man, however, with his ambivalent appreciation of both the domestic and the romantic, assumed that it was his privilege to have both, and felt no conflict. He would have been shocked if his mistress had tried to interfere in his domestic life. He would have been astonished by any display of jealousy on the part of his wife.

This is how it was before the war. Many women still fall into one of these two categories, but a third kind of woman can be found in the Japan

---

* The *koto* is a lutelike stringed instrument played kneeling on the floor, and the *samisen* resembles a mandolin.

Kishi has helped to build, one who has mastered some of the essentials of both groups. She has a spirit of individuality that has canceled much of the indebtedness she previously felt to men. This spirit was born during the war when young women tasted independence for the first time working in arms factories, ironically manufacturing guns and grenades for use against those who were to give impetus to their emancipation. And it was nurtured in no small degree by the example of liberal Western social tradition during the Occupation.

Japanese girls were not oblivious to the way battle-hardened American colonels were pushed around by their demanding wives, nor did they miss an opportunity to learn about life in America as pictured by Hollywood—the power of the female through controlled use of her sex, the glamor of divorce, the virtues of unfaithfulness. But they also learned that a woman could be educated without necessarily losing her femininity, and that men and women could share common topics of conversation at social gatherings (though Japanese ladies, still unused to their new status, tend to remain demure and silent at mixed affairs).

The sudden shock of this overnight change has severely shaken the family strata of the Japanese social structure, understandably fostering certain evils; for example, an increasing number of prostitutes and cabaret hostesses, and a soaring divorce rate. At the same time, however, women today have voting privileges, equal legal status with men, the right to enter all state universities (one out of every five university students is a girl). More than twenty women sit in parliament, more than three hundred, in municipal assemblies. There is even a woman mayor. Girls from the finest families are today working in offices and department stores, though in many cases doing little more than serving tea for executives, while others are bus conductors, usherettes and elevator operators.

The inter-class wedding of Crown Prince Akihito and Michiko Shoda underscored another lesion in Japan's social network—the altered relationship between the Imperial family and the people. With a commoner now a member of the royal family, the spiritual aura that has traditionally surrounded the Emperor and his family has virtually disappeared. Faith in the divine origin of the Emperor had already been severely shaken when the Emperor himself, under orders from General MacArthur, had denied his divine ancestry. Only the most loyal subjects had remained firm, arguing that the Emperor had made the disclaimer under duress. But the recent marriage, which means that future Emperors will have commoner blood, represents a final rejection of the theory that the Sovereign is infallible and the source of all good.

On New Year's Day, endless lines of people twist their way through the magnificent gardens, past the swan-decorated ponds, and over the arched bridges of the Imperial Palace grounds in Tokyo, where they gather in a huge grassy interior plaza to catch a glimpse of the Emperor as he greets them with languid waves from the balcony of a small structure specially built for the purpose. As the Sovereign appears, an almost awkward silence settles over the crowd, embarrassingly broken by scattered, hesitant applause. Someone cries out, "That's him. He looks just like his picture, doesn't he?" Smiling parents lift their children up to see the gentle little man with the large eyeglasses. Photography enthusiasts stand on large rocks or boxes to snap a picture of him. Schoolboys chew on bean-paste candy. Visiting American sailors chat with pretty girls dressed in their colorful holiday kimonos.

Such a scene could not have been imagined in prewar days, when the Emperor's rare appearances elicited hysterical cries of *banzai!*, set off an orgy of bowing, and produced radiant looks on the faces of people who thought themselves touched with a magic wand. Today, the greater part of the population esteems and loves him, and, now that he is viewed as a common mortal, with an intimacy that never existed when they worshipped him as a distant spiritual image. But most Japanese, particularly the youth, feel a sense of obligation toward him hardly more binding than the *giri* due an in-law.

The prewar leaders of Japan were just as obligated to obey the Emperor as anyone else, and if the Sovereign had flatly declared himself against the war, their hands would have been tied. But typical of the vagaries of Japanese tradition, he would not have done this even though he may have desired to, for while he, alone among all Japanese, is, theoretically, indebted to no living mortal, he feels a sense of obligation toward Imperial tradition almost as strong as that felt by his prewar subjects toward him. And Imperial tradition calls for him to follow the advice of those responsible for his protection. The militarists, therefore, enjoyed a double advantage when they agreed to go to war. Imperial sanction of the decision was virtually automatic, and the sanction of the Emperor meant the unanimous support of the public.

Official policies get automatic Imperial approval today, exactly as they did when Tojo was in command, but this no longer means overwhelming public sympathy for them, for the Sovereign's stamp of approval is now recognized as the simple formality it is. Whereas up to V-J Day the people received *on* from the government, the representative of the Emperor, the government now receives *on* from the people.

Kishi has always been more rational in meeting his obligations than most Japanese, never repaying his debts blindly, but first deciding whether such repayment might conflict with a higher, if less concrete, obligation. When he directed the industrialization of Manchuria in the 1930's, for what he considered the good of Japan, he stripped his uncle, Yosuke Matsuoka, who was President of the South Manchurian Railway Company, of much of his power in the Japanese-controlled state. And when Tojo asked Kishi to resign from his cabinet post to ease his own political position after Japan started suffering reverses in the war, Kishi, though indebted to Tojo for his rapid promotion, refused to obey, on the grounds that if Tojo remained in power, he would prolong the war to the detriment of the nation.

No less important than Japan's domestic revolution has been the change in relationship between Japan and Southeast Asia. Japan's pre-war conception of itself as a "superior" nation led its leaders, Kishi among them, to believe that it had the moral right, as well as the economic need, to dominate the other countries of Asia. Thus Japan tried to establish a hierarchal Greater East Asia Co-Prosperity Sphere parallel in structure to the Japanese internal social order, with itself at the top. When the other nations refused to co-operate in organizing such a community, Japan, which genuinely believed it was acting in the interests of all concerned, turned upon them with the same vicious intolerance, only more brutal in form because of the lack of environmental controls abroad, that was directed toward Japanese who refused to fall into the local community mold. The Japanese did not understand the rights of individuals, nor of individual nations.

Today the Japan of Kishi realizes that it can only partake of Asian "co-prosperity" if all its neighbors are treated as equals. The Japanese are more understanding of relationships with their wartime "inferiors." Unbegrudgingly, Japan is paying them heavy reparations for war damage, giving them technical aid, training their students in Japanese schools, and investing quite heavily in their development projects. When President Garcia of the Philippines visited Japan in 1958, he was welcomed so warmly that one of his aides sighed, "I only wish we were treated like this at home."

This change in attitude is neither a contradiction of Japanese character, nor has it hidden motives of future Japanese ambitions. Japan is pursuing some of the same ends that it hoped to accomplish before the war. It has the same economic need to develop the Southeast Asian nations and thereby enlarge the market for trade. The difference is merely that the

Japanese now realize that this can be done more effectively by peaceful democratic means.

Thus, internally and externally, Japan's traditional concept of hierarchy and the chains of obligation needed to assure its rigidity are gradually being overhauled—with Kishi one of the mechanics. The same Kishi who not many years ago kept Japan's economy going with raw materials stolen from its neighbors. The irony of the situation is obvious.

However that may be, the sudden switch of Kishi—and Japan—from one world to another, has been nothing new. Japan has drastically shifted philosophies and political systems in the past. Opportunism? Perhaps. But based on the sincere conviction that the nation had to change in order to advance itself. Kishi, too, seeks Japan's advancement, but no longer within the distorted context of a false and tragic dream.

CHAPTER II

SHAPING OF THE SWORD

JAPAN'S PRESENT EFFORT to import Western institutions, ideas, and technology almost faster than they can be absorbed represents one of the most spectacular cultural revolutions in history. But Japan itself does not find this great face-lifting operation a phenomenon, for it has abundantly demonstrated in the past its ability to swallow foreign civilizations whole and adapt them to its own ends. This does not mean that Japan has borrowed more from abroad than other nations have. France is hardly an undiluted concentration of Gallic institutions, nor does modern Italy greatly resemble the Holy Roman Empire. The United States is an even more undefinable mixture of cultures. Japan, indeed, can boast of greater cultural purity than most countries. Its traditional religion, art, architecture, and literature, while containing alien influences, are as unique as any in the world. But Japan has been singled out as a nation of borrowers because of the conspicuous nature of its borrowing process.

Other states have changed gradually, almost imperceptibly. Japan has done so in concentrated spurts. Intermittent periods of national insulation have been followed by the wholesale introduction of foreign products and concepts. From the seventh to the ninth centuries, the nation imported Chinese culture on a vast scale, converting itself from a primitive, anarchic clan society into a feudal empire of refined tastes and rigid moral standards with a deep awareness of its national identity. Then, in the nineteenth century, after living for a thousand years in medieval seclusion, it

24

brought in Western technology with equally little restraint, and transmuted itself within a few decades into a highly industrialized state.

In both cases, revolution came after contact with more advanced civilizations revealed to a startled Japan, isolated and stagnant, the extent of its backwardness. The shock produced a dynamic force, compounded of fear and pride, that made possible the miraculous feats of adaptation. On the one hand, Japan feared eventual military domination by the advanced countries if it did not learn and use for its own benefit their secrets of power. On the other, it experienced a great surge of national pride, an irresistible desire, nourished by Shinto doctrines, to prove itself the equal, if not the superior, of any other nation.

Defeat in the Second World War has created a pacifism in Japan that has, up to now, ruled out militarism as a factor in the country's present transformation. Pride is still a powerful element, but it no longer can be equated with the egoism and arrogance that were inevitably bred in a people fed on the notion that hierarchy is the natural order of society. Rather, it has, since the war, been primed by the peaceful challenge of rehabilitation, developing, to a large extent, into the kind of harmless vanity that Westerners feel when contemplating their constructive achievements. But if the circumstances of this reformation differ greatly from those surrounding the two previous national metamorphoses, the unique ability of the Japanese to adapt foreign innovations to their own purposes has remained constant. In the nation's past, therefore, lies, to no small degree, the key to an understanding of the Japan Prime Minister Kishi has helped to build.

Japan, prior to the seventh century, was in large measure uncivilized by Western standards. The principal inhabitants were aboriginal Ainus, a Caucasian race that occupied the island areas north of present-day Tokyo, and, from about the first century, immigrants from China, Korea, and the Malay Islands, who settled in southern and central Japan. These newcomers established small clan societies, each ruled by a high priest or priestess. By the fourth century, one great clan, centered in the Yamato Plain in southern Honshu, had won control of central and western Japan and had formed a loose and restless federation of clans under the supreme authority of the Yamato priest-chief.

This primitive clan-nation initially became interested in the flowering culture of China when Korean immigrants—refugees from Chinese oppression, Buddhist monks hoping to convert the Shintoist Japanese, and adventurers who had heard of the rich rice-lands across the sea—brought

with them the system of Chinese characters, which gave the Yamato race
its first means of written communication. Intercourse with China started
with some regularity in the late sixth century when Regent Prince
Shotoku took power in Yamato as the man behind the Throne. (The
concept of a puppet monarch had already been introduced.) Deeply influenced by Korean monks, Prince Shotoku fostered the spread of Buddhism throughout the country. Many Japanese were immediately attracted
to this complex religion, which filled their spiritual needs far more effectively than Shintoism, yet did not conflict with the simple, animistic
tenets of this indigenous faith. The mysterious rituals of the Buddhist
ceremony appealed to the superstitious masses, while the revolutionary
concepts of Hell and Heaven intrigued the intellectuals.

With the advent of Buddhism in Yamato, related aspects of Chinese
civilization flowed in at an ever-increasing rate. One Korean monk, Kwal-
leuk, played a particularly important role in awakening the nation to
China's cultural riches, bringing with him numerous books, never before
available, on customs, art, science and philosophy. While Kwal-leuk's
students dreamed of the day when they might visit the fantastic world
described to them, the Yamato leaders drew up plans for bringing its
benefits to their island nation, tailored to fit Japanese needs. The Yamato
chiefs were convinced that Japan had to raise its standards of civilization
if it were to survive as an independent entity. Only by importing Chinese
culture, they reasoned, could Japan provide itself with the military and
governmental instruments necessary to unite all clans under their control
and build defenses adequate to meet a possible future attack from China.
Aside from such practical considerations, their pride was deeply stung by
the realization that their people were so far behind the Chinese.

In the year 607, a representative was sent to visit the Chinese Emperor
Yang Ti. This was Japan's first formal effort to establish direct contact
with China. In the following year, Shotoku dispatched two priests and two
noblemen to the mainland to study Chinese civilization and bring back a
detailed report. The four scholars returned thirty years later with a
voluminous account of their findings, supplemented by the writings of
innumerable Chinese sages. The stage was at last set for the *Taika*—the
Great Reform. The *Taika* was inaugurated in 645 with the relentless,
systematic approach of a bricklayer building a house. No sooner was a
page of the thirty-year report digested by the nation's leaders than a new
reform was instituted. The Yamato state was converted into an Empire
on the Chinese model, with the reigning high priest promoting himself to
Emperor. The machinery of state administration, embracing the Con-

fucian civil service system, was imported intact, down to the caps and insignia worn by officials to denote rank. Provincial governorships and new systems of law and taxation were created. Land was redistributed on a more equitable basis. Military conscription was introduced. Chinese literature and art, flavored with the Buddhist influence, taught the warrior clansmen appreciation of poetry and delicately composed water paintings.

But Japanese importations were not indiscriminate. The leaders tried to use only what was considered adaptable to Japanese needs and traditions, in some cases rejecting in advance, in others swallowing whole and then discarding what could not be assimilated. The Chinese concept of an Imperial system with overtones of divinity was borrowed, but the notion that each individual Emperor had to demonstrate the virtues expected of the Son of Heaven or else make way for another pretender was rejected, for the Japanese from the earliest Yamato days had been led to believe in the sacredness of the dynasty in power. Japan tried but failed to absorb China's highly centralized administrative system completely, though the fact that so complex a theory of government could be applied at all in this clan-splintered country strongly attested to the nation's capacity for accommodation.

Within a century, most Chinese ideas and institutions had been incorporated in the new Japanese culture, and could, over a leisurely period, be shaped, pruned, twisted, and combined to fit Japanese requirements. Gradually the nation developed a distinctive social structure, governmental system, and art all of its own, a civilization fashioned, like the one budding today, from the most usable products of two worlds.

But this process extended over many centuries, with traditions and innovations often blending, as time went on, only with great difficulty and almost immeasurable slowness. One reason for this diminishing rate of progress was the indifferent attitude of the successive governments to the main purpose behind the Great Reform—political and military unity. The Confucian bureaucracy installed in Japan initially had reduced the power of the individual clans, and their loyalty to the central government might have been permanently secured if the state leaders had followed through with their plans to set up a strong conscript army that could control the clans. However, the Court, under the direction of the Fujiwara family, which ruled the nation in the Emperor's name from the tenth to the twelfth centuries, was more interested in the artistic and cultural imports from China than in the political and military. While Kyoto and Nara, the new Japanese capitals, echoed with the fragile strains of the flute and *samisen* played at sumptuous ceremonial palace gatherings, the rest of Japan resounded with the clash of swords as the various clans met in battle to determine who would take over the decadent central government.

Finally, in the twelfth century, one great feudal chieftain, Minamoto Yoritomo,* won sufficient control of the nation to set up a Shogunate, a dynastic military dictatorship, under which he usurped, as Shogun, the Emperor's powers, though not his Throne. (The Imperial system was inviolate to every Japanese, whatever his politics or ambitions.) For seven centuries thereafter under this dual system of rule the Emperor was kept a virtual prisoner in his castle in Kyoto, almost forgotten by the people. Shogun Yoritomo and his descendants, ruling the Empire from Edo (the original name of Tokyo), managed to keep peace for about a century, achieving unprecedented unity in the thirteenth century when the clans joined together in the face of an attempted Mongol invasion of Japan— the long-feared threat from China had materialized. This invasion failed mainly because of a storm, which is described in Japanese lore as a *kamikaze,* or divine wind, that miraculously sank the Mongol armada.

No longer threatened from the outside, the clans were soon locked in bitter conflict again, and for more than three hundred years the history of Japan was a romantic tangle, told and retold in Japanese poetry, of samurai battles, clan intrigues, and heroic suicides. In the late sixteenth century, there emerged from this perpetual struggle for glory and power a military dictator, Shogun Oda Nobunaga, powerful enough to fasten his control over more than half the country. When he was assassinated in 1582, his lieutenant, Toyotomi Hideyoshi, an even more extraordinary figure, crushed the resistance of the remaining opposition. The son of a peasant, Hideyoshi was a dynamic, courageous man and a military genius. He accomplished the remarkable feat of forcing his way to the top of the stratified, samurai-dominated clan pyramid and then unified the whole country under a single government for the first time in Japanese history.

By the end of the sixteenth century, when Hideyoshi died, Japan had finally completed the process of assimilating what had been borrowed from Chinese civilization. Buddhism had taken deep root, but its philosophical concepts had been modified, with the accent on ceremony and emotional ingratiation rather than on the meditative soul-searching preached by the early immigrant priests. Japanese art and literature had attained a uniqueness in form, even while reflecting the Chinese influence.

---

* Names of Japanese who died before the Meiji Restoration in 1868 will, in accordance with Japanese custom, be used in this book with the family name first.

The Confucian Treatise on Filial Piety, carried to an extreme, had become the social bible of Japan, the carefully forged chain that held the hierarchal feudal society together. And now with the achievement of national unity, the Confucian theory of absolute government could be effectively applied, backed by the most powerful national army in the Far East. Under Hideyoshi's command, 200,000 troops had crossed the straits of Tsushima in 1592 in a brilliantly staged invasion of China and Korea. Although this expedition had failed, largely because of logistical oversights, it was the first clear indication that Japan was destined to play a strong role in the political future of Asia. A new nation, more closely knit than ever before and with a culture in many ways as rich and original as that of the country from which it had obtained its raw material, had emerged.

Then, before the Japanese could reflect on the enormity of their cultural accomplishment, they found themselves agitated by new, entirely unfamiliar stirrings. The first tremors were felt in 1542, when a Portuguese trading vessel landed on the island of Tanega, south of Kyushu. The Portuguese sold trinkets to the natives, who crowded the shore to ogle these strangers from another world. The most curious "trinket" of all to the startled Japanese was the arquebus. From this Japan learned the use of gunpowder.

Seven years later, in 1549, another Portuguese ship anchored in the port of Kagoshima at the southern tip of Kyushu. Again the Japanese turned out to wonder and stare at the visitors. Francis Xavier of the Society of Jesus stepped ashore and remained there to preach to the Japanese something that was to prove even more explosive than gunpowder—Christianity.

By the time of Hideyoshi's death, samurai forces were equipped with arquebuses as well as swords, Japanese Catholic priests, among three hundred thousand converts, were teaching the new faith at the Imperial Court, and commerce had begun with several Western nations. The seeds of a new civilization had been planted. The Japanese were awed by an utterly strange culture that offered at once to save their souls and to destroy their enemies, both with unprecedented dispatch.* Not since the Korean priests of the seventh century arrived in Yamato with boatloads of books on Chinese laws, government, religion, and philosophy had the Japanese imagination been so stimulated. It appeared that a second great era of cultural adaptation was about to begin.

* It is important to remember that Christianity and Western science were simultaneous introductions and therefore resulted in an unintended anachronism.

But if the high priests of Yamato had welcomed the influx of Chinese culture into the country, Hideyoshi had no such kind inclinations toward the infiltration of Western civilization. For one thing, he lacked the motivations that had propelled the Great Reform. Having won control of all Japan, he didn't need innovations from the West to help him attain such a goal. And his armies were, he was sure, now strong enough to throw back any enemy that might be foolish enough to attempt an invasion of Japan, a condition of security that his ancient predecessors had never been able to attain.

Furthermore, he saw little indication that the West could enrich Japanese civilization as the Chinese had done. On the contrary, Hideyoshi believed, Western ideas, unlike those of the Chinese, to be rigid, unmalleable, and resistant to any compromise with Japanese tradition. Christianity, with its absolute moral values, could not adapt itself to assimilation with Buddhism and Shintoism, which judged good and evil on a relative basis. Nor could the Shinto gods, which had come to be considered the reincarnation of Buddha, ever be accepted as the reincarnation of Christ. Christianity preached that all men were equal, and that loyalty to Christ was a greater moral obligation than loyalty to one's feudal lord—concepts that could destroy Japan's hierarchal web. Also, Hideyoshi thought, not without some justification, Christian missionaries were not just priests, but political agents for the Western governments.

Hideyoshi, having convinced himself of the dangers of Westernization, banned the spread of Christianity and, while permitting the development of foreign trade, controlled such commerce carefully to make sure that Japan would profit from it without being corrupted. After he died, another brilliant general, Tokugawa Ieyasu, took over the Shogunate, defeating most of Hideyoshi's followers in a bloody battle at Sekigahara in 1600. He consolidated his control with the fall of Osaka Castle, where Hideyoshi's son had been resisting. Ieyasu, determined to establish a lasting dynasty, decided that the best way to achieve this goal would be to carry Hideyoshi's anti-Western policy to its logical extreme—complete exclusion of all foreign influence. Otherwise, sooner or later this influence would develop into massive cultural infiltration, which, in turn, would mean disintegration of Japan's social system and the Tokugawa dynasty.

Ieyasu and his descendants intensified Hideyoshi's anti-Christian policy, killing and torturing those who refused to disavow the new faith. Persecution reached a dramatic climax in 1637 when a defiant group of Christians, armed with arquebuses, fortified themselves at Shimabara in Kyushu, and, after holding out for a considerable period against sword-bearing Shogunate forces many times their number, were finally slaughtered when they ran out of ammunition. Simultaneously, the Shogun decreed, "For the Future, let none, so long as the Sun illuminates the world, presume to sail to Japan, not even in the quality of ambassadors, and this declaration is never to be revoked on pain of death." With this proclamation, all foreign trade and intercourse, except for the barest commercial exchange with Dutch merchants, was severed. To seal tight Japan's isolation, the government forbade the construction of sea-going ships, prescribed the death penalty for people who tried to leave the country, and denied re-entry to the few Japanese who happened to be abroad. Japan had, to all intents and purposes, seceded from the world.

With the establishment of a stable dynasty as their central aim, the Tokugawa rulers proceeded, with brutal thoroughness, to petrify Japan's social and political structure. All creative tendencies were cruelly suppressed, all existing institutions uncompromisingly frozen. The feudal system was not only retained, but its hierarchy rendered utterly inflexible. Whereas previously the four castes—samurai, peasant, artisan, and merchant—were relatively fluid in nature, permitting, for example, a peasant like Hideyoshi to reach even the position of Shogun, nobody could now shift from one to the other.

The principle of *giri* solidified into the very purpose of living as most people devoted themselves completely to meeting the unavoidable obligations attached to their place in society. This was particularly true of the samurai class. In pre-Tokugawa days, it had not been uncommon for samurai to switch clan loyalties, depending on the material and other advantages involved. Under the Tokugawa, the moral standards among the warriors became so rigid that suicide developed into the natural method of atoning for one's failure or inability to repay a debt to his superiors.

The warrior owed much to his superiors, especially his lord, or *daimyo,* who, for his part, was obligated to support the samurai and his family. The warrior's code of honor, rooted in *giri,* became known as *Bushido,* or the Way of the Samurai. As a Japanese writer, Jukichi Inouye, has described *Bushido,* the samurai "looked upon it as shame to themselves when their lord was hard pressed . . . their own shame was the shame upon their parents, their family, their house and their whole clan, and with this idea deeply impressed upon their minds, the samurai, no matter of what rank, held their lives light as feathers when compared with the weight they attached to the maintenance of a spotless name." The peasant, on the other hand, was indebted to both the samurai and the lord for keeping him, though he often rebelled against their authority. The artisans and merchants were least concerned with *giri,* for, occupying the lowliest ranks of society, they had little family honor to defend.

The extent to which *giri* dominated life was reflected in the pathetic paradox of the *Forty-Seven Ronin,* masterless samurai, a favorite story of most Japanese, including Kishi. At the turn of the eighteenth century, Asano Naganori, Lord of Ako, was insulted by a Shogunate official, Kira Kozuke. To repay *giri* to his name, Lord Asano attacked the latter with his sword, wounding him. But while liquidating one *on,* or obligation, Asano acquired another—from the Tokugawa, whose lieutenant he had assaulted. To repay this debt, Lord Asano had to commit *hara-kiri.*

The story does not end there. Asano's forty-seven samurai retainers, grief-stricken at the death of their lord, pledged to assassinate Kira in repayment of their *giri* to the spirit of their dead master. Posing as drunken, dishonorable *hinin,* or social outcasts, to avoid arousing suspicions of their purpose, they broke into Kira's house and slew him. Having avenged their lord, they ripped open their own bellies in final tribute to the code by which they had lived. For they, like their master, had violated *giri* to their Tokugawa Shogun, and death was the only way out of the paradox.

The inflexibility of the Tokugawa system was mirrored not only in *giri,* but in laws that regulated almost every phase of one's life. Enrollment in a Buddhist temple was mandatory. The cost of wedding presents and the proper size of children's dolls were prescribed. Women were forbidden to employ hairdressers to arrange their hair. The Japanese, a dynamic, adventurous, individualistic people before the Tokugawa period, were, under the regulatory pressures of the government, gradually converted over a period of two hundred and fifty years into docile puppets incapable of acting without reference to the rules of their society.

Only a few clans resisted this relentless pressure toward conformity. Among these were the members of the Choshu clan that occupied southwestern Honshu—the ancestors of Nobusuke Kishi. The proud samurai of Choshu had opposed Tokugawa rule from the first, having been among Ieyasu's bitterest enemies. As so-called "outside vassals," they were isolated from the strategic positions of the realm and subjected to restrictions that were enforced far more strictly than in the case of the more co-operative clans. It was forbidden for the clans to build fortifications. Instead, they had to construct expensive public works which kept them too poor to finance a revolt. To make sure of their obedience the government instituted the world's first efficient secret police system. As further assurance against an uprising, feudal barons had to live part of the year in the Shogunate capital of Edo, and leave members of their families there as hostages during the rest of the year.

The Choshu clansmen grew increasingly restless, not only because they were unable to throw off the yoke of the Tokugawa, but because they found it impossible to adjust to the state of peace that had been clamped on the country. They were warriors without wars to fight. This reflected what was basically wrong with the Tokugawa system. Feudalism was an order rooted in bellicosity and war. Yet, with peace the feudal structure had become more unalterable than ever. The samurai at the top of the class pyramid, unable to practice his occupation, had become a social parasite, a jobless, obsolete figure who could find satisfaction only in dreams of bygone battles fought by his forefathers.

The samurai still had the right, indeed, the obligation, to wear a sword, and he could still use it, without fear of punishment, to cut down any commoner who happened to irritate him. But of what value was this hollow, meaningless privilege when the samurai was deprived of his true military function and reduced in many cases to poverty? He could always squeeze additional levies of rice from the peasants—the Japanese economy was still based largely on this commodity—but such action often invited more trouble than it was worth. The peasants were already overburdened with the demands, decrees, and regulations imposed on them by clan and Shogunate. They were even forbidden to use such minor samurai luxuries as paper raincoats, umbrellas, or perfumed hair oil. Many peasants began to rebel against their masters, despite the certainty of a death penalty, or to flee to the cities, also at the risk of execution, to look for jobs in the myriad of shops that were springing up.

Ironically enough, as the nineteenth century dawned, the lowly merchants were the only Japanese benefiting from the Tokugawa policy. As the warriors grew poorer, the businessmen became richer through their control of the rice market and by lending money to the samurai at high interest rates. Even the Shogunate, steeped in the corruption and court intrigues fostered by more than two hundred years of uninterrupted Tokugawa rule and staggered by the cost of keeping countless retainers and their families, had found it expedient, if not necessary, to borrow heavily from them—sometimes in return for the granting of samurai status.

The merchants were not lost for ways to enjoy their new-found wealth and social position, either, creating a new and strange bourgeois culture —which they described in highly unorthodox "realistic" novels—from their world of geishas, brothels, Kabuki plays, and other evolving pleasures of urban life. The merchant class, the lowest in the Japanese caste system, lived on a better scale, at least in material terms, than their superiors. Yet even the merchants voiced dissatisfaction with the regime. The money economy they were swiftly developing had outgrown the Tokugawa system. There were fortunes to be made in trade with the outside world that was sealed off from them. Significantly, with each loan rendered the Shogunate, the merchants' influence grew.

The samurai, however, were the most determined to end Tokugawa rule, not because they desired contact with the foreigner, but because they wanted to usurp for themselves the benefits attached to the power so long enjoyed by others. As they sought means to achieve this goal, the more scholarly of the samurai began to study Confucian philosophy, and the more they read, the deeper they delved into the long-forgotten facts and legends of Japanese history. These scholars courageously reminded the public of Japan's "divine" past, and for the first time in seven hundred years people began to wonder why the voice of the Emperor, descendant of Amatarasu, the Sun Goddess, was never heard. With Choshu among the leaders, the clans rallied with a cry which they hoped could topple the shaky Tokugawa regime: "Restore the Emperor!"

While Tokugawa power slowly crumbled under the innumerable pressures building up within the country, the government was suddenly faced with a threat from outside. Foreigners—"barbarians" as they were called —were trying to break the isolation which had protected the Tokugawa regime. On a misty July morning in 1853, Japanese fishermen and seaside inhabitants gaped unbelievingly as four paddle-wheeled monsters crawled up the coast coughing, it seemed, volcanic smoke.

A few days later, American Commodore Matthew C. Perry stepped ashore in formal military dress and delivered a letter addressed to the Emperor from President Fillmore, demanding that Japan inaugurate trade with the United States, treat shipwrecked sailors humanely, and grant American steamers access to coal and provisions. Promising to return soon for an answer, he departed, leaving the government in a state of near-panic and sharply divided on the course to follow.

Perry reappeared in February 1854, and the Shogun, in the name of the Emperor, agreed to all the demands except that for an "immediate" trade agreement. Then, at a great ceremonial banquet, Perry showered the Shogun with gifts, including a model steam train and telegraph sets that pointedly illustrated America's technical achievements. Reluctantly, apprehensively, Japan's leaders celebrated the disintegration of the sealed shell in which the nation had been mummified for two hundred and fifty years.

But there was no celebration in Choshu. Many other clans, vaguely aware of Western military power, agreed that compromise with Perry was necessary, at least until Japan could build up its defenses sufficiently to drive the foreigners out again. Choshu, however, demanded complete rejection of the American ultimatum and continued seclusion. When its wishes were ignored by the Shogun, it intensified its attacks on him with a new slogan: "Revere the Emperor and Expel the Barbarian."

Its fanatical nationalist campaign was led by a brilliant young Choshu samurai named Yoshida Shoin, who hated both the foreigners and the Tokugawa, but worshiped the Emperor, whom he vowed would regain his ancient status. Even as a child he had been obsessed with the idea of restoration. At eleven years of age, he had delivered lectures on the divine origin of Japan in the court of his *daimyo*. "I have a purpose and am determined to carry it out, even though Mount Fuji crumbles and the rivers are exhausted," Yoshida Shoin told his fellow-clansmen.

When Perry landed in Japan, Yoshida, then twenty-three, violently opposed acceptance of his demands. But although he wanted to keep the foreigners out of Japan, Yoshida, anticipating history, also saw the need for Japanese scholars to go abroad and learn the sources of Western technical strength—as his forefathers had gone to China to study Chinese civilization twelve centuries earlier. Yoshida Shoin believed that it was necessary to introduce Western technology into Japan so that Japan could later attack and defeat the barbarians with their own weapons and means of destruction. Further blueprinting the future, he advocated expansion into Manchuria, Formosa, Korea, and the Ryukyu and Kurile Islands. Among the many followers who flocked around him was another leading Choshu patriot, Nobuaki Sato, the great-grandfather of Nobusuke Kishi.

Yoshida, hoping to study abroad himself, made five abortive attempts to swim out to Perry's vessels and board one of them as a stowaway. Finally, he was caught by Shogunate forces and turned over for punishment to his own clan authorities, who were forced to keep him under house arrest. Accused later by the Tokugawa of organizing a plot to overthrow the government, he was imprisoned, and, in the words of a devoted follower, "By the hand of the headsman, his refined and burning and reform-loving spirit was severed from his five-foot body and caused to ascend to the high heaven." But Yoshida had made another remarkably accurate prophecy before he died. In a poem, he wrote:

Although my body is cast out to decay,
On the Musashi plain,
*Yet my Japanese spirit will remain.**

In 1863, four years after Yoshida's death, the *daimyo* of Choshu, Lord Mori, decided on a showdown with his domestic and alien enemies. His brave warriors would throw the "barbarians" out themselves, at the same time placing the cowardly Shogunate in an untenable position. Mori's plan was to prevent the passage of all foreign vessels through the legendary Gates of Bakan, the Straits of Shimonoseki separating Honshu from Kyushu, which the clan controlled. Mounting ancient smooth-bore muzzle-loading guns and mortars on a string of forts that rimmed the shoreline, the Choshu samurai, ready for their first unsuspecting victim, glowed with the same sense of anticipation that their descendant, Kishi, was to experience less than eighty years later as he awaited news of the attack on Pearl Harbor. The samurai saw nothing unprincipled in a surprise attack if it could lead to military success. The only immorality in warfare was to lose.

The first vessel Lord Mori sighted was a small American steamer, the *Pembroke,* which emerged from the Inland Sea and anchored off Shimonoseki near the mouth of the straits. With darkness descending, the ship's crew decided to wait until morning to proceed through the narrow waterway. Later that night, a small craft loaded with samurai drew up to shore between the American vessel and the entrance to the straits, while simultaneously, a gun sounded, signaling a series of blasts from guns all along the shore. The crew of the *Pembroke,* though puzzled, saw no cause for alarm. But at dawn, the steamer, as it started toward the narrows, was suddenly rocked by exploding shells—fired from the small craft. Only slightly damaged, the *Pembroke* sailed full-steam through the straits before it could suffer further damage. Lord Mori's samurai had lost their prey, but they had made their point—which was further stressed in the next few weeks with attacks on French and Dutch vessels.

After Western protests to the Shogunate proved unavailing, an American sloop, the *Wyoming,* blasted its way through the narrow passage, engaging in battle three primitive Choshu warships and the shore batteries. When it had run the channel, it turned around and threaded the course once again to impress on Lord Mori and his warriors the futility of the blockade. The *Wyoming* limped out of the straits, battered but afloat, leaving behind three sunken Choshu ships and a mass of debris where fortifications had once stood. This feat by the *Wyoming* set in motion the

* The Musashi plain is the area in which Tokyo is located.

psychological wheels of a revolution far different and infinitely broader in scope than anyone might have imagined. Perhaps, as Yoshida Shoin had said, thought the Choshu leaders, Japan could profit from an understanding of what made Western weapons so much more effective than their own. For the first time the samurai recognized that their own weapons and battle techniques were outmoded.

Meanwhile, the Emperor, though having regained many of his powers from the Shogunate with the support of the Choshu clan, angrily ordered Choshu representatives out of his court in Kyoto for provoking the feared Westerners. The Choshu leaders, stunned by this sudden threat to their plans to win control of Japan, decided that this was the time to seize the reins of government. They plotted to kidnap the Sovereign and replace the Tokugawa as his advisers. They would then automatically be the nation's rulers, in accordance with the historical axiom that whoever controlled the Emperor controlled his empire. Once under their "protection," the Emperor, by tradition, could no longer openly oppose their views, while the Tokugawa would, in effect, become the rebels.

On August 20, 1864, two thousand sword-swinging Choshu samurai fought their way into the Palace grounds in the face of bitter resistance by the Shogun's forces, ironically defending the Emperor. Greatly outnumbered, as the Shogun received reinforcements, the Choshu samurai were finally beaten back, leaving the streets of Kyoto littered with dead and wounded, including Choshu military leaders who committed *hara-kiri* for having disgraced their lord. The first major clan revolt since the days of Ieyasu had failed. Nor was this the end of Choshu's troubles. Even as the battle of Kyoto raged, the foreign powers were demanding guarantees that there would be no further obstruction at Shimonoseki.

At about this time, two young followers of Yoshida Shoin, Hirobumi Ito and Kaoru Inouye, arrived in London after stowing away in a British vessel. Their aim was to accomplish what Yoshida had failed to do, to master the sciences of the foreigner so that they could be adapted to the aim of keeping the foreigners out of Japan. But as soon as they observed at first hand the technical miracles wrought by the West, they realized their mission was utterly unrealistic, at least for the time being. Reading in the London *Times* of the trouble at Shimonoseki, the two youths immediately returned to Japan to warn Lord Mori of the dangers Choshu faced if it did not abandon its foolhardy policies.

Mori, though having learned to respect Western weapons, proudly refused to heed their advice, and, as a result, a combined force of French, British, Dutch, and American vessels liquidated the Choshu batteries.

Finally convinced of the hopelessness of his situation, Mori promised to open the Shimonoseki Straits and pay a large indemnity for damage that had been done to foreign ships. The time had come, he concluded, to change tactics. The "barbarians" could not be thrown out, or even prevented from attacking Japan, until Japan had guns and ships as powerful as those that had subdued Choshu. Yoshida Shoin had indeed been right—the nation had to borrow from the West the means to fight the West, though it was now evident that contact with foreigners could not be confined to scholars studying abroad. Japan would have to open its doors to foreign trade. Only the development of commercial intercourse on a broad scale would hasten the day when Japan would be capable of defending itself against foreign domination. The Choshu clan knew that that day would come, if not in their lifetime, in their children's, or their grandchildren's. It might even take a century to assimilate Western technological developments and to prepare for the final showdown with the West.

With this as their eventual objective, Choshu turned to the more immediate problem of the Tokugawa. Since routing the Choshu forces in Kyoto, the Shogun had regained considerable strength and prestige and was now prepared to attack the clan on its own ground to crush what remained of its rebellious spirit. Lord Mori, weary from the disasters of Kyoto and Shimonoseki, was ready to surrender to the Shogun, believing that the Choshu samurai could not possibly win the forthcoming battle. But a young Choshu military genius, Takasugi Shinsaku, led a revolt against Lord Mori and his deputies, and, taking control of the clan, vowed to defend the lands of Choshu to the last man. Takasugi, taking advantage of the fresh attitude held by the clan toward the barbarians, bought the newest type rifles from abroad and distributed them to the first Japanese troops ever organized on the Western model. Cracking the previously inflexible caste system, twenty-five-year-old Takasugi, a small, thin man with close-cropped hair that made him look like a boy, formed his army mainly with cloth-uniformed peasant commoners rather than the traditional armor-plated samurai warriors.

Well-disciplined and well-paid, the *Kiheitai,* or modern cavalry, as the new Choshu army was called, proved far superior to the Shogun's medieval sword-wielding forces that attacked in July, 1866. Finally, after the clans collaborating with the Shogunate withdrew their support, the government sued for peace. Kishi's forefathers had assured the fall not only of the Tokugawa, but of the feudal system with its tight caste structure. Japan, it was now obvious to all Japanese, would have to remodel itself, in form if not in spirit, in the image of the barbarian West it had tried for so long to ignore.

Choshu and other leading clans, including the powerful Satsuma clan of southern Kyushu, joined in drawing up plans for an alliance under which all would place their troops at the disposal of the Emperor, a twelve-year-old boy popularly known as Meiji (Emperor Komei, his father, had died in February, 1867), and ordered the Shogun, Keiki, to resign. Helpless to resist, the Shogun replied:

"I confess with shame that the present unsatisfactory condition of affairs is due to my shortcomings and incompetence. Now that foreign intercourse is becoming more extensive, unless the administration is directed from a single central authority, the foundations of the state will be imperiled. If, however, the old evils be amended, and the administrative authority restored to the Imperial Court, if national deliberations be conducted on a broad basis and the Imperial decision secured, and if the Empire be sustained by the harmonious efforts of the whole people, then our country will be able to maintain its rank and dignity among the nations of the earth."

The last of the Tokugawa thereupon resigned, and on January 3, 1868, the young Emperor, before a meeting of clan leaders, solemnly announced the abolition of the Shogunate and the restoration to the Imperial House of the powers that had been usurped seven hundred years earlier by Minamoto Yoritomo, the first Shogun.

The Meiji Era, the second momentous period of reform in Japanese history, had begun, and the nation again embarked on a policy of massive importations, to be shaped and adjusted, during the process of digestion, to meet Japan's needs within the framework of its tradition and spirit.

The new government was led by a Choshu-dominated oligarchy of young, brilliant, idealistic samurai far removed in character from their fathers and grandfathers who had dreamed of overthrowing the Tokugawa simply so they, rather than the Tokugawa, could enjoy the fruits of power. These new leaders had one objective in mind: to build Japan into a great nation that would win the recognition of the world. The degree of power which Japan should strive to attain had not yet been determined. Some thought only in terms of making Japan strong enough to be able to defend the home islands against foreign attack. Others dreamed, as had Yoshida Shoin, of absorbing neighboring areas. Whatever was to be Japan's ultimate aim, all agreed that Japan, in reforming itself, had to consider every change in a military light. This basic policy was reflected in the words of Koin Kido, one of the young leaders from Choshu:

"If we wish the restoration of a new government to be realized and the prestige of our Emperor to be elevated abroad, we must establish the basis of government by allotting three-fifths of the expenses for military purposes, one-fifth for the government, and one-fifth for relief and for the people."

The Meiji chiefs were wise enough to realize that a powerful military could only be built on a completely new foundation. Feudalism had to be replaced with a unified system of society. The political structure had to be centralized. Modern industries would have to be imported virtually intact from abroad. There was not sufficient time for Japan to start at the bottom. Japan could not produce high-quality guns and efficient soldiers unless it underwent a thorough social, political, and economic revolution based on massive innovations from the West.

But this revolution would be more selective than the Great Reform, in which Japan had drawn from all phases of Chinese civilization. Imports this time would be limited mainly to technical items and would exclude disruptive ideological doctrines. At the same time, Japan would again fit the reforms into the Japanese cultural mold. It would select, reject, alter, blend. And guiding this great absorption process would be one overriding factor: would the reform help to build Japan into a strong military power?

The general framework of the revolution was proclaimed in a Charter Oath providing that:

"1. An assembly widely convoked shall be established, and thus great stress shall be laid upon public discussion.

"2. The welfare of the whole nation shall be promoted by the everlasting efforts of both the governing and the governed classes.

"3. All subjects, civil and military officers, as well as other people, shall do their best and never grow weary in accomplishing their legitimate purposes.

"4. All absurd usages shall be abandoned; justice and righteousness shall regulate all action.

"5. Knowledge shall be sought for all over the world and thus shall be strengthened the foundation of the Imperial polity."

No sooner had these broad principles been announced than the government began filling in the details with hundreds of decrees. The caste system was abolished, with the samurai encouraged to put away his sword and to cut off his topknot. The nobility were forced to brush clean their traditionally blackened teeth and to stop shaving their eyebrows. The *daimyo* had to turn over their domains to the Emperor. Religious and other basic freedoms were guaranteed the people. A national bank, stock exchange, and postal system were established. Lighthouses were built, and modern newspapers started. The Western calendar, a government civil service, and revised legal and tax systems were introduced.

Such reforms were always announced in the name of the Emperor, and the Sovereign himself, for the first time in hundreds of years, appeared among the people, exhorting them to devote themselves to their revolutionary task. The young samurai leaders exerted every effort to glorify the Emperor in the eyes of the public, for he was the key to the national unity and patriotic fervor so essential to the success of their plan to compress centuries of progress into a few decades. Through him, the disciplined thought-patterns of the past, if not overly disturbed by the infiltration of Western democratic philosophy, could be used to thrust Japan bodily into a modern, mechanized future. During the long period of Imperial seclusion, the primary loyalty of the people had been channeled to the feudal lords, and, in a lesser degree, to the Shogun. Now this fierce sense of obligation, potentially a vise-tight binding force on the whole community, had to be re-diverted to the Emperor. The spiritual raw material was there. If a man would willingly die for his lord, a person of mortal heritage, they reasoned, then his loyalty to the Sovereign, descendant of the Sun Goddess, could be nurtured to similar extremes.

One of the vehicles used for the promotion of Emperor-worship was the schoolroom. Japan inaugurated for the first time a system of universal education, with attendance obligatory in the primary grades. Western teaching methods were adopted, but twisted into an instrument that would produce technically competent vassals devoted to one end—enhancement of the glory of Emperor and State. State Shinto was distinguished from the Shinto religion and, under the guise of teaching temporal tradition, instructors interwove the fiction of the Sun Goddess with convenient facts of history.

Few peasants and other commoners were able to remain in school beyond the primary level, but their indoctrination was continued in the armed forces, which were recruited, under a military conscription law, mainly from the peasant ranks. The new warriors spent almost as much time in their barracks listening to lectures on the medieval past as in the field learning Western military tactics and the use of Western weapons. Although they had never developed under the feudal system the sense of obligation to their superiors that had so dominated the life of the samurai, the peasants, viewing themselves as the new samurai, eagerly embraced the moral traditions of their fighting predecessors.

This gigantic effort to harness the ethics and mores of a feudal civilization to the institutions and technology of the modern world was reflected even more dramatically in industry. The merchants, who toward the end of the Tokugawa period had to finance the government, now found themselves financed by the government. For no individual enterprisers were able to meet the costs of the tremendous industrial schemes envisaged by the new leaders. There was no time for building a foundation of small factories and light industries. Instead, the government, with technical aid from abroad, poured funds into the construction of huge paper and cotton spinning mills, silk factories, shipbuilding facilities, munitions plants, railroads, and public utilities. When these industries had been sufficiently developed, the government turned them over to favored private firms, laying the groundwork for the growth of the giant family-controlled combines, the *Zaibatsu,* which were to play so important a role in preparing Japan for the Second World War.

The sudden superimposition of great industries on a society that still had one foot in the feudal age created a social-economic monstrosity unique in the world. Peasant workers who had never seen a machine before began operating the latest and most complicated equipment from the West. Their employers paid them almost no salary, but furnished them with food and living quarters and advised them on their family affairs. These modern feudal lords flourished, for the combination of Western science and cheap labor proved to be a highly profitable marriage.

But as skillful as the Meiji leaders were in creating a new, unified society, founded on old principles but spiced with Western technological ingredients, they gradually found themselves faced with considerable resistance. Small merchants and home manufacturers not favored by the government with subsidies and other economic advantages were going out of business. Landowners had to pay enormous land taxes, virtually carrying the burden of the reform program. They also suffered from a government retrenchment program that sent rice prices downward, resulting in a large number of local peasant rebellions reminiscent of Tokugawa days.

Many samurai who hadn't been able to adjust to a world without war found it even more difficult adjusting to a world without caste, though they were designated as "gentry" to compensate for the loss of their special privileges. These unhappy samurai eventually found a champion in Saigo Takamori, a leader of the Satsuma clan, who had played an important role in overthrowing the Tokugawa. A charter member of the first Meiji government, Saigo Takamori had favored unifying the nation under the Emperor but wanted the samurai as a class to keep its superior status. When his colleagues overruled his demand that Japanese forces take control of Korea (they agreed in principle but thought it wiser to wait until Japan had consolidated its new strength more securely), Saigo quit the government, and shortly afterward led a desperate last-gasp samurai revolt. Confronted with the entire national army, well-trained and newly-equipped, Saigo and his warriors, Japan's last fighting swordsmen, were destroyed.

Their fierce resistance, however, captured the imagination of the romantically minded Japanese, contributing to the growth of political opposition to the government. The oppositionists, including many discarded members of the government, fought to weaken their former colleagues in the only way left to them. They demanded a constitution providing for a "Western-style" popular assembly. Ironically, there was little popular demand, even among the most discontented groups, for such an institution, which was too far removed from anything the people had ever known before. But the leaders of the new Japan calculated that this might be the answer to the growing national restlessness.

A constitution could, in fact, serve a dual purpose. Composed in such a way as to reinforce the power of the Emperor (in reality that of his oligarchical advisors), it would simultaneously offer a veneer of democracy to those people who were likely to become contaminated in the future by foreign ideological concepts. The Japanese could hardly cry for a democratic constitution if they already possessed one. The move was a shrewd maneuver, increasing the powers of the Emperor through the careful composition of a "democratic" constitution. Even the opposition had never advocated giving the people real democracy. As its leading member, Taisuke Itagaki, explained, "If the Council Chamber [parliament] is established, we do not propose that the franchise should at once be made universal. We would only give it in the first instance to the samurai and the rich farmers and merchants."

A special committee, led by Prime Minister Hirobumi Ito and including Foreign Minister Kaoru Inouye, began drawing up Japan's first constitution in 1886. Ito and Inouye had come a long way since Tokugawa days, when they had stowed away in a British vessel to study the science of the foreigner. The deep impression left on them, particularly on Ito, by the technological achievements of the West constituted no small influence on the speed and scope of Japan's new revolution.

Right after the Restoration, Ito was chosen, at the age of twenty-nine, Governor of Hyogo (now the city of Kobe) to permit him to deal with foreign traders entering this port. Two years later, as Vice-Minister of Finance, he went to the United States to study its monetary system. Then, as part of a political research team, he returned to America and also visited Europe, where he was deeply influenced by Bismarck's Prussian philosophy. On becoming Minister of Public Works, he supervised construction of a national railroad system and installation of a telegraph system. Later, he went back to Germany to study its authoritarian Constitution. In 1885, Ito, only forty-four years of age, took over as the first Prime Minister of a reorganized government based on the cabinet system, and devoted himself to the task of composing a constitution for Japan, without the benefit of a constituent assembly to assist him.

The document that finally emerged was a masterful adaptation of Prussian concepts. As Prince Ito (he was dubbed a Prince by the Emperor) pointed out:

> "It will be evident that as the supreme right is one and indivisible, the legislative power remains in the hands of the Sovereign and is not bestowed on the people. . . . But the Sovereign may permit the representative body to take part in the process of practically applying the legislative right. . . . Nothing being law without a concurrence of views between the Sovereign and the people, the latter elect representatives to meet at an appointed place and carry out the view of the Sovereign."

The constitution was thus a gift from the Emperor to his subjects, a political toy attached to an Imperial string and manipulated by the oligarchical rulers. The powers of the House of Representatives, the only elective body provided for, were severely limited, and as a guarantee that this branch of the Diet, or parliament, would stay in line, an appointive upper house, the House of Peers, was given virtual veto power over the lower house. Furthermore, the ruling clique, in the name of the Emperor, could prevent any future efforts to reduce the Sovereign's power through a provision making it possible only for him to amend the constitution.

Probably the most important constitutional feature of all was an omission. No reference was made to the principle of collective government responsibility. As a result, the Ministers of Army and Navy, when they wanted to by-pass their civilian cabinet colleagues, would be able to go directly to the Emperor, the Supreme Commander of the armed forces, for approval of their plans. In addition, these ministers had to be active military officers, making it possible for either service to prevent formation of a cabinet by withholding approval of candidates for these posts. The military, as the Second World War and the events leading up to it so tragically illustrated, had the final legal say on government policy.

To Prince Ito, the constitution represented a logical compromise between two extreme principles. He had, on the one hand, thrown a few crumbs of democracy to a people beginning to stir with discontent, and on the other, appeased the militarists, who had feared the effects of giving the people even the right to free speech or public debate. Ito staunchly believed in authoritarian rule based on popular worship of the Emperor, for this was the key to retention of the traditional Japanese hierarchal social system, although on a far less rigid plane than in the Tokugawa era.

This system would, in fact, help to render the Diet impotent, Ito was convinced, to perhaps an even greater degree than the constitution itself, for the individual was not used to making decisions in Japan, whether on politics or on family matters, but always shaped his judgment to fit into the mold of group opinion as determined by elders and superiors. The lack of individual responsibility in parliament would certainly benefit the oligarchy. In any event, the Constitution now legally assured continuation, even solidification, of the Japanese social system within a modern political framework. And such a framework was necessary if Japan was to achieve its true destiny as outlined by Yoshida Shoin and envisaged at this stage of the revolution by almost all the Japanese leaders—a place in the sun, in the international hierarchy, worthy of its superior heritage.

Even so, Ito was wary of the militarists, who, like Saigo, wanted to achieve this goal too swiftly, without proper consideration of the obstacles confronting Japan. The militarists, however, were too powerful to defy, and would have ultimate control of the nation in any case. There was little to be gained, therefore, by restricting their power constitutionally. Indeed, no constitution could be promulgated at all without their support. And so Ito agreed to get in step with the militarists, much as a fellow clansman yet unborn, Nobusuke Kishi, was to do many years later.

Ito learned that he had made one miscalculation. No sooner were the first Diet elections held in 1890 than deputies, representing new people's parties, used their freedom of debate to considerable advantage. They severely criticized the government for many of its policies and even tried, though unsuccessfully, to censure the leaders and slash the budget. The oligarchy, in retaliation, dissolved House after House, but each new election produced equally articulate opposition, increasing the worries of Ito and his fellows that eventually they would not be able to withstand the pressures of public opinion, even if only about one per cent of the people were enfranchised.

In desperation, the nation's leaders ordered prefectural governors and police to "support" the election of their candidates, but this only back-fired in a scandal of riots and killings. Finally, Ito used the prestige of the Emperor to force obedience from the Diet, advising the Sovereign to ask the Diet members personally to co-operate with the government on specific issues. This produced, at least temporarily, the desired results, but the oligarchy by now well realized that the constitution, with its contradictory principles of parliamentarianism and authoritarianism, was a political hornet's nest. Ito and his colleagues had failed to adapt this Western concept successfully to what they considered Japanese tradition. They had not counted on the fact that a little freedom would only lead to the demand for more, even among a people unfamiliar with freedom.

But the government, with the militarists exerting pressure, found the way to bring unity to the nation again. The time had come, it was judged, to show the people what the Meiji Restoration had wrought in but two decades, to prove to them that the economic, social, and political reforms instituted had produced a national miracle. Even Prince Ito was convinced that Japan should now test the great military establishment that was the essence of this miracle.

Forcing the decadent Manchu government of China, which was falsely reputed as a Great Power at the time, into a war over domination of Korea in 1895, Japan's modern samurai overran Chinese forces in that country, southern Manchuria, and the city of Weihaiwei in China proper. The Chinese fleet was destroyed. The peace treaty that was signed in 1895 recognized Korea's independence and gave Japan control of Formosa, the Pescadores, and the Liaotung Peninsula in southern Manchuria, as well as a large indemnity.

Japan's leaders beamed. The victory over China had unified the nation as never before. Even more important, they had won the recognition and respect of a startled world that had still imagined Japan as the backward, underdeveloped nation it had been only a few years earlier. True, only a jostle had been necessary to collapse China's corruption-ridden house of matches, and the real military test, perhaps involving control of China itself, was yet to come. But there was time. If not the present leaders, then their descendants would finish the job of winning for Japan the place in the sun it deserved. Had the Japanese not been able, throughout their long history, to adapt themselves to circumstances and gradually improve their country's status in the world?

One year later, in 1896, Nobusuke Kishi, a child of Choshu, was born.

CHAPTER III

❧

RICE CAKES AND HAND GRENADES

HIGH ON A ROLLING rice-green hill in Yamaguchi City, capital of Yamaguchi Prefecture, there stands a small Shinto temple shaded by a few trees. Nearby eight identical unpainted wood-and-paper houses, each partially concealed behind a neatly clipped cryptogram hedge, stretch away from the shrine like sentinels guarding the gods. These dwellings, which comprise the village of Hakkenya, appropriately meaning "eight houses" in Japanese, sheltered Lord Mori's brave samurai warriors in the Tokugawa era. On November 13, 1896, in the house farthest from the temple, the second son of Hidesuke and Moyo Sato, descendants of these samurai, was born.

The baby, named Nobusuke, entered a gay, noisy—and crowded—household. He was coddled and spoiled by a family circle that embraced a brother, several sisters and uncles, and a student boarder. And he received additional attention from the student friends of his Uncle Matsui, a student himself, who were constantly streaming into the house, often staying for the night. There was always space for one more on the *tatami* in Matsui's room. Wild and boisterous were these young men, but Moyo, when she wasn't busy nursing her baby, cared for them as she did for her own children.

When Nobusuke was one month old, Moyo took him to the local Shinto shrine, where the priest, in a brief ceremony, blessed mother and son and introduced the child to the patron deities who had willed his

47

survival after birth, in particular Hachiman, the god of war, the Satos' guardian god. Despite the priest's blessings, Moyo, even before Nobusuke was old enough to display a will of his own by reaching out his tiny arms to her and thus earn the right to be taken into her bed (he had lain on his own little mattress since birth), fell ill with diphtheria. The child, therefore, was left to be spoiled and pampered by the younger members of the household, who prepared his milk and changed his irritating padded diapers. And whenever he began to cry, his sisters would play *jang-ken-pon,* "stone, paper, scissors," to determine whose turn it was to carry the child. It was the losers' duty to strap him on the back of the winner with a broad double sash.

Nobusuke's father seldom joined in this to-do over his son. An official in the Yamaguchi Prefectural government, Hidesuke, a small man with a long, thin face that seemed to ask only for the chance to live his life over again, usually returned home tired and discouraged. Hidesuke, despite his efforts, was not looked upon with much favor by his superiors, and there appeared to be little possibility of promotion. He had another problem too—his wife. Moyo was a remarkable woman—intelligent, magnetic, strong-willed. But that was the trouble. These weren't the proper qualities for a Japanese wife. It had been awkward enough for him to accept the role of an adopted husband and to take her family name.

It had all started when his family, the Kishis, sent him to study Chinese classics with Moyo's father at the nearby Sato home when both families lived in the village of Tabuse near Yamaguchi City. Before he knew what was happening, the Satos had adopted him, married him off to their daughter, and integrated him into their household. Being a younger son, he could understand his father's willingness to see him absorbed by a family like the Satos, who were of higher samurai standing than the Kishis, but it was extraordinary, indeed, for the Satos to adopt a husband for Moyo and thereby permit *her* to perpetuate the house of Sato when she had three brothers who could have done this.

At the time of the marriage, Hidesuke had not been unhappy about the arrangement. His wife was a pretty almond-eyed girl of fourteen and would be an heiress when her father died. Furthermore, he had thought his adoption into the Sato family would permit him to continue his studies under Moyo's father and clear the way for him to receive a university education. Within a year after the marriage, however, his father-in-law was elected to the prefectural legislature and moved with his wife to Yamaguchi City, where the legislature convened. Hidesuke, trapped by the needs of his swiftly growing family (his wife had already given birth to one child and was expecting another), had to devote all his time to "rice-winning" and was unable to realize his dream of higher learning.

He opened a sake brewery next door to the Sato house. But, at his wife's instigation, since she did not approve of his being a sake merchant, he shut it down and took his family to Yamaguchi City, where his father-in-law obtained a "more respectable" government job for him. Hidesuke did not feel that he was sufficiently educated for this government post, but Moyo was always badgering him to improve himself and live up to his samurai heritage. In many ways, of course, she was a good wife. After all, had she not presented him with two sons? But it was not easy catering to the whims of an heiress. Nor to be indebted to his wife for his job and made to feel that what social standing he had was because of her.

Moreover, Moyo's whims were not really whims, but commandments in the house of Sato. Many Westerners have a mistaken idea of the Japanese woman and her role within the family. It is true that in public Japanese women are humble, courteous, and silent. But, once behind the paper walls of their homes, they usually have a good deal to say about running the household. Few, however, exert their wills as forcefully as Moyo did. Theoretically, Hidesuke, as a male, was head of the house. He was the first to be served at mealtime and the first to use the family bath; and he was legal owner of the family property. But Moyo, through her strength of personality, always had the last word on matters of family policy. Still, she exerted her influence, not with blunt demand, but with a shrewdly concocted brew of political acumen and feminine wile. The brother of Moyo's sister-in-law, Yosuke Matsuoka, who was destined one day to be Foreign Minister, once told her, "If women could enter the political arena, you, Moyo, would, without doubt, be prime minister."

It could therefore be expected that Moyo would bring up her children in a disciplinary manner highly untypical of most Japanese mothers. The average mother may gently scold her child or threaten to withdraw her love from him, but she seldom spanks him or takes other strong measures to impress on him the differences between right and wrong. That will come later, she tells herself, even as the child is poking holes through the paper walls of the house. It should be noted, however, that the Japanese mother does not take this attitude of leniency for the same reasons as many modern American women do, but because she knows that there is a more thorough and unrelenting discipline awaiting her children—that great machine of indebtedness that will bind them to the Japanese community. Most Japanese children, therefore, have a less disciplined childhood than most Western children, but this childhood ends more abruptly and at an earlier age.

Moyo, whose high cheekbones were accentuated by tightly drawn lips that reflected her iron will, was not the average Japanese mother, for her "proper place" lay on a higher ledge in the social hierarchy. She had won her place in competition with three men, her own brothers. Thus, the weight of her debt to family and society far exceeded that of the average woman, and she reacted accordingly. She was determined that her children would start earlier than most to learn their duties to the demanding world into which they were born. Though she herself had received little education, they—at least the boys—were going to be given the best possible schooling. She had decided that her children's "place" was at the top, and to get there, they had to be prepared for the abnormally heavy burdens which such achievement would entail.

"My father was a man of gentle disposition," Kishi says, reflecting on his childhood. "He and my mother were poles apart in character. Among the relatives, she was spoken of as a woman of remarkable spirit. The fostering of us, the children, was always the job of our strong-minded mother."

When Nobusuke was two years old, the Satos moved back to Tabuse and reopened the sake brewery. Hidesuke's bureaucratic job simply hadn't worked out. He had been handicapped, as he had feared, by the lack of higher education, an important consideration in government when promotions were handed out. Moyo was not happy about this turn of events, convinced that the place for a man of samurai blood was either in the government or the military—not in commerce. Before the Restoration it had been below the dignity of a samurai to do his own shopping or even to be seen handling money. And here was her husband, a samurai, content to be a sake merchant!

Things, of course, had changed under the Meiji regime. With the feudal clans virtually destroyed, jobless warriors had had no choice but to drift into commerce. And the Meiji leaders had lent prestige to the commercial class by encouraging its development. But a strong stigma was still attached to it; business was suitable, perhaps, for the average Japanese, but not for a samurai.

Hidesuke took a simpler view of all this than his wife. He could never get far as a bureaucrat, and the family had to live. He even resented the years he had wasted in Yamaguchi City, since he had known that he would not succeed. As a merchant, however, he felt sure that he could provide for his family. His wife would just have to make the best of it.

And Moyo did take her defeat with grace. She decided that it would be better for her husband to be a successful merchant than a failure in government. Things would be different with her children, she assured herself. They would be generals or ministers, as befitted the descendants of samurai.

Although business at least held out the prospect of material reward, even this compensation was denied the Satos in the first year or so after the reopening of their brewery. Hidesuke brooded over his financial difficulties. He began to develop the same fear of failure that he had felt while living in Yamaguchi City. But Moyo refused to despair, maintaining even in their darkest hours the front of an aristocratic lady. Whenever she went into town she wore her finest kimono, though she went out less and less to avoid being seen too often in the few such kimonos she possessed. She would not let poverty change her way of living or her demeanor in public.

Everybody in the village knew of the Satos' misfortune, and Moyo knew they knew, but her pride and the esteem in which the Sato name was held forced many of the villagers—some far more successful professionally and financially than the Satos—to act as if they accepted the fiction she lived as fact. Whenever the villagers met Moyo, they bowed low before her in the manner reserved for the aristocracy. Even strangers she passed in the street respectfully moved aside for her, awed by the graceful movement of her slim body as she clip-clopped along in short, sure steps on her stilted *geta;* by the placid expression on her delicately chiseled face; by the slight upward tilt of her head, which might have belonged to a stone goddess.

Moyo made sure that hard times did not dilute in the slightest her children's pride in their ancestry. "Never forget," she constantly reminded them, "we are of samurai lineage. We are the descendants of the Imperial Governor of Shimane."

The child Nobusuke was to remember the Governor of Shimane, but in a different guise, as his Great-grandfather Nobuaki Sato. One of his clearest memories is of this old man, with kindly eyes and a leathery wrinkled face, who was also his godfather. He had been present at Nobusuke's birth and had asked that the child be named after him. Thus, the prefix *nobu,* which means "faith," was used in the baby's name. Nobusuke became the old man's favorite great-grandchild.

Often, the elder Sato, who was confined to his bed with palsy shortly after the child's birth, asked that his great-grandson be brought to his bedside. After one such request, Moyo set out on foot with Nobusuke and his sister, Otose, toward Nobuaki's sprawling villa, located in a seaside village about three miles away on the other side of a mountain pass. As the children were too young to walk this distance—Nobusuke was only four—Moyo hired a workman to carry them, each bundled in a straw-rope net hung from either end of a bamboo pole balanced on the man's shoulder. It was like being inside of a kettle and at the same time swinging through the air. Kishi remembers how people would burst into laughter as they saw him pass, only his slim face peeping out from the bulging net. Though he smiles now at the recollection, he recalls, too, that it was his first taste of the agony of ridicule. But he remembers best seeing his great-grandfather, who was propped up against a pile of quilts. He remembers the pride the old man nourished, the pride that made him see in this child, so many generations removed from himself, the future image of a man. "My dear great-grandson, you shall one day be the glory of the Satos," Nobuaki Sato told the boy.

The Governor of Shimane, who was in his late eighties, died while Nobusuke was still a small child. Yet Nobusuke was greatly influenced by him. Though the visits had been few, Moyo left little untold about his great-grandfather's career. Yoshida Shoin had been his most intimate friend. Deeply influenced by Yoshida, Nobuaki developed a strong sense of nationalism, which intensified his support of the Restoration movement. He was named Governor of Shimane Prefecture by Royal Ordinance immediately following the Restoration, receiving this appointment despite the heated demands of numerous *daimyo* for equivalent positions to help compensate for the transfer of their lands to the Emperor. And for his services, he was awarded the rank of the Fifth Grade of Merit of the Imperial Court.

Young Nobusuke often imagined his great-grandfather as he had traveled from place to place in the splendor and pomp that had been reserved for the *daimyo* in Tokugawa days—dressed in the finest silk kimono, wearing a black feather in his hat, and riding in a soft-cushioned, lacquered palanquin carried on the shoulders of four powerful bearers. Most of all, he took pride in his great-grandfather's close relations with such important leaders as Prince Ito and Kaoru Inouye. When the aging Sato retired in the early 1880's, these and other important figures visited him at his grand seaside villa and exchanged poems with him, as was the custom of the day. Deeply engraved in Nobusuke's mind were the symbolic words his great-grandfather inscribed on a scroll he fashioned from the letters he had received over the years from Choshu patriots: *Taore te nochi yamu*—"Fight to the last drop of blood."

One spring morning in 1903, Nobusuke awakened, crawled out of bed, put on his best kimono, then, after nervously gulping down a breakfast of pickled fish and rice, took under his arms the several small paper-bound textbooks his sister, Otose, had used before him, and quietly shuffled along beside his father on the gravel path leading to Kuniki Primary School.

On arriving, Nobusuke bid *sayonara* to his father, removed his straw sandals, leaving them in the small lobby inside the door, and went to register in the school office. He was told the number of his classroom, which he entered, seating himself cross-legged on the *tatami* behind one of the low tablelike desks that was still vacant. When the teacher, a middle-aged man with a stern countenance, came in, Nobusuke, with the other children, rose and bowed.

Nobusuke noted with a sense of relief, born of a strange companionship in discomfort, that the other beginning pupils looked at least as apprehensive as he felt. There were about forty in his class, with boys and girls seated on separate sides of the room. Altogether, approximately one hundred pupils, divided among the first four grades, were enrolled in the school, which consisted of two wooden double-story buildings, one with the teachers' offices and students' lounging quarters, the other with the classrooms.

Nobusuke, after overcoming his initial fear, soon began to enjoy school, and, as his mother had predicted, he was usually at the top of his class. He was particularly adept at reading and writing, though it was no easy job memorizing hundreds of multiple-stroked Chinese characters, or learning to use a writing brush so that each stroke would have a distinctive grace. He also excelled in arithmetic, and learned with great skill to flick along metal wires the wood marbles of the abacus, the traditional oriental counting-board.

But the subject that interested him most was one called "morals," which was based upon the contents of the Imperial Rescript on Education issued in 1890. In Nobusuke's classroom, as in all others throughout Japan, a copy of this rescript hung on the wall next to a portrait of the Emperor, describing the duties and obligations of the Japanese subject to the Imperial Ancestors, the Emperor, the state, and society. As part of the "morals" course, Nobusuke memorized his textbook on Confucian ethics, learned the virtue of courage through stories of great samurai heroes, and partook in discussions of State Shinto, which stressed the godly attributes of the Emperor, who, although a mortal himself, nevertheless was a direct descendant of the gods.

Shinto reached deep into the Japanese heritage, perhaps not back to the beginning of time, as orthodox believers claim, but at least as far back as the Yamato state. Shinto, which means "Way of the Gods," was to the Yamato settlers a simple worship of the wonders of nature, such as an oddly twisted tree or a particularly high mountain. In later centuries, this worship of nature was gradually extended to embrace what was described as the greatest wonder of all—the divine birth of Japan. This was a significant political feat which did much to shape the history of Japan by giving the Japanese people a sense of national destiny. The story of this birth, as described in the Shinto Bible, *Nihonki,* Chronicles of Japan, captured the imagination of the sensitive young Nobusuke far more than any fairy tale his mother had ever told him, and it was all the more exciting because, from his viewpoint, it was a "true" fairy tale.

Once upon a time a god and goddess, Izanagi and Izanami, searching the earthly abyss below from the Floating Bridge of Heaven, poked a jeweled spear into the ocean, then withdrew it. The brine dripping from the point of the spear solidified and formed an island. The divine couple descended the Stairway of Heaven to this island, settled down, and gave birth to all the islands of Japan, as well as to many deities, including the Sun Goddess, Amaterasu, who eventually sent her grandson down to rule her island sisters, telling him, "The Luxuriant Land of Reed Plains is a country which our descendants are to inherit. Go, therefore, Our Imperial Grandson, and rule over it. And may our Imperial lineage continue unbroken and prosperous, co-eternal with Heaven and Earth. . . ."

Equipped with three divine symbols of authority—a sword for justice, jewels for mercy, and a mirror (into which the Sun Goddess herself had looked) for truth—the young god landed on a Japanese mountain, and some time later—in the seventh century B.C., according to legend—saw his earth-born son, Jimmu, crowned Emperor of Japan, the first of a line of Emperors that even today supposedly remains unbroken. Japan was thus endowed with godly virtues denied the rest of the world, which had never known the divine kiss of Amaterasu.

In the third grade, Nobusuke learned about the position and responsibilities of the Empress, and what was meant by "the fundamental character of the Japanese Empire," the relation of the Imperial Family to the people. It can be seen that Japanese education proceeded gradually to set the trap, through appealing to their imagination, which would eventually make the children aware of what each one of them owed the world —from the Sun Goddess to the casual acquaintance down the street. Not until much later, however, would the children be taught the ways by which they were to start repaying their obligations.

Nobusuke's grades suffered only in the non-academic subjects of singing and drawing. Though he liked to sing the folk and patriotic songs in which his teacher led the class with arm-swinging enthusiasm, he simply could not hold a tune. He was even more perturbed about his drawing because of the competition offered by the boy sitting next to him. This boy was especially talented in drawing horses, and could portray the animal quite expertly from any angle, either standing or running, while Nobusuke could only draw the left profile of a stationary horse, no matter how hard he tried to imagine it from other angles. He often tore his drawings into such tiny pieces that his fingers ached from the effort. It made him furious to know that no matter how hard he worked at drawing, he would never be able to equal that which the boy who sat next to him did with such ease.

The pride which his mother had instilled in him often got him into trouble. When he first started school, he haughtily expected—and usually received—the respect of the other children, for he was a Sato, the descendant of an Imperial Governor. Most of the other children in the village came from lowly tenant-farm families that had been feudal vassals in Tokugawa days. He often misbehaved more than the other children, and was aggressive and quarrelsome with his classmates, particularly if they showed any disrespect for him or the Sato name. Most of them tried to avoid getting into a fight with someone of such honored ancestry. When Nobusuke did fight, it was usually with older and stronger boys. The chances of losing were considerable, but this did not matter to him in these cases, for he was fighting in defense of his name, and this was a matter of principle. The teachers themselves were greatly impressed by his family background. He was never required to stand in a corner as punishment. In fact, they chose him *kyucho,* or monitor, whose function it was to pass on orders from the teacher to the class, though he was selected as much for his excellent grades as for his family name.

The behavior of the class took a notable turn for the worse when a woman teacher, something new in Japan, was added to the all-male faculty. If most of the children could not be controlled by their own mothers, they certainly could not be harnessed by a female stranger. Nobusuke, like the others, treated her with the utmost disrespect. His position as *kyucho* gave him special opportunities to harass her and make her work even more difficult. He knew that she would not dare to complain to his parents. He knew, too, that the other teachers were not likely to have much sympathy for her. Quite probably, the woman teacher would have been forced to resign, which would have made Nobusuke a hero in the eyes of his classmates, if it had not been for a peculiar incident.

As representative of the class, he once accompanied her to the house of a deceased pupil, a poor peasant boy, to offer condolences to the child's family. The bereaved mother, pain in her reddened eyes, greeted them at the door, falling to her knees and humbly bowing her head almost to the floor. Nobusuke presented her with a large bouquet of camellias. Then the boy and his teacher removed their sandals and followed her shuffling figure into a small but clean parlor where the father, clad in kimono, squatted at a table grimly, blankly, sipping a tiny glass of sake.

He invited the visitors to sit down while the wife vanished into the kitchen to prepare tea and bean paste delicacies. Nobusuke looked around the room. How small this peasant's house was. The *kakemono* hanging in the *tokonoma* was obviously painted by an amateur, and the flower arrangement setting it off hardly compared in beauty with his mother's. The paper walls were ripped in places, the *tatami* on which he sat was worn and stained with use, and even the sake was low-grade.

"Please accept the condolences of the class," said the teacher with lowered eyes. "Your son shall be sadly missed."

Somewhat later, Nobusuke, on his fifth cup of sake, felt an intense resentment. What right did this lowly woman have to speak for the class? Why had he humbled himself by entering this poor farmer's house? He felt no real sorrow for his deceased classmate. He had never associated with him. On a sudden impulse, mainly to embarrass his teacher, he exploded into a loud burst of meaningless laughter. Silence, taut and dreadful, followed. Nobusuke was seized with anguish at the sight of the shocked, grieving faces of the father and mother—she had just entered with a trayful of refreshments. He could bear even less the horrified expression of his teacher. He felt as if he had just pierced her with a sword. The teacher got up, bowed clumsily to the elderly couple, and ran to the door as fast as her tight kimono would permit. Nobusuke begged forgiveness of the stunned parents, and followed the teacher out.

The youth severely reproached himself for this breach of good manners and taste, which could have tarnished his family name if he had been a little older. He was all the more miserable because his teacher never disciplined him for it. Somehow, he would have to repay *giri,* even if it meant showing her as much respect as was due a man. And thus, rather unwillingly, he became responsible, through his shame and sense of debt to her, for helping her to keep discipline in the classroom. Although he still did not approve of a woman as a teacher, he felt that he had to help her. In a curious way, Nobusuke had one of his first tastes of *on*.

However, the nature of a boy is not likely to be changed by any single incident. He remained proud, haughty, and troublesome. His arrogance was never more stimulated than by one particular classmate who often played hooky from school. A poverty-stricken peasant's son, Michio Matsumoto, had to spend many of the days when he should have been in school working on his father's farm. His father was ill and unable to manage the farm alone. But the teachers, unaware of the circumstances, were angered by the frequent absences of the boy, though they could do little about it—only scold him or make him stand in a corner. Any severe discipline would have been contrary to Japanese school tradition.

The kind of indoctrination the Japanese use and the way the sense of community obligation is developed in young men can be seen in this instance. The teachers, instead of disciplining Michio themselves, made Nobusuke and his classmates aware that this boy's absence from school reflected on them, that it represented a black mark against the group. Then the teachers left it to class pressure to remedy the situation. The class responded immediately by ostracizing the boy, refusing to speak to him or allow him to participate in their games. The other pupils often misbehaved, too, and they were well aware of this fact, but they attended school regularly in accordance with a formal school edict, and so they had the right to demand that this boy also heed the letter, if not necessarily the spirit, of the rules.

Nobusuke, as monitor, was especially irked about this classmate—and a mere peasant's son at that—who so openly disregarded the group norm of behavior, deliberately ignoring his obligation to the class. He would show him. One day when the boy did turn up for school, Nobusuke, with a sarcastic gleam in his eye, confronted him after class just outside the school.

"Matsumoto," he said, "Why weren't you in school yesterday?"

"I—I couldn't," Michio muttered hesitatingly.

"You deserve to be punished," said Nobusuke with deep indignation, and he tore off the boy's cotton sash that he wore around his dirty, tattered kimono, and threw it high into a tree, while other children who had gathered at the scene began to laugh. Young Matsumoto crossed his arms to keep his kimono from opening, and, without the slightest protest, started down the road toward his home, trying to hold back his tears.

For a split second, Nobusuke exhibited a shocked, rather numb expression, but when he saw the other children laughing, his face lit up in a broad smile and he felt more important than ever.

The following day, the peasant boy showed up at school again, this time with an old torn sash around his kimono. Nobusuke approached him. "We are happy to see that you came to school today," he said, twisting his lips into a cruel smile and throwing an ironical glance at the crowd of children who had again gathered around. "But we must make sure that you've learned your lesson. . . ." He ripped the already torn sash from Matsumoto, leaving the boy once more exposed to ridicule. This time, the child ran off weeping aloud, again to the sound of rollicking laughter.

The sinking feeling Nobusuke had experienced the day before returned. Then someone slapped him on the back and said, "You know how to deal with those who do not know *giri*."

Shortly afterward, Michio's father died and Nobusuke learned the true reason why the boy had not been able to attend school regularly. Nobusuke felt as if he had been tricked by his position as *kyucho* into inflicting unfair punishment on the boy. Yet he knew, too, that no one had told him to punish Matsumoto, nor to carry the punishment to such lengths. He had done it because he had believed that it was his right and his privilege, and, to be honest, because he enjoyed looking important in the eyes of his classmates.

On the first day that Michio returned to school after his father's death, he was wearing, not a sash, but a straw rope around his waist. The sight of it brought back the latent pain in Nobusuke's heart, which seemed, in a flash, to spread all through his body. His mind reeled before the full force of what suddenly burst before him as stark tragedy. In the middle of class, he stood up and asked the teacher to excuse him because of "illness."

Nobusuke walked along the gravel path leading home, picking up pebbles and throwing them with the strength born of deep inner turbulence at trees on the roadside. He seemed to feel some relief when the tiny missiles landed solidly. When he reached the river, where he so often went fishing with his friends, he threw himself on the muddy grass bank, his head facing the water. He tore a patch of grass up by the roots and scattered the green reeds in the river as if they symbolically represented bits of his tortured self. They caused tiny ripples on the smooth surface. Nobusuke gazed into this vast jelly-like mirror, studying the distorted reflection of his own face, as if appraising an incomprehensible painting. Finally, unable to contain himself any longer, he dug his fingers into the soft, wet earth, clenched his dirt-filled fists, and burst into bitter sobs.

"There remains in me that ingrained lesson of humility even today," Kishi says. "I learned also the truth of what it meant to be a Sato, a samurai, for although I would gladly have stripped the sash from my own waist and have flung it into the river, although I would have gladly dishonored myself before my classmates to redeem the wrong I had done to Matsumoto, yet I could not do this because it would have reflected on the Sato name."

For some time after this, Nobusuke's interest in school waned. Though he got top grades, he seldom opened a book once school was out, despite his mother's exhortations. He spent his evenings talking, joking, and playing with neighborhood friends in the garden. Often he challenged them to contests in top-spinning, pasteboard dump, *go,* or backgammon, which he invariably won. But he never competed with them in *sumo* wrestling or running, for he was poor at these sports, and he didn't want to lose. There was no sense in risking disgrace unnecessarily. He particularly did not want his own parents to see him lose. His mother, however, cared little about wrestling or running. It was his education that she was concerned with. She was determined that he gain "knowledge" as well as good grades. "How you shame the Satos," she would say in a low, cutting voice. Sometimes she went to such lengths as spanking him or cauterizing his arm with a joss stick, a wood-dust incense rod. Although he would scream with the short-lived pain, this kind of punishment seldom did much good. He was not the sort of boy who could be forced. Locking him in the storehouse had even less effect, for he would simply lie down on a quilt and go to sleep.

During the summer vacation, Nobusuke could usually be found, dressed in cotton shorts, by the river, either swimming with his friends, or fishing for dace and eels with Uncle Matsui, who was now attending university in Tokyo but spent part of the summer in Tabuse. In autumn, the boy roamed the nearby hills to gather mushrooms, which would be cooked for supper in the evening; and in the spring, often with delicate, pale-pink cherry blossoms fluttering to earth all about him, he collected sweet-smelling bracken to decorate the house. Sometimes he would proceed on such ventures with his baby brother, Eisaku, strapped to his back, enjoying the infant's company in the loneliness of the vast green countryside.

But winter for Nobusuke was the best season of all, for then he would go hunting for birds, ducks, and rabbits. His hunting methods were those of the trapper. One of his tricks was to spill bird-lime near a cage placed next to rose bushes or plum blossoms or under nectar-rich trees, using a tame bird as a lure. A wild bird would get caught in the lime, and Nobusuke, hiding near the cage, would capture it, wash its feet, and deposit it in the cage, though he always set free the female white-eyes, or Japanese bunting, for they could not sing as well as the males, nor could they match in beauty the latter, with their yellow-streaked breasts.

Nobusuke usually went duck-hunting at night, setting up limed bamboo traps in the rice fields and waiting for ducks to fly into them as they swooped down to earth. When rabbit hunting, he would stake out his net in a likely place, then send hounds to search the rabbits out and chase them into the net.

Winter also meant the delights of the New Year season. Toward the end of the year, Nobusuke's father would bring in many workers from neighboring villages to brew sake from rice provided by nearby farmers. The Sato home would become a beehive of activity and echo with exciting sounds: the gay, rhythmic sound of the workers singing folk tunes as they polished the rice in the water mill adjoining the house; the squeaky, grinding sound of the water wheel attached to the wall just outside Nobusuke's room; the whispering sound of the dense clouds of vapor that filled the brewery in the evening while the rice was being steamed in huge vats in preparation for malting; the sound of laughter as the Sato children rushed into the brewery every morning to be treated to delicious *mochi,* or rice cakes, which the workers baked, from samplings of the sake rice, over the fire around which they squatted, warming themselves in the cold winter air.

The taste of *mochi* was the taste of winter to Nobusuke. Shortly after the sake workers arrived, the time came to turn out holiday rice cakes by the score. They were baked for various festival days throughout the year, but not on such a scale as during the New Year season. The young brewery workers, when they had time, would pound steamed rice into cakes for the family, but most of the work was left to rice-cake specialists who went from house to house offering their services and were hired to make, not only ordinary *mochi,* but rice cakes mixed with millet, sugar, salt, or soybeans. The pounding of the steamed rice would begin before daybreak, and by noon Moyo, together with hired women and the children, would be cutting the cake into small round morsels. Nobusuke always volunteered to help, enjoying the feel of the soft, spongy steamed rice in his hands.

A kind of rice porridge called *shohjiru* was also made during the New Year season and used in a ceremony intended to ensure good harvests. After Nobusuke and another member of the family made a cut in the trunk of a fruit tree in the garden, one of them would say aloud to the tree, "Will you bear fruit or not?" The other would reply, "I will! I will!" Then they would pour the porridge into the gash, and the stage was set for a good harvest of persimmons, oranges, or other fruits.

The New Year's game of *toro, toro* was the most fun of all. After supper, Nobusuke and the other young Satos would prepare a trayful of rice cakes, seaweed-wrapped fish, and other foods, and then tiptoe to some nearby house, slide open the door, and deposit the tray on the *tatami,* crying *"toro, toro"* as they ran and hid. As was the custom, the recipient of the food would empty the tray and return it to the spot where it had been left, heaped with other rice cakes and goodies. The children would "secretly" take the tray and carry it back to their rooms to divide and eat the delicacies, thus learning in this delightful way the virtues of good-neighborliness.

The New Year was not merely a season of festivities. All old business, including most debts, monetary and moral, had to be liquidated before the New Year. The house was made absolutely clean, with pine and bamboo, symbols of longevity, decorating the gateway, and citrus fruit, rice straw, and ferns placed over the door. When the New Year came, life began anew, to the splashing of a ceremonial first bath and the smacking of lips that delighted in the taste of special delicacies like *fuku-cha,* green tea with a pickled apricot, which was to prevent illness, *toso,* a sweet rice wine into which was dipped a little silk bag of such medicinal herbs and spices as pepper, ginger, cinnamon, red beans, rhubarb, and bellflower root, and *zoni,* a rice-cake soup containing chicken or duck, vegetables, and greens. During the holidays, the first three days of the year, Nobusuke wore a brand-new kimono as he greeted visiting friends and relatives bearing gifts, and then, with his family, returned the visits and equivalent gifts.

There were also important religious ceremonies to be observed during the New Year holidays. The ancestral spirits of a Japanese family are just as much a part of the household as their living descendants. Immortality is probably a more real concept to the Japanese than to Westerners. Many Americans have only a fingers-crossed hopefulness that they will find a life-after-death, while the Japanese keep their ancestors alive in their hearts and their memories. With the help of the cobwebbed remains of a paper fan, fish, and a piece of hemp ceremonially placed on the ridgepole of the house, the spirits protected the Sato family from harm, and in return, the family paid them homage with a mixture of Buddhist and Shinto ritual observance conducted every morning.

Services were not only held in the home. Almost daily, Moyo and her children humbly honored their guardian god, the god of war, at nearby Hachiman Shrine. They would first wash their hands at a sacred fountain, then, on entering, contribute to the offering box, clap hands, bow a moment, pray, clap hands again, and leave. Many were the times that Nobu-suke played games—usually "soldier"—in the shade of the trees that surrounded the austere temple of Hachiman, the deified spirit of an ancient war-loving Emperor.

There were many other shrines in the area also, State Shinto as well as "religious" shrines. At the official temples, ceremonies were performed only during festivals and state occasions. There was a hierarchy of about five thousand such shrines in Japan, the most important being Ise, which was dedicated to the Sun Goddess, and Yasukuni, where the spirits of soldiers who died in battle for the Emperor were deified. Ise established the link between the Emperor and his divine ancestors, while Yasukuni underscored the axiom that to die for the Emperor was the greatest honor one could achieve.

Life in Tabuse, as elsewhere in Japan, centered around the shrine. Gay, colorful lantern-decorated festivals were held at planting time to implore the god of a particular temple to bless the village crop, and before the harvest to thank him for having done so. People came from all around to participate in these ceremonies. Temporary booths were set up near the shrine where the children would buy toys, cakes, or bean-paste candy often molded into the shapes of animals by the proprietor before their joyous eyes. Tumblers thrilled the crowds; artists, using colored sand, drew pictures of people on the ground, and sometimes Shinto dances and dramas were performed by amateur players who wore masks of the demon and swung long gleaming swords, drawing laughter from the spectators even during scenes of deepest tragedy.

At one of these festivals, several miles from his home, Nobusuke, in the care of a neighbor, got lost in the crowd when he stopped to purchase a few sen worth of fried bean curd. As evening approached, he started toward his home, though not sure of the direction. Soon he found himself alone and frightened, with only the moon to guide him through the darkness. Even the moon played tricks on him, its glow filtering through the rustling trees on either side of the road in grotesque patterns.

In the distance, he thought he saw a string of fires, like flashing lanterns, bobbing along the horizon, a sight that filled him with terror. He remembered his mother telling him that bewitching foxes often left behind them a row of fires just like that as they sped along with the wind. He halted for a moment and pondered whether to run back toward the festival or continue on. He decided to keep going.

He recalled the experience of his grandmother, who often came from Yamaguchi City to see his family. One evening, returning from a visit to a neighboring village with her servant, who was weighted down with a large box of bean curd, a gift from her hosts, she decided to take a short cut home through a thick wood; but she and her servant soon found themselves hopelessly lost. Suddenly, they sighted an old herb peddler carrying an open umbrella. Nobusuke's grandmother asked the way to her village. "You are heading in the wrong direction," the man said. "Come here and I will lead you home." But something in the man's manner made Nobusuke's grandmother distrust him and she and her servant hurried away. They finally emerged from the wood and found the road home.

The next day a rumor spread in the village that the man in the forest was in reality a fox that had tried to trick Nobusuke's grandmother out of her bean curd, the fox's favorite dish, according to Japanese tradition. The next night, she put the bean curd outside the house to see if the fox would come for it. In the morning, it was gone.

As Nobusuke nervously reflected on this tale, he realized that the "row of fires" he saw were lights emanating from the houses of a village—his own. He was so glad not to be lost that he ran across the fields and all the way home. Not until he was inside the house did he note that he had dropped or lost the box of bean curd. To this day Kishi, as a politician, has retained his respect for the cleverness of the fox, the subtle ways in which the creature is able to satisfy his appetite for bean curd.

While Nobusuke grew up in a world brocaded with remnants of samurai verse, jeweled spears, and rice-cake offerings to the god of war, the rulers of Japan were weaving these ideological threads into a hard national fabric. They were trying to reinforce the myth of Japan's divinity with the steel filament of international recognition. They had made a good start with the crushing military victory over China in 1895,

shortly before Kishi's birth, and by 1899 all Western nations had relinquished their extraterritorial rights in Japan.

But Japan was becoming an object of fear as well as of respect. Russia in particular was alarmed. Japanese occupation of the Liaotung
Peninsula in China threatened its plan to conquer Manchuria and Korea.
Germany and France also wanted stronger footholds in the Far East.
These three nations demanded that Japan return the Liaotung area to
China, and the Japanese, unable to resist such concerted pressure,
agreed. In 1898 the three Western powers themselves extended their
own interests in China, with Russia moving into Liaotung, which Japan
had just evacuated.

What had hitherto been largely a desire for world status on the part
of Japan became a matter of honor, pride and vengeance. The Japanese could, without bitterness, accept defeat in the face of superior power,
but trickery was another matter. They were determined to wipe away the
stain of this humiliation which Russia had engineered. "Abide the time
by sleeping on beds of thorns and feeding on gall," the government told
the people as they prepared themselves for the inevitable showdown.

Japan found a willing instrument of vengeance in Great Britain, which
also feared the colonial ambitions of Russia. An Anglo-Japanese alliance
was concluded in 1902, calling for each to help the other should either
of the two nations, while already at war with one power, be attacked by
a second. The alliance guaranteed Japan that it would not have to fight
alone if, in the event of a war with Russia, the latter brought its own
allies into the conflict.

Japan decided to open war with Russia at an Imperial Conference on
February 4, 1904. When the meeting was over, Prince Ito, who was then
the President of the Privy Council, asked Viscount Kentaro Kaneko, a
Privy Councilor, to go to the United States to win American support for
Japan, but the Viscount was reluctant to undertake the assignment. He
later recorded his conversation with Ito:

> "You do not wish to go because you are not certain of success. Is
> that so?"
> "Even so, Your Grace."
> "Then I must tell you something," said Prince Ito. "We are going
> to war, but there is not one of us who believes we can be successful.
> Neither in the Army, nor the Navy, nor in the Ministry of Finance is
> there a single person who thinks we can win. Before we decided to
> declare war, I went and talked with the authorities at both the Army
> and Navy offices, and they all agreed that there was no chance of
> victory. But that does not alter the fact that if Russia is left alone, she

will go on to take complete possession of Manchuria and, after that, would invade Korea, and eventually threaten even Japan. In these circumstances, there is no alternative. We are bound to fight, even at the price of our very national existence. It is futile to discuss the outcome, success or failure. I, for one, am perfectly willing to surrender all I have and enjoy to the service of His Majesty, since all I have or hold is but a gift from him. For the very existence of our country is at stake, and no argument can be more weighty. I say frankly I expect no success.

"The same argument applies to you. All you have and hold you also owe to His Majesty, and we must place his cause above all other considerations. Take my hand, and let us work together, be the odds what they may. I have taken my resolution. Should all our army be driven back from Manchuria, should all our ships of war be sent to the bottom of Tsushima Strait, and should the Russians press on to attack our country itself, then I should shoulder a gun and join the ranks. On the coast of San-in or of Kyushu I would fight as long as I could stand and refuse to yield an inch of ground to the Russians. You remember how, when the Mongols raided our country in ancient times, Hojo Tokimune, who was then military regent, declared himself ready, if need be, to join the ranks and go into the front line; and how he told his wife that she would have to come to Kyushu with him in order to cook rice porridge for the soldiers. So would I, if the occasion arises, tell my own wife, even as Tokimune did, to come to San-in or Kyushu with me to provide rice porridge for our men fighting against the Russians. I'd take up my gun and fight and die with the rest. With my mind so made up, I refuse to worry any more about failure or success. So why should you be anxious about success? Just go, and do the best you can to win the American people over to our cause. That is all I ask of you."

Viscount Kaneko was so deeply moved by Prince Ito's words that he undertook the mission to the United States. Less than forty years later, these words were still remembered by Nobusuke Kishi as he debated with himself the question of whether Japan should go to war with the United States.

The Japanese Navy, striking without warning, knocked out most of the Russian fleet at Port Arthur and Chemulpo. The Czar was caught by surprise, not having dreamed that Japan would dare to take on so powerful a nation as Russia, or to do it with so blatant a disregard for international "rules of war."

Hachiman became the most popular god in Tabuse, and elsewhere throughout the nation, as Japan's warrior sons undertook the first important leg of the long road to the sun. The Satos and their neighbors went more often than before to pay homage in Hachiman Shrine, and

Nobusuke and his classmates, armed with wooden swords and stone "hand grenades," played soldier within his divine shadow. These were exciting days for Nobusuke and his friends, especially with news sifting in of victory after victory. Nobusuke built up a library from the books his Uncle Matsui sent him concerning the lives of the noted Japanese generals. He carried these books to school, reading them between lessons, and he re-read them at night by the light of an oil lamp as he lay in bed.

In the evenings, townsmen were always dropping in at the Sato house to discuss the allocation of war bonds and other matters pertaining to the civilian war effort. Nobusuke, who was not allowed to sit in on these sessions, would open the door of his room slightly and watch the people as they talked, their serious expressions and anxious voices making him realize that war was not only a matter of marching bands and glorious victories, but of finance, supplies, transportation problems, and civilian privation. When little black urns of ashes—the remains of dead soldiers—started arriving, the ugly side of war struck home. Sometimes, Nobusuke and his classmates were let out of school to participate in mass funerals for the returned dead, and inevitably, the village heads and elders offered identical eulogies on every such occasion. Nobusuke memorized most of the words, the last few being: "May their souls come down from heaven to accept our sincere condolences." After each funeral, the children were treated to bean-jam bread.

Then came New Year's Day, 1905. The Satos had risen early that morning, and, as was the custom on this sacred holiday, stood by the windows at dawn bowing and clapping their hands in honor of Japan's patroness, the Sun Goddess. After a delicious ceremonial breakfast of *fuku-cha, toso* and *zoni,* Nobusuke went back to the new book he was reading, a holiday gift from Uncle Matsui—the biography of General Nogi, who was now leading the Japanese armies in Manchuria.

So deep was his concentration that he hardly heard a voice from the front garden crying, "Nobusuke! Nobusuke!" Finally, as the voice grew louder, the boy closed his book and ran to the door. He slid it open and saw his friend Shuichi.

"What's the matter?" Nobusuke asked. "Why are you screaming so?"

"Haven't you heard?" cried the visitor. "General Nogi has captured Port Arthur."

Nobusuke's long, slender face remained immobile. "I told you he would," he said, shrugging. "Didn't I say we have the best army in the world—better than the Russians or anybody?"

"Come on out," said his friend. "Everybody is celebrating."

Nobusuke disappeared behind the paper door, and in a few minutes, clad in his new holiday kimono and bamboo sandals, was walking with Shuichi down the narrow road leading to the center of the village. Tabuse was alive with joy and gaiety. The two boys passed a group of women dressed in decorous kimonos around which were wound splendidly brocaded *obi* belts knotted in back into huge butterfly-wing bows, their hair intricately woven in the basket-like geisha style, with an enormous bun on top. *"Omedeto!* Happy New Year," Nobusuke called out to them.

Still further along, they stopped to watch a group of young girls, who, unaccustomed to being observed by young men, were laughing and giggling as they daintily manipulated their wooden paddles in the New Year's game of *hanetsuki,* sending a shuttlecock drifting in slow arcs across a grass court. In a nearby field, some of Nobusuke's friends were flying kites, specks of color bobbing in the misty sky like stars out of orbit. "Did you hear about Port Arthur?" one of them yelled.

"Yes," called Nobusuke. "What a fine New Year's gift for our Emperor!"

An old man with a small, pointed white beard and gnarled body which he supported with a stick hobbled toward them, waving colored pieces of paper. "Boys," he cried in a frayed voice, "buy one of these and you shall have pleasant dreams tonight. You will dream of cherry blossoms, or of *Fujisan,* or of a bird. Put it under your pillow tonight and enjoy good luck throughout the year."

Nobusuke and Shuichi each bought a slip of paper on which was printed a picture of a ship whose passengers were the seven gods of fortune, and whose cargo included several precious signs of fortune: gold, silver, coral, crystal, agate, emerald, pearl, and a book of great learning.

"What do you want to dream about tonight, Nobusuke?" Shuichi asked.

"General Nogi, of course," Nobusuke answered. "Isn't he Japan's greatest soldier?"

The boys wandered on until they came to a rice paddy bordered by bamboo poles from which fluttered the flags of more than a score of nations. Dozens of children were dancing and playing around the poles, splashing barefoot in the paddy water and screaming *"Banzai! Banzai!"*

"Let's play soldier," Shuichi suggested. "All the kids are out today. Enough for a whole army."

"All right," agreed Nobusuke. "I'll be general."

"I want to be general this time," protested his companion. "It was my idea. Besides, I have a new samurai sword. My father made it for me out of wood."

Nobusuke reddened. "You may have a wooden samurai sword, but remember, I come from a samurai family that used real swords. My great-grandfather was the first governor of Shimane, and someday I shall be a *real* general."

The two boys walked along in silence for a few moments. Almost unconsciously, Nobusuke was allowing time for his haughty words to sink in. Then he said with finality, "I shall either be general or I won't play."

Shuichi finally conceded and Nobusuke played, but with the bitterness of a boy, yearning to be a grown man, who knew he had still many years to wait.

The Japanese armies relentlessly followed up their Port Arthur victory, pouring northward into Manchuria as the Czar's battered forces retreated, depending for reinforcements and supplies on a single-track railway thousands of miles long. In May, 1905, Russia's European fleet, arriving from the Baltic Sea, was destroyed by the Japanese Navy in the Korean Straits. This was the knockout blow, since it gave the Japanese complete domination of the sea. Russia, suing for peace, agreed in a peace treaty signed in Portsmouth, New Hampshire, under the auspices of President Theodore Roosevelt, to recognize Japanese supremacy in Korea, transfer to Japan its Liaotung Peninsula lease and the South Manchurian Railway, and cede half of Sakhalin Island.

The Satos, like most Japanese, were, at first, dissatisfied with what they considered a "soft" peace in the light of Japan's overwhelming victory. And there was some resentment toward the United States for having insisted that Japan exercise "moderation," using, it was felt, financial pressure to force its will on the Japanese. Banks in the United States which had furnished considerable credit during the early phases of the war suddenly, and rather mysteriously, grew less generous as the Japanese exhibited their unsuspected military power. Though Theodore Roosevelt had favored a Japanese victory to offset Russian strength in the Far East, he had begun to see Japan as ultimately a worse threat to American interests in Asia than Russia.

But as hometown soldiers triumphantly returned to *banzai* greetings, their tunics glittering with ribbons and their pockets bulging with souvenirs for their families and friends, the feeling of bitterness began to wane. Japan, after all, had avenged itself. Its faith in the gods had been justified. As a foreign military critic had commented, "Japan has

been victorious because she had learned that war is a business, not
merely of the soldier or of the sailor, but of the nation as a whole." The
victory of the Japanese was a triumph of a people over a government. In
less than four decades, the nation, rising as one man, had climbed from
the debris of Shimonoseki to a top rung on the ladder of world power
and prestige. And now that Japan finally had a solid foothold on
the Asian mainland, it was clear which road to the sun was the shortest.

As Japan floated in the glory of victory in its first major war with a
power of the Western world, Nobusuke continued his preliminary training for a role in the new and rising empire. After completing four years
of primary school, the compulsory education ceiling in Japan at that
time, he switched to Nishida Advanced Primary School, which com-
prised the fifth and sixth grades. Few of his classmates accompanied him,
for most of them, coming from poor peasant families, had to go to
work on their farms. Though faced with far stiffer competition in more
difficult courses—history, geography, and science were added to the
curriculum—Nobusuke maintained his position at the top of his class.

School actually became easier for him now than in the lower elementary grades, for he had never before had a teacher like Mr. Nukita.
Mr. Nukita taught the boy far more than textbook facts; he taught him
tolerance and understanding. Nobusuke one day was given a large sum
of money by his father to deposit in the bank, but before reaching his
destination he stopped at the post office and inadvertently left the money
wrapped in a paper bag, on a table while mailing a letter. When he returned it was gone.

Panic gripped him. He questioned every person in the post office, but
nobody had noticed the disappearance of the package. Finally Nobusuke
started toward home, embarrassed, ashamed, and afraid of what his
parents would say. He contemplated running away. Only the knowledge
that fleeing was a worse disgrace gave him the strength to go to his
father and admit that he had lost the money. If he fled, he would be an
outcast, a *hinin,* wherever he went. People would shun him, suspect him.
He would, he decided, spend whatever portion of his life was required
paying the money back. He found his father in the parlor squatting on a
cushion in a corner reading a newspaper. Hidesuke looked up as his son
entered.

"Father," Nobusuke said, "I—I've got something to tell you. Something—very bad."

"Yes, son," Hidesuke replied, removing his round wire-rimmed
spectacles.

"It's the money . . ."

"Did you deposit it?" his father asked.

"No, I stopped off at the post office to mail a letter. I left the money on a table and somebody took it."

Hidesuke did not reply immediately. His fingers rather nervously played with the rims of his glasses, adjusting them. "This calls for a conversation between men," he said, "but I think you should have your mother in to advise you what to say."

He called in Moyo and explained what had happened. Without changing expression, she turned toward Nobusuke, then said simply, in her usual restrained but demanding voice, "Apologize to your father." When Nobusuke had offered apologies in a trembling voice, his eyes still lowered, Hidesuke, feeling great compassion for the boy in his humiliation, replied, "I still trust you, my son. Only be more careful after this. We are not rich people, you know."

After a pause, Moyo said, as if nothing really important had occurred, "Dinner will be ready in a few minutes."

The kind, forgiving attitude of his parents shocked Nobusuke. He felt much more strongly than if he had been punished the need to find or to replace the missing money. Since it would take him years to earn that amount of money, and since he did not know where to begin looking for the thief, he sought the help of Yamato, the fortuneteller. Yamato, who lived in a small house at the edge of town, was reputed for his inaccurate predictions, but people went to see him anyway, for his prophecies always filled them with hope and happy tidings. And in matters which, like a coin, had only two sides, he was at least sometimes right, and therefore deserved a certain respect.

"Oinari-sama, the fox god, will help us find the thief," Yamato said, "but we must offer a few sen to show our appreciation to Oinari-sama."

When Nobusuke had taken money from his pocket and given it, the fortuneteller knelt and prayed briefly before a small altar dedicated to the spirit of the fox god. Then he took a dish filled with vinegar from the altar and chanted softly as he moved his bony hands in an impressive circular motion over it. Nobusuke noticed that a snail at the bottom of the dish slowly moved toward the surface as the chant progressed, its movement supposedly indicating the direction in which the thief had fled. But though Yamato could point his arm in the direction in which the thief had gone, he was too far away to be able to get a clear view of his face. "He is a man with an evil face and narrow hands," said Yamato.

"He will try to steal again and will be caught. You may rest assured that he will be severely punished."

The visit with Yamato convinced Nobusuke that he was not likely to catch the thief, but the bitterness of the loss of the money remained with him. He went many times to the post office, hoping somehow that there, where the theft had taken place, he would perhaps again encounter the thief, or someone who might have seen the money taken.

One day Mr. Nukita, his teacher, who had noticed the change in the boy, asked him what was the matter, and Nobusuke told him about the theft. "I'll never trust anybody again," he said.

The teacher replied, "It's true there's an old saying that one shouldn't trust strangers. But it is a false saying. No man is perfect, but you must always look for the good in him. You must not doubt or fear him just because you have been hurt once. Or you shall be unhappy, not just for the moment, but for the rest of your life."

This talk had a profound effect on Nobusuke. He began to look, as Mr. Nukita had advised, for the good in people—friends and strangers —and found that he liked people better, and that they liked him better, too. He was no longer uneasy about the responsibility of carrying his father's money to the bank. He was more careful than he had been in the past, but he was not suspicious and distrustful.

CHAPTER IV

SEEKING THE SLOT

T HE TIME now drew near for Nobusuke to seek his proper place in the great social web that promised him, while throbbing with the tension of entrapment, a snug, indestructible niche of security. In a way, Nobusuke looked forward to being settled in this niche, philosophizing that if something was inevitable it was probably good, but he nevertheless shuddered at the thought of losing the chaotic, relatively unfettered freedom that he could afford to enjoy only as a child. Even more frightening was the struggle ahead to discover his proper place. For if it was to be near the top, the climb would be full of agony and bitterness bred by intense competition, and, with personal and family honor so deeply involved, of festering wounds if he fell short of his goal. He comforted himself with the thought that when the competition ended, he would fall into his slot, whatever it was, as an anarchic *pachinko** ball bouncing against many obstacles finally comes to rest in the cavity for which it is destined. This, after all, was the logical, the unavoidable, order of things.

Nobusuke moved in with his Uncle Matsui, who now lived in Okayama, a good distance from Tabuse, so that he might attend the superior Uchiyamashimo Primary School, where he could best prepare himself for

---

* *Pachinko* is a Japanese pin ball game in which the ball falls vertically. Played in special *pachinko* parlors, the game is one of the most popular forms of entertainment in Japan.

the hard middle-school entrance examination ahead. Nobusuke was delighted to live with his uncle, a younger brother of Moyo, who had stayed with the boy's family in Yamaguchi City. Later, they had gone fishing together many times during the summers in Tabuse. Matsui was obligated to take Nobusuke in repayment for favors that had been bestowed upon him by the Satos, but he would gladly have done this even if *giri* had not been involved.

Matsui's home—he purchased it when, after obtaining a degree in medicine at the Imperial University of Tokyo, he took a job teaching obstetrics at Okayama Medical College—was even more crowded than had been the Sato home in Yamaguchi City. Living with him in addition to his own wife and children were his many brothers, sisters, and nieces, including Nobusuke's two sisters. His home, like the one in Yamaguchi City, was always brimming over with visiting students, who were also beneficiaries of his generosity. All of Matsui's spare yen went for the education of his relatives and young friends. In return, they had only to listen quietly while the doctor, who was avidly interested in politics, expounded his political views. The house was located near an old feudal castle that was surrounded by a lotus-speckled moat, a fine place for dragonfly hunting in the summer. Uncle Matsui treated Nobusuke like a long lost son, buying him many gifts, including khaki knee breeches and bamboo sandals, which made him the envy of his class—most pupils wore plain Japanese kimonos and straw sandals they fashioned themselves. Matsui also taught his nephew the finer points of gardening, having won several prizes for the huge morning glories he meticulously cultivated in his garden.

But gentle and tender-hearted as Matsui was, he insisted that Nobusuke be brought up in a manly way. Whenever the boy would carry one of his two baby cousins on his back, the father would tell his wife, Shizue, "Don't let him do that. Do you want him to grow up to be a nursemaid?" Matsui, a powerfully built man who had starred in baseball and crew in his own school days, urged his nephew to participate in sports, purchasing him as enticements a tennis racquet and a baseball bat and glove. Nobusuke used them, though reluctantly, for he knew he would never excel in these sports. When he entered middle school, he was required to enroll in judo and fencing courses. In judo he became an expert in the art of falling down safely, and managed to defend himself with skill, but he learned little about how to put another man down. Still, Nobusuke had pluck, once wrestling an elephantine classmate who was destined to become a great *sumo* champion. He lost magnificently.

The fight to enter middle school represented the beginning of the great lifetime struggle to keep one's family name free of humiliation or dishonor. It was humiliating indeed to fail an entrance examination, and the competition was all the more bitter because of the individual ranking system used. Okayama Middle School was one of the most difficult middle schools in Japan to enter, with only about one out of four competitors making the grade.

Before the examination, Nobusuke, encouraged by his uncle, studied day and night—a new experience in discipline for him. Late one night, Matsui entered the boy's room and, finding him asleep on the *tatami* beside his books, gently shook him. "This isn't the time for sleep," he said. "You must study."

His nephew rubbed his eyes, moaning, "But I'm tired. I want to sleep."

Matsui replied sternly, "There is no want or need in the world that you cannot conquer if you make the effort. You must discipline yourself to do even what you consider is impossible. That is the only way to succeed in life."

Nobusuke, who had had little competition in Primary School in Tabuse, knew that he was not as well prepared for the examination as some of the other boys. When he had finally taken the test, he dragged himself home from school, pale with fear that he had failed. He even considered committing suicide if the results were negative. But within the next few days he learned that he had passed. He went immediately to the tailor's and ordered a black brass-buttoned uniform and peaked cap, which middle-school students wore as a means of de-emphasizing the importance of social rank in school. The very sight of the uniform filled him with pride.

Uncle Matsui was almost as happy as his nephew. "I knew you would bring honor to the Sato family," he told him. "And I hope you will always be at the top of your class."

"I wonder if all boys' lives are as up and down as mine was," Kishi said to me when I was questioning him about his childhood. "One day I would be on top of the world, and the next I would do something stupid, thoughtless or clumsy, and so lose the honor it had taken me so long to achieve. All my studying for examinations, all the happiness I felt at the sight of my uniform, all this vanished because of a little red teapot."

This teapot belonged to Uncle Matsui, whose mother had given it to him when he was a child. He always used it to make green tea in his room over a *hibachi*. One afternoon Nobusuke happened to glance into the room, unoccupied at the time. The aroma emanating from the teapot smelled good. He entered and knelt down on the *tatami,* sure that his uncle wouldn't mind if he enjoyed a cup of his tea. As he poured, the lid fell on a wooden tray and broke. Panicked, Nobusuke hurried out of the room. Later, Matsui found the broken object and inquired around the house how the accident had happened.

"I don't know anything about it," Nobusuke lied.

The youth could hardly look Matsui in the eye. He saw written on his face, not anger, which he could have borne, but only deep sadness.

Uncle Matsui, only thirty-five, fell ill with pneumonia and died in April, 1911. Nobusuke was stricken with grief. He owed so much to his uncle, since the very day he was born. Matsui had spoiled him with gifts, gone fishing with him, worried about him, taken him into his home. All this added up to far more than his uncle owed his family or himself. And what had he done to repay Matsui? What was his *giri?* A broken teapot-lid and an unforgivable lie. And now it was too late. His *on* was all the more painful to bear because he wore it for someone he loved so dearly. It was not only simple *giri* that he owed dear Uncle Matsui, but his very heart and soul. What hurt Nobusuke most was the knowledge that his uncle would so willingly have forgiven him.

As Matsui's body lay wrapped in a kimono on a *futon* in his room, surrounded by his kneeling, heartbroken family, Nobusuke at first remained outside the door, unable to face, in his guilt, either the living or the dead. He watched the scene of mourning through a sliver of opening where the door failed to touch the wall. Finally, despite his shame, he entered and fell to his knees beside the corpse, taking his uncle's cold hand in his own, gently patting it several times, then kissing it.

A few days after Matsui's death, Nobusuke was whisked away from Okayama to start a new life in Yamaguchi City, his birthplace. Another uncle, Yosaku Yoshida, husband of Moyo's younger sister, Sawa, offered to care for the boy and see him through Yamaguchi Middle School. Once the decision was made, Yosaku immediately went to Okayama and took his nephew back with him. Nobusuke thus left the home he loved so dearly without even attending Matsui's funeral or saying good-by to his friends and teachers.

Matsui's death had left him in a state of semishock, and for several weeks afterward he was completely apathetic about his fortunes or his future. Day after day, he would lock himself in his room and weep aloud as he lay on the *tatami*. At night he dreamed of Matsui working in his garden among his giant morning glories, or helping him pull in a catch of dace from the river. Sometimes the boy would have nightmares, with monsters shaped like teapots chasing him. He would awaken, crying, "Uncle, Uncle, I'm sorry, please forgive me."

Uncle Yosaku, whose round heavily lined face seemed hardened into a perpetual frown, differed sharply in personality and character from Matsui, and these differences were accentuated by the fact that Yosaku, in his fifties, was much older. A history teacher at Yamaguchi Middle School, he was a serious man, an ardent intellectual, who seldom smiled or saw humor in life, devoting himself entirely to academic pursuits. On returning home from school, he would immediately enter his den, squat down, and on a low desk cluttered with research papers, go to work with brush and ink on a manuscript. He had a deep interest in the history of Yamaguchi and the surrounding areas. For recreation, he studied Japanese and Chinese poetry and collected water paintings. He was very strict with his own children—three sons and a daughter. If Moyo dominated her household, her younger sister had little to say in hers, one reason perhaps why Yosaku had succeeded in the field of his choice, whereas Hidesuke had failed.

Nobusuke was at first frightened by the harsh authoritarian tone of Yosaku. He tried to avoid him, which was not too difficult, for he did not actually live in his uncle's house. Two of Yosaku's students were living in the only unoccupied room, so Nobusuke had been put into a rooming house next door, together with another student. He went to his uncle's house only for meals or whenever his uncle summoned him to appear.

Nobusuke spent his vacations with his family in Tabuse. He always looked forward to these homecomings—until he arrived on one occasion and discovered he was, in a sense, disowned. No sooner had he entered the house and bowed to his father in greeting when Hidesuke, sitting on a cushion by his *hibachi*, tapping a small pipe in the palm of his hand, said to him in the compassionate tone of one who knew from personal experience of the pain he was about to cause, "My son, the time has come when you should get to know your new family."

"My new family, Father?" Nobusuke exclaimed, stirred with sudden misgivings. "You—you mean the Kishis?"

He had suspected his fate for a long time. He was being adopted into the family of his father's elder brother, Nobumasa, as the prospective husband of his ten-year-old cousin, Yoshiko. This had to be. Nobusuke, as the second son in the Sato family, could not be the Sato heir, while on the other hand, his adoptive family had only three girls, no boys. Nobusuke was a natural choice to fill the male gap. Japanese tradition requires that such a gap be filled by adoption, as well as by marriage if there are only daughters, in order that the family name can be perpetuated and the ancestral spirits eternally honored.

So Nobusuke took the name, Kishi, which his father had given up when he himself had been adopted into the Sato family as Moyo's husband. Thus, two generations had swapped names and ancestral lines. The youth was not happy about this, despite his long conditioning to the eventuality, for he was proud of the name Sato. How many times his mother had told him never to forget that he was a Sato, the descendant of famous samurai, and now he was to lose the luster of this name for one far less impressive, and he would have to pay homage to the ancestors of his new family rather than to the Sato spirits.

But what would be hardest to bear was the fact that he was to be permanently separated from his real family. This was all the more frightening when one considered that his adoptive family contained four females—his foster mother and her three daughters—and only one male, his seventy-year-old grandfather. Only the year before, after adoption arrangements had already been made, his prospective foster father had died. It was bad enough, perhaps even a little degrading, for a young man to live in the house of his mother-in-law, but to accept all the obligations that the situation would eventually force upon him was almost terrifying. He was alone among a tribe of women who would try to rule over him and yet make him responsible for them.

Nobusuke realized that his real parents would also suffer. He could see the sadness in his father's eyes as Hidesuke told him the news of his adoption. When he saw Moyo a few minutes later, he wanted to run into her arms and beg her to keep him, but that was not the way of the samurai. Nor did he want to cause his mother any more distress than he knew she felt. Her face had never been more serene or inscrutable, an unmistakable sign that she was hiding a deep anguish. And her voice was softer than usual as she inquired about his studies and grades, completely ignoring the subject that was disturbing both of them so profoundly. He answered her with the same casualness that she displayed. Such conversation at a time like this spoke more eloquently of the depth of their feelings than if they had emotionally revealed them.

Nobusuke spent most of his vacation at the Satos', sleeping there every night. He only visited the Kishis at the insistence of his parents, though he knew he was now obligated to at least act the role of a son to his foster mother, but he would hardly look at his prospective wife, Yoshiko. He wasn't sure whether this was due to embarrassment or resentment at having to take her name. As the family knelt on cushions around the dinner table in silence, Yoshiko, a gentle girl with a shy smile, would steal frequent glances at him as she scooped mounds of rice into her tiny mouth with her chopsticks, turning away with an air of unconcern whenever his gaze met hers. Neither, it seemed, could quite imagine the other as his, or her, lifetime mate.

Moreover, Nobusuke could not acclimate himself to the gloomy atmosphere of a house which suffered from physical decay, womanish over-tidiness, and the absence of male authority. The house, over a century old, showed its age, with most of the rooms somehow dark even when the sun was shining in. Several rusty lances lay on the transom over the front door, and other ancient relics could be found inside. The Kishis maintained many old-fashioned customs. When placing a candle on the altar of the household shrine, they used flint to light a fire, believing matches too impure for the purpose. As electric lights were not yet available in this part of the town, flickering paper lanterns were used, adding to the dreariness of the house.

The atmosphere here, Nobusuke thought, certainly differed from the carefree, careless spirit that pervaded the relatively modern Sato house-hold, or the gaiety and energy of the dormitory-like home of Uncle Matsui. Yet, oddly enough, his foster mother, Chiyo, was reputed as a "very progressive" woman, too much so for the strong traditionalists. She had been graduated from a teacher's college at a time when only a handful of women—which did not even include a woman of such in-telligence and background as Moyo—attended middle school. Chiyo sometimes startled the village by appearing in Western-style dresses she fashioned out of kimono cloth.

Nobusuke, however, did derive one joy from his reluctant visits with his adoptive family—the wonderful garden at the rear of the house and the large camphor-wood veranda overlooking it. This garden, an unusually beautiful composition, formed a magnificently fresh and color-ful contrast to the gloominess of the house. At lunchtime, Nobusuke sat on the veranda like a young prince while Grandfather, with his shaky, withered hands, prepared the most delicious bean curd baked in *miso,* or soy sauce. The boy began to sense that there were advantages to being the only young male in the house, privileges and rights which would soon be his. Still, Nobusuke was only too glad when vacation was over and he could return to school, which somehow seemed to relieve him of the terrible tension born of his new family relationships.

Far more study was required in middle school than in primary school. For one thing, subjects were much harder, including English and European history and geography, which offered him his first taste of Western influence. And with the tougher competition, a photographic memory and a quick mind alone were not enough to get top grades. For the first time he decided to devote himself wholeheartedly to study. This decision stemmed partly from Uncle Yosaku's stern, demanding attitude, but a more important factor was the bittersweet knowledge that Uncle Matsui's fondest desire had been to see him at the top of his class. Nobusuke remembered Matsui's words, "There is no want or need in the world that you cannot conquer if you make the effort." He vowed to please the beloved spirit of his uncle.

Assigned to a classroom of students chosen on the basis of height, he topped the whole school—in terms of academic standing if not size— in the first examination. This did not enhance his popularity among the other students, to whom the name Sato (Nobusuke continued to use his original family name in school) had little of the magic effect it had had in the more feudal-minded Tabuse. They were jealous that a newcomer had won highest honors. And they found an excuse for taunting him in his lack of athletic skill. Nobusuke loved to go on long walks, and, on Sundays, to climb nearby mountains, and he enjoyed playing in the garden of the local shrine and hunting fireflies when they were out. But he still avoided competitive sports, though, remembering Uncle Matsui's emphasis on athletics, he sometimes played tennis and baseball and studied judo and fencing. He also ran in the school's annual seven-mile marathon race, which was compulsory for all students, finishing among the last.

The attitude of his fellows deeply hurt Nobusuke. But certainly he would not deliberately sacrifice his grades to please them. Still, there had to be some way to earn their admiration. One day, unwittingly, he found it. A student in his class had misbehaved and a notice announcing his suspension had been tacked to the class bulletin board—but someone took it down, probably to save the boy "face." The teacher was furious.

"Who took the notice down?" he demanded.

No one responded.

"Very well," the instructor said, "the whole class will remain after school every day for a week—or until the guilty one admits his error."

Utter silence prevailed for several moments. Then Nobusuke rose slowly and said in a halting voice, "Teacher, I took the notice down. I apologize."

Silence again. This time it was broken by quiet sobbing among the students, who knew that he was innocent. But Nobusuke did not know that they knew. He trembled as he thought of the disgrace he would be bringing on his whole family if he were suspended. And Yosaku was a teacher in this very school. Maybe he shouldn't have taken the blame after all, he told himself. In fact, he wasn't quite sure why he was doing it, why he was trying to show his loyalty before a group of boys who had exhibited little love for him. Yet somehow he sensed he was doing the right thing. And he did not intend to back down.

The teacher finally spoke, addressing the class as a whole. "Let's see to it that such nonsense does not happen again. Nobusuke, I accept your apology, and I thank you for showing us all that there are times when a lie has some honor to it." He continued with his lessons as if nothing had happened.

A year after Nobusuke entered Yamaguchi Middle School—on July 30, 1912—the Emperor Meiji died. The Emperor's vigorous personality had been reflected in the great revolutionary policies his protectors had instituted in his name. Ever since the overthrow of the Tokugawa, when the Sovereign was only twelve years old, he had been the living symbol of the new Japan, the Japan that the gods had destined to find its rightful place in the sun. In the span of his lifetime, Japan had developed from a weak feudal state into a great modern power commanding the respect of the world.

The emotional impact of the Emperor's death reached its zenith on the day of his funeral. On that day, while millions mourned, General Nogi, the hero of the Russo-Japanese war, and his wife, fell to their knees, and, in the old samurai tradition of self-immolation on the death of one's lord, committed *hara-kiri* so that they could continue serving their master in the world of spirits.

This dramatic event, together with the death of the Emperor himself, released a surge of nationalistic sentiment in Japan rivaling the fanaticism that had followed the victory against the Russians. It was a nationalism composed of two seemingly contradictory elements: the dynamism of a new modern society in the midst of revolution, and the glory of a stagnant, but spiritually vigorous, feudal past. Mixed together, these two ingredients formed a powerful, and potentially explosive, political potion.

Nobusuke was himself on the point of exploding when he read the comment in a British newspaper that Japan had reached its maximum state of development and, with the Emperor's death, would enter a period of decline. He was equally infuriated by the charge of a Japanese scholar that General Nogi's suicide was a "step backwards into feudal medievalism."

Nobusuke sat down and wrote a reply to the scholar's "stupid" comments, entitling it, "In Memory of General Nogi." He submitted it in class as a composition assignment, which his teacher commended and pinned on the wall as a model example of "patriotism and logic." It read:

"General Nogi died the death of a true samurai. It is this samurai spirit that shall carry Japan to ever greater heights. I count the day of his death as one of the most important in my progress toward manhood. I sensed then for the first time that I was destined to serve Japan with whatever small talents I possessed. That is a great concept for a boy to understand—that his country is as real as his home, that his countrymen are as real as his own brothers and sisters. And I owe much of this understanding to General Nogi."

The emotion of the moment at first strengthened Nobusuke's childhood desire to become a great general. Then, suddenly, he wanted to join the Navy. He was influenced in part by the success of his elder brother, Ichiro, who was chalking up the highest marks ever recorded in the history of the Imperial Naval Academy, and also by his enjoyment on school boat excursions. But as the time approached when he had to make up his mind whether to enter a military preparatory school or a high school to study for a future in government, he began to turn against the idea of a military career. One reason was his rather delicate physical condition and distaste for athletics, which he feared might block his path to the top. Also, he was impressed by the success of his uncle-in-law, Matsuoka, who was a career diplomat, and he remembered the deep interest that Uncle Matsui had displayed in politics. But it was not easy making up his mind what he wanted to do, especially with the pressures that were exerted on the students by military leaders in the district. Generals visited the school and spoke of Choshu's glorious army tradition, and although naval tradition was strongest in Satsuma, admirals also solicited future officers, both offering as an enticement to lend tuition and expense money to students who would "choose the road to glory."

Nobusuke, despite the offers of the militarists and the pleadings of his friends, most of whom chose this road, finally decided he would enter high school and pursue a political career. One general, who had hoped to corral the boy, angrily told him, "You have made a big mistake.

There's no excuse for a brilliant young man like you, born in Choshu, choosing a civilian career. Our future lies in the hands of the military." But Nobusuke had made up his mind. After all, he thought, could he not, as a civilian leader, work together with the military, as Prince Ito had done?

Nobusuke, after completing his five years of middle school, graduated as the best student in his class, winning this honor by driving himself furiously—particularly in his last year—in competition with another brilliant student. So intense did the rivalry become that Nobusuke once cheated in an examination in drawing, his weak spot. Though this was discovered, he overcame the black mark and finally nosed out his rival when his English teacher gave him an unprecedented grade of 101 per cent. All Nobusuke had wanted to do was learn, but, instead, he had been forced to make the competitive aspect of school his main concern. The pressures exerted upon him by his teachers and his friends, and the ranting of Uncle Yosaku had made him feel as if they were threatening rather than encouraging him.

"Don't forget," Yosaku would say in his flat, persistent voice, "the honor of the whole family is at stake. And the fact that I teach at the school makes the matter all the more delicate."

Now, with the family honor temporarily upheld, the time came for a new, and even more nerve-shattering, turn of the screw—the high-school entrance examination. High school in Japan at the time was a college-level institution intended strictly as preparation for entrance into an Imperial university. Nobusuke applied for entry into tradition-bound Tokyo First Senior High School, which was the highest-rated high school in Japan and intended mainly for students hoping to get into government service. Students who survived the academic rigors of this institution and then of the Imperial University of Tokyo, where Nobusuke planned to go later, stood the best chance of being recruited into the plum positions in the bureaucracy. The youth, determined to launch his career enjoying the maximum advantage, packed his things and went to Tokyo to prepare himself for the new competitive struggle ahead.

He settled in a student boardinghouse and enrolled in a special school devoted to getting students through the examination successfully. This school, he soon discovered, was hardly conducive to the discipline required for concentrated study. No one cared whether he was late for class, or if he came at all. Thus, still overwound from the intense middle-school rivalry, Nobusuke neglected his lessons for movies, plays, and long walks through Tokyo. He was enjoying his first real taste of freedom since childhood, and he was somewhat annoyed at himself for his lack of self-discipline. "Can I only do my studies when I have someone like Uncle Yosaku shouting at me?" he asked himself. But just as Nobusuke had begun to take hold of himself, his studies suffered further when he fell ill with beriberi.

Examination day found Nobusuke only partially prepared—a realization that struck him with crushing force the moment he entered the testing room. When he came out, he felt even more miserable. Adding to his apprehension was the warning of an older student who told him, "The best middle-school students in the provinces can't compare with the average student from Tokyo schools. So, if you think you passed, you may not have. And if you think you didn't do well, you probably did even worse."

Nobusuke went home to Tabuse to await word of his fate. He bitterly reproached himself. If only he could feel, he reflected, that it didn't really matter whether he passed or not, or that passing would be only a matter of personal satisfaction, but there were so many people who depended on his success. As he lay sick in bed at the Kishis—he had finally agreed to move into the home of his adoptive family—he brooded in silence and refused to eat. This was partly due to a loss of appetite, partly to an odd resentment of the Kishis' efforts to comfort him, which he found hypocritical in view of the disdain in which they would inevitably hold him when they learned of his failure.

He waited and waited for confirmation of this failure. Finally he received a letter from a student friend in Tokyo, which read, "Nobusuke, you have been accepted as a student of German law. . . . You are very lucky. Your name is almost at the bottom of the list. . . ."

Nobusuke immediately summoned the entire Kishi family into the room and made a formal announcement of his acceptance. He did not tell them how narrowly he had escaped failure. Then, when the rest of the family had left the room, the youth told Yoshiko, "When we're married, I'm going to make you proud of me."

A brief reddening of the girl's cheeks betrayed the effect of this remark. She bowed her head and shoulders slightly and half ran out of the room, too embarrassed, if in a pleasurable way, even to reply. It was the first time that Nobusuke had ever indicated that he was satisfied with the girl who had been chosen to be his wife.

Nobusuke did not stay ill long. Within a week he embarked, with several friends who had also passed the examination, on a celebration of their acceptance. During his middle-school days, he had sometimes visited the boardinghouse of an uninhibited classmate who had induced him to drink considerable sake, as well as to smoke. He was, therefore, quite familiar with the more stimulating methods of enjoying oneself. Equipped with an adequate supply of sake, cigarettes, rice, and noodles, Nobusuke and his companions found themselves a lonely beach cove far enough away from home so that no one they knew would be likely to encounter them. And for three days, the length of time the sake lasted, they did nothing but eat, drink, and sleep. "How we hated to leave that private whirling little world of rice wine where one's soul becomes so eloquent and one's body becomes so shamefully unmanageable," Kishi says.

In September, 1914, shortly after the outbreak of World War I in Europe, Nobusuke returned to Tokyo and moved into a school dormitory, where all first-year students were required to live. The dormitory was a sprawling wooden structure two stories high, with the lower floor arranged for study purposes, and the upper floor divided into sleeping quarters. Nobusuke was assigned to a large matted room containing thirteen students from various parts of Japan.

The dormitories were managed by the students themselves, who elected a government made up of representatives from the various rooms. But another association, this one self-appointed, assumed the task of ensuring discipline among the students, reprimanding and even beating those guilty of such acts as returning from town after "lights out." It was dedicated to making sure that every student abided by the established regulations and moral standards. Nobusuke, like many other students, was rather aghast at these strong-arm methods of exerting group pressure, though he agreed that each student should be made to feel—if by more civilized means—a sense of responsibility toward the dormitory community.

"My own experience in bringing dishonor to the farm boy who had failed to attend class regularly had made me doubt the wisdom of allowing students to inflict punishment," Kishi says. "And to whip or to beat has never, in my opinion, been the best way of making a boy into a man."

But Nobusuke enjoyed most aspects of his high school life. Unlike the more provincial middle school, high school—and especially the dormitory experience—offered him constant opportunity to engage in intellectual discussions on philosophy, art, the origins of the war in progress, and the pursuit of things eternal. For the first time, he found himself among students of mental capacities comparable to his own. Furthermore, high-school life, with its overtones of oriental bohemianism, was more carefree than the university would be, lacking the pressures that lay in thoughts of job-hunting and in highly technical studies.

The courses offered at the high school—law, literature, science, and medicine—were not of a very technical nature. Though Kishi's major subject was German law, little of the technical processes were taught, the German language taking up much of his time. Nobusuke, who had been third from the bottom in the entrance examination, jumped to third from the top at the end of his first year. And he managed to do this without undergoing the tremendous strain he had experienced in middle school, spending more time at the theater than did most students and showing an avid interest in several young actresses. He also found time to do considerable outside reading, especially enjoying novels and philosophical essays. One reason why he was able to earn high grades despite such extracurricular activities was that he had developed extremely effective methods of study. As one classmate explained, "While most of us were still memorizing facts, he was doing his own thinking."

During Kishi's second year, Yoshiko, accompanied by her mother, moved to Tokyo to attend a girls' school, and the youth went to live with them. After a year of dormitory life, he was more than willing to return to the comforts and privileges of a home. The new Kishi house, a small four-room structure, often took on the aspect of a dormitory, with Nobusuke's friends streaming in for chats on philosophy, politics, or a game of go. Kishi was extremely generous, frequently helping his classmates when they were in financial straits. All he had to live on himself was about twelve dollars a month, but he discovered that Yoshiko's kimonos could be exchanged for sizable sums of money at the local pawn shop. Since Yoshiko had a large number of kimonos, she never knew when one was missing—until one day she caught her future husband and his friends ransacking her wardrobe.

"What are you doing?" she cried.

Nobusuke's friends dropped their silken loot and ran out of the house.

"Yoshiko, you see. . . ." Nobusuke began.

"What were you doing with my kimonos?" she asked.

Cornered, Nobusuke finally answered, "I was giving a couple of your kimonos to my friends. They desperately needed the money. But you shouldn't worry about it. I have done this several times before and I always get them back."

"Oh, Nobusuke, how could you do such a thing?" Yoshiko asked.

Kishi shrugged. "What harm did it do you? You ought to be glad that I was able to help my friends when they were in need. In a sense, I was helping the country, too. With the money they obtain with the kimonos they can buy things and thus contribute to the national economy."

"But can't you see how it embarrasses me to know that my kimonos have been in pawn shops?"

Kishi replied sternly, trying to hide his own embarrassment with bluster, "I can see that you put a small virtue above large ones. I can see that you will become a woman with a tight hand and a narrow mind."

Yoshiko, wordlessly but in sobs, turned and dashed into her own room, sliding the door shut behind her.

Churning with a mixed sense of guilt, regret, and relief, Nobusuke went back to his books, wondering why women lacked all understanding of men.

CHAPTER V

❦

CAUGHT IN THE STORM

KISHI ENTERED the Imperial University of Tokyo in 1917 at the age of twenty and was swept into a cauldron of ideological ferment. The campus, which embraced a cluster of old brown-brick Gothic buildings, became the focal point of one of the fiercest national struggles to shake Japan since the Meiji Restoration. Autocratic nationalists, pledged to maintain the political, economic, and social status quo, collided head-on with a fledgling liberal movement that threatened to revolutionize Japan's intricate hierarchal society.

The nationalists, Kishi soon learned, had to cope with two swiftly growing alien influences. One was the Bolshevik revolt in Russia, which was stimulating enthusiasm for socialist concepts, principally among the intellectuals and budding labor unions. Simultaneously, the democratic idealism preached by American President Woodrow Wilson was making a powerful impact. Wilson's attacks on Prussian authoritarianism and militarism seemed to many Japanese to be highly relevant to the situation in Japan, for the government was still dominated by the generals and oligarchs, even though the political parties were growing in strength.

These dynamic modern influences provoked sharp reactions on the part of the nationalists, who wanted to stamp them out altogether, or in some cases, to interweave them with the traditional threads of Japanese society. Nationalist resistance was reinforced by Japanese military moves in the Far East. Japan, having entered the First World War on the side of the Allies in 1914, enriched itself with the spoils of war to a large extent at the expense of China, which was forced to accept most of the Twenty-One Demands made by Tokyo. These demands included the transfer to Japan of German rights in Shantung, economic concessions in Mongolia and Manchuria, and control of the railways in Manchuria and the iron mines near Hankow. In addition, Japan occupied the German Pacific Islands. In 1918, under pressure of the militarists, Japan sent an expedition of several divisions to Siberia "to protect Allied interests" against the Bolshevik revolutionaries, though Britain, the United States—and the Japanese cabinet itself—had been opposed to this scheme, which was obviously aggressive in intent.

The bitter struggle between the forces of liberalism and traditionalism created tension in almost every classroom Kishi attended. Students argued with each other and instructors fervently expressed their own pointed opinions in their lectures. Kishi was particularly intrigued by the running debate between two of his law professors, both of whom were considered among the top constitutional authorities in the country, over the question of the Emperor's relation to the State. Dr. Shinkichi Uesugi held that under the Meiji Constitution the traditional national structure had to be preserved, with absolute sovereignty remaining in the Emperor's hands. Dr. Tatsukichi Minobe maintained with equal ardor that the Constitution could and should be interpreted to make the Emperor an organ of the State responsible to the people.

Most of Kishi's fellow students joined political groups revolving around these two concepts, with Dr. Uesugi leading the nationalists and Dr. Sakuzo Yoshino, a famous professor of political science, organizing those with democratic leanings. Dr. Yoshino co-ordinated his movement with a liberal freshman group called the *Shin-Jin-Kai,* or Awakened Man Society, and with similar democratic organizations founded by Dr. Fukuda at Tokyo Commercial College and by Dr. Kawakami at the Imperial University of Kyoto.

Nonetheless, the fear of expulsion, a heavy price to pay in a country where a college education was almost indispensable to success, kept many of the students from active participation in the democratic movement, which was causing the government and university administrators no little concern. But other liberals, like the nationalists, held numerous meetings, often on the gravel plaza in the shadow of the towering clock steeple atop the administration building. Liberal rallies, however, were sometimes interrupted by nationalist-inspired violence and police intervention. Some nationalists, in their fanaticism, even refused to don the black uniforms that the great majority of students, including Kishi, wore, preferring instead the traditional kimono. Many more angrily protested the fact that most classes were conducted in English, German, or other foreign languages, which they thought implied recognition of Western cultural superiority.

Kishi was at first startled by his sudden exposure to almost uninhibited political conflict. In his pre-college days, he and his classmates had largely taken for granted the traditional national structure of the Japanese State. Most of their political discussions had involved only details of how it could best work. No one had ever questioned the powers and rights of the Emperor. But at *Todai,* as the Imperial University of Tokyo was popularly known, this issue was being publicly debated, and both the defenders and attackers of the prevailing system fought with a vigor that seemed to reflect a deep-seated doubt of its ability to survive.

Despite the tendency of his fellows to embrace wholeheartedly either one concept or the other, Kishi tried to remain detached. Yet he could not shake off the influence of his Choshu samurai heritage. He knew that his mother, Moyo, Great-grandfather Sato, Yoshida Shoin, and Prince Ito all would have been on the side of Dr. Uesugi. Dr. Minobe's argument, which constituted almost a complete refutation of everything that Kishi had learned about Japanese culture and history, was, on the other hand, too radical for him. He therefore accepted Uesugi's thesis in principle, though his basically humanist instincts, fed by contact with Western philosophies, rebelled against the professor's demand that the Emperor must remain a cloistered image, kept distant from the people by his traditional advisers. The Emperor should retain absolute power, Kishi thought, but as a popular monarch rather than as a vague object of worship. There had to be a compromise between the mysticism of the past and the reality of the present.

Kishi thus refused to join Dr. Uesugi's nationalist organization, called the *Mokuyo-kai,* or Thursday Meeting Group. He reached this decision despite the pressure of many of his friends, most of them Choshu-born like himself, and his warm relationship with Uesugi, who considered Kishi his brightest pupil.

Oddly enough, Kishi's closest friend, Sakae Wagatsuma (now one of Japan's leading authorities on civil law), was a liberal. Kishi had finished second to Wagatsuma in the competition for grades in high school. Entering the university together, they had remained at the top of the academic ladder, far above all the other students in their class. In personality, Kishi and Wagatsuma, though equally brilliant, could hardly

have been less alike. Kishi was ambitious, proud, rational; Wagatsuma
was modest, unpolished, often abstract in his thinking. Even their study
methods differed considerably. Wagatsuma inquired into every detail,
however insignificant or useless, while Kishi grasped the essence of
the subject and then dissected it into the essential details only. But they
found common ground in their tendency to pursue idealistic aims, divergent though these aims were.

Kishi derived his greatest mental stimulation from his discussions
with Wagatsuma, whose theories of democracy, he was convinced, were
entirely unsuitable for Japan, though sometimes presented with challenging logic. Their personal debates, conducted in and out of the classroom, usually centered on the interpretation of some point of law, and
kept the instructors and other students in a constant state of mute fasci-
nation.

During vacation periods, they often went to seaside resorts together,
loaded down with reference books, to study for their examinations, but
a good deal of their time was consumed in their running ideological discussion. Sometimes, it went on until after midnight, when they would
bathe together in the large, steaming community hotel bath, arguing as
they soaped and rinsed themselves on the grated wooden bathroom floor
or bounced around in the bath pool.

Occasionally, the two "educated each other," as other students jok-
ingly commented, while relaxing under a tree by a small lake on the
campus, or at Kishi's house, where Kishi now lived alone with Yoshiko,
his prospective wife, and a maid. Once, Wagatsuma recalls, while Yoshiko, who was still attending school, occupied herself with household
duties, he asked Kishi, "Do you really believe that in this modern era,
when democracy is spreading throughout the world, Japan can, and
should, maintain its system of Imperial absolutism? Are you not willing
to make any concession to world trend of thought?"

Kishi, with a grimace, replied, "You know very well that I am not an
extremist. Of course we cannot ignore modern trends! But neither can
we ignore Japanese tradition, the thing that makes Japan what it is,
different from other countries. The Emperor is the symbol of our unity.
The greatness attributed to him has made the Japanese spirit strong. If
we legally limit his power, we are, in the eyes of the people, limiting the
good that flows from his greatness."

"Therefore," Wagatsuma intervened with a note of mockery, "his
power should be limitless!"

"No, that does not necessarily follow," Kishi responded. "There should be limitations on his power, but not legal ones. The limitations should be of a traditional nature. The Emperor, as you well know, has never acted on his own, but always on the advice of his advisers. Up to now, these advisers, mostly plutocrats and nobles, have not been close enough to the people, therefore the Emperor has also been too distant from his subjects. Professor Uesugi thinks this is the proper relationship between the Emperor and the people. I disagree with him. I think that the Emperor should in the future be popularized, that his advisers should consist of the true representatives of the people. In that way, the Emperor would retain his greatness in the eyes of the people and still remain their master, but at the same time he would be indirectly subject to their will. On the other hand, if the Emperor's decisions were legally subject to parliamentary approval, he would lose much of the prestige that is the heart of the unifying Japanese spirit."

Wagatsuma rubbed his chin. "That is all very well, but the Emperor is a human being. One need not worry about a good and wise Emperor taking advantage of the absolute power he now theoretically holds. But suppose some day in the future the Emperor proves to be a man lacking scruples and tries to use his power for bad ends. The Constitution, as it is now interpreted, would permit him to do this. The people have no safeguards. We are entirely dependent on the character of the man who happens to be Emperor."

"But tradition," replied Kishi, "is so strong in Japan that it is really quite unrealistic to talk about an Emperor using his power arbitrarily as kings and czars have done in Europe. The Emperor's power can always be curbed by his advisers. The problem is to have his advisers rooted in the people. But in any event, the Emperor should retain ultimate power. That is Japanese tradition and what the people themselves want."

While Kishi advocated a relatively moderate brand of nationalism in his discussions with Wagatsuma, his other friends, mostly from the same middle school and senior to him, relentlessly prodded him to contribute his prestige to Dr. Uesugi's organization. He was misguided in his moderate views, they told him, but this could be overlooked by the Choshu student community if he joined the group. It wasn't necessary, they pointed out, for a member to agree one hundred per cent with Dr. Uesugi. Kishi began to give way. He was reluctant to weaken the solidarity of the Choshu faction at the university.

Furthermore, he did agree with much that Dr. Uesugi supported, and he liked the professor personally, occasionally chatting with him about constitutional matters in his office. He was attracted by Uesugi's solemn charm and air of grandeur as he stood before the class, dressed appropriately in a formal kimono, and staunchly defended Japan's glorious heritage in his cool, incisive manner. Dr. Uesugi was by nature a humble, rather inconspicuous, scholarly man. People who had known him in years past could hardly recognize him in the role of a modern samurai. But, with the threat to Japanese traditionalism growing, he had become an increasingly fervent and aggressive opponent of reform. And were not the great men of Japanese history, Kishi asked himself, nourished more on pride and inspiration than on reason? Was this not the spirit of his own ancestors? He finally decided to join Uesugi's group, but with considerable misgivings. "I hoped to make the nationalists more moderate in their views. I suppose I represented compromise at a time when no compromise was possible," Kishi says.

Kishi discovered that his tendency to favor a less rigid traditionalism than Uesugi supported was by no means a unique inclination. A number of "radical" nationalist movements had been initiated that combined the elements of conservatism and modernism. One of the most important was an agrarian effort, which had been spurred by peasant "rice riots" resulting from wartime inflation, to better the economic and political position of the rural areas. Led by Gondo Seikyo, this movement called for a return to rural autonomy and an agrarian-centered economy that would operate within a decentralized society, and assure the peasants a fair share of the nation's wealth.

The brand of nationalism, however, that appealed most to Kishi was the "national socialism" preached by Ikki Kita and his disciples, in particular Shumei Okawa, who was in later years to form a nationalist movement of his own. The national socialists wanted a highly centralized, industrial-centered state. Kishi and his nationalist friends occasionally visited Kita at his Tokyo home.

"I was simply overwhelmed by the revolutionary spirit of Ikki Kita," Kishi says. "He was not one of those ordinary rightists you found everywhere, but was pre-eminent both in his character and his vision. Ikki Kita was indeed one of the persons who profoundly influenced me during my university days."

Kita, a brilliant but arrogant and egocentric man, was fanatically dedicated to his cause. Still young, only in his thirties, he had recently returned from China, where he had served as a member of the Black Dragon Society, an organization designed to pave the way for Japanese expansion on the Asian mainland. He had contributed his services to the great rebel, Sun Yat-sen, who successfully led the Chinese revolution of

1912, in the hope of gaining for Japan economic and territorial advantages in a new, more unified China. But, frustrated in this aim—at least until the outbreak of the First World War gave Japan the opportunity to move into Shantung—he returned home to help strengthen the nation's resistance to the infiltration of such foreign ideologies as "democracy" and "communism."

Kita, in Kishi's opinion, had worked out just the right formula to accomplish this. He called for reconstruction of Japan's traditional social order by fusing within it the elements of socialism, individualism, and liberalism. This, Kita reasoned, would eliminate the popular discontent that had nourished the "Western movements." The details of this plan were contained in a publication entitled, *A General Outline for the Reconstruction of Japan,* which Kita published clandestinely in view of its revolutionary character. Kishi managed to borrow a copy, which he reproduced word for word with brush and ink before returning. He studied the work as a priest might read the Bible, thrilling to its nationalistic inspiration and, what seemed to him, its thoroughly realistic approach. The pamphlet spelled out in detail the ideas that he himself had entertained about the ideal Japanese polity.

Kishi was particularly impressed with Kita's view on the relationship of the Emperor and the people. The publication stated:

> The fundamental character of Japan is the main element uniting the Japanese people, and, at the same time, is the very foundation on which our country will develop. Therefore, we Japanese people should make every possible effort to keep the national character of our country safe from the ravages of a destructive revolution. However, we must avoid falling victim to an idealism isolated from the people by purifying this constitutional idiomorphism to an excessive degree. If the Emperor cannot find a place among the common people of Japan, the glory of the fundamental character of our country cannot be preserved. Thus, we should do away with all institutions lending to the separation of the Emperor from his people."

Kita's plan called for the Emperor to suspend the Constitution for three years, dissolve the Diet, dismiss his Privy Council and inner court advisers, and declare martial law, thereby underscoring his supreme position in the nation. Then, a tightly knit group of military leaders, the need of which Kita had perceived from his participation in the Chinese revolution, would be elected from the reserve army corps and take over the government from the "corrupt" politicians, elder statesmen, and plutocrats. Once this junta was in power, a new Imperial advisory board of fifty "great men" from all walks of life would be appointed, and a refurbished Diet, to which these advisers would not be responsible, would, as a sop to the democrats, be elected by universal manhood suffrage but would be unable to discuss basic reform policies approved by the Sovereign.

Some of the main reforms, Kishi read approvingly, would be in the economic sphere. The junta would expropriate all private property exceeding a fixed limit to be set for each household and all industrial property over a specified value, with the excess land being sold to landless farmers. The confiscated industrial property would be retained by the state. A system, Kita said, that placed too much economic and political power in the hands of a few individuals was "evil." On the other hand, he maintained that the ownership of private property was essential for the freedom of the individual and that private ownership of industry was necessary to stimulate economic activity and creative genius. Any socialist ideology which did not respect private property, he added, reflected the thinking of the "early communist ages."

Kita's call for a broader distribution of wealth did not involve only the wealth in Japan, which he saw as too limited to permit real prosperity, but that of neighboring countries as well. He justified an expansionist policy with an argument which seemed to Kishi quite logical:

"England is a powerful millionaire who has holdings over the entire world, and Russia is a huge landholder with lands throughout the northern half of the globe. So why doesn't Japan, which is made up of scattered island chains and which is in the position of a proletariat among nations, have the right to start a war, in the name of justice, in order to seize possessions from these monopolies? There are self-contradictions in the fundamental thoughts of those European and American socialists who approve of proletarian class struggle within a country but who consider international proletarian war as chauvinism or militarism."

Consistent with these sentiments, Kita advocated fostering the emigration of Chinese, Indians, and Koreans to such places as Australia and Siberia. He favored the occupation of Manchuria and Siberia, and attacking Russia "for the security of the Japan Sea, Korea, and China," this being the "logical conclusion" of the Russo-Japanese War of 1905. Further, a large naval force would be built up to secure Japan's First World War winnings in China and the Pacific against possible American and British encroachment. In his drive against foreign influence, Kita even advocated abolition of English as a second language and a campaign against all "imported sports," such as baseball.

The call for a revitalized glorification of the Emperor, an elite military government, and a more nationalistic foreign policy gratified the demands of Kishi's Choshu heritage. At the same time, the socialist aspects of the economic plan gave ample quarter to his humanistic instincts, while the provisions for individual enterprise constituted a bulwark against communism. Kishi felt that Kita was perhaps too strong in his anti-Western sentiments. Yet, he could understand these sentiments. Had not the Western leaders, including Woodrow Wilson, the hero of the democrats, rejected Japan's demand, so basically just, that a clause guaranteeing "racial equality" be included in the League of Nations covenant? Kita had succeeded, at least on paper, in fitting the meritorious aspects of socialism into the traditional Japanese polity. He had found the logical compromise between the concepts of conservatism and liberalism that were so dangerously vying with each other for the soul of Japan. One day, Kishi was confident, Kita's plan would prevail.

It became more and more clear to Kishi that Dr. Uesugi's "status quo" movement, which had been renamed *Gokoku Doshi-kai,* the Society of Comrades for the Elevation of the Country, was outdated and entirely lacking in imagination. Statesmen of Prince Ito's caliber no longer existed, and the quarreling little men running the government were far too busy scheming to keep themselves in power to think about their responsibilities to the nation. The leadership of young militarists like his Choshu forefathers, who had restored the Emperor fifty years before, was needed to revitalize Japan's political and economic structure. When the Army embarked on its anti-Bolshevik Siberian adventure in 1918, Kishi was far from unhappy. It had forced the hand of the reluctant oligarchy Dr. Uesugi was pledged to support.

But Kishi, though attracted to authoritarian doctrines, was, paradoxically, repulsed by the use of force to eliminate opposition. He disagreed with "democrats" like Minobe and Yoshino, yet he retained considerable respect for them. Kishi's gradual estrangement from the Uesugi group was influenced by the intolerance it displayed toward the liberals. As the democratic movement grew stronger in Japan, and particularly at the university, counter-propaganda by the government-backed traditionalists soon developed into attempts at outright suppression.

Police tactics were reflected in the fate that befell two liberal newspapers, the *Osaka Asahi* and the *Tokyo Asahi,* which had openly opposed the "dictatorship" of the ruling oligarchy and the aggression of the militarists who ordered Japan's intervention in Siberia. The *Osaka Asahi* was indicted on the trumped-up charge of disturbing the public peace after it criticized the government for suppressing news of the "rice riots." When the publishers of this newspaper agreed to apologize publicly for its anti-government view and dismiss its liberal employees, most of the staff members of the Tokyo paper, quitting *en masse,* bitterly denounced this act of "cowardice," as well as the "despicable actions of their Tokyo colleagues who seek to curry favor by truckling to the wishes of the bureaucrats."

On the campus of the university, Dr. Yoshino was threatened and abused following publication of a magazine article he wrote entitled, "The Ethical Significance of Worship at the Shrines." Yoshino indirectly attacked State Shinto by recounting a story about a friend who had explained to his son that the souls of dead soldiers were enshrined at Yasukuni Shrine because the soldiers had died for the Emperor. When the child asked if the soul of a former family servant who had been killed in a skirmish in China was enshrined at Yasukuni, the father replied that it was. "Even though he was a bad man who lied and stole?" asked the child. "Yes," answered the father, who then wondered if he had done the right thing teaching the boy that a sinner was to be worshiped as a deity if only he died for the Emperor. To the Western mind, this may seem no great criticism, but to the Japanese it constituted a form of slander and impiety. It cast overtones of doubt upon the divinity of the Emperor and of those who died for him, which the traditionalists stoutly maintained as a sacred religious and political truth.

Even more abhorrent to Kishi than the treatment accorded Dr. Yoshino was the fate of Dr. Tatsuo Morito, another progressive professor. Dr. Morito created a sensation on the campus, and throughout Japan, with the publication of an article in a university journal called, "A Study of the Social Thought of Kropotkin." Dr. Uesugi's group and other nationalist organizations, accusing Dr. Morito of propagating the anarchistic ideas of Kropotkin, held mass protest meetings and demanded that he be expelled from the university. The police arrested Morito, who not only lost his job, but was tried and sentenced to a brief term in jail, despite bitter protests by the liberal groups. Kishi was amused to note that the nationalist organizations, in trying to keep Kropotkin's writings out of circulation, made them best-sellers in the local book stores. But he was not amused by the outcome of the Morito case, which he considered an unwarranted example of police oppression.

Besides, though he disagreed with Kropotkin's advocacy of complete abolition of private property, he considered the principle of private property by no means indisputable. As Ikki Kita had said, "private ownership of property should be reformed with the times. Such reform would not be in conflict with the fundamental character of the nation." The *Gokoku-Doshi-Kai* and similar nationalist groups had condemned Morito for a "crime" that had nothing to do with nationalistic principles. The gulf between his own thinking and that of Dr. Uesugi, Kishi decided, was simply too great to bridge. Thus, despite the efforts of leading members to keep him in the professor's organization, he resigned.

His resignation, he found, not only relieved him from a troubling moral strain—he no longer had to cheer and applaud statements that he didn't fully believe—but left him more time to devote to his studies. Majoring in German law, he became a model student, unlike many of his friends, who were too involved in the political storm to be able to concentrate very hard on dry academic research. As no special textbooks accompanied his courses, he always listened to his instructors with extreme attention, being forced to depend at examination time largely on the information contained in his scrawled notes.

He felt a deep sense of responsibility not only to himself, but to his high school, which traditionally produced the best students at the university, and especially to his family. As a mature man he was expected to be even more conscious of his filial duties than in his younger days. Beyond all this, Kishi found that he had never enjoyed studying as much as he now did among Japan's greatest scholars and finest students. "Without the inspiration of great men, who in turn leave their honor in the hands of younger men, the world would be a jungle. I knew I was among the best Japan could offer and I was determined to be worthy of the hours they gave to me. I only regret that I did not learn more, especially of literature and the arts. But after all, the university was intended primarily to prepare me for a career, not to broaden my cultural background."

Kishi knew he wanted to be a civil servant, but he wasn't certain what ministry he should join. Most aspiring bureaucrats applied for jobs in the Home or Finance Ministries, which traditionally enjoyed the greatest prestige. But with so many students moving into these ministries, he would have to face not only stiff competition but the hazards of political favoritism in working his way to the top. He decided to wait until graduation to make up his mind, though he was disturbed somewhat by this uncertainty.

Meanwhile, he braced himself for the Higher Civil Service examination, an especially difficult test primarily concerned with law, which he was required to pass in his second year in order to qualify for eventual promotion to the upper government levels. Kishi, together with Wagatsuma and several other students, rented a vacant teahouse at the former site of Kamega Castle in the village of Inawashiro, Fukushima Prefecture, and settled down for the summer to study for this important examination. Wagatsuma, who intended to pursue an academic career and did not have to take the civil service test, nevertheless prepared for it as an excuse to spend the summer with his friend, Kishi.

The teahouse was situated at the top of a hill, with Mount Bandai towering on one side and Lake Inawashiro shimmering on the other. The mayor of the town, to whom the boys had a letter of introduction, treated them, as did the local populace, with the courtesy reserved for distinguished guests. It was no small honor for a rural village to enjoy the presence of students of the Imperial University of Tokyo, from which most of Japan's leaders emerged. The peasants, still influenced by the feudal past, continued to pay homage to the "samurai."

Before the examination, Kishi was unusually tense and nervous, for this test, as no other, would directly affect the pattern of his career. He realized more clearly than ever now how miserable his father, cheated of a university education, must have been as a petty bureaucrat in the Yamaguchi government, doomed to remain permanently at a lowly level, while men of better education and technical skills steadily rose in rank. It was little wonder that he had returned to the business of brewing sake.

Kishi passed the examination with a high mark. In fact, so impressive was his scholastic record in general that shortly before his graduation Dr. Uesugi called him into his office and urged him to choose an academic career. "I hope you will consider remaining at the university after your graduation," the professor told him. "You have an important future here. I am getting old and tired, and soon I shall have to give up lecturing. I would like you to succeed me as a lecturer on constitutional law."

Dr. Uesugi well knew that Kishi had withdrawn from his political organization because he could not agree with many of its policies, yet he was offering the young man the chance to be his successor. Startled, Kishi replied, "I am most honored that you should consider me for such a post. But I do not believe I am qualified to pursue a scholar's career."

"You are not a scholar yet," Uesugi said with a smile. "So you are in no position to judge whether you have the qualifications to be a scholar. I am a scholar, and it is my opinion that you can become one, too."

Kishi felt cornered. If he contradicted the professor, he would be discourteous. He lied, "Regrettably, Dr. Uesugi, my parents are opposed to my following an academic career."

The professor frowned. He could not ask the boy to disobey the wishes of his parents. "Perhaps if I spoke to them they might change their minds."

"I really do not believe they will," Kishi said. "They have always wanted me to enter the government service."

Uesugi did not reply, and Kishi was uncertain whether this meant he would or would not make a plea to his family. But shortly afterward, when he visited Tabuse, he asked his family to reject any proposal Uesugi might advance that he remain at the university. Kishi explained to his mother, Moyo, that he did not feel suited to the life of a scholar. He wanted to take an active role in bringing power and glory to Japan, in the tradition of Prince Ito and other Choshu statesmen. Furthermore, he said, it would be unfair to accept a post offered him by a man whose views were considerably divergent from his own. "If I did not enter the government service," he told his mother with a smile, "I would probably go into business so that I could earn millions of yen to spend on you."

Kishi regretted that he had had to lie to Dr. Uesugi so that he could turn down his proposal without hurting his feelings. (A few years later, when the professor died, he visited his grave and apologized.) But he was flattered by the offer, especially in view of the fact that Dr. Uesugi might more logically have chosen as his successor a member of his own organization. He could only surmise that the professor himself had begun to doubt the ultratraditionalist theories he preached, but, unable to modify his teachings without losing "face," had hoped to solve the problem by selecting his best "reformist" pupil to fill his shoes.

Although there was no doubt in the young man's mind about the kind of career he intended to pursue, there remained considerable question as graduation approached about what branch of the government he should or would be able to enter. He still thought he might apply for entry into the Home or Financial Ministries, but he was reluctant to take his place in line with so many other candidates, many of whom came from influential families. The move he made now would determine the course of his career, and he couldn't afford to make a mistake. The Ministries of Home and Finance carried the greatest prestige, but this did not promise him the kind of personal prestige he wanted. The important thing to Kishi was not, as to many of his colleagues, prestige by association, but the speed with which he could attain high place.

Finally, he sought advice from an old and distinguished friend of the family, Mannosuke Kamiyama, who had in his lifetime been a high official in several ministries. Kamiyama urged him to enter the Home Ministry with such fervor that Kishi almost decided then and there to abide by this suggestion. But one evening, a student friend introduced him to Kinji Nagamitsu, chief of the stock exchange bureau of the lowly rated Ministry of Agriculture and Commerce. Impressed with Kishi, Nagamitsu offered him a job in his bureau after graduation. When he noted Kishi's hesitation, he explained to him the growing importance of the stock exchange office.

Kishi had entered the university in the midst of an unprecedented economic boom, stimulated by munitions and other war profits. After the war, however, the country began to feel the effects of the unsettled economic conditions in other parts of the world. Now the whole attention of the financial world was focused on the stock exchange as a barometer of the economic climate. Therefore, Nagamitsu told Kishi, he would be entering a ministry of increasing significance that was bound to expand.

Kishi, quick to note the better possibilities of promotion in this ministry than in the popular ones where the seniority system would be more rigid a factor, decided to apply for a position in Nagamitsu's office. In his eagerness, he made the mistake of applying even before he found time to consult again with Kamiyama, who had advised him to enter the Home Ministry. This was a serious breach of *giri* that hurt and angered Kamiyama, and Kishi found it no easy matter to persuade him to accept his apologies. This experience offered Kishi a sharp reminder that he had to show greater respect for his elders and superiors if he wanted others to respect him.

As graduation neared, Kishi and Yoshiko visited Tabuse, where they culminated a nine-year engagement with a modest marriage ceremony at the local Shinto temple, followed by a small reception at the Kishi home at which tea and bean curd were served. Only relatives and close friends were invited. This represented a sharp departure from the usual Japanese practice of holding a grand wedding, though such unorthodoxy was not uncommon in cases where the groom was an "adopted husband" and had therefore lived in the same house with his prospective wife for many years before the marriage. "We have not the memory," Kishi says, "of that sense of happy excitement that is usually felt at a wedding." After a short honeymoon at a resort in Yamaguchi, the couple returned to their house in Tokyo, and life went on as if nothing had changed—except that Yoshiko, it seemed to Kishi, radiated a warmth and loveliness he had never noted before.

Then, after graduation—he and Wagatsuma finished at the top of their class—Kishi took his place, with a mixed sense of apprehension and self-confidence, in the society he was expected to serve within the rigidly prescribed confines of a near-feudal hierarchy. He was prepared to accept the slow, mechanical nature of advancement under this system, but was equally ready to take advantage of any opportunities that might present themselves to accelerate his rise. He would somehow find the proper compromise between hierarchal restriction and ambition. When one classmate advised him that his career would suffer from the lack of prestige attached to the Ministry of Agriculture and Commerce, Kishi summed up his attitude with the half-serious reply:

"I'm entering it so that it *will* have more prestige."

CHAPTER VI

PRELUDE TO GLORY

K ISHI LEARNED SOMETHING of the inflexible demands of the society he was about to enter immediately after his graduation. He and Yoshiko had gone to Tabuse for a vacation, during which Kishi hoped to recover from the strain of the last hectic months in college. He assumed it was quite normal for someone emerging from the tensions of school life to enjoy an interval of relaxation before launching his career, and therefore hadn't bothered to consult with his prospective employers. But a few days after his arrival in Tabuse, he received a telegram from the Ministry of Agriculture and Commerce ordering him to return to Tokyo and report for work at once. And from the tone of the wire it appeared his new bosses were considerably irritated.

The couple left hastily for Tokyo, where Kishi found his worst anxieties confirmed. Greeted coldly, he was pointedly reminded that all other recruits from college had reported in the day after graduation. Kishi was deeply concerned about this "black mark" on his record, earned even before his career had begun. As he began work in April, 1920, he realized as he never had before that he could not afford to make mistakes in the future if he was eventually to attain a position of power.

Kishi entered a civil service that was among the most powerful in the world. Ever since the seventh century, when Japan modeled its bureaucracy on the Confucian system of China, Japanese bureaucrats had wielded tremendous influence in national politics. They had achieved their peak

102

of strength during the Meiji period, when the oligarchy of young idealistic leaders were greatly dependent on them for the administration of Japan's technical revolution. The bureaucrats, a proud and homogeneous caste, did not hesitate to use their indispensability as a political lever. Kishi, in the tradition of his profession, was now determined to become indispensable. Starting as a clerk in the stock exchange control branch of the ministry, he spent most of his time gathering routine foreign trade statistics from the various other ministry departments for analysis by experts in his bureau.

Lowly as this job was, it gave him a good opportunity to study the depressed condition of the Japanese economy. The postwar decline in demand for military goods had resulted in sharp steel price reductions, factory shutdowns, and increasing unemployment. This situation was aggravated by Japan's stationing of troops in Shantung, which stimulated Chinese boycotts of Japanese goods, while Western businessmen were re-entering the Chinese market and reinvesting in the country.

The seriousness of this recession, Kishi observed, was reflected in the growing restlessness of the workers, who joined labor unions on a large scale for the first time. More than 30,000 workers went on strike in 1921 at the Kawasaki Shipyard in Kobe in the biggest walkout Japan had ever seen, while other strikes, often involving violence, added to the national confusion. Such conditions gave birth to the Japanese Communist Party in 1922. But oddly enough most unions—as well as intellectual groups—sought an answer to their economic and social grievances, not in extremist doctrines, but in democracy. This tendency was fostered by the increasingly liberal policies of the government, which had begun to respond to the demands of the "democrats." The rise to the premiership in 1918 of Takashi Hara, the first commoner prime minister in Japanese history, symbolized the democratic trend. On the other hand, Hara's assassination in November, 1921, revealed the desperation of the nationalists in their struggle to stem the liberal tide.

Kishi followed economic and political trends more with the eye of the disinterested technician than that of the passionate observer he had been in college. Like most of the bureaucrats, who tended to be arrogant and authoritarian, he opposed the growing democratic movement, with its accent on disorder and its disregard for Japanese tradition. But in his present position, he believed, he would best serve his interests if, within the limits of human passivity, he remained untouched by the political currents swirling about him. When he neared the top, then he would be in a position to influence policy, in a discreet subtle way, of course. He would use the techniques that the bureaucrats traditionally use—he would ride the current wave while simultaneously trying to reverse it. But for the time being, he decided, he would condition himself to the aloofness that his status required.

Kishi soon impressed his superiors with his legalistic mind and his eye for detail. Within a few months he was moved into an unanticipated opening, paying twice his starting salary, that normally would have been filled by a "two-year" man. In the summer of 1922, he was appointed to a job in the prized Documents and Archives Section of the ministry's secretariat, one of the rarest of positions within his range of qualification. Partly due to luck, partly to his exceptional ability, Kishi had succeeded in skirting the barriers of the strict seniority system. So far, in planning his career, he had calculated correctly. And his remarkable advance was particularly satisfying in view of the birth to Yoshiko, in November, 1921, of a son, Nobukazu. The extra yen Kishi earned in these days of recession would make it much easier for him to raise a growing family in the proper manner.

Although Kishi's new job was not high-ranking in terms of hierarchy, it was probably the most important "minor" position in the ministry. All documents intended for the Minister or Vice-Minister were screened by the Documents and Archives Section before they were sent on to them, and Kishi was one of two councilors who did the screening. In this capacity, he had a great deal to say about what reports and requests should or should not be approved for examination by the policy-makers. In addition, he conducted research for all-important ministry conferences. He was in a position, however insignificant on the organizational chart, to exert an indirect influence on policy itself. He also had the opportunity to study the activities of all the bureaus in the ministry.

Kishi consolidated his position by making many friends, some in very high places, who were attracted by his clear, rational thinking and his practical—as well as theoretical—knowledge of law and government, a rare attribute among Japanese bureaucrats. He also displayed remarkable powers of persuasion. When a draft plan for a reorganized chamber of commerce was sent to him for survey, he convinced the proud official who had drawn it up and initially resisted any alterations that the plan should be broadened to provide for a chamber of commerce *and industry*. "Kishi-san always took the broad view," says Shinji Yoshino, his section chief at the time.

So brilliantly did Kishi perform his duties that he was about the only man in his department who never drew words of abuse from the blunt, often ill-tempered Yoshino, whose celebrated elder brother, Dr. Sakuzo Yoshino, had failed to stir Kishi with his lectures on democracy at college. And Kishi did his best to maintain this uniquely serene relationship. He knew that to move ahead swiftly in the bureaucracy, one had to attach himself to the coattails of a superior who would pull him up the ladder with him. This was the way almost all bureaucrats reached the top. One had to have not only ability, but a powerful patron.

Kishi discreetly refrained from discussing politics with Yoshino, who was, like his brother, liberal-minded. And whenever he wanted to see Yoshino, he would first peek into his office to ascertain if the weather was fine or cloudy. If it was fine, he went in, stated his business, and then slipped out again. If it was cloudy, he returned to his own office and waited until later. If the business was urgent he sent someone else in. There was nothing wrong, Kishi thought, with using tact in dealing with a superior, particularly if the superior sometimes appeared unreasonable. Yet, though Kishi recognized the importance of Yoshino's patronage, he had no intention of trying to win over his boss simply with favors and a humble attitude. A relationship based only on ties of *giri,* which would have satisfied most ambitious bureaucrats, held little appeal for him. He liked and admired Yoshino and wanted to develop a genuine friendship with him, rooted in mutual respect. And he succeeded. Yoshino told me recently when I asked him why he had never spoken harshly to Kishi, "How can one speak harshly to someone if he never makes a mistake? Anyway, it's dangerous to argue with a man who can usually convince you that black is white."

As Kishi had hoped, discretion, ability, and luck, in potent combination, greatly accelerated the pace of his advance. A new opportunity presented itself when the government decided to split the Ministry of Agriculture and Commerce into two separate units. As Kishi's section drew up the plans for this reorganization, he had the chance to help determine his own future, getting himself transferred, together with Yoshino, to the Documents and Archives Section of the new Ministry of Commerce and Industry. Kishi, who had shared his old councilor job now had the position all to himself, which considerably increased his influence.

One evening in 1925, a few weeks after the ministerial reform, Kishi returned home from work especially cheerful in spirit. It was spring and the air was scented with the flowers that blossomed behind every wall and hedge in the neighborhood. It was also a holiday, Boys' Day, the day when youths were traditionally honored and encouraged to grow into strong, courageous, patriotic men. Strings of colored carp-shaped flags, the symbol of the festival, were strung across the narrow streets, and children dressed in their holiday finery played under the fluttering banners. Kishi looked forward to seeing his son.

But when he entered the house, he found that Nobukazu, who had not been feeling well for several days, had taken a turn for the worse. He had trouble moving one of his legs. The doctor was called, and after examining Nobukazu, hesitantly announced that the child had polio and might never be able to walk again. Kishi and his wife were shattered by this news. "I felt," Mrs. Kishi recalls, "unspeakable sorrow and despair. For some time I even avoided going out. . . . I could not stand the sight of other children playing merrily and cheerfully. . . ." But neither she nor Kishi gave up hope that their son would recover. Every night they massaged his paralyzed limb, and they also hired a professional masseur for this purpose and had the child take electric treatments.

"Father and I were never terribly close," Nobukazu told me, nostalgically recalling his boyhood. "He was always very busy, and when he came home he was tired and just wanted to sit and read. He left it to mother to bring us (referring to himself and his younger sister, Yoko) up. Even on his days off, he would usually not stay at home, but would go fishing with friends. And he would hardly ever give us any spending money. Sometimes, of course, he would take us out, usually on a Sunday or a holiday. He would take us to the zoo, and then maybe to a restaurant. Either he or mother would carry me, as I couldn't walk very well. But those pleasant occasions were rare, and sometimes I would wonder if Father really loved me.

"But, one day, I found a pawn ticket on his desk. I knew then how he obtained the money to pay for my electric treatments—by pawning many of his possessions. I remember how I cried when I realized what he had done. I knew then how much Father really loved me."

The faith of Nobukazu's parents was not misplaced, for the boy gradually began to walk again, although with a limp.

Kishi, after his son was stricken, became more determined than ever to move swiftly to the top, for he needed the money to pay for the expensive treatments required for the child. Yoshino also wanted to see him advance as quickly as possible, but was a bit concerned that his "protégé" might be handicapped in the future by his lack of a thorough knowledge of international economics, which was partly due to the skimpy training he had had in English.

When the Japanese government decided to participate in the 1926 Philadelphia World's Fair, Yoshino, whose section was in charge of arrangements, offered to send Kishi to America to supervise construction of, and to manage, the Japanese pavilion. This would give him an opportunity, he told Kishi, to improve his English and learn something about the United States. Kishi jumped at this chance to see the "outside world" for the first time. He had long dreamed of doing so, but he had never imagined that he would be sent on an overseas mission until he had reached a higher echelon of government.

Kishi sailed for the United States, disembarking in Seattle and making side trips to Texas and Washington, D.C., before arriving in Philadelphia. He found that managing the Japanese exhibits, which featured a million dollar pagoda made entirely of Mikimoto pearls, was a demanding but interesting job. He met and worked with a number of well-known Japanese personalities, including the Hollywood actor Sessue Hayakawa. He also studied modern American dancing and learned how to play golf, which, on his return to Japan, he played with his associates—those he knew he could beat. He sometimes indulged in the strange game of poker with diplomatic friends, though he would have preferred chess, which involved less chance and more method.

Kishi was deeply hurt and disappointed when he discovered evidences of racial prejudice in the United States. After he had rented a house for himself and his Japanese aides near Fairmont Park, neighbors raised a howl of protest to the landlord that no Orientals were wanted in the area. Instead of moving out, Kishi invited the neighbors over to dinner, and they were so shocked that they came. By the time dinner, which included several Japanese dishes, was over, the guests were magnetized by his charm and his stories (told mostly through an interpreter, as he didn't yet trust his English) about life in Japan. "I never realized," one housewife said, "that people from Japan could be so intelligent and sensible." Kishi thought that he had scored something of a diplomatic coup, but he also realized more clearly than ever the extent of the gulf between the two races. And he regretted that he was being considered, at best, as an exceptional visitor from a strange and rather primitive land.

Despite a few such unpleasant experiences, Kishi was deeply impressed by the United States—its over-all friendliness, its size, its energy and imagination. He marveled at the clean parks, which contrasted sharply with the paper-strewn parks in Japan, and he admired the relative politeness of American subway passengers, as compared to the animal-like aggressiveness of Japanese trying to squeeze into trains and buses. But he was impressed most of all by America's industry and high living standards.

"I had studied the American economic structure and knew something of its hugeness from published production figures," he told me. "Now I saw for the first time what those figures meant. I visited the Ford automobile plant, the U.S. Steel Corporation, the Stetson Hat Company, the coal mines of Pennsylvania. I saw forests of oil wells in Texas, whereas one could only see individual trees in Japan. I was overwhelmed, and completely discouraged about Japan's stage of industrial development. On the way home, I toured Europe, and received the impression that Japan would do better to pattern its economic development after that of Germany, a 'have-not' nation like Japan, than after that of the United States."

If Kishi was "overwhelmed" by American industry, he was confounded by some of the elements that were supposed to compose "American democracy." The highly materialistic values, the independent attitude of the women, the loosely woven family system, which was almost too loose to be called a "system"—these were all strange things, and while they might be all right for America, he dreaded the thought of their absorption into the Japanese way of life. On returning to Japan in the spring of 1927, he found himself speaking better English, but he wondered if he had greatly increased his understanding of America, of those peculiar qualities of character and soul that made a nation what it was.

Kishi found Japan in a tense mood on his arrival home. While he had been away, Nationalist troops in China, under Chiang Kai-shek, in a drive to wipe out resisting war lords and communists and unify the nation, had moved into Nanking, and in the fighting that occurred, many Japanese, as well as British and Americans, were killed or wounded and considerable foreign property was destroyed. United States and British vessels bombed the Nationalist positions, but the Japanese took no retaliatory measures. Shortly afterward, Japanese naval officials in Hankow were insulted, but still the Japanese government made no strong representations. These incidents, however, were all that the Japanese traditionalists needed to revive their nationalist movement.

Throughout the 1920's this movement had been in a disadvantageous position as peaceful foreign policies and embryonic democratic institutions blossomed. Under the influence of Foreign Minister Kijuro Shidehara, Japan, having evacuated the Shantung area, had adopted a highly conciliatory attitude toward China. No foreign power, Shidehara insisted, could ever impose a political or social structure on the Chinese people, nor was it ethical to make the attempt. Domestically, the government even passed a universal manhood suffrage law in 1925, increasing the electorate from 3.3 million to fourteen million. The liberal forces gained so much ground that soldiers discovered they enjoyed greater prestige in civilian clothes than in their uniforms. Reflecting the times, the government reduced the Army's strength by four divisions. At the same time, naval sacrifices were agreed to at international disarmament conferences in Washington and London.

These policies did not mean that Japan had suddenly been converted into a Western-style democracy. The new electoral law was accompanied by a Law for the Maintenance of Public Peace, which read, "Those who organize an association for the purpose of changing the national polity or the form of government, or denying the system of private property, or those who join it with a knowledge of its purposes, shall be punished with penal servitude or confinement for not more than ten years." Further, with Diet members still considering themselves more responsible to the Emperor than to their electors, the influence on policy of the corrupt old political and financial cliques continued to supersede that of the people. The traditional Japanese pattern of obligations had not yet substantially changed.

An impressive start toward democracy had, nonetheless, been made, impressive enough to induce the frustrated militarists, particularly the junior officers, to organize an underground opposition to the government, armed with the philosophies of Ikki Kita and his disciple, Shumei Okawa, both of whom Kishi had idolized at college. Okawa created a sensation in 1924 with the publication of a book invoking the ancient concepts of *Hakko Ichiu* and *Kodo* to justify morally the launching by Japan of a Divine Mission to rule, not only Asia, but the world. *Hakko Ichiu* literally meant the Eight Corners of the Universe under One Roof, or making the world one big family (though originally it may have been intended to signify unity of only the eight islands of Japan). *Kodo,* or the Imperial Way, meant that this aim could be achieved through absolute obedience and loyalty to the Emperor, on whom all aspects of national life—politics, economics, culture and defense—were to be focused. Japan, as the first state to come into being, argued Okawa, had a divine right to rule mankind.

Okawa's doctrine, an extension of Kita's, greatly influenced the young militarists. Army officers formed the *Tenken To,* or Heavenly Swords Society, and naval leaders, the *Osui Kai,* which announced that its purpose was to "establish the Great Japanese Empire in conformity with the spirit of the foundation of Japan and to unify the world with morality and righteousness." These organizations grew in strength following the incidents that took place in China as Chiang Kai-shek struggled northward. With Japan's honor sullied, they managed to stir up public opinion sufficiently to overthrow the Shidehara-dominated cabinet. When the succeeding, less liberal government sent troops into Shantung to protect Japanese interests, fighting broke out and the local Japanese commander, without instructions, demanded a formal apology from Chiang, resulting in a further degeneration of relations between the two countries. This was most seriously reflected in a new Chinese boycott of Japanese goods.

The boycott was a vital economic blow to Japan and underscored, in the minds of the militarists, the need to control China, quite aside from their belief that Japan had the moral right, as an "elder brother," to exert such authority. The unsettled economic conditions that had plagued the nation throughout the 1920's began to grow critical toward the end of the decade, with the bitter winds of depression blowing in from the Western world. Japan's silk markets—silk had been its most profitable export—collapsed, and the economy floundered; unemployment reached new heights, and numerous smaller firms went bankrupt and were swallowed up by the *Zaibatsu,* Japan's huge combines.

The younger officers, in particular, most of whom came from rural areas where the distress was greatest, were more determined than ever to win for Japan its proper share of the world's wealth, as well as respect. China was its natural market, its natural source of raw materials, its natural annex of settlement for relief of the growing overpopulation problem. Yet, while the sufferings of their families grew, they could only watch in panic as Chiang Kai-shek, now a confirmed enemy, continued moving northward toward Manchuria and Mongolia, where Japan still retained precarious economic footholds. And standing by, waiting to profit from all this, in their view, were the greedy Western businessmen who had for so long exploited Asia for their own benefit.

Kishi personally did not escape the ravages of the depression that engulfed Japan. He needed money now as never before, not only to pay for the continuing treatments for his son, but to provide for an expanding family, which now included a little girl, Yoko, born in 1928. Though he was earning little enough, the government, desperately trying to make ends meet, embarked in 1929 on an economic retrenchment program under which civil service salaries were to be reduced. Each minister was to determine the extent of reduction he considered reasonable for the personnel of his ministry. The Minister of Commerce and Industry decided on a ten per cent cut.

Kishi violently opposed any wage decrease whatsoever. His opposition gradually developed into outright defiance as he watched Nobukazu hobble around, and as he thought of his juniors who had to support larger families on salaries much lower than his. But it was a dangerous matter, defying one's superiors. His Choshu ancestors, men like Yoshida Shoin, often defied the Tokugawa, but until their final victory they had paid a high price for their boldness. As for himself, he would have to offer his resignation if he challenged his bosses, win or lose, to permit the Minister to save "face." Defiance, therefore, might mean an end to the career that was his life and livelihood, an ironic possibility in view of his carefulness in the past to deny his superiors any grounds for criticizing him or balking his advance. Yet, after intensive reflection, he decided to take this risk. Pleasing one's superiors on administrative and other minor matters was one thing. But this was not a minor matter, nor just a question of money. Principle was involved. The poor, uninfluential people at the bottom of the hierarchy, those who could least afford to do so, were being made to carry the burden of bad times.

Kishi called a meeting of the civil servants in his ministry and told them that he planned to ask the Minister to rescind the salary reduction order. They unanimously supported him, entrusting him with their letters of resignation for use as a bargaining wedge, though he had not requested this. If the Minister would not listen to reason, all those present at the gathering—about fifty—would resign *en masse,* completely disrupting the work of the ministry.

Kishi, delighted with this backing, wrote to Minister Yukio Saku-rauchi, stating that as representative of the civil servants in the ministry he was obliged to press for a rescission of the order in question. The Minister immediately summoned him to a midnight meeting at his official residence. On his arrival, Kishi repeated the request he had made in the name of the employees, whose resignations, he indicated, he was author-ized to submit if necessary.

"Kishi-san," said the Minister, "I know how you and the others feel, but I have no choice. I must carry out the order. However, I would con-sider a compromise. The Ministries of Railways and of Postal Services have already dealt with the matter on a compromise basis. Certainly you cannot expect the personnel of this ministry to stand alone in their refusal to accept any reduction. I myself will take a *twenty* per cent cut in salary."

Kishi, incensed by what he considered tasteless condescension, replied, "Sir, ministers do not have to live on their salaries. Some would choose to keep their jobs even if they were not paid at all. On the other hand, the civil servants must live entirely on their salaries. Therefore, it does not follow that if a minister accepts a twenty per cent cut, his underlings should have to take a ten per cent reduction."

The Minister's eyes sharpened with rage. "I don't care if every one of you resigns. I shall bring the Ministry down in ruins before I give in to you. Do you understand?"

Kishi replied, "If you wish to destroy the Ministry, I shall help you."

Then, realizing the futility of further conversation, he left, wondering if perhaps he should not have considered the compromise proposal. He discussed the matter with his colleagues, who favored acceptance as the wisest thing to do under the circumstances. Kishi then saw the Minister again, and an agreement was reached whereby the ten per cent reduction would be compensated to some degree by increased year-end bonuses and severance payments.

Kishi then submitted his resignation, fully expecting it to be accepted. He began considering a career in business, having made many business contacts in his job, when the Vice-Minister telephoned him and said, "If we accepted your resignation, we would probably have another revolt on our hands. Do you want to wreck the ministry?" Kishi remained on the job.

His rise in the bureaucracy was, as it turned out, accelerated rather than slowed down by the depression. Japan, desperately clinging to what foreign markets remained, tried to maintain its prices and profits through the frantic formation of larger cartels and trusts. But centralization of industry was only a partial solution. The nation's factories were, on the whole, operated with outdated machinery and methods, resulting in extremely low productivity. It had been possible to compete on the world market previously because of the cheapness of Japanese labor, but now, when markets were so scarce, international competition would only be possible with greater productivity.

A provisional Industrial Rationalization Bureau was established in the Ministry of Commerce and Industry, with an owl-faced man named Koichi Kido, great-grandson of Koin Kido, one of the original Choshu engineers of the Meiji Restoration, as its chief. Kishi, who drew up the plans for the new department, was directly under him in authority. His first assignment was to attend a World Power Conference in Berlin and, at the same time, investigate Germany's industrial rationalization program, after which Japan planned to model its own.

Kishi was excited about this opportunity to visit Europe. But the trip was marred by an embarrassing incident that occurred en route on the Trans-Siberian Railroad train. He awoke in his compartment to find his wallet, which contained several hundred dollars as well as valuable travel documents, missing from his coat. The thief was found after an intensive search, but before he could be apprehended he jumped off the train, chased by the conductor and a dining-car waiter. The culprit was finally caught and Kishi got his wallet back, but he writhed in humiliation, particularly when he learned his colleagues had reported the incident to the ministry. He had started on this important mission by losing "face." For although the Japanese have sympathy for a man who has been the victim of an armed robbery, they tend to laugh at and ridicule a man who has permitted a thief to outwit him or catch him unawares.

But by the time Kishi returned home in late 1930 after several months abroad, the incident had been forgotten. Instead, Kishi found his superiors acclaiming him for the results of his trip, which produced exhaustive industrial reports, not only from Germany, but from Britain, France, Italy, and Switzerland. He had returned with the knowledge indispensable to a successful rationalization process at home, and with the methods, it was hoped, of avoiding economic collapse.

Kishi arrived back at a time of crisis indeed. Prime Minister Hamaguchi had just been assassinated by the scheming militarists, whose power had been restricted by Hamaguchi's cabinet. And the militarists received considerable help from civilian supporters in the nationalist effort to profit from the seething unrest of the great depression. Rabble-rousers, led by Shumei Okawa, barnstormed the country, appealing to the workers and peasants to join in a "people's movement" to throw out the big capitalists and the "corrupt" politicians and transfer their power to the military. These appeals ironically gained popularity as Kishi instituted his rationalization program, which, "in the interests of efficiency," strengthened the hold of the capitalists over industry. Pragmatism, Kishi decided, had to take precedence over idealism at a time like this.

Meanwhile, the militarists organized a new secret society called the *Sakura Kai,* or Cherry Blossom Society, which pledged to use force if necessary to implement Okawa's demands. Its members could not, stated the prospectus of the organization, tolerate the immorality of the Elder Statesmen, the irresponsibility of the press, the unemployment in the cities, the great distress in the rural areas, the radicalism of many intellectuals, the lack of patriotism in the universities, the self-seeking attitude of the bureaucrats, and most important of all, the treachery of the *Zaibatsu* leaders and politicians who, it was claimed, were growing rich at the expense of the people. This society, allied with Okawa, planned to follow up the Hamaguchi assassination with others, but were forced to give up the idea when several highly placed military officials backed out of the plan at the last minute.

The plotters then decided that they could press their demands in an equally sensational manner by forcing a "basic solution of the Manchurian problem," which, they hoped, would bring an end to the depression and, incidentally, create more and better jobs for themselves. Since Japan defeated Russia early in the century, it had enjoyed a unique position in Manchuria, tightened and reinforced by a number of agreements with China. It administered a part of Manchuria, called the Leased Territory, with almost full rights of sovereignty. The Japanese-owned South Manchurian Railway, moreover, controlled railway areas that embraced many towns, including important sections of Mukden and Changchun, administering in these places the schools, taxes, police, and public utilities. To assure against interference with Japanese rule, the Kwantung Army was stationed in the Leased Territory, Railway Guards protected the railway areas, and Consular Police were maintained in all these zones.

The Lytton Commission, which investigated Japanese activities in Manchuria for the League of Nations, reported:

> "There is probably nowhere in the world an exact parallel to this situation, no example of a country enjoying in the territory of a neighboring state such extensive administrative privileges. A situation of this kind could conceivably be maintained, without leading to incessant complications and disputes, if it were freely desired or accepted by both sides, and if it were the sign and embodiment of a well-considered policy of close collaboration in the economic and political spheres. But in the absence of such conditions, it could only lead to friction and conflict. . . ."

With Chiang Kai-shek threatening Japanese privileges in Manchuria, this friction and conflict grew. The time had finally come, the Cherry Blossom Society thought, for decisive action that would not only solve the Manchurian problem once and for all, but the domestic one as well. On the night of September 18, 1931, its plot, supported by the Kwantung Army and leaders of the War Ministry, was set in motion with an explosion that was to rock the world. A bomb was detonated by the Japanese on the tracks of the South Manchurian Railway near Mukden. The Kwantung Army blamed the incident on Chiang's agents and, forcing the Japanese government to accept a *fait accompli,* swarmed over all southern Manchuria in two days and swallowed up the rest of the province by the following January.

The Manchurian Incident was to most Japanese, bitter, frustrated, disillusioned by the uninspiring tenets of democracy, very much like a spectacular new sunrise. The Sun Goddess was suddenly resurrected. National socialist parties mushroomed, with conservatives attracted by the accent on "national," and the workers, who abandoned the two proletariat political parties *en masse,* drawn by the appealing combination of nationalism and socialism. The democrats found themselves passively supporting these movements because they could not resist the wave of public approval. Those who did offer opposition learned their possible fate when Prime Minister Inukai, after speaking against the occupation of Manchuria, was, like his predecessor, Hamaguchi, assassinated in May, 1932. With the appointment of a nonparty premier to replace him, the military now had an iron boot in the political door.

Kishi, like most Japanese, by no means disapproved of the aggression in Manchuria. His years as a civil servant had mellowed his college-day sympathy for Ikki Kita's militaristic solution to Japan's problems. In fact, since embarking on his career, he had not given much thought to political policies in general, which were, after all, beyond the ken of his bureaucratic niche. But the shock of Manchuria suddenly awakened his nationalist instincts, relighting the glory of his samurai heritage. He did not concern himself greatly with the justification of the Army's action. But he was deeply impressed by the overnight change in the national atmosphere. A restless, demoralized people, dazed by the depression and lacking strong leadership, had come alive.

His thoughts drifted back to his childhood—the glorious days of victory in the Russo-Japanese War, the samurai pride forever displayed by Great-grandfather Sato and his mother. Dear Moyo. She was, to a large degree, responsible for everything he was. She had instilled in him from his earliest years the spirit of his ancestors, never letting him forget that he was a product of Choshu, the greatest of all samurai clans, and, therefore, obligated far more than most people to bring glory and honor to his family. He had done so little to repay *ko* to his mother, visiting and writing her far too seldom. Even when he was able to make it down to Tabuse, he never saw much of her. A good deal of the time he was either at the Kishis or going to local meetings and sake parties with his old friends.

When, in 1931, Moyo fell ill, Kishi went to Tabuse and brought her to Tokyo, securing for her, after extraordinary difficulties, one of the two first-class rooms in the overcrowded Imperial University of Tokyo Hospital. He told the family doctor, "I've always been the least helpful to my parents of all the children in the family. I'm grateful that I've been able to offer Mother this small bit of comfort."

Moyo, after she had recovered from the illness, returned to Tabuse, only to have a serious relapse. Kishi rushed down to see her, as did the rest of the scattered family, including his elder brother, Ichiro, who had become a Vice-Admiral, and his younger brother, Eisaku, then an official in the Ministry of Railways. Kishi imagined his mother as she had been twenty years before—a figure of grace, with a smooth, silken complexion and the commanding dignity of a goddess, righteous and devout in her idealistic views, thoroughly obsessed with the futures of her children. Now she was a gray-haired woman with sunken cheeks and thin, shriveled hands. Yet, in her eyes there still glowed the spirit of the figure in Kishi's imagination. And when he knelt beside her on the *tatami,* Moyo said, almost in a whisper, "My son, I'm proud of you—I'm proud of all my children. Not one of you will be a failure." She exerted a slight pressure on her son's hand, then remained silent, staring at him with a barely perceptible smile.

As the doctor did not view her case with great urgency, Kishi, after spending several days at his mother's bedside, left by train for Tokyo, thinking that she would soon regain her health. But when he arrived home, he found a telegram waiting for him. Moyo had died.

The addition of Manchuria, or Manchoukuo, as the puppet state was called, to the Japanese Empire resulted in a marked increase in the activities of Kishi's Ministry of Commerce and Industry. Appointed a section chief in the Ministry's Industrial Bureau in 1933, Kishi selected a special mission to investigate industrial possibilities and embark on preliminary construction in Manchoukuo, to which Japan, encouraged by the militarists, now looked for an answer to both its economic ills and its ideological longings.

In 1935, Kishi, promoted to the directorship of the bureau, helped the Japanese General Staff draw up a five-year National Defense Plan for the expansion of the armaments industry and a six-year program for the re-equipment of the armed forces. But he continued to concentrate on Manchoukuo, formulating, in conjunction with his staff in the territory, a five-year plan for its industrial development. He received profound satisfaction from this assignment. He had dreamed all his life of playing an important role in the development and glorification of Japan. Now he had the opportunity to test for the first time the revolutionary concept of national socialism, under which the government would supervise strategic industries.

Eventually, this principle, if it worked in Manchoukuo, might be applied in Japan itself.

The question of reform in Japan had, in fact, already become a political issue stormy enough to split the militarists. The Young Officers Group, the radical-minded sons of impoverished farm families, intensified their support of the Kita plan for the military overthrow of the financial cliques and political parties in power. They demanded the immediate introduction in Japan of the kind of national socialism that Kishi was trying to bring to Manchoukuo. They argued that such a program had to be established without delay to strengthen the nation's capacity for carrying out its "divine" mission. The more conservative senior, high-level officers, known as the *Toseiha,* or Control Group, also favored the expansion of the Japanese Empire, but did not believe that drastic economic and social reform at home was required to facilitate it.

When the *Toseiha* began purging Young Officers from important military positions, one of the latter calmly walked into the office of General Nagata, head of the Bureau of Military Affairs, and plunged a sword into him. Shortly afterward, on February 26, 1936, an all-out attempt was made by the Young Officers to deliver a *coup de grace* to both their civilian and military enemies and take the Emperor under their own wing. They would re-enact, they hoped, what Kishi's Choshu ancestors had done in the rebellion against the Tokugawa. With Ikki Kita himself among the leaders, the First Army Division, which the Control Group had planned to "exile" to Manchoukuo because of its sympathy with the Young Officers, revolted.

In a lightning move, rebel troops occupied the War Ministry, the Diet Building, and other strategic points in Tokyo. Finance Minister Takahashi, Lord Keeper of the Privy Seal Admiral Saito, and General Watanabe, Military Education Inspector General, were assassinated. Premier Admiral Okada, another intended victim, escaped death by disguising himself in a woman's kimono.

Martial law was declared, and the Emperor commanded the rebels to surrender, finally bringing the fighting to an end after three days of terror. Thirteen officers and six civilians, including Ikki Kita, were executed, five officers were sentenced to life imprisonment, and others committed *hara-kiri.* The national socialist movement suffered a severe setback. But the rebels, in the military sense, had nevertheless furthered their cause. For they had made it possible for their seniors to strengthen their political control at the expense of the Emperor's civilian advisers.

The revolt had a powerful but confused emotional impact on Kishi. On the one hand, as a bureaucrat working with the politicians, and also as a basically moderate person, he did not approve of cold-blooded assassination as a means of achieving an end. On the other hand, he was sympathetic to the rebel cause, and was saddened to hear that a great man like Ikki Kita, who had exerted so profound an influence on him, had been executed like a common criminal.

Having seldom associated with the peasants or occupied himself with their problems, Kishi did not fully understand the important role that rural discontent had played in generating the conspiracy. But he did understand the anger of the national socialists against the politicians and businessmen, many of whom were, as charged, corrupt, weak men conscious only of power and profit. Moreover, it was understandable that the Young Officers were impatient to destroy the decadent materialistic Western influences in China and replace them with the rich spiritual values of Japan, which alone could bring happiness and prosperity to its neighbors. It was time, indeed, that the strings of national unity were drawn tighter, with every individual Japanese feeling himself as part of the whole. And this could only be achieved, as Kita had said, through social and economic reform.

Kishi, however, more cautious in his views than he had been in his university days, did not favor rushing too fast or too far along the socialist path. Big private capitalism could possibly serve the same purpose as national socialism—another expression for state capitalism—if it were big and unified enough and were oriented, under strict government regulation, to meet national needs on a planned basis. Nevertheless, he thought, outright state control of the vital, strategic industries would permit more efficient planning and therefore seemed preferable.

Spurred by the spirit of the abortive coup, Kishi helped to organize a reform movement among a number of civil servant colleagues which worked closely with Kita followers in the Army. Most bureaucrats were reluctant to co-operate with the military, not so much because they opposed its aims as because it threatened their power. But Kishi was not worried about this threat. He was so valuable a technician, he was convinced, that his advice would be sought no matter who was in power. The New Bureaucrats, as the reform group called itself, adopted as their emblem the "Showa Restoration" flag (Showa is the name of the current Imperial era) under which the Young Officers had revolted. They intensified the campaign, on a peaceful basis, to nationalize, or partially nationalize, the *Zaibatsu,* under their direction. This program represented, the New Bureaucrats dramatically claimed, simply a "restoration" to the

Emperor of ultimate power over industry, a task which had not been completed under the Meiji Restoration.

As Kishi's influence grew, he suddenly found himself a victim of it. He and Yoshino, who was now Vice-Minister of Commerce and Industry, had become a combination far more powerful in matters of policy-making than would normally be true of bureaucrats in their positions. It began to be whispered about in government circles that the ministry would "fall apart" without their services. This certainly did not endear them to Minister Gotaro Ogawa, who was threatened with becoming a mere figurehead or puppet in the areas of his own authority.

Furthermore, in the eyes of the Minister, Kishi and Yoshino were showing off their importance to an unwarranted degree in the geisha houses. It was, of course, the privilege of high officials to visit such places occasionally. In Japan, only clerks came directly home from work every night. Men of social and political standing were almost obligated to be seen in the expensive places of entertainment with business and government associates. Still, too much was too much, and Kishi, in particular, cut quite a figure among the geishas as he severed for a few hours his bonds of responsibility and transformed himself, with the help of a few glasses of sake, from a tense, serious-minded human machine into a gay, carefree, relaxed human being. He joked with the geishas and sent them into orgies of giggling with his uncanny ability to build matchstick castles, win games of "stone-paper-scissors," and emerge unscathed from contests in which a flaming piece of paper was handed around the table until someone's fingers were burned.

Minister Ogawa's fear and dissatisfaction, moreover, were aggravated by Kishi's association with the New Bureaucrats, who were hardly favorably disposed to veteran politicians like himself. Everybody should know his place, Ogawa thought, and his two subordinates had evidently forgotten theirs. He had, in fact, been wary of them since he first took office. His predecessor, Minister Takukichi Kawasaki, had warned him, "You will not be able to carry out the functions of your post satisfactorily unless you take a strong hand with Yoshino and Kishi. In particular, watch out for Kishi. Don't forget how much trouble he caused about the reduction of salaries." Ogawa decided that the time had come to "take a strong hand."

One day, Yoshino called Kishi to his office and told him gravely, "I have just spoken with the Minister. He wants to transfer us out of Tokyo. I have been offered the job of directing development in northern Japan. As for you, Ogawa asked me to advise you to take an assignment in Manchoukuo. I told him that if he wanted to dismiss you, he should deal with you in person."

Kishi was bitterly disappointed, but not overly surprised. Having drawn up development plans for Manchoukuo, he was an obvious choice to help in their implementation. Also, he was one of the few highly placed bureaucrats in the Ministry of Commerce and Industry who was known to be co-operative with the Army. Yoshino had long thought that Kishi would have a unique opportunity for advancement in Manchoukuo, where he would be freer of the bonds of the highly restrictive seniority system. Kishi would be a big fish in the small Manchoukuo pond. Almost a year before, Naoki Hoshino, head of Manchoukuo's General Affairs Bureau, which administered the puppet government under the military, had visited Tokyo and told Yoshino, "The elementary state of economic development is now over in Manchoukuo, and it is time to carry out full-scale development of its economy and industry. But no ordinary staff can do this efficiently. We need better personnel than we have. Can you suggest some people?"

Yoshino recommended Kishi, but expressed doubt that he would willingly take the assignment. And Yoshino was right. Kishi, when approached, indicated he would rather not take the job "immediately." Nevertheless, he anticipated that sooner or later he would have to submit to military pressure. He even felt a sense of obligation to go to Manchoukuo. He had promised the men he had assigned there that he would eventually join them. He had, quite frankly, told them this to calm their fear that such an assignment was equivalent to "banishment." For in the early years, Japanese civil servants viewed Manchoukuo with the same uneasiness that Englishmen once viewed Australia. Now it was he who was being "banished." Manchoukuo by no means seemed to Kishi, as it did to Yoshino, like the most direct route to the top. But even if he were able to argue Ogawa into letting him stay in Tokyo, how far could he advance under him? The Minister was certain to delay his promotion and might even take away certain powers and authority which he already possessed.

While Kishi pondered his future, Ogawa asked to see him at his official residence. The Minister, greeting him as if he were his best friend, said, "Kishi-san, I'd like you to go to Manchoukuo. The military authorities have been pleading with me to send you and I think it would be a good idea if you accepted."

Kishi, irritated by the Minister's seemingly false air of good will, asked, "Is this an order or simply a proposal which I am free to accept or reject?"

Ogawa smiled. "It is not an order in the strict sense of the word. It is the proposal of the military authorities. As you know, the administration of our ministry is tied quite closely to military policy. Therefore, we cannot help but comply with their wishes to some degree. I hope you realize this."

Kishi absorbed this evasive explanation coldly, answering, "I judge then that it is an order. I feel that I have little choice but to accept."

"You will only have to stay in Manchoukuo for a year or so," said Ogawa. "Now that isn't so bad, is it? You're one of our best people, and we will miss you. We will be waiting for you to come back to us."

Kishi replied acidly, "Frankly speaking, I have no wish to return. You should understand that I am complying with your request only because it is a matter of principle with me that I do what I am ordered to do. But now that I am going, I have no desire to return after a limited assignment, as apprentices do. I really don't care if I perish there."

When Kishi had left, Ogawa, his triumph soured with indignation, wrote in a report explaining his subordinate's transfer to Manchoukuo: ". . . He has embarrassed the Ministry by indulging too frequently in unnecessary pleasures and comforts."

CHAPTER VII

❧❦❧

THE LIGHT OF CIVILIZATION

As THE AIRLINER from Tokyo winged northwest over Korea toward Manchoukuo, Nobusuke Kishi pressed his face to the round little window by his seat, searching the horizon. Finally, in the distance, Kishi glimpsed the town of Mukden, ancient home of the Manchu dynasty that had ruled China until it was overthrown by Sun Yat-sen in 1912. He recognized it from the modern buildings and tall factory smokestacks exhaling the black breath of industry.

Near here had been fought some of the momentous battles of the Russo-Japanese War, battles won by one of Choshu's greatest heroes, General Nogi. Kishi reflected on the joy he had experienced when news came of the General's New Year's Day capture of Port Arthur. He could still recall the angry, proud words he had written when criticism had been leveled against General Nogi for having committed *hara-kiri* after the death of the Emperor Meiji. "It is this samurai spirit that shall carry Japan to ever greater heights. . . ." Now here he was himself in the land that General Nogi had freed from the Russians. Whatever doubts he had entertained about the wisdom of going to Manchoukuo disappeared. He, Nobusuke Kishi, now had the opportunity to help complete the sacred mission that General Nogi had initiated—bringing the Japanese spirit to Japan's younger Asian brothers.

As he peered through the thick-paned window, the great central plain of Manchoukuo stretched to infinity. Within view were the trappings of two contrasting worlds—ancient China and modern Japan. Tiny, intensively cultivated farm plots blended into a magnificent terrestrial design of greens, yellows, and browns, through which twisted, like cracks in a mosaic, narrow, murky rivers that emptied into the Sea of Japan or the Gulf of Pechili. Straw-hatted peasants, as their fathers and grandfathers had done before them, guided wooden plows drawn by horses, oxen, donkeys, or Manchurian ponies; some pulled their own plows. Their produce—soya beans, millet, maize, wheat, buckwheat, barley, rice, flax, hemp, ramie, cotton, and tobacco—was transported to the towns in Japanese-made trucks on Japanese-built highways or in trains that moved along the tracks of the South Manchurian Railway.

Kishi felt a surge of pride as he saw evidence and examples of the civilization which the Japanese had brought to this "primitive" country. But he was also apprehensive as he noted the "protected villages" of mud-and-wattle huts, where populations of whole areas had recently been concentrated in order to prevent them from helping the 10,000 or more Manchurian bandits, mostly communists, he was sure, who were conducting guerrilla warfare against the Japanese. A high mud wall surrounded each village, around which a deep ditch was dug. On top of the wall, barbed wire was strung and, surrounding the barrier, blockhouses with corrugated iron roofs were situated at intervals. As villagers, Kishi knew, were not trusted to carry arms but were expected to telephone the closest Japanese detachment whenever bandits appeared, he was not surprised that this elaborate defense system, according to reports he had received, was not highly effective.

Kishi was also disturbed to see steel and concrete pillboxes at all bridgeheads, tunnel entrances, and railroad stations. Japanese troops stood guard over the gangs of railroad workers along the tracks, making the stations resemble prison camps. At night, lights in the smaller stations were kept out except when trains, many of them manned by machine-gun units, came through. Sometimes armored cars piloted the trains. Apparently the bandit situation was worse than he had been led to believe by army officials in Tokyo. "How foolish the guerrillas were," Kishi thought. "Did they not realize that the Japanese were here to help them, not to hurt them? The Japanese were bringing them roads, factories, dams, modern cities, literally lifting them out of the feudal age, just as the Choshu patriots had done in Japan itself in the past seventy years."

The airliner finally came within sight of the new Manchoukuo capital of Hsinking, Kishi's destination. Only a few years before, Hsinking had been a little farm village of mud huts and dirt roads. Now there were broad tree-shaded boulevards lined with modern apartment and office buildings. There were artificial lakes and parks, and new houses, though, of course, still many mud huts. Kishi hardly noticed a scene near the airport of thousands of raggedly dressed men, women and children—forced laborers—working on a road under the eye of Japanese soldiers.

When the plane landed, Kishi was greeted by several colleagues whom he had sent to Manchoukuo in previous years. Etsusaburo Shiina, who was in charge of the mining sector of the Manchoukuo government Industrial Department, said, "We're certainly happy to see you. We've been waiting for you to join us for a long time."

Kishi grinned. "Does that mean I am welcome? Or does it mean that you have been waiting to see me suffer the same fate to which I condemned you?"

Shiina laughed aloud. "I had never thought of it *exactly* that way."

In a festive mood, the group climbed into an official automobile and the chauffeur sent the car roaring down the road. "General Itagaki (the Kwantung Chief of Staff) is anxious to welcome you," Shiina said. "You're going to meet a lot of generals here. It's not like Tokyo. Here, we're practically in the Army."

Kishi was upset by this remark. He realized, of course, that Manchoukuo was, to all intents and purposes, controlled by the Kwantung Army. He knew, too, that the Army had been pressing for his services. But he was determined not to become a "yes man" for the military. His job— as Vice-Minister of the Industrial Department of Manchoukuo—was to help create a strong, industrialized country. This job required vision and imagination, attributes not usually found in the inflexible mind of the soldier. Naturally it was necessary for the Army to play an important role here. Close co-operation between Japan and Manchoukuo was essential to bring well-being and prosperity to both countries, and such a relationship was only possible, as the bandit threat illustrated, through utilization of military power. But if the Army had to be used, he would not be used by the Army.

Later in the day, after freshening up at his quarters, Kishi, accompanied by Shiina, went to meet General Seishiro Itagaki at military headquarters. He found the outer office bustling with callers, including some officers, but mostly civilians, who stood in long lines before several reception desks.

"What are all these civilians doing here?" Kishi asked.

"Most of them are businessmen," Shiina replied. "They have to go through a lot of military red tape before they can get things done here."

Kishi shook his head slightly in agitated surprise. "Why? Since when is business a function of the military?"

General Itagaki was notified of Kishi's arrival, and the visitor, leaving his colleague in the lobby, was led by an aide through a labyrinth of corridors, crowded with civilians, to the General's office. As Kishi entered and bowed, Itagaki, whose tight-jawed face was distinguished by heavy eyebrows and a brush mustache, got up from his desk and showed him to a chair. Kishi was a bit nervous, for he knew from General Itagaki's reputation that he was not an easy man to deal with. A rabid nationalist and iron-fisted authoritarian, he had played a leading role in the preparation and execution of the Mukden Incident that had opened the way for Japan to take control of Manchuria. He was shrewd and cunning, too. On the day of the incident, the War Ministry had sent General Tatekawa to Mukden to investigate reports, though not too ardently, that such a plot was being planned. Itagaki, then a colonel in Kwantung headquarters, had greeted the visitor, dined with him, and left him at an inn to be entertained by geishas while the bomb burst.

Kishi came right to the point: "I fully understand, General, that the Kwantung Army has responsibility for the maintenance of public peace in Manchoukuo. But it is my view that economic and industrial problems should be in the hands of civilian officials like myself. I sincerely hope that we will be entrusted with authority over such affairs and that the military will not interfere with this authority. We will, of course, follow the basic political policies laid down by the Kwantung Army."

General Itagaki remained silent, his thick eyebrows raised slightly, as if he were startled by such directness. "To be quite frank," Kishi continued, "I was surprised to see businessmen crowding the lobby and corridors of this building. I rather feel that they should be coming to the Industrial Department, not to the military. However, if you feel unable to accept my views, I would fully understand the selection of another more suitable man to fill the job intended for me."

Kishi was aware that Itagaki might accept his resignation before he had even started on his new job. He was no less aware of the difficulties which would arise if he had to return to Tokyo and work under Ogawa, whom he had also angered with his frank approach. Nevertheless, if he was to succeed in his mission in Manchoukuo, he had to make it clear from the start that he would not be a mere puppet of the military.

The General finally said, without expression, "Kishi-san, you're free to run matters as you wish within your own department."

"Thank you," said Kishi, greatly relieved.

"As a matter of fact, the Army will be more than grateful for all the assistance that you can give us," continued Itagaki. "We do not want these businessmen cluttering up our offices. They are a nuisance. The fact is that they come to us because it is natural for civilians to believe that the military can offer them special favors and privileges." He paused. "Does that make clear our problem?"

Kishi bowed and departed happily. He had made an excellent beginning.

He found that other Kwantung leaders also exhibited co-operative attitudes. After waiting more than a year for his services, they were prepared to meet, to a considerable degree, his unusually forthright demands. Bureaucrats with his exceptional ability who could be trusted by the military were rare, and they didn't want to lose him.

Kishi was particularly impressed by General Hideki Tojo, Commander of the Military Police, the *Kempei Tai,* who was known by his colleagues as The Razor because of his sharp temperament. Tojo's pointed, frozen features might have been chipped from stone. But underneath the hard, inanimate expression was hidden an unyielding nationalistic zeal, a cold white flame that burned with as much intensity as any fire—and was not as likely to be whipped up by wind or quenched by water as the kind of passion found in most men. Nor did Kishi fail to gauge Tojo's inordinate personal ambition, perhaps because he was of a similar nature in this respect.

In Tokyo, Kishi had heard Tojo discussed as a man with a bright future. True, his career had been undistinguished for almost thirty years, and only two years before, in 1934, he had blundered when, as Chief of the Military Inquiry Department in Tokyo, he told the press that "the United States, Russia and China, knowing that Japan is likely to be confronted with various international difficulties in November, 1935, are steadily preparing for war." The Kwantung Army, embarrassed by this hint of its plans for November, 1935, had forced him to announce that he really meant the "general period of 1935-1936." But on being sent to Manchoukuo to head the Japanese Gestapo there, he soon made up for his error with his highly efficient police tactics. The files in his red-brick headquarters were crammed with information about every Kwantung officer, and those suspected of disloyalty were often disposed of with dispatch in dank torture cells.

Moreover, the General was popular among both the senior and junior officers. He was conservative enough to please his superiors, yet displayed a radical aggressiveness satisfactory to the young hotheads. Kishi was now convinced, both by this response of other army officers to him, and by his own observation of his character, that the Tokyo reports had not exaggerated his potentialities.

Kishi discovered that Manchoukuo was a bureaucrat's paradise. The government provided him with a large Japanese-style house, which, he was sure, would please Yoshiko, who was to follow him to Manchoukuo shortly, leaving the children with their grandmother in Tabuse. He was granted allowances several times his basic salary. And he had prestige here, too; he wasn't an anonymous cog in the great governmental wheel as he had been in Tokyo. In Confucian style, he wore a gold band around his hat and arm to denote his rank and was treated by Manchu collaborators like a *daimyo* of feudal times. They bowed to him, seldom argued with his decisions, and seemed to display a remarkable understanding of the hierarchal practices that, in Japan's view, constituted the natural foundation for a true and just social order.

Also, unlike Tokyo, Kishi could attend any number of geisha parties without fear of censure by his superiors for "pretentious" conduct. He took full advantage of this extra measure of freedom, and the lovely young geishas imported from Japan to ease the "hardships" endured by high officials in this pioneer state were as delighted with his company as he was with theirs. His popularity and exploits among these entertainers soon became legendary, particularly after what came to be known as the "Hair-Counting Incident."

At one party, Kishi examined the hand of a young geisha sitting next to him and remarked that it was the hand of a child. The girl, smiling coquettishly, replied that a diamond ring on the finger would make it look like a woman's. Kishi promised to give her a diamond ring, provided she was able to win a little game. Pointing to a distinguished colleague with a nearly bald head, he explained that to earn the ring she had only to count the hairs that remained on his head without the man becoming aware of what she was doing. The girl beamed. It looked easy. She knelt beside him and made her presence agreeable to him. Then, while he drank sake and talked, she leaned over his shoulder and began counting hairs. But he would never keep his head still long enough for her to complete the count. Finally, after failing many times, and noticing that the man was beginning to be annoyed by the way she hovered over him and kept staring at his head, she burst into tears, acknowledging failure.

The man, on learning why she had cuddled up to him, cried, "I feel ten years younger. It is wonderful to know that I have more hair than she could count. Perhaps *I* should offer her a diamond ring, don't you think?"

Kishi presented the geisha with a brand-new kimono, a consolation prize, which she happily accepted. From that time on, it seemed to him, every geisha in Manchoukuo offered to try her hand at counting the hair of his friends.

Kishi and his fellow Japanese lived like *daimyo* despite the fact that Manchoukuo, in theory, was a sovereign country. Japan, under an agreement concluded in 1932, accorded Manchoukuo formal recognition, while calling for it to co-operate with the Japanese and acquiesce in the continued presence of Japanese troops. Executive and legislative authority was ostensibly exercised by Manchu Emperor Kang Teh. However, his powers were subject to approval by a State Council headed by Prime Minister Chang Ching-hu. This State Council was composed of several cabinet departments, each nominally led by a Chinese minister but actually controlled by a Japanese vice-minister (Kishi was thus Vice-Minister of the Industrial Department) and a Japanese-dominated General Affairs Bureau. Over-all civilian authority resided with a General Affairs Board, whose director was a Japanese, Naoki Hoshino.

Superimposed on this civilian power structure was the Kwantung Army, with General-Ambassador Kenkichi Ueda at its head, flanked by Chief of Staff General Itagaki and Military Police Chief General Tojo. Although this Manchoukuo hierarchy virtually determined policy in the state, the General-Ambassador was responsible, if rather loosely, to the Manchoukuo Affairs Board in Tokyo, which was presided over by the Minister of War.

Among the civilians, Kishi as the highest-ranking Japanese industrial leader, was second only to Hoshino, a short heavy-set man with long, thinning hair and an imperious demeanor, accentuated by a pair of large thick shell-rimmed glasses, who had sold his home in Tokyo before coming to Manchoukuo in 1932 in the expectation of remaining there for the rest of his life. Kishi's main job was to supervise implementation of the Five-Year-Plan which he had helped draw up in Tokyo. This plan was designed to lay a solid foundation for the exploitation of industrial resources so that Manchoukuo would be able to supply itself with all vital commodities in the event of an emergency, and at the same time provide Japan with many of the raw materials it needed, particularly for war industries. It called for the production of munitions, automobiles, and rolling stock; the development of such basic enterprises as iron and steel, liquid fuel manufacture, and the exploitation of agricultural resources required for national defense. Among the largest projects envisioned were two huge hydro-electric dams, one on the Yalu River, the other on the Sungari River.

The plan was announced shortly after Kishi arrived in Manchoukuo. There were, however, financial difficulties which were causing serious delay in putting it into operation. The necessary capital was simply not available. The real source of this problem, Kishi well realized, was the hatred harbored by the young Kwantung officers from peasant families for the great *Zaibatsu* capitalists. The influence of these officers (although considerably reduced in Japan as the result of the abortive "February 26th" coup) was still great in the Kwantung Army, and even the senior officers in Manchoukuo were sympathetic to their views. Now that the Army had under its thumb an area "of its own," it saw an opportunity to experiment with the principles of national socialism for which Ikki Kita had died.

Stirred by Kita's idealism, the militarists wanted to use Manchoukuo for the salvation of Japan's poverty-stricken farmers, its unemployed, and its medium and small industrialists and merchants. They were determined that the *Zaibatsu* would never set foot in Manchoukuo, though they did permit limited investment by newer firms. Conversely, the *Zaibatsu* were not overanxious to come to Manchoukuo, fearing Army domination and finding investment opportunities in a swiftly arming Japan more inviting than in what they considered risky foreign projects.

The Kwantung leaders had long sought an alternative to the private capitalists in the largely state-controlled South Manchurian Railroad Company (SMRC), which had been established in 1907 as a corporate enterprise to represent the sum total of special rights that Japan had won in Manchuria as the result of the Russo-Japanese War. The main organ for prosecution of Japan's national policy on the Asian mainland since then, the SMRC, had developed into an arterial system of railways, harbors, ports, mines, oil, and hotels, while engaging in industrial, economic, transport and communications, and cultural and educational activities. Although its great tentacles were supposed to embrace only Japan's Leased Territory in Liaotung up to 1931, all of Manchuria, and even parts of North and South China felt their "civilizing" grasp. The SMRC constituted one of the largest capital resource units in the world.

But many of the enterprises it operated, such as a coal liquification plant at Fushun, were highly unprofitable. And after the invasion of Manchuria, the Kwantung Army, hoping to develop a complex of war industries under its own direct control, burdened the company with many additional unfeasible and marginal enterprises. The SMRC was obliged to assume control of the former Chinese railways in Manchuria, many of them in poor financial condition, and had been given the job of building new strategic railroads, mostly through thinly populated areas. It was also required to finance and manage more than a score of new state-regulated industrial concerns.

By the time Kishi arrived in Manchoukuo, the foundation for the Army's industrial plans had been laid, and the SMRC was tottering under its burden. Kishi's primary task was to find additional sources of capital to put his Five-Year-Plan into effect—within the highly restrictive framework of national socialism. This was a most delicate matter. It required him to walk a fine line between the idealism of the Army and the realism of hard economics.

Despite the difficulty in plotting such a course, he enjoyed the challenge, for the compromise required coincided with his own concept of the best economic system for Japan and its territories. It would draw from both the radical principles espoused by Kita and the conservative policies Kishi had practiced during his many years of experience in government economics. An ideal, if it was to work, had to be wedded to reality. And the reality was that neither the Japanese nor the Manchoukuo governments were financially capable of supporting the Five-Year-Plan through the SMRC or any other state organ. Large-scale private investment was essential. He would have to persuade the military to permit such investment, and, on the other hand, persuade the private investors to submit to some government regulation. Therein, it seemed to Kishi, lay the logical answer.

But he soon learned that in such an answer also lay a deeply disturbing personal problem. The president of the South Manchurian Railway Company, Yosuke Matsuoka, happened to be an uncle by marriage to him—a brother of Uncle Matsui's wife, Shizue. And Matsuoka, who had been a director of the SMRC for fifteen years before his appointment to the top post in 1935, was not anxious to relinquish the monopoly which he had helped to build.

Kishi had a profound respect for his uncle, who had reached his high place in Japan's political hierarchy via an extremely unusual route. At the age of thirteen, three years before Kishi's birth, he went to the United States, attending grammar school in Portland, Oregon, high school in Oakland, California, and the University of Oregon law school. He thereby escaped the pressures and hazards of the kind of competition that wreaked havoc on the nervous systems of most Japanese students, perhaps one reason why he was more carefree and less tense than most of his compatriots. But Matsuoka had to make compensating sacrifices. He had to pay his way through school by indulging in such menial labor as gardening and waiting on tables, work which few men of Choshu samurai heritage like himself would stoop to do. And because of the lack of a Japanese education, he had greater obstacles to overcome in pursuing his career than did most of his competitors. Yet, from the time he returned to Japan at the age of twenty-two, he moved steadily ahead in the diplomatic world, his brilliance and shrewdness making up for the handicap.

In 1919, Matsuoka was sent as a delegate to the Paris Peace Conference, and in 1931, as chief delegate to the Plenary Session of the League of Nations, which was considering the Lytton Report on Japan's "aggression" in Manchuria. Kishi had been proud of his uncle as he thundered, "Some of the people of Europe and America may wish even to crucify Japan in the twentieth century. We are prepared to be crucified. But we do believe, and firmly believe, that in a very few years, world opinion will be changed and we also shall be understood by the world as Jesus of Nazareth was." Though the League condemned Japan regardless, Matsuoka returned home a hero, and was presented with a case of sake and a cask of fish by the Emperor. Matsuoka, despite his American education, was a true Japanese idealist, Kishi thought, ready to make any sacrifice for the rejuvenation of the nation's spirit. He had even resigned from the Diet in 1933 to work for the dissolution of all political parties in the interest of national security and unity.

Kishi frequently saw his uncle, a pudgy-faced man with a large black mustache, after his arrival in Manchoukuo and they reminisced often about Kishi's childhood days when Matsuoka and his wife would visit either his mother's or Matsui's home. "Moyo," Matsuoka told him, "was one of the greatest women I have ever known."

But when they talked business, Kishi would be torn by conflict. "I am certainly delighted that you are here," Matsuoka said as they sat one day in a coffee house. "It's always nice to work with someone in the family. Together we shall contribute greatly to the future of Manchoukuo."

"But do you think the SMRC can handle a bigger economic burden than it is now carrying?" Kishi asked.

Matsuoka laughed. "Of course we can. We need more aid from the government, that's all. Our new rail lines and subsidiary companies will gradually show more profit. The SMRC has managed to overcome all obstacles for thirty years. It has carried the light of civilization into Manchoukuo. There's no reason why it cannot continue to do so."

Kishi considered this view entirely unrealistic. He understood his

uncle's desire—certainly a natural one—to keep what authority he had
accumulated. After all, he had been a director of the SMRC for fifteen
years before his appointment as president in 1935. It would be difficult
telling Matsuoka, an elder member of his family who had been on close
terms with his mother and Uncle Matsui, that he would have to relinquish much of his power and prestige. In a sense, Kishi thought, he would
be violating *giri* to a relative, but he was also obligated to Japan to help
develop Manchoukuo. He did not agree with his uncle's observation that
it was "nice to work with someone in the family."

Though deeply perturbed, Kishi's rational instincts overcame his personal sentiments. He advised Hoshino of the need to bring in massive
private investments, and together they began urging the military leaders
to modify their stand against the *Zaibatsu*. But they were rebuffed. "We
must have money!" said Kishi. "You cannot escape that fact." "Yes. But
not from the *Zaibatsu*." As an alternative, suggested the generals, with
incredible naïveté, in Kishi's opinion, the families of soldiers killed in past
battles should be encouraged to buy shares in Manchoukuo development
projects.

Kishi found the military increasingly obstructive in other ways, too. He
was enraged when word came to him that General Ueda had, without consulting him, negotiated to send large quantities of iron ore to Japan.
Kishi instructed one of his aides to tell newsmen that this was a mistake
in view of the fact that the iron and steel mills in Manchoukuo were
operating at far below capacity. General Ueda, angered by this "act of
insubordination," demanded that the minor official be fired.

Kishi had had enough. He called on General Ueda and said, "Sir, I
was told by General Itagaki when I arrived in Manchoukuo that I was
to have full responsibility for the determination of industrial policy here.
Yet you have made a commitment on the iron ore project without consulting me. Now you wish to have my subordinate dismissed, though what
he told the newspapers was the truth. Sending our iron ore to Japan for
refinement would be uneconomic. While our factories are starving for
work, we would have to pay for the freighting of raw material to Japan.
This is obviously illogical. Therefore, in my view, so would be the firing
of the official in question. If you insist on his dismissal, I am afraid I shall
have to resign myself, for it would be clear to me that I am being denied
the right to carry out the responsibilities of my office as I see fit."

General Ueda, a cranky man who had lost a leg in 1932 when an embittered Korean tossed a grenade at him during a brief Japanese occupation of Shanghai, found himself in a delicate position. He had gone on

record as approving the proposal to ship iron ore to Japan. And he had demanded the dismissal of the man who publicly criticized this decision. But the Army, in his name, had also committed itself to let Kishi determine all matters pertaining to industrial policy.

"We soldiers," he finally started, "are often criticized for lacking charity. But we can be charitable. I shall excuse your subordinate this time, though he committed the grave offense of insulting His Imperial Majesty's armed forces. No doubt his rashness stemmed from a misinterpretation of the report on the iron ore situation. Actually, nothing definite has been decided and matters are still to be negotiated."

Kishi then took his leave, still too agitated to fully appreciate his triumph. For although General Ueda had refused to admit that the mistake had been his own, he had virtually ceded to Kishi the right to countermand his proposal, a major and highly unusual concession for a high army officer to make. This incident, Kishi happily discovered, also had the effect of loosening the Army's rigid opposition to his policy proposals —perhaps because the generals were afraid he might confront them again with the embarrassing choice of agreeing with him or accepting his resignation.

He was particularly gratified that they were willing to consider a compromise plan for private investment in Manchoukuo. The plan was to keep the old trusts out, but to bring in one of the new *Zaibatsu*— sprawling industrial giants that had sprung up in the last few years—to establish a large holding company to carry out the development of heavy industries under a system of integrated management. Unlike the older combines, the new ones confined their activities almost entirely to iron, steel, light metal, and chemical industries, the very ones the Army desired to foster. Also, their shares were widely distributed rather than concentrated in the hands of a single family, as with the old firms, thus avoiding conflict with the military's anti-plutocratic stand. Getting down to specifics, Kishi expressed the opinion that the most desirable of these new trusts was Nippon Sangyo Kabushiki Kaisha, known as Nissan, which was headed by one of Japan's most imaginative and progressive businessmen —Gisuke Aikawa. Aikawa's reputation for managerial and technical efficiency might even attract foreign capital, Kishi warily suggested.

"Aikawa is doing so well in Japan that he may not be interested in further ventures in Manchoukuo," he added. "But I think it would be a good idea if we invited him here to discuss the matter."

The generals agreed that nothing could be lost by exchanging views with Aikawa. Kishi, elated, immediately invited Aikawa to Manchoukuo.

Aikawa was no stranger to Kishi. Both were of Choshu heritage, and their families had known each other long before either man was born. Kishi's foster mother had, in fact, been Aikawa's teacher in primary school. "He was the smartest pupil in the class," she had told her adopted son. Aikawa lived up to that early reputation by becoming one of the richest men in Japan. Taking advantage of the inflation boom and of the increased military budgets that followed the invasion of Manchuria in 1931, he had created overnight the enormous Nissan empire, which, capitalized at more than 500 million yen ($125 million), embraced such diversified interests as iron, machinery, glycerine, whaling, nitrogen fertilizers, gold and coal mining, accident insurance, shipping, fishing, industrial chemicals, and automobiles. But his principal profits came from sales to the military, and, being a man of vision, he realized this would remain the principal source of future profits as well.

On his friend's arrival in Manchoukuo, Kishi impressed upon him the advantages of coming to this virgin state. "There is a wonderful future for you in Manchoukuo. We are just starting to build."

Aikawa, a slender man with a thin, tense face, replied, "That may be so, but it would be difficult to divide Nissan between Japan and Manchoukuo."

"Well, then, simply transfer Nissan to Manchoukuo lock, stock, and barrel."

"But that is impossible. Manchoukuo is a foreign country, and under Japanese law a Japanese firm, as you well know, cannot transfer itself to a foreign country and retain its status as a juridical person."

Kishi, his eyes gleaming, responded, "That won't be a problem. As the old saying goes, we have an opportunity that comes but once in a thousand years. Japan is relinquishing its extraterritorial rights to this country on December 1, 1937. If you moved into Manchoukuo before that date, Nissan would become a Manchoukuo company under that arrangement."

Aikawa smiled. "I'll have to think about it. And I presume the military will, too."

The military thought about it—and balked under pressure from Matsuoka and the young officers, who preferred to continue stumbling along with the SMRC rather than permit capitalists to get a foothold in the area. Kishi, who was promoted by Hoshino to the position of Vice-Director of the General Affairs Bureau, found little solace in his increased power. Without the necessary funds, it was barely possible to get the Five-Year-Plan off the ground. Then, overnight, the situation changed.

On the night of July 7, 1937, Kishi was at home with Yoshiko, who had arrived in Manchoukuo in the spring. He sat listening to the radio when an announcer broke into the program to report that a "new incident" had occurred at the Marco Polo bridge at Lukouchiao near the town of Wanping in North China. The Chinese had, "without provocation," attacked Japanese forces legally stationed in the area under the Boxer Protocol, said the Japanese announcer. A Chinese radio station soon afterward reported that Japanese troops "provoked the attack by conducting maneuvers beyond the zone where foreign troops were permitted to be stationed under the Protocol, a situation which the Chinese could not ignore in view of the strategic importance of the area. The Japanese troops had threatened a connecting railroad between the Peiping-Tientsin and Peiping-Hankow main lines."

This "incident," Kishi soon learned, was far more consequential than previous ones. Though Japanese commanders had originally planned only to force the withdrawal of Chinese troops from the area, the tension swiftly gathered momentum. While the Japanese ambassador to Nanking tried to reach a local settlement with the Chinese—on Japanese terms—China appealed for support to the Western Powers, charging that Japan had violated its treaty obligations. Meanwhile, Japanese reinforcements were moved in from Manchoukuo and Korea. Then, Japanese troops in North China attacked and destroyed Chinese units near Peking and began to occupy the whole Tientsin-Peking region. Japanese officers in the field, duplicating what they had done after the Mukden Incident, forced a reluctant government at home to agree to the extension of hostilities. By the end of July, Peking and Tientsin had fallen, and by mid-August Shanghai was under attack and Inner Mongolia had been pierced, with invading troops occupying Kalgan, China's principal railway connection with Russia.

Kishi harbored mixed feelings about these developments. Chinese nationalism had without doubt, he was convinced, reached a point where it seriously threatened Japan's interests in China. The ultimate goal of Chiang Kai-shek was not only to retake Manchoukuo, but to eliminate every vestige of Japanese influence from the mainland. And this danger had increased since the end of 1936, when Chiang, who had been captured by the dissident Chinese communists at Sian, was freed on the understanding that the Nationalists and the Reds would work together to drive out the Japanese. This "entente" was, of course, loose and superficial, but it still meant a more concerted threat to the Japanese. The present clash had therefore been inevitable, thought Kishi. The Chinese had stupidly provoked it.

Even so, he would have preferred that the Japanese military had exercised greater restraint. China was a huge country with a huge population. It might not be easy subduing such a giant. Nor was it necessarily in Japan's best interest, strategic or economic, to stretch its forces thinly over so great and hostile an area. Furthermore, despite Chinese provocation, the need for protection of Japanese interests, and the fact that Japan wanted to guide China along a more modern and rewarding path, the military subjugation of China, Kishi told me recently, "did not seem justified, either from a legal or a moral viewpoint." But, he rationalizes, "Manchoukuo was another story. Aside from the fact that it was manageable in size and rich in resources, Japan had the legal right to the so-called Leased Territory and therefore the moral right to control the rest of Manchuria in the light of the threat posed for the legally held area by the Chinese and Russians."

Manchoukuo suddenly found itself the base of battle operations, and as pressures mounted for a speed-up of industrialization and exploitation of raw materials required for war purposes, Kishi met constantly with other civilian and military leaders. General Tojo, who had replaced Itagaki as Chief of Staff when the latter was promoted to a high position in the War Ministry in Tokyo, attended some of these meetings, but not very often. Usually bald, bullet-headed General Tadashi Katakura represented the Army at the conferences. Kishi seldom saw Tojo on a social basis either, for his intense, mystical personality did not blend well with Kishi's cool, rational nature. Nor, for that matter, did Tojo's wife, who was vain and ambitious, find much in common with gentle, retiring Yoshiko, preferring the company of Mrs. Hoshino.

But Kishi and Tojo had a profound respect for each other's professional ability, and Kishi noted that their administrative methods were alike in some respects. Both paid unusual attention to detail. Tojo took copious notes at every talk Kishi ever had with him, and often referred back to them at future conferences, almost hoping, it seemed, to catch him contradicting himself. Further, Kishi was more and more captivated by Tojo's nationalist fervor. It was perhaps exaggerated and could lead to unfortunate emotionally based political decisions, but it was still refreshing to see in him the rebirth of the true Japanese spirit, unstifled by modern rules of logic.

Kishi's admiration for Tojo eased the difficulties of working closely with the Army. The need for such co-operation was confirmed by the increased costs of the revised Five-Year-Plan. Kishi was—as an economist rather than a militarist—disappointed that Manchoukuo could not be developed in accordance with natural economic factors. But he was fully aware of the necessity for the "waste" that would be involved in war projects. Development would cost double what it should, yet, ironically, the war would make money available. And, in any event, long-term prospects now looked more favorable than they had at first. Once China was defeated, a Japan-Manchoukuo-North China economic bloc could perhaps be set up that would greatly improve economic conditions in all these areas.

Kishi no longer had any trouble convincing the military that Aikawa should be asked to transfer his Nissan interests to Manchoukuo. Such a transfer was clearly the only means of meeting the provisions of the expanded Five-Year-Plan, particularly in view of the new and serious drain on Japanese government resources that the China war entailed. With even the young officers prepared to compromise under the emergency circumstances, Kishi knew the only serious opposition would come from Matsuoka, his uncle. He proposed to Aikawa, Tojo, Hoshino, and their assistants that conferences held to draw up final plans for the revolutionary venture be kept secret from Matsuoka. When they expressed surprise that he would treat his own uncle in such a manner, Kishi explained with a contrived air of coldness, "I would want the talks to be kept secret from the SMRC whether or not its president were a relative. If we let my uncle in on our plans, he would inevitably try to squash them. And they are absolutely necessary in the interests of Japan and Manchoukuo."

At the secret meetings, it was decided that a Manchoukuo Heavy Industry Company, to be popularly known as Mangyo, would be formed with Nissan as its nucleus, to exploit iron, gold and silver mines, to produce pig iron and steel, and set up various factories. The company would be capitalized at 450 million yuan, one-half subscribed by the Manchoukuo government, which guaranteed Aikawa a six per cent return for ten years and protection for the free transaction of the company's shares on the stock market. By these terms, Aikawa was assured of a minimum rate of profit and protected against fluctuations in the market value of the shares. This would allow Aikawa, in turn, to offer attractive terms to other potential Japanese investors, as well as foreign interests, particularly American and German. The new concern would absorb most of the existing industrial firms under state control, including many subsidiaries of the South Manchurian Railway Company. All of these enterprises would be managed by experienced Nissan industrialists rather than, as in the past, by political appointees.

When the negotiations were concluded, Kishi felt a tremendous sense of satisfaction, but also a sinking sensation. At his own suggestion, the talks had been carried on behind the back of his uncle. Immediately after the announcement of the Mangyo project, Matsuoka sent his board director, Nakanishi, to see Kishi in a belated effort to persuade him to call off the arrangement.

"Matsuoka-san," said Nakanishi, "has asked me to request of you in all sincerity that further consideration be given to this matter. He wants me to remind you of the glorious achievements of the SMRC during the last thirty years, of its tireless role in building up Manchuria long before any other interests ever gave this area a thought. And he is particularly disappointed because this disservice to the SMRC is being championed by a member of his own family."

Kishi replied that, profoundly troubled as he was, he could be honest neither with himself nor with the governments of Japan and Manchoukuo if he tried to reverse the decision. He hoped his uncle, whom he greatly respected, would understand this and forgive him. Nakanishi departed with this message, and a few hours later Kishi, sitting in his office, was handed a copy of a public statement issued by Matsuoka. Anticipating an announcement of his uncle's resignation, he nervously read:

"The governments of Japan and Manchoukuo have formulated a plan for the establishment of a corporation to carry on the development of Manchoukuo's heavy industries in accordance with policy common to both countries. This is indeed a great step toward the accelerated development and expansion of Manchoukuo's heavy industries. In response to the urgent demand of both Japan and Manchoukuo, the South Manchurian Railway Company has been a pioneer in the exploration of Manchuria's resources during the past thirty years. It is a pleasure to recollect that my company has contributed its share, and that share has been of no mean proportions, to the establishment of heavy industries.

"In the current period of spectacular expansion, a new state-supported corporation is to be organized for the exclusive purpose of developing heavy industries. It may be said that my company has fulfilled adequately its pioneer mission of exploring these industries in Manchoukuo. At a time when, in the course of the state's rapid growth, new fields of activity are being opened up for my company, it is only logical that these industries for which we have successfully completed our pioneering work should be removed from our control. It has been a policy of my company, in force for some time, to sell off to the public at large the shares of its subsidiaries. It is therefore only natural that when a semi-governmental corporation is formed for the exclusive purpose of speeding up development of heavy industries, my company should as far as possible transfer thereto such of our enterprises as come within its sphere.

"From the higher standpoint of state policy and in sympathy with the measures which have been adopted by the two governments, my company is prepared to give to the new corporation all of the co-operation necessary for the achievement of its aims. Negotiations in regard to the particular enterprises concerned will be conducted after the new corporation has been formed."

Kishi put down the announcement, which he realized was a pathetic effort to save "face." He scrawled out a statement for the press:

". . . This plan [for the development of heavy industries] has received the approval of the Japanese government and the endorsement of the South Manchurian Railway Company. It is our belief that, in carrying on these activities, the new corporation will have the full co-operation of the SMRC."

Kishi was at last equipped with the financial means to carry out his Five-Year-Plan. He became one of the main cogs in a five-man power wheel popularly known as the *niki sansuke*. This expression meant "two '*ki's*' and three '*sukes*,'" referring to the two political leaders, Hide*ki* Tojo and Nao*ki* Hoshino, and the three industrial chiefs, Nobu*suke* Kishi, Gi*suke* Aikawa, and Yo*suke* Matsuoka, who was still playing an important, if reduced, role in the development of Manchoukuo.

The economic transfusion provided by the transfer of Nissan to Manchoukuo could hardly have come at a more propitious time. For the China Affair* was spreading with the relentlessness of fire in a dry forest. Commanders cried for an increasing flow of supplies and equipment to permit their armies to maintain their momentum. As they advanced, the Japanese, in an orgy of wanton destruction, indiscriminately bombed Chinese cities and even attacked the *U.S.S. Panay* and *H.M.S. Ladybird* on the Yangtze River as these vessels were evacuating Americans and British trapped in a siege of Nanking, the capital of Free China.

The orgy reached a peak of fury with the fall of this city in what has become known as the rape of Nanking. While gay lantern parades wound grotesquely through pillaged streets in celebration, small bands of soldiers, many of them drunk, roamed the city committing savage crimes.

* The Japanese leaders referred to the fighting in China as an "affair" rather than as a war, never having officially declared war on that country. They were not willing to concede that the bloodshed was anything more than a prolonged "incident" of a relatively minor nature.

They burned down homes, looted, murdered. They raped young girls and old women, committing acts of a sadistic and abnormal nature, then killed and mutilated their victims. The Japanese soldier, who lived by an inflexible moral code while within his own society, had no scruples about his conduct abroad, where he found himself suddenly free of the rules of his community. On the other hand, his commanders, calculating that brutality would break the Chinese spirit, closed their eyes to the atrocities, actually authorizing the murder of all male inhabitants of the city on the grounds that many of them were probably soldiers who had discarded their uniforms. In all, about 200,000 Chinese soldiers and civilians were killed during the first six weeks of Japanese occupation.

Though the officers presiding over these scenes of bestiality tried to keep the news from seeping through to the outside world, including Japan (for fear of the effect it would have on Japanese public morale), Kishi and his colleagues learned from various military contacts that the Japanese troops had "failed to measure up to the proper standards of discipline." But as a matter of moral convenience, they tended to discount atrocity stories as exaggerated. After all, soldiers, in the excitement of victory, were likely to commit indiscretions. It was a natural, if not a laudable, reaction. Prime Minister Konoye, who must have been aware of the situation in Nanking, apparently judged the behavior of the soldiers acceptable, having attributed the victory in a radio announcement to the "Emperor's august virtue" and the greatness of Japan's fighting men.

And there was certainly nothing brutal, Kishi observed, in the statement of General Matsui, Commander-in-Chief in Central China, issued at a religious service the day after his triumphal ceremonial entry into Nanking:

> "I extend much sympathy to millions of innocent people . . . who have suffered the evils of war. Now the flag of the Rising Sun is floating high over Nanking, and the Imperial Way is shining in the southern parts of the Yangtze-Kiang. The dawn of the renaissance of the East is on the verge of appearing. On this occasion I hope for reconsideration of the situation by the four hundred million people of China."

Kishi explained to me, "The militarists kept the true picture of Japanese atrocities from civilians like myself. And although, of course, some of the facts leaked out nevertheless, I heard them in a distorted light and had no idea of the widespread character of the atrocities. If I had been familiar with the actual situation, I would have been enraged and deeply ashamed. But I can't state now whether I would have protested, or resigned, if I had known. I say this in the context of the atmosphere that prevailed at the time. A protest then would have been considered an act of disloyalty to the Emperor and might well have meant arrest and death. It was simply natural for people to accept the shortcomings of militarism as necessary, or acceptable, evils. And as we in Manchoukuo were constantly in danger of being attacked by guerrillas, we tended all the more—and I think this was only human—to overlook, or regard as exaggerated, reports on our troop behavior in China."

On one occasion, Kishi maintains, he did take a serious risk in an effort to prevent an atrocity. "Upon learning that the military planned to set a whole Manchurian village afire to root out several bandits believed to be hiding there, I strongly appealed to the military leaders to abandon the project. To my great relief, they agreed to do so."

Kishi added, "By no means can the terrible crimes committed by many Japanese soldiers be justified, but *do you feel that the atomic bombings were morally more proper than some of the Japanese atrocities?*"

Kishi and his partners, like General Matsui, were hopeful about an early peace as they rushed plans to increase Manchoukuo's war production in case their hopes did not materialize. Japan, as the price of peace, now asked only that Chiang agree to the independence of Manchoukuo and the "temporary" stationing of Japanese troops in North and Central China and Inner Mongolia. It also offered apologies to the United States and Britain for the attacks on their gunboats in order to ease their antagonism toward Japan and keep them from active intervention.

But when Chiang ignored Japan's peace proposals, moving his capital further inland, and the Western powers intensified their protests, however toothless, against "Japanese aggression," the *niki sansuke* realized that on the success of its supporting operations could depend, to a large degree, the future of the war. And the importance of these operations increased in relation to the multiplying demands made on the home economy, as Japan strained to maintain its large armies in China and furnish the bulk of capital goods needed for Manchoukuo's industrial program. Further, preparations had to be made for a possible larger-scale war. Many officials, including Kishi and Tojo, estimated that while war with the Western Powers might be averted, at least for the time being, Japan was almost certain to come into armed conflict with the Soviet Union, whose interests were more directly affected by the Japanese military campaign in China.

Mangyo wasted no time extending its control over such existing corporations in Manchoukuo as the Showa Steel Works, Manchuria Coal Mining Company, Manchuria Light Metals Company, and Dowa Auto-

mobile Company, augmenting their capital and improving their equipment. It also set up new firms like the Manchoukuo Mining Company
(gold, silver, copper, and other metals), Manchoukuo Aircraft Company
(airplane parts), Manchoukuo Magnesium Company (metallic magnesium), Tungpientao Development Company (coal and iron mining
and development of other minerals and natural resources in the Tungpientao area), Manchoukuo Automobile Company, Kyowa Iron Mining
Company, and Penhsihu Coal and Iron Works. Simultaneously, Mangyo
intensified exploratory mineral, metal, and farm crop surveys.

But the Manchoukuo leaders ran into many unanticipated difficulties,
stemming in part from clashes of personality and ideology. Kishi and his
fellow bureaucrats, applying the principles of national socialism, made
Aikawa long for the relative economic freedom which his industries had
known in Japan. They limited his authority over the subsidiary companies
that he had expected to dominate and controlled the prices of goods exported to Japan, thereby keeping down Mangyo's profits. On the other
hand, both Kishi and Aikawa were frustrated by the constant interference
in industry by unqualified army advisers, by the failure of Matsuoka to
give the co-operation he had promised, and by the delay in shipments of
vital capital goods from the homeland.

It was even harder buying such goods abroad in view of Japan's small
foreign exchange reserves. Increased sales of Manchoukuo farm products
were supposed to finance their purchase, but agricultural production was
handicapped by poor wheat crops, the system of "protected villages,"
which required farmers to spend part of their time as policemen, increased
taxes on Chinese farmers who, in protest, deliberately kept down their
yields or fled to North China, restrictions on Chinese immigration into
Manchoukuo, and the failure of the Manchoukuo government to entice
many immigrant farmers from Japan despite an elaborate settlement
program.

Adding to the troubles of Kishi and Aikawa was a serious shortage
of industrial personnel, particularly engineers, and though Kishi resorted
to the revolutionary practice of shifting specialists around in accordance
with the need (previously when a man was not working at a particular
job for which he had been trained he would be kept idle until his special
skill was required), the personnel gaps still could not be adequately filled.

No less disappointing to the Manchoukuo "clique" was the failure to
attract foreign, particularly American, capital. Potential American investors were impressed by the business methods of Aikawa, who displayed
a management efficiency, imagination, and dynamism rare in Japanese

industry. But they were discouraged by the United States government's policy of nonrecognition of the Manchoukuo regime, especially following the "Marco Polo Incident," and also by the monopolistic practices of the Kishi-led planners, however appealing were their offers on paper.

Kishi was especially disappointed by the failure of negotiations with Thomas J. Watson, president of the International Business Machines Corporation and the International Chamber of Commerce. Kishi had been seeking a loan of fifty million dollars, which was to be applied to the development of Manchoukuo heavy industries through the purchase of American machinery. Washington and the American press exerted sufficient pressure on Watson to force him to drop all consideration of the project. Kishi knew then that the possibility of obtaining United States capital had evaporated.

In the face of these multiple difficulties, the *niki sansuke* was compelled to modify even further its scheme for the establishment of a self-contained industrial base in Manchoukuo in order to gear the economy of the puppet state more closely to that of Japan, concentrating on the production of minerals for export to Japan and of semifinished goods for processing in the home country.

In the fall of 1939, Kishi, in the midst of these troubles, learned that he was to be recalled from Manchoukuo. Hoshino informed him with his usual down-to-earth bluster that several times in the past year Tokyo had requested that he be sent home to take over an important job. But because he was urgently needed in Manchoukuo, Hoshino said, he had rejected every request without even conferring with him. Kishi astonished Hoshino by displaying an attitude of utter indifference. With a placid expression, he replied, "I can fully understand your actions."

"Do you want to return to Tokyo?" Hoshino asked.

"I will be satisfied whether I remain here or am sent back. My future is for you and Tokyo to decide."

"Tokyo has just asked me again for you. They are going to make you Vice-Minister of Commerce and Industry. What do you say to that?"

"I'm not really sure," Kishi said.

His reaction was mixed indeed. The promotion held obvious advantages. He would now be but a step away from the top position in his field. And he would be freer of military interference in Japan. But he would miss the respect and acclaim he received in Manchoukuo, which could never be equaled within the great Tokyo bureaucracy. More important, he was largely responsible for the recent industrial expansion in Manchoukuo, and it did not seem right that he should suddenly abandon this work. As restricted as his program had been by wartime conditions, he had helped perform an industrial miracle. Up to 1931, Japan had invested 1,617 million yen ($404 million) in Manchurian enterprises, 50 per cent contributed by the SMRC. By 1938, this figure had jumped to 3,441 million yen ($860 million), and would reach 4,500 million yen ($1.1 billion) by the end of 1939.

Thus, with mixed emotions, Kishi and Yoshiko, after their "exile" in Manchoukuo, left for home. In Dairen, before boarding a ship, Kishi told newspapermen of his role in the development of Manchoukuo:

"The industrial world of Manchoukuo is a piece of work which I created. I have an infinite affection for this creation of mine. It shall remain close to my heart always."

CHAPTER VIII

❧⑤❧

JUMPING OFF THE VERANDA

KISHI RETURNED to a Japan steeped in economic conflict and confusion. The *Zaibatsu* were still powerful and resisted every effort of the military, who were now virtually in control of the country, to reduce their power. Both the military and the trusts agreed that the expanding war economy should be unified, but each had its own ideas about how to do it. The military chiefs wanted to tighten government regulation of industry to make sure the economy would be geared to the "national interest" rather than to private profits. The industrialists pressed for the formation of huge, monopolistic cartels, under their own control, which would provide them with both increased production and profits.

With these two great forces locked in a stalemate, the national scene was one of chaos. Any businessman with enough money could buy raw materials reserved for "essential" industries. Production of war supplies remained far below capacity as the industrialists tried to force the government to pay higher prices for equipment and manufactured goods. Wages were rigidly frozen, but price controls supposedly applied were illusory.

Kishi, whose main job as Vice-Minister of Commerce and Industry was to supervise the conversion of peacetime industries into war industries, supported the military program, which, after all, had, under his guidance, proved successful in Manchoukuo. But as a matter of practical necessity, he was prepared to compromise with the *Zaibatsu*. They were simply too influential to be forced into line.

To put the businessmen in an equally conciliatory mood, he often entertained them, usually at geisha parties but sometimes at home. When they dined at his house, they were usually surprised to find themselves sitting on chairs around a high table rather than on the floor. This unorthodoxy, Kishi would explain to them, was one of the concessions he had made to the comfort of a young guest he had brought with him from Manchoukuo, the sixteen-year-old son of the Minister of the Manchoukuo Industrial Department. When the youth, whom Kishi was putting through school in repayment for kindnesses rendered him by his father, found some difficulty adjusting to Japanese customs, Kishi agreed to arrange his house in Manchu style to some extent.

The effort by the military to fasten a grip on the *Zaibatsu,* Kishi well realized, was only one part of a co-ordinated plan to gain full control of Japan's national life. The Army directed the war in China almost without reference to the civilian leaders, and even forced administrative shifts in the government to make sure its supporters monopolized the key positions. Further, it encouraged Prime Minister Konoye to push through the Diet a National General Mobilization Act permitting the government to mobilize all the people and resources of the nation, to control goods, services, and finances, to censor the press and other information media, hire and dismiss workers, prevent strikes, dictate working conditions, and, in theory, regulate and operate war industries.

Consistent with his national socialist tendencies, Kishi was sympathetic to this program of national unification under what amounted to military dictatorship. Although his experiences in Manchoukuo had exposed to him the exasperating rigidity of the military mind, it had also revealed the undiluted idealism and sincerity of the Army leaders, who, however impetuous and naïve, were a welcome contrast to the devious, greedy politicians and businessmen—those so-called "moderates" with whom he was working again. When he could forget their arrogance and inflexibility, Kishi viewed the militarists as latter-day samurai, filled with the romantic nationalistic notions of his forefathers. In this role they served admirably as an ideological spearhead in the campaign to awaken the Japanese people to their national destiny, and simultaneously could become a useful instrument for the establishment of a peaceful, orderly Asia.

But even as Kishi dreamed the dream of his ancestors, he did not permit himself to be blinded to reality. Japanese troops seemed powerless,

as he had feared, to subdue the whole of China. The country was perhaps too vast to conquer. Japanese troops would advance inland, but only
to expose themselves to flanking attacks. There were too many endless
stretches of rice paddy, too many Chinese peasants, armed with shotguns,
hidden in haystacks. Not to mention the regular Chinese troops equipped
with modern weapons supplied by Britain and the United States. China
posed much the same problem for the Japanese that Russia had for
Napoleon.

Kishi was relieved to learn that the military had begun to realize how
much wasted effort and wealth were going into the China Affair. The
generals no longer undertook large-scale operations to vanquish new
regions of China, but devoted themselves mainly to keeping order in the
occupied zones (which were organized into a puppet state under Wang
Ching-wei), bombing strategic areas in the interior for psychological
purposes, mopping up guerrilla forces that hampered the movement of
food and raw materials to the cities, and conducting local offensives to
break up Chinese troop concentrations in key areas. The China Affair
had been straining the Japanese economy at the expense of Japanese
preparations for possible war with Russia or the United States and
Britain, a situation that severely threatened Japan's security. Actually,
only 40 per cent of military appropriations were devoted to the China
war, but even this was too much under the circumstances, the senior officers concluded, at the risk of antagonizing their less pragmatic juniors.
Japan had to be ready for war with any big power by 1942 at the latest.
By then, the Army judged, Japan's military and industrial strength would
match that of Russia in the Far East. But economics was not the only
factor in the decision to ease up in China. There was no sense tempting
Stalin to join forces with China before Japan was prepared to fight him.

But Kishi was not at all confident that a mere slow-down of military
operations would settle the China Affair. He believed that Japan would
best serve its own interests, at least for the time being, by withdrawing its
troops from South China, and perhaps even from portions of the North
—but on the condition that Manchoukuo remain an "independent" state
under Japanese tutelage. Such a solution would permit Japan to conserve
its strength for a possible bigger engagement, while confirming, once and
for all Japan's right to Manchoukuo. Manchoukuo, of course, could
never be given up. It was Japan's future. Japan might lose a certain
amount of "face" in the pursuance of such a program, but if Chiang Kai-
shek accepted it, the nation would still have profited, and might even

win Western recognition of Manchoukuo,* and possibly economic aid. In any event, Japan would have an opportunity to develop the full industrial potential of Manchoukuo. Once this state became a powerful, self-sufficient industrial zone, Japan would be in a better position to embark, if this were desirable, on further Asian adventures. On the other hand, continuation of the China war, on however limited a scale, would not only handicap the economies of both Japan and Manchoukuo, but might also prematurely provoke a war with America and Britain, or even more likely, with Russia. Kishi thus hoped that the retrenchment of military activities in China would lead to a settlement with that country.

The news that the Second World War had broken out in Europe was received with joy in official Japanese circles. Neither Britain, whose very survival was at stake, nor the Soviet Union, which sat precariously on the edge of the war, were likely now to interfere with Japan's activities in Asia. This was the time, thought Kishi and other Japanese leaders, to strengthen ties with Germany and Italy and stand up firmly to the United States, the only other power still posing a serious threat to Japanese policies. But if Japan was to take full advantage of the developments in Europe to strengthen its defense posture, the national economy would have to be unified and operated on a planned basis. What was needed now, Kishi reflected, was the kind of idealistic, closely knit ruling team that had existed in Manchoukuo. Hardly had he expressed this thought to his friends when, in July, 1940, a new government was formed by Prime Minister Prince Konoye—composed largely of the Manchoukuo team.

Konoye, a descendant of an old noble family, considered himself a "moderate," and was, in fact, supported by most moderates—politicians and businessmen with a relatively realistic awareness of the risks that would be involved in a war with the Western powers or Russia. The Zaibatsu officials, in particular, were concerned about these risks. Such a major conflict would, of course, mean greater profits from the manufacture of armaments. But what good would these profits be in the long run if Japan lost the war? Anyway, as was proved in the Manchoukuo experiment, the military would do all in its power to keep the old combines out of newly acquired areas, or at least try to limit their profits, if Japan succeeded in overruning Southeast Asia. Actually, normal trade with independent Asian countries seemed to hold greater prospects for increased profits than dealing with the Army during an occupation of these countries.

Still, the moderates did not, in principle, oppose expansion in Asia,

* The United States never recognized the Japanese occupation of Manchuria.

but preferred to wait for an opportune occasion, such as the possible involvement of America in the European War. If this war involved the United States, the moderates believed, Japan would encounter no opposition, except possibly diplomatic protests, to its military plans. This view did not differ greatly from that held by Kishi, but he accommodated himself to military policy with less serious reservations than Konoye and his backers because of a feeling, stirred by the ghosts of Choshu, that the military perhaps understood Japan's destiny better than men like himself, who may have been too concerned with considerations of "logic" and "rationalism." Japan's strength had to be calculated not only in terms of material wealth, but of spiritual resources as well.

Konoye, a weak and confused man, became, without intending to, a tool of the militarists and other extreme nationalists. His method of "keeping them in check" was to appease their demands, however opposed he might be to them. Typically, in forming his new government, he appointed General Tojo as War Minister, Matsuoka as Foreign Minister, and Hoshino as President of the Planning Board. The fervently nationalist Manchurian "clique" in large measure took over the government.

While the new cabinet was being formed, Matsuoka informed his nephew, Kishi, that Konoye wanted to appoint him President of the Planning Board, an organ whose function was to co-ordinate all aspects of the national economy in preparation for war. "The Prime Minister," Matsuoka said, "attaches so much importance to the Board that its president will also hold the post of Minister without Portfolio."

Kishi was gripped by excitement. He was being offered a cabinet post, a goal he had coveted since youth. His first impulse was to accept. Then he considered the almost impossible task that faced the Planning Board, and decided to reject the offer. With the *Zaibatsu* so bitterly resisting government regulation, the board would have little opportunity to accomplish the planning it was supposed to do. He might, therefore, fail at his first cabinet post, and this would be a blot his career could not afford. Besides, he would be jumping ahead of his old boss, Hoshino, who was still in Manchoukuo, which the latter might justifiably resent. Furthermore, he was in the middle of a vital job at the Ministry of Commerce and Industry. He could wait. He would make the final jump to the top when he was more certain of staying there. Turning down the offer, Kishi asked his uncle to recommend to Konoye the appointment of Hoshino to the position.

A few days later, Matsuoka again summoned Kishi and told him that his recommendation had been accepted, but that Konoye still wanted him in the cabinet. "Since you feel obligated to remain with the Ministry of Commerce and Industry, the Prime Minister would like you to head that ministry," Matsuoka declared. "Then you could carry on with your present work, but in a higher capacity."

Kishi, to his uncle's surprise, rejected this offer, too, for basically the same reason he turned down the first. Since it was well known that he favored the military, he would be a prime target of the *Zaibatsu*. He suggested that a businessman be named to the post as a means of winning the co-operation of the industrialists. "What is needed now is someone who will seem to favor the *Zaibatsu*," Kishi told his uncle. "I can work better now for the regulation of industry by staying behind the scenes."

But the pressure on Kishi to accept the cabinet office was strong. Konoye himself called for him and requested, without success, that he reconsider his reply. Finally, the Prime Minister said, "I would prefer that you accepted the post, but since you won't, I will let you choose your boss. For I expect you to wield the real power." Kishi was delighted with this opportunity to direct his ministry without having to bear the responsibility for possible failure of its policies. He readily agreed to the Prime Minister's suggestion that a businessman, Ichizo Kobayashi, be offered the post.

Kobayashi was the son of a humble peasant family who had, remarkably enough, worked his way into high financial circles. He probably could be handled easier than most other businessmen who had been born into wealth and were more aware of their influential place in society. Kishi thus found himself in a unique situation. Having been entrusted by the Prime Minister with the real power in the ministry, he did not feel the sense of obligation to his superior, Kobayashi, that he normally would have felt. In fact, Kobayashi was, at least technically, obligated to Kishi, although he was not supposed to know about the circumstances which led to his appointment. When the new Minister did hear rumors about these circumstances, Kishi learned that his position was not only unique, but highly disadvantageous.

Kobayashi, overwhelmed by the idea that a peasant boy like himself had suddenly been catapulted to the top rank of national leadership, installed in office in the Emperor's presence, was at first bewildered by the responsibilities of his post. But Kobayashi was also a proud, aggressive man with a mind of his own, and he deeply resented Kishi for planning to dominate the ministry. Moreover, he was encouraged to defy Kishi by the *Zaibatsu* interests, which were still determined to remain free of government regulation. The conflict between the two men was further aggravated by the failure of Kishi to offer his resignation, as subordinates customarily did when a new chief came to power. It was generally considered one of the privileges of a cabinet member to select his own staff, or at least to confirm the existing appointments. But Kishi had not taken the risk of being dismissed, particularly after he discovered that Kobayashi knew how and why he had been appointed Minister.

Soon after taking over his post, Kobayashi startled Kishi with a remarkably frank clarification of their relationship: "I am well known as a fighter. I am also famous for never losing a fight. The reason is simple. I never pick a fight unless I know I will win. I've thought over the situation here and I've come to the conclusion that in an all-out fight with you, whether I win or lose, I stand to lose in the end. If I managed to have you dismissed from your job, the ministry staff might refuse to co-operate with me. On the other hand, if I tried and failed to have you dismissed, I would lose 'face.' So I do not intend to fight you."

Kishi interpreted this declaration as a warning that Kobayashi was, in fact, ready for a fight if necessary. And the struggle, if there was one, would be bitterly waged. Kishi realized that he had met a man who was as ambitious and unused to losing as himself. He was not unaware of the irony of having accepted as his superior a man with a character similar to his own.

Kishi and Kobayashi almost immediately came to loggerheads over the question of economic controls. Kobayashi, with the *Zaibatsu* solidly behind him, would not budge in his contention that regulation of industry had to be kept to a minimum. Kishi, supported by Konoye and the militarists, was adamant in his belief that establishment of a totalitarian economic structure was essential—particularly after the adoption by the Japanese government of an ambitious program for spreading the Imperial influence in Asia.

Previously, Japan had concerned itself only with extending and consolidating its authority in China and developing the resources of Manchoukuo. But as Hitler registered success after success in Europe, the new government feared that Germany might claim the British, French, and Dutch Far Eastern colonies as the spoils of war. This fear gave rise to the realization that Japan could profit from the European war by picking off these colonies, since they were no longer defendable by the mother countries. Now was the opportune time, it was decided, for Japan to expand its influence to embrace a Greater East Asia Co-Prosperity Sphere, within which each nation would be allotted its "proper place" by the Emperor.

To set the stage for this program, Foreign Minister Matsuoka, who had long favored strengthening ties with Germany and Italy, negotiated the entry of Japan in the Axis, or Tripartite Treaty of Alliance, in September, 1940. Japan had spurned an effort by Hitler to bring it into the pact the year before, fearing at that time that membership in such an alliance would involve the risk of war—before the country was ready for it—with Russia or Great Britain and the United States. But Hitler, it was now clear, needed no help in the Battle of Britain, and the pact specifically stated that it in no way affected the "political status which exists at present as between each of the three contracting parties and the Soviet Union." Thus, the alliance could involve Japan in war only with the United States, which, if it attacked the European Axis partners, would find itself at war with Japan as well. And even this risk was more than compensated by the obligation placed on Germany and Italy to come to the aid of the Japanese if America attacked Japan.

Furthermore, the alliance would possibly help to solve the problem of the China Affair. On the one hand, Japan, with bigger conquests in mind, could continue reducing the scope of the wasteful war in China without antagonizing the young officers. For Japanese troops and supplies in China had to be freed for use in other areas. On the other hand, Chiang Kai-shek, confronted with a diplomatically strengthened Japan and encouraged by a softening Japanese policy in China, might see the futility and foolishness of further resistance.

But most important of all to Japan's leaders, their country, in return for its recognition of German and Italian dominance in Europe, was recognized under the pact as the undisputed leader of the Far East. In effect, the alliance prevented Germany from making any territorial claims in Asia. It cleared the way, except for possible American interference, for the establishment of a Greater East Asia Co-Prosperity Sphere.

Kishi was now faced with the most difficult and demanding task of his life. It was his job to help build an economy that could support this new foreign policy—a policy which required, in fact, mobilization for possible war with the United States, and, though less likely now, with Russia. True, Japan would not be obligated to fight the U.S.S.R. if it became involved in a war with Germany and Italy. But if Stalin decided to move in the Far East, the Axis Pact, conversely, would be valueless to Japan.

Kishi and Kobayashi sparred ceaselessly over the most propitious means of preparing Japan to meet all needs and contingencies. Then, Kishi found an opening when his boss went off on an urgent mission to the Dutch East Indies to negotiate with the Dutch for the supply of petroleum, which the armed forces in China were crying for. He joined Hoshino and other economic officials in drawing up a plan calling for the establishment of a New Economic Structure based on the Manchoukuo model. Under this drastic program for bureaucratic control of the nation's economy, management was to be separated from capital, and the various cartels were to be reorganized, strengthened, and directed by cabinet appointees with virtual dictatorial powers to implement policies drawn up by the government on the advice of the military. One of the most far-reaching of these policies was to provide for the conscription of 250,000 women, including geishas and prostitutes, into the factories.

When Kobayashi returned to Japan, Kishi reported to him what had been done in his absence. The Minister, barely able to suppress his fury, icily told Kishi, "I'm not interested in your report. I have my own ideas on how the economy should be run and I don't want to hear yours." At a conference of the Planning Board attended by cabinet members, Kobayashi angrily demanded that the proposed plan be scrapped, crying, "Many of the provisions in this plan smack of communism."

This charge had a peculiar effect on the cabinet members. It virtually accused the designers of the New Economic Structure of being communist. And in Japan, at this time, a communist was a criminal. The militarists and their supporters trembled. They knew the *Zaibatsu,* in order to discredit them, would take up the charge that the armed forces, while supposedly suppressing communism, were, in reality, putting it into practice. Kobayashi had won at least a partial victory. His opponents agreed to delete provisions of the plan that he had labeled communistic. Immediately afterward he boasted to a group of businessmen, "The original draft was based on communism, so we had to revise it."

Kishi, bursting with anger, and fearful that his reputation would be ruined by the taint of communism, asked Hoshino to call another cabinet meeting to permit him to prove that no communist concepts were involved in the plan. Hoshino, who had himself helped formulate the program and therefore also feared the effects of the charge, tried to convene such a meeting, but War Minister Tojo, another initial supporter of the controversial draft, strongly opposed such a move. "Nothing could be more absurd," he told Hoshino. "If we held such a meeting, the matter would only become more complicated."

But Kobayashi and his *Zaibatsu* friends, forcing the conference that Kishi, paradoxically, had hoped would clear his name, made a new series of charges and generally reaped havoc (as Tojo had feared) from the new discussions. The economic plan went back to the experts for new compromise revisions, and though the *Zaibatsu* finally had to submit to some control measures, their propaganda efforts resulted in an order by the panicky national leaders for the arrest of several scapegoat officials who had helped Kishi and Hoshino draw up the original blueprint. Kobayashi, gloatingly magnanimous in his victory, told Kishi, "All right, you win. I will sign any documents you propose in the future without even bothering to look at them." Kishi smiled bitterly. For him, the battle had only begun. And he knew that Kobayashi had no intention of relaxing the advantage which he had gained. Still, Kishi had managed to get certain controls put upon the *Zaibatsu,* even though at a heavy price to himself.

And so the battle continued, with each man stealthily maneuvering to destroy the other. Kishi was convinced that further government controls were necessary if Japan's increasing military requirements were to be met. Meanwhile, Kobayashi, who was just as determined that industry should have few or no regulations imposed on it, finally decided, on the advice of Home Minister Kiichiro Hiranuma, another political enemy of Kishi's, to engage in an open fight with the man he wasn't sure he could beat.

On reaching this decision, he was so impatient to implement it that he personally went to Kishi's house the following morning to deliver the news to his assistant. Yoshiko fell to her knees and bowed as the visitor asked to see her husband. "I am afraid he is in bed with a bad cold," she said.

"Then would you please deliver him a note and ask for a reply," the Minister said, removing his shoes and following her into the reception room, where he sat down on a cushion. He scrawled on a sheet of paper, "It has become evident that co-operation between us is impossible. Therefore, I should like you to submit a letter of resignation."

Yoshiko shuffled into the bedroom and handed the note to Kishi, who, exhibiting a troubled look, wrote on another piece of paper, "I must consult with a number of people before I decide whether I should resign or not. I'll think about the matter when I recover from my cold."

Kobayashi, after reading the reply, got up and walked out of the house in a rage, his feet only partially deposited in his shoes. Kishi had humiliated him, sent him away like an office boy. He could only regain "face" now through vengeance, and this he vowed to have.

Kishi immediately consulted with Tojo and Matsuoka about the question of his resignation and both agreed to support him—if Prime Minister Konoye did. Kishi then wrote to Konoye asking for an audience, and received a reply that the Prime Minister had no time to see him but would speak to him briefly over the telephone. Disappointed at this coolness, Kishi nervously telephoned the Premier and asked him what he should do about Kobayashi's demand for his resignation. After a pause, Konoye brusquely said, "In the event of a quarrel between a minister and his assistant, it is natural for the assistant to resign."

Kishi was stunned by this response. Had not Konoye told him that he, Kishi, would be the real boss of the ministry and could even choose his superior? Now the Prime Minister was saying that Kobayashi had every right to fire him. It was the communist issue, of course. Konoye hoped that by getting rid of Kishi he could remove the political odor that Kobayashi had created. Crestfallen, Kishi sat down and wrote a letter of resignation, emphasizing, in an effort to clear his name, that he was resigning because he disagreed with the policies of the government, not in acknowledgment of communist tendencies. Kishi had suffered his first important political defeat.

But defeat for Kishi did not mean victory for Kobayashi. The Minister found himself up against a stone wall of non-co-operation within his ministry as Kishi's supporters, mainly the influential New Bureaucrats, pledged themselves to end the reign of the *"Zaibatsu* man." Meanwhile, Kishi himself joined Diet backers in digging into Kobayashi's past to root out any possible scandal that could be used to oust him. Finally, an array of charges were made against Kobayashi in the Diet. He had secretly shown a copy of the confidential original control draft to his business friends. He had evaded taxes. He had been involved in scandalous episodes with stage girls.*

Kobayashi was compelled to resign.

Hoshino was also forced out in a delicate balancing act by the government to keep peace with the *Zaibatsu*. Kishi regretted this, but he was happy to have settled accounts with Kobayashi, and was convinced that it was only a matter of time until he would be back in the ruling circle. Even if Prince Konoye had turned against him, he still had the support of Tojo and Matsuoka, who recognized his value to the government, and their power seemed to be growing.

Kishi decided that, meanwhile, he would further educate and prepare himself for the moment when he would be called back to duty. At his own expense, he embarked on a tour of occupied China to study the possibilities of strengthening economic co-operation with that area, on which

---

* Kobayashi controlled, among other enterprises, the famous Takarazuka all-girl revue, which in 1959 toured the United States.

Japan was heavily dependent for raw materials. His self-appointed mission took him to Shanghai, Nanking, Hankow, Peking, Tientsin, Chokako, and Daido. Kishi urged Chinese businessmen to help their Japanese "brothers" increase production of such critically needed items as fine-grade iron ore, which constituted about half of Japan's total imports, coal, which represented half of the nation's coal purchases, salt, and raw cotton.

On his return to Japan, Kishi found that Matsuoka's prestige, which had soared when he had concluded the Axis Treaty, was further enhanced with the signing, in March, 1941, of a Soviet-Japanese Neutrality Pact. Now that Japan's northern flank was finally secure, only the United States remained as an important barrier to Japanese ambitions in East Asia. Washington continued to block the Japanese peace effort in China, sending increased aid to Chiang Kai-shek. A bit of saber-rattling, Matsuoka believed, might do the trick. If not, the saber might actually have to be applied.

"Matsuoka diplomacy" set off a new explosion of nationalist sentiment in Japan, and Kishi was not immune to its fury. He longed to play an important role in the national mission, even while harboring reservations about its practicality. He did not want to go to war against a country as materially powerful as the United States. But if Japan wouldn't back down in its foreign policy, and if America intensified its pressure on Japan to do so, what choice would his country have except to resort to the force of arms? Japan, he thought, should do everything it could within the bounds of political feasibility to avoid war with America, but it also had to be ready for war if it came.

Spiritual mobilization, he observed, was swiftly gaining momentum. Not since the days of the Russo-Japanese War had the people displayed such enthusiasm for national traditions as they exhibited on February 11, 1941, the anniversary of the divine founding of the Japanese Empire. The most important ceremony took place at the Imperial Palace, where the nation's political, military, and religious leaders and members of the court gathered in a white-wood hall decorated with branches of the sacred Sakaki tree to join the Emperor, who was bedecked in traditional ceremonial robes, in praying to his godly ancestors. Simultaneously, millions of Japanese, including the Kishis, crowded into shrines throughout Japan to express in more humble fashion their own reverence to the gods. On the same day, almost 200,000 flag-waving youths, military cadets, worker representatives of the new Industrial National Service Federation, and delegates from other organizations, most of them proudly shouldering rifles and smartly dressed in khaki, blue, or green uniforms, paraded to the graveled Palace plaza to bow *en masse* before the Emperor and thunderously compress the sentiments of the nation into a single word, thrice repeated: *"Banzai!"*

Home Minister Hiranuma told a Tokyo lecture audience that same evening, "Japan's national polity is unique in the world. Heaven sent down [the grandson of the Sun Goddess] with a message that their posterity should reign over and govern Japan for ages eternal. It was on this day, 2601 years ago, that our first Emperor, Jimmu, ascended the throne. Dynasties of foreign countries were created by men, but Japan has a sacred Throne inherited from the Imperial Ancestors. Japanese Imperial Rule, therefore, is an extension of Heaven. Dynasties created by men may collapse, but the Heaven-created Throne is beyond the power of men."

Elaborating on this theme, the newspapers reminded the public that "on this day, Japan's first Emperor . . . issued the famous Rescript involving the *Hakko Ichiu* principle. *Thereafter the Capital (Japan) may be extended so as to embrace all the six cardinal points, and the eight cords may be covered so as to form a roof. Will this not be well?* The Jimmu proclamation can be vivified in national activities as the spirit of the founding of the Empire."

The term *Hakko Ichiu* began to be used frequently. At the inaugural meeting in July, 1944, of the Great Japan East Asia League, an organization established to intensify public support of the government's foreign policy, an address read for Prime Minister Konoye, who, though president of the group, was mysteriously absent, helped to clarify Japan's ultimate aim as dictated by the militarists: "Shining as the sun and stars is the goal of the Japanese Empire. The spirit of universal brotherhood denoted in *Hakko Ichiu* is embodied in concrete form in the Greater East Asia Co-Prosperity Sphere. It is the greatest honor and the life mission of every Japanese to do his part in its construction. But our movement must not stop at the realization of a co-prosperity sphere in East Asia alone. *We must prosecute the movement for all time, and so realize peace and security for the whole world* now torn by violence and swept by conflagration."

Hakko Ichiu, idealistically, called for a universal brotherhood that would envelop all nations under the supreme guidance of the Emperor, and Kishi thought it was wise to instill this concept into the thinking of the people. As for himself, he realized it was mere fantasy to consider Japan's destiny in universal terms at this time, for the nation would have enough difficulty achieving a Greater East Asia Co-Prosperity Sphere. In the face of Western resistance, it was hardly likely that the Japanese could extend this doctrine of universal brotherhood beyond Asia and the islands of the western Pacific. Even if the British Empire fell, there was the problem of correlating *Hakko Ichiu* with German and Italian ambitions. Hitler and Mussolini, whose movements were similar to Japan's except for their lack of a spiritual foundation, certainly could not be expected to place their empires under the Japanese Imperial roof. It was far more realistic, at least for the foreseeable future, to view the world order in terms of division into spheres of influence, with Japan ruling Asia, as, indeed, the Tripartite Treaty provided. But the preaching of *Hakko Ichiu* could, nevertheless, be valuable in tightening the moral sinews of the nation.

Also useful, Kishi believed, was the propagation of the doctrine, *Shimmin no Michi,* The Way of the Subject, which was contained in a publication put out by the Education Ministry for distribution in all schools and organizations. His daughter, Yoko, who had to devote an increasing amount of her homework to the study of "morals," brought this booklet home from school one day, and her father, thumbing through it, found it to be a neatly-organized exposition of the traditional Japanese ethical code. It was far more complete and systematized than any such book he had ever studied in his own youth and was, of course, brought up to date, describing with clarity the Western threat to Japan's "heavenly" rooted culture and ambitions. The publication read:

> "The concepts that have formed the foundation of the Western civilization since the early period of the modern age are individualism, liberalism, and materialism. These concepts regard the strong preying on the weak as reasonable, unstintedly promote epicurean desires, seek a highly expanded material life, and stimulate competition for acquiring colonies and securing trade, thereby leading the world toward a veritable hell of fighting and bloodshed. . . . [In view of this inherent danger in Western civilization, it is Japan's duty to construct] a new world order based on moral principles . . . to enlighten China, to strengthen Sino-Japanese unity, and to realize co-existence and co-prosperity. . . . [The situation requires a] highly geared and centralized defense state and the strengthening of the total national war framework. . . . Unless a country is systematized, even in peacetime, so that the total power of the state and the people is constantly concentrated on the final objectives of the country, and the highest capacities displayed, that country is predestined to be deposed even before taking up arms.

> "The first prerequisite of filial piety is to fulfill the duty of subjects to guard and maintain the Imperial Throne in observance of the be-

queathed will of their ancestors. . . . Unless men offer their lives and cast aside their personal desires for money and fame, they cannot perform their unswerving services and duties to the state and place it in a secure position in time of emergency, thereby answering the Imperial Will. . . . This is the very moment that the Japanese nation should thoroughly understand the fundamental character of the Empire, eliminate selfish and utilitarian ideas, encourage service to the state as the highest duty of national morality, prior to all other obligations, maintain keen insight into the international situation, and fulfill the duty of the people with indomitable will and unflinching determination, thereby diffusing the glorious and great principles of the Japanese Empire to the world."

Kishi was stirred by the intensity of the idealism expressed in the publication. It was perhaps a bit overemotional, like the speeches Dr. Uesugi used to make at college, and, just as in his college days, he could not accept the implication that the Emperor was infallible. But for the average person, this, like the doctrine of *Hakko Ichiu,* was good propaganda.

The central agency for the dissemination of such propaganda was the government-controlled Imperial Rule Assistance Political Association, which not only played the role of a political party—it had swallowed up all others—but also gradually exerted control over most of the nation's cultural, educational, and to some extent, business, activities. Among its functions was the sponsorship of mass meetings featuring top government and industrial speakers, and the operation of a youth organization, which instilled nationalist dogma into its members while serving as an emergency militia.

Sometimes, to help in this massive morale-raising campaign, particularly among businessmen, Kishi himself delivered public lectures, usually glowing with enthusiasm about the nation's basic economic strength. He didn't feel he was propagandizing, but simply telling the truth. The government—due partly to his own efforts—had indeed done a remarkable job mobilizing Japan's material strength for a possible war with the West, despite insufficient industrial unification and the drain of the China Affair. In one lecture to businessmen, he said:

"At this juncture it is necessary for all men in financial circles to be convinced of the great economic power of Japan. Some people in this country regard the present China Affair as a war of consumption, as Britain and America do, but it is a gross mistake to think that the economic strength of Japan has been weakened as a result of the war. It is true that the battle lines in China stretch far and wide, but *the*

*total of materials being consumed by the war in China today is only
ten per cent of the goods Japan is now producing.* Moreover, it is to be
noted that a part of that ten per cent is being used for construction work
on the continent—in Manchoukuo, North China, Inner Mongolia, and
Hainan Island. The remainder, or 90 per cent of the materials, including planes, guns, tanks, automobiles, hides and leather, foodstuffs,
and all other items Japan may need for the defense of the country, is
being stored."

Kishi's audience gasped in surprise. This was the first public indication
of how extensive had been Japan's preparations for a greater war. Kishi
went on:

"A real war of consumption is still to come. We must, therefore, do
our utmost to organize a highly geared defense state in order to fortify
this country against an eat-or-be-eaten war such as is being fought by
Germany and the Soviets today. For a country with the small production facilities and the meager resources with which Japan started, our
present status is a formidable achievement. And Japan is proud of the
fact that she has been able to do all this by her own efforts, without
foreign loans. How has she done it? She has done it using the same
methods by which Hitler has been able to arm Germany. She has put
the whole nation to work building up a war industry and a war machine on the principle of 'Guns before butter, and damn the expense!'"

The businessmen present, though still cool toward Kishi for his "control" policies, applauded his speech enthusiastically. For no matter how
Japan had managed to achieve its favorable economic position in this time
of crisis, it had done so. No patriotic Japanese could help but be proud
of this great accomplishment.

Plans for launching a war in the Pacific were already being drawn up
by the nation's leaders, who had been shocked into action by the unexpected German invasion of the Soviet Union in June, 1941. At an Imperial
Conference held on July 2nd, it was decided that the time was ripe for a
spectacular move. Not all the leaders agreed on what the best move
would be. Matsuoka, who had lost "face" because he had not foreseen
the German attack before he signed the Neutrality Pact with Russia,
favored an immediate invasion of Siberia, which, at least, would be consistent with his past appeals for close Axis ties. But the Army, led by
Tojo, and some of the Navy chiefs, argued that Japan was not obligated
to help Germany under the Axis Pact. They felt that it would be wiser
to advance southward into Indo-China and Siam, where they would meet
almost no opposition, even at the risk of a war with the United States and
Great Britain. Other naval figures opposed such a risk because of Japan's

lack of sufficient oil and other resources, though adherents of the plan maintained that the only way to obtain enough of these items was to gain control of the areas in the south where they were available.

Konoye supported the cautious naval group, feeling that Japan should win the war in China before embarking on other ventures. By that time, America might be involved in the European war and be too preoccupied to concern itself with the Far East. But Tojo and his military supporters, pressed by the powerful Young Officers' clique, were adamant that the time had come to act, and the opposition, fearful of being branded as cowards, finally agreed. The Japanese armies would move southward. Japan would observe the Neutrality Pact with Russia—until it became clear that Germany was on the verge of victory, at which time an attack would be launched on Siberia.*

All that Kishi and other private Japanese citizens were told about the Imperial Conference was that "a fundamental national policy to be adopted in meeting the prevailing situation has been decided." But they soon learned what this policy was when, shortly after, Konoye formed a new cabinet without Matsuoka. France's Vichy government was forced to let Japanese troops into Indo-China. Kishi needed no explanation for this move. Japan had to assure itself of an adequate supply of raw materials in case of an expanded war. Of course, this action might bring such a war closer, but unless the United States decided to withdraw support from China, there would probably be a war anyway. It was better to fight earlier from a strong position than later from a weak one.

Kishi was not surprised when the United States, in retaliation for the Indo-China invasion, imposed an economic embargo on Japan, freezing all Japanese assets abroad and virtually cutting off trade with the country. He knew that Japan had to reach an agreement with the United States soon or fight. It simply could not, for any extended period of time, endure the effects of an embargo without seriously endangering its ability to wage a major war.

At the same time, the embargo, Kishi was sure, would only reinforce the determination of the military, as well as the public, not to compromise with the United States, for now a matter of "face" was involved. "If the purpose of the embargo," Kishi told me in retrospect, "was to force the

* This demonstrates the failure of the Japanese to recognize how closely the success of their own military operations would be linked with the progress of the fighting in Europe. Although the Japanese recognized the opportunity which the war in Europe presented, they never considered it as having any real bearing upon their own plans. The failure to see the war very clearly in world-wide terms contributed to the eventual outcome of World War II.

militarists to withdraw troops from China and Indo-China, this purpose was tragically defeated. America unfortunately didn't understand the Japanese mind. As far as Japan was concerned, the embargo was practically tantamount to a declaration of war, for the government leaders were placed in a position where they couldn't make any significant concessions at all without losing 'face.' However wrong our actions may have been, you Americans, perhaps without realizing it, prodded us into war."

Konoye, also realizing that the time had come for a showdown with the United States, proposed a meeting with President Roosevelt on some Pacific island, but the President informed Japanese Ambassador Admiral Kichisaburo Nomura that he would agree to such a conference only if Japan clarified its "true intentions." On September 6, 1941, Japan's leaders met secretly in the presence of the Emperor to settle the question of peace or war once and for all. Konoye and most other members of the cabinet favored further diplomatic explorations. Tojo and his militarist partners demanded a decision to go to war. Finally, the Emperor, who had been sitting in painful silence, true to the tradition of his exalted station, announced to the shocked gathering that he would read a poem that his grandfather, the Emperor Meiji, had once composed:

Though I consider the surrounding seas as my brothers, why is it that the waves should rise so high?

Hirohito commented, "I have always read and appreciated this poem, and kept in my heart the Emperor Meiji's spirit of peace. It has been my wish to perpetuate this spirit."

Konoye smiled faintly, but Tojo fumed. The General could not openly flaunt the Emperor's virtual command to exert new efforts in the cause of peace. A compromise solution was thus decided on. Negotiations would continue with the United States, but if an accord was not reached by early October, 1941, a definite decision would be taken regarding war with that country. Meanwhile, war preparations would be accelerated.

When an interchange of notes between Washington and Tokyo simply produced a renewed American demand that Japanese troops be withdrawn from the mainland, the Ministers of War, Navy, and Foreign Affairs met at Konoye's home on October 12, 1941, to determine Japan's next move. All but War Minister Tojo still had reservations about going to war. And they had been encouraged to hold out against war if possible by Marquis Koichi Kido, Kishi's superior in the Ministry of Commerce and Industry some years before, who was now Lord Keeper of the Privy Seal, the Emperor's chief adviser. Foreign Minister Toyoda, who had replaced Matsuoka, suggested to Tojo that Japan "meet" Washington's demand for a withdrawal of Japanese troops from China by agreeing to this "in principle," with the stipulation that the process be spread over a period of many years. No actual withdrawal would have to take place, he implied. But Tojo shouted angrily, "We can accept no compromise on principle. After all the sacrifices we have made in China the Army won't agree to any withdrawals. Army morale would not survive it." Tojo's threat was clear. Failure to decide on war with the United States could produce an Army coup, which would probably mean liquidation of those opposing the military view.

With the moderates in near panic, Konoye, finally mustering the courage that had failed him for so long, made a desperate plea to Tojo at a meeting between the two men held later in the Prime Minister's house. Konoye asked his guest, "What hopes do you have of bringing war with the United States and Great Britain to a close once you begin it? This, I believe, is the only point from which our negotiations with America can be considered."

Evading the question, Tojo replied with agitation, "Even if my job depended on it, I could not order the withdrawal of our troops from China. What America wants is hegemony in the Far East. Once we make a concession to her, there is no telling what she will demand next."

When Konoye pointed out America's superiority in material resources, Tojo said, "There was no certainty of victory in the war with Russia in 1904, or in China, either. Besides, there are a large number of people of German descent in America who won't fight against their mother country. Nor can one ignore the possibility of widespread strikes in American war plants once war starts. The Premier of Japan should have enough courage to jump off the veranda of the Kiyomizu Temple."*

"If this concerned me alone, I would not hesitate," replied Konoye. "But we are considering, not the fate of an individual, but of a nation with a history of three thousand years. We cannot go into reckless national adventures as if they were private exploits."

Tojo departed, containing his rage only with difficulty. In view of the opposition he had encountered, he was now determined to get rid of Konoye, and this he would do by politically isolating him. First, he would deal with the uncommitted Navy. Through an emissary, he let Konoye know that "if the Navy comes out openly in favor of a peaceful settlement, the Army will bow to its wishes. After all, it is the Navy and not the

* The Kiyomizu Temple stands at the edge of a cliff in Kyoto. Tojo meant that Konoye should be willing to take a chance even though the odds were heavy.

Army that would have to fight the United States." But as Tojo had calculated, the naval leaders would not make such a statement for fear of
being labeled cowardly. Nor was Marquis Kido, who dreaded the possibility of a military coup, prepared openly to support the Prime Minister.
Therefore, on October 16, 1941, Konoye resigned.

Kishi immediately got in touch with some of his high-placed friends
and learned that Tojo stood the best chance to head the next cabinet.
Several Elder Statesmen who feared this would mean war were opposed
to his selection, but Kido, the most influential of the "kingmakers,"
favored him. Tojo was, argued Kido wishfully, the only man who could
prevent war. He was a necessary compromise between the relatively moderate but less influential senior officers and the fanatical war-minded
juniors who were ready to provoke an international incident that would
inevitably lead to war. Tojo became Prime Minister on October 18, 1941.

Only a few hours after taking over his post, Tojo summoned Kishi to
his official residence and offered him the position of Minister of Commerce and Industry. Kishi unhesitatingly accepted the offer. As he left
Tojo's office, his heart beat with excitement and he smiled to himself. He
recalled how he had turned down the same offer made by Konoye the
year before. For a short time that decision had seemed a costly mistake.
But everything had turned out well after all. He was back in government
again, and would probably have less trouble carrying out his policies
than he would have had under Konoye's regime, for with the nation on the
threshold of war, businessmen would certainly be more amenable to compromise. His economic policies could probably be instituted as emergency
measures and then gradually made part of a stable system.

Later that day, Kishi, immaculately dressed in a cutaway and striped
trousers, made an appearance—the first of his life—before the Emperor,
who presented him, and the other new cabinet officers, with certificates
of appointment. He was filled with deep pride when his turn came to
enter the audience room from the antechamber in which he and his colleagues were waiting. But when he saw the Emperor, pale and tired, waiting to greet him, he was suddenly overwhelmed with humility. After Kishi
had bowed, the Sovereign, his eyes brooding behind his large glasses, un-
rolled a certificate handed to him by a chamberlain and quietly said,
"Nobusuke Kishi, I appoint you Minister of Commerce and Industry."
When the chamberlain had bestowed the certificate upon him, Kishi
bowed and left.

On arriving home, he found his house crowded with friends who had
dropped over to congratulate him. While the guests drank and enter-

tained themselves, Kishi and his wife knelt before the household shrine, and, with the certificate of appointment placed on the altar, reported the honor which had befallen Kishi to their ancestors and silently prayed that the new Minister might succeed in the important task that lay ahead. Kishi thought of Moyo, knowing that his mother would have been proud of him. When prayers were over, he asked Yoshiko with a smile, "Did you pray hard for me?" "Yes," she whispered, "for you—and for peace."

On returning to his guests, Kishi found several newspapermen waiting for him. He read to them a statement he had prepared earlier:

"Since I left the Ministry of Commerce and Industry last January, the situation has undergone considerable changes at home and abroad. To cope with these changed conditions, I shall institute a new policy to meet the future development of commerce and industry. During my absence from the ministry I had many chances to meet with people of various circles and gained invaluable experience. What impressed me most is that the people at present are looking for the government to indicate clearly in which direction the industrial circles should go.

"I hereby pledge to the people that all policies published in the name of the Minister of Commerce and Industry will be carried out, regardless of the expense involved. In the stringent conditions that exist at present, the government must avoid taking useless precautions. The government must act promptly and effectively. No time should be lost in the administration of national affairs in time of war. . . ."

The next morning, Kishi proudly read his words in every newspaper. In one, the *Asahi Shimbun,* there was even an editorial about it. But as he scanned it, his pride suddenly turned to pique. It said:

"We look to Minister Kishi for some sort of reform, but feel an uncertainty concerning his future policies because of his past career. . . . When he retired from his post of Vice-Minister of Commerce and Industry this spring he raised more disturbance than was warranted. . . . One of his outstanding remarks is, 'I hereby pledge to the people that all policies published in the name of the Minister of Commerce and Industry will be carried out, regardless of the expense involved.' His statement is full of burning youthful ardor and these remarks could emanate only from Minister Kishi. It is obvious that he intends to invigorate and brighten the outlook of industrial circles. To this no one can have any objection. However, as a means of execution he objects to extreme precaution and prefers rough and ready measures. He says that he will revise any policy which he believes wrong.

"If this be so, we fear that his policies may fail completely. Although the present condition of the country demands prompt action rather than hesitation, a single wrong step at this critical juncture would result in dire consequences. Kishi's conduct would be excusable in an immature minister but the people expect a man like him to carry on with due deliberation. . . ."

So he was expected to act "with due deliberation," Kishi thought; in other words, to continue the same musty, weak-kneed policies of the past, when in this time of crisis decisiveness, imagination, and even ruthlessness were required. He would show them!

As soon as he took over his job, Kishi rocked the ministry with his demand for the resignation of many of its highest officials, replacing them in a number of cases with members of the old Manchoukuo team. Shiina was promoted to the position of Vice-Minister. Veteran politicians and bureaucrats were shocked by the swiftness and scope of this reorganization, the most drastic personnel surgery performed in the ministry since its birth. Usually when ministers wanted to get rid of their subordinates, they did so by gradual stages, whenever other positions were available to which the men could be transferred. Good bureaucratic jobs were at a premium and it was cruel to dismiss professional employees unless they had other prospects, as Kishi himself had discovered when he had been forced to resign his job as Vice-Minister. He had had to wait several months to get back into the government. Also, the minister had certain obligations to his subordinates, just as the reverse was true. Kishi considered all this, but with Japan now in a virtual state of emergency, common sense dictated that traditional attitudes be abandoned.

When Shiina himself began to question the wisdom of so complete an overhaul, Kishi explained with cold logic, "If we are to fulfill our duties, I have no choice but to act as I have been doing. Personal affections must be sacrificed. Previous ministers, as you know, kept many people on the payroll who didn't do a good job. This sort of treatment may be kindly, but it is also ruinous to the government. When a man is given a certain position, he must be able to live up to the trust and responsibility that the job requires. If the work is too much for him, he should be asked to resign—particularly in times like this. And that is the real kindness—both to himself and to those he is serving."

While Kishi reorganized his ministry for possible war with the United States, he found himself in the grip of a new crisis of conscience. Could he fully support, or even condone, a policy of war? The core of the matter was China. War could only be avoided if the United States lifted its embargo unconditionally or if Japanese troops were withdrawn from China. But America showed no sign of giving in, and there was no possibility of a troop withdrawal, which, if ordered, would certainly set off a revolt by the Young Officers. They were, Kishi thought, morally justified in wanting war. America was trying to prevent the stabilization of East Asia, of which Japan was the natural leader, for its own selfish economic ends. But if their desire was just, was it rational? The answer would be in the affirmative—*if* Japan could be reasonably certain of victory.

How certain was victory? Kishi pondered this question as he worked in his office, as he visited factories, as he lay restlessly in bed at night, as he ate his meals while Yoshiko furtively, worriedly, saw the conflict written in his face. He turned over in his mind scores of facts and statistics. How many planes was America producing? How much oil? What was the rubber yield in the Dutch East Indies, the tin output in Malaya?

As he had informed the military, the petroleum situation, in particular, was growing desperate. The civilian supply, however strictly controlled, would be completely exhausted by the summer of 1942, and the military supply would be so low by the summer of 1943 that the Navy could not operate. The petroleum available in Japan, mostly in South Sakhalin, represented only a drop in the bucket in relation to what was needed. And if production of oil was to be substantially increased, such large sums of money would have to be spent on new facilities that it would be necessary to cut back armament and other war industries for the purpose. Even then an adequate supply of petroleum could not be obtained. Beyond all this, America and its British and Dutch allies would certainly tighten the blockade of Japan as time went on.

As for armament, Kishi realized that Japan lacked some of the modern weapons of the West. Many of the nation's top Army officers, thinking of their divisions in feudal terms, had, until recently, been dangerously confident that mass *banzai* charges in the spirit of the "true samurai" would prove more effective against the enemy than tanks, bombers, and big guns. Fortunately, they had learned a lesson during border conflicts with the Russians in 1938 and 1939 at Changkufeng and Nomonhan, in which the Japanese discovered that rifles and old artillery were no match for the more advanced weapons employed by the U.S.S.R. Japan's factories were now turning out tanks and other modern equipment, which, supplementing the nation's invincible infantry, would probably suffice to frustrate what few ground attacks would be launched by the West. The Navy and Air Force, which would do most of the fighting, were in first-class shape. Japan's naval officers, many of them trained in Britain and the United States, were among the most competent in the world, and the size of the Japanese fleet was comparable to that of the American. Japan's

Air Force was, if anything, larger than that of the United States, though Kishi had to admit that the quality of American planes was superior.

How prepared was America for war? It was quite obvious from a study of American industry that its potential strength was far greater than that of Japan. Perhaps America was short of rubber, but it could probably scrape through with imports from South America and reclaimed and synthetic rubber. As for the mobilization of its industrial potential, the United States had almost completed conversion and expansion of its facilities to meet the war needs of its allies in Europe, and these facilities could be used to carry on a war against Japan.

Japan certainly couldn't win a war which required occupation of the United States, but perhaps it could win a restricted war if it succeeded in conquering the Southeast Asian area, with its rich supplies of petroleum and other raw materials. Then the United States would probably find it so difficult, if not impossible, to dislodge Japan from the region that it would agree to stop interfering in Far Eastern affairs. China, once cut off from Western economic and moral support, would crumble. With the resources of Southeast Asia available, Japan could wage war for more than a year, perhaps two. Naturally there was always the possibility of unforeseen dangers. Kishi had heard reports that America—as well as Germany—was conducting research on a powerful bomb that harnessed atomic energy, but it seemed certain that no such weapon could be perfected within the next few years. Based on what was known at the moment, Japan *could* win a Pacific war.

Furthermore, the risks involved in war had to be studied from more than a statistical and materialistic point of view. The Japanese spirit could be the decisive factor. The Americans were no match for the Japanese in this area of strength. "We did not realize that the American people were as unified as they proved to be," Kishi told me in a frank appraisal of his attitude at the time. "We were misled by the fact that Americans are of many different races and originally came from many different lands. We thought that those of German blood, in particular, would refuse to co-operate in your war effort. Also, we calculated, as odd as it may seem, that your wealth would work to your disadvantage. A wealthy man, at least in Japan, will seldom fight a poor man with great enthusiasm. He is too satisfied with life to risk injury to himself. He has too little to gain from the poor man. On the other hand, a hungry man will fight like a tiger, for he has little to lose and everything to gain."

Perhaps the Young Officers were right, Kishi concluded. Perhaps it *was* time for Japan to jump off the veranda of the Kiyomizu Temple.

Armed with facts and figures prepared by Kishi and other economic experts, Tojo and his fellow militarists pressed for a government decision to go to war by the end of November. Foreign Minister Shigenori Togo, whom Tojo had brought into his cabinet to appease the moderates, alone called for continued negotiations with the United States. Togo warned that America and Britain had tremendous industrial potentials and would fight tenaciously, whereas Japan could expect no aid from Germany and Italy. He argued that it would be foolish to decide on war because of the prospect of early victories. "After all, if one wins ninety-nine battles and loses the hundredth, one loses the war." Moreover, he added, it would not be keeping faith with the people to decide on war without assurance of final victory, especially while there was still some possibility that negotiations might succeed.

Kishi wanted to side with Togo but found himself unable to do so when he re-examined the petroleum situation and the effects of the embargo. He was, therefore, quite satisfied when, at another Imperial Conference, a compromise was reached. Japan would make war on the United States and Great Britain *if pending negotiations with them failed*. A final proposal was sent to the Japanese Ambassador in Washington with the order that agreement had to be obtained, if at all, by November 25, 1941. But Kishi's small hope that a miracle would suddenly occur was reflected in a speech he delivered to the Chamber of Commerce and Industry on November 21st, warning that Japan must mobilize the total strength of the country. While acknowledging that the extension of state controls had resulted in conflict between the government and business, he maintained that Japan was far more powerful now than prior to the fighting in China.

The deadline came, and, as expected, no accord had been reached. On December 1, 1941, Kishi attended another Imperial Conference, and signed his name to a resolution of war.

On December 7th (Japan time), Vice-Admiral Ichiro Sato, who had recently retired from the Navy because of illness after serving as commander of Fort Ryojun at Port Arthur, called at the office of his brother, Kishi, and asked angrily, "How long are we going to continue these ridiculous negotiations with America? When will the war start?"

"I can only say," Kishi replied with a smile, "that the day probably isn't too far off. The Imperial Diet will be convoked on December 15th. And it is customary for the Imperial order for the opening to be issued about a week in advance—perhaps tomorrow."

Sato, startled, looked at his brother, then returned his smile. He knew that a declaration of war would automatically be followed by a convocation of the Diet, and the announcement of such a meeting would probably not be made before war started because of the danger of tipping off the enemy. "This is the news I have been waiting for," he said. "This is what the Navy has been building toward for the past ten years."

Kishi returned home late that night, ate his dinner in almost complete silence, then went to bed but couldn't fall asleep, tossing and turning, getting up at intervals for a glass of water or a stroll around the garden. Yoshiko wasn't able to sleep, either. Her husband had told her nothing, but she sensed that something was in the offing. Finally, at about four A.M., the telephone in the next room rang. Yoshiko started to get up, but Kishi, turning on the light, went to answer it himself.

He returned shortly and said, "I've got to go to a cabinet meeting immediately."

"It must be something very important."

"Yes. I'm afraid it's war."

CHAPTER IX

❦

THE DIVINE SMILE

MINUTES LATER Kishi was dressed. While the maid knelt and tied his shoelaces, Yoshiko stood by the door shivering in the cold morning air, her arms folded tightly in her kimono sleeves. Kishi noted her anxious expression. War meant killing, and it was understandable that women would be oversensitive about that, realizing less clearly than men that sometimes extreme measures were required to attain virtuous ends. He said, "There will be grave days ahead, Yoshiko. But all will end well."

He found his car waiting, and ordered the driver to take him to the Prime Minister's official residence as fast as possible. He felt an odd, exhilarating sensation as the automobile sped through the hushed emptiness of sleeping Tokyo toward a sliver of orange sunlight on the horizon. Kishi lapsed momentarily into a world of fantasy. Amaterasu, the Sun Goddess, was smiling upon her children at this fateful moment in their history. The car finally pulled into the court of the Prime Minister's residence, bringing Kishi back with a start to the world of flesh and politics.

As Kishi entered the conference room he found himself in an electric atmosphere. But if his colleagues, who sat around a circular table, seemed to be elated, they also appeared to be anxious. Naoki Hoshino, now Chief Secretary in the Tojo cabinet, had not revealed the purpose of the meeting when he had telephoned them. But as all had heard before from private sources that Japan would attack the United States momentarily— though the military had tried to keep this fact a secret even from the

171

highest civilian leaders—they assumed this was the reason for the dawn conference.

Tojo, his face inscrutable as always, opened the meeting with the remark, "This is a most important conference." He then called on Navy Minister Shigetaro Shimada for a report. Shimada, with a bland expression, confirmed what all had expected. Pearl Harbor had been bombed. Shimada said, "Reports indicate good results. The enemy has suffered heavy damage."

Kishi and the others relaxed. None of them were stricken with moral compunctions about the means that had been employed to launch a war. Even Foreign Minister Togo, who had protested to the military, when he had learned of its plans, that a surprise attack would be contrary to internationally accepted rules of war, now basked in the success of the operation. After all, they reasoned, was not this attack in the tradition of the Shimonoseki Affair, in which Kishi's Choshu ancestors fired without warning on an American ship as it had entered the straits? Had not Japan's gallant soldiers started the Russo-Japanese War with a surprise bombardment of the Russian fleet? The larger, materially more powerful nations could afford to abide by the meaningless "rules of war." Japan, a small island country with scant resources, a mere David fighting a Goliath, could not. It had to use every weapon at its command—and this included gaining the iniative while the enemy was still asleep. War, as Japan's history had borne out, was not immoral—only defeat was. And, if Japan did not fully exploit every advantage, it would risk defeat.

After Shimada's report, Hoshino read the Imperial Rescript of War drawn up for submission to the Emperor and passed it around the table for examination while discussion of its contents went on. Later in the morning, members of the cabinet joined with the Privy Councilors, the Emperor's formal advisers, in the Palace for further informal talks on the Rescript, and a second joint meeting, this one formal, was held early in the afternoon in the presence of the Emperor. Kishi noted that all the speakers praised the document, and in similar terms, though one Councilor, Seikin Ikeda, did propose a minor alteration. Observing that the two enemy nations were referred to in the Rescript as the "United States" and "Great Britain," Ikeda said that politeness required that their formal names, the "United States of America" and the "United Kingdom of Great Britain," be used instead. His proposal was turned down.

Late that afternoon, Kan'ichi Nakayasu, an old friend of Kishi, visited the Minister at his office. The two men had known each other since middle-school days when Nakayasu, who was now a successful businessman, had earned Kishi's grudging respect by regularly humiliating him in fencing contests. Kishi often discussed matters of state with his bluff, rotund, good-humored comrade, particularly if they pertained to economics.

"Is the radio report that we bombed Pearl Harbor true?" Nakayasu asked.

"Yes," replied Kishi with a smile, "the war has started at last."

"But does the government know what it is doing? I visited the United States only a few years ago and inspected many factories. Their production capacity is enormous."

"We realize that," Kishi said. "But we think Japan will be able to consolidate its position before America can achieve its potential. Washington will almost certainly make peace on terms favorable to us rather than commit millions to death in a prolonged battle for the Pacific."

"It sounds risky to me," said Nakayasu.

"Japan had no choice. And we have little to lose. The American blockade cut off most of our oil supply. If we waited any longer, we soon would not have the means to fight a war. Japan would be at the mercy of the colonial powers. By starting the war now and winning control of East Asia, we will be able to assure ourselves an almost unlimited supply of oil and other raw materials."

Nakayasu was still not convinced. "I'm afraid that one night enemy planes will rain bombs on us."

"You can take comfort in the fact that although the quality of their planes may be superior to ours, there isn't much difference in numbers."

"Yes, but I hope you have not underestimated America's ability to increase its production greatly in a very short time, and also its will to fight to a conclusive decision."

On this cynical note, Nakayasu bade goodbye. Kishi was disturbed by the visitor's parting words, which he himself feared might be true. But his optimism returned when a messenger delivered a copy of the Imperial Rescript just issued, officially declaring war on the United States and Great Britain:

". . . To ensure the stability of Eastern Asia and to contribute to world peace is the far-sighted policy which was formulated by our great, illustrious, Imperial grandsire and by our great Imperial sire succeeding him and which we take constantly to heart. To cultivate friendship among the nations and to enjoy prosperity in common with all nations has always been the guiding principle of our Empire's foreign policy. . . . Hallowed spirits of Imperial ancestors guarding us from above, we rely upon the loyalty and courage of our subjects in our confident expectation that the task bequeathed by our forefathers will be carried forward and that the sources of evil will be speedily eradicated and enduring peace immutably established in Eastern Asia, preserving thereby the glory of our Empire."

This was a good, a just war, Kishi reflected. He believed his country was fighting not only for itself, but for its neighbors as well. Japan was the light of Asia. It would provide Asia with a new moral order free of corrupting Western influences. Nakayasu, he told himself, should look at the brighter side of the picture.

Japan's dream of conquest began to materialize with relentless momentum. The Pearl Harbor attack had put the United States Pacific Fleet out of action, clearing the way for Japan to extend its embrace throughout East Asia almost without interference. First Guam fell, then Wake Island, Hong Kong, the Philippines, the Dutch East Indies, Malaya, Burma, and Singapore. Thailand, unoccupied by Allied troops as were the other areas, reluctantly opened its doors to the invaders. By the summer of 1942, Japan appeared to have fulfilled its vow to occupy Greater East Asia, with its soldiers in control of territory thousands of miles from their homeland, spread out across the Pacific and Asia, as Kishi liked to think of it, like a huge fan of light at dawn.

Kishi was proud to be in the key position he held at this golden moment in history, a moment in which his descendants would glory for the next million years. And he had achieved this position at the remarkably early age of forty-five. He owed his success, he felt, to his exceptional ability as a bureaucrat and an economist. But it was not enough for one to be highly competent in his field. Kishi wanted recognition not only for his professional attributes, but for himself. He wanted to be popular, to feel that the people, as well as the government, approved of him. This was not only a matter of personal gratification, but of national import. It was proper—and certainly beneficial to the war effort—that in this difficult period there should be a tighter bond than ever between the rulers and the ruled, an expression of complete solidarity in support of the national cause. Kishi therefore decided to enter the Diet election of April, 1942, when Japan was experiencing its most feverish moments of victory delirium.

Kishi had previously considered inaugurating a new political party, which he had hoped to head. Tomio Muto, a former high official in the Manchoukuo government, says that Kishi approached him for help in recruiting "four or five men from Manchoukuo to run in the coming general election and to participate in the organization of a new party."

When Kishi indicated that there was no suitable candidate for the presidency of such a party, Muto, guessing his intention, suggested that Kishi himself become president. Kishi readily agreed. The plan, according to Muto, had been on Kishi's mind since his return from Manchoukuo. Other ex-Manchoukuo leaders, including Hoshino, also developed an interest in the idea, but it never got beyond the planning stage. The group finally merged in the Imperial Rule Assistance Political Association, the huge totalitarian party subservient to Tojo, which automatically backed Kishi because of his cabinet status.

Some of Kishi's colleagues, who enjoyed their power with or without the public's affection, thought his decision to run in the election unwise because he would be risking the prestige of his cabinet office. Many people ran for parliament in the hope of being brought into the cabinet one day, but it was not common for someone to enter the Diet elections after this objective had been attained. Kishi, however, thought the risk worth taking. With the support of IRAPA, his chances were good. He took no active interest in this monolithic organization and never attended an IRAPA meeting. But he by no means spurned its support. Though he could understand the vexation of some of his "liberal" friends, such as Jusoh Miwa of the banned Social Mass Party, with Tojo's dictatorial policies, he also appreciated the need for maximum national unity during this critical period when political bickering could be disastrous for Japan. But to prove that friendship went deeper than politics, he offered to obtain IRAPA support for Miwa if he wanted to run for the Diet, an opportunity which the latter politely rejected.

Kishi found that it was hardly necessary to use either pressure or propaganda to achieve national unity, for, with Japanese troops irresistibly sweeping across Asia, even most "liberals" were voluntarily jumping on Tojo's bandwagon. There was no substitute for success. Nevertheless, there were a small number of candidates who continued to resist official policies, even though subject to strong government pressures. One radio broadcast warned, "Careful watch must be kept on speeches which might encourage dissatisfaction toward the policy of Japan, unnecessary criticisms of wartime policy, or criticisms directed to social problems in relation to the economic hardships due to the shortage of material."

TOKKO, Tojo's special political police, did not hesitate to coerce candidates who refused to obey, threatening, and sometimes arresting, and even torturing, them. Because this kind of coercion did exist, Kishi felt it was even more important to win popular approval. He campaigned vigorously in his Yamaguchi constituency, speaking in crowded meeting halls and from the back of a sound truck at street corners, with banners labeled "Vote for Kishi" draped across the vehicle. He flavored his speeches with the usual references to Japan's battlefield gains, but tried to impress the people that he was one of them rather than above them— a concession to the democratic spirit highly uncharacteristic of the IRAPA. To dramatize this "equality," he spoke at most meetings standing on the floor rather than on a raised platform so that he would not have to look down on his audience.

Kishi was elected easily, and the great bulk of his pro-government colleagues were also swept into the Diet, though a few oppositionists, despite police intimidation, managed to win. Among the successful rebels was the strongly antiwar liberal, Yukio Ozaki, and the anti-Tojo Nazi-style fascist, Seigo Nakano, both of whom the IRAPA had bitterly fought.

Kishi was delighted on learning of his victory. "I have had some very happy moments in my life," he says, "when I graduated from the university with honors, when I passed the Higher Civil Service examination, when I was appointed Minister of Commerce and Industry. But my election to the Diet was somehow more satisfying than all of those accomplishments."

Having won the "confidence of the people," Kishi returned to his ministerial duties determined to live up to their trust in him. He, and the other national leaders, could not rest on the laurels earned for them by the soldiers in the battlefield, Kishi thought. A careful study of long-range war plans and prospects had to be undertaken. Japan could ill afford to make a miscalculation. He immediately made a thorough examination of the Japanese economy, his field of responsibility, and the deeper he probed, the more concerned he became about the future. Japan's war machine had not yet met with substantial resistance, offering little surface justification for such concern. But Kishi, looking beyond the sensationalism of the newspaper headlines, saw in blunt, cold statistical terms the closing gap between the military power of Japan and that of its awakened enemies. The odds mounted against Japan each day, even while Japanese soldiers were advancing almost at will. It was only a matter of time until, as Nakayasu feared, America's material strength would exceed that of Japan. He had realized this before the war started, but now that the days were actually ticking off, the situation seemed far more urgent.

Territorially speaking, Kishi thought, Japan had largely achieved its goal. Only the troublesome hold-out regions of China prevented Japan from dominating the entire East Asia sphere. It would take decades to digest the lands already occupied, and perhaps even longer before they could be adequately developed. Was it not time now, while Japan's bargaining power was so tremendous, to bring the war to a halt and concentrate on the "co-prosperity" aspect of the Japanese program, which could never be achieved under wartime conditions?

There were a few other Japanese leaders, he knew, who entertained similar views—notably Prince Konoye. But not many, even among those who had originally opposed war, were interested in cold statistics and economic probabilities at a time like this. Kishi himself sometimes felt that the war should be continued, for a while yet anyway, until America was more thoroughly convinced of the futility of its cause. It was not easy to determine the propitious moment for making a peace offer—on Japanese terms, of course. Kishi had no idea how strongly the American people felt about the Japanese aggression in the Pacific, especially the surprise attack on Pearl Harbor and the bitter surrender at Bataan.

After an intense struggle with himself, Kishi concluded that Japan should at least feel out the Allies about a peace agreement. Each military and naval victory gave Japan added bargaining power, but at the same time, Kishi was aware that a Japanese defeat, even a minor one, could make a peace offer at terms favorable to Japan more difficult. Yet Kishi knew that he personally could do little about the situation. The militarists were running the government and the war, and Tojo certainly had no intention of calling for peace when everything was going his way. The military mind was not geared to stop wars when there was more to be gained by further fighting. The very suggestion of a peace offer at this time would probably rile Tojo. But Kishi decided, as the man largely responsible for the operation of the nation's war economy, it was his duty to communicate his sentiments to the Prime Minister.

Shortly after the fall of Singapore Kishi advised Tojo that in view of Japan's limited economic potential it would be wise to seek an early end to hostilities. The Allies, he pointed out, might well look with favor on a peace based on the present status quo, which, after all, would give Japan almost everything it wanted. Tojo listened in frigid silence, then replied that, if the Allies were growing in strength, Japan's economic potential was also expanding rapidly with the availability of Southeast Asia's resources. Furthermore, he added, it would be difficult convincing his subordinates, particularly the young officers, that they should lay down their arms in the midst of overwhelming victories.

"No," he concluded, "the time is not yet ripe to seek an end to the war. The China problem has not been entirely settled, and military gains elsewhere have to be consolidated. Japan must destroy the remainder of the American fleet, and then inflict on the Americans and British, when they try to retake what they have lost, such a crushing defeat that they will realize completely the uselessness of further assaults. Only then will it be time to make peace."

Kishi knew further argument was useless. And he was hampered by the fact that he himself believed Japan could extend its control even further in Asia and the Pacific. Perhaps Tojo was right. After several more defeats, the Allies might agree to Japanese peace terms. But Kishi could not remove from his mind the unavoidable conclusion that Japan was unnecessarily taking a chance.

This reservation changed into a definite uneasiness during the summer of 1942, when Japan suffered its first major defeat of the war in a naval battle off Midway Island. Japanese carriers and battleships had confidently steamed toward the island to complete the destruction of the United States Pacific Fleet. When the battle was over, the Japanese armada had retreated—minus four first-line aircraft carriers. Pearl Harbor had, in a sense, been undone in a single blow. Japan's precious margin of naval superiority had been destroyed.

Kishi was, however, relieved to learn that Tojo had decided to shift his approach to China as the war began to take an unfavorable turn. A few months before, the Army had planned to abandon its "holding position" in China and mount a major offensive against Chungking, the capital of Chiang Kai-shek's Free China. But with the reverses in the Pacific resulting in the withdrawal of Japanese troops from China for reassignment to critical areas, the assault was canceled. Instead, a "new China policy" was formulated, which Kishi fully supported. This new policy, at least on paper, called for the treatment of occupied China on a "basis of equality," political and economic. It was hoped that this would either win over Chiang or weaken his support, and pave the way for a loosening of control over other captive Asian nations. The Japanese had no intention of replacing their concept of hierarchy with true equality in the relationship between Japan and its neighbors, but they were prepared to offer important concessions to the nationalist aspirations of the people of this vast area.

While Kishi strongly favored this policy, he had in mind a different objective than did Tojo and his fellow militarists. The generals saw the collaboration of the conquered peoples as a factor that would give Japan the impetus it needed to finish off the Allies in the Pacific, but Kishi hoped that a liberal attitude toward these peoples would facilitate an early negotiated peace. If the Japanese could turn their fellow Asians into real allies, which, after all, was Japan's ultimate aim in any event, the United

States and Britain would soon realize the hopelessness of their military position and possibly the hollowness of their "moral" objections to the Japanese plan for a united and prosperous Asia. It is perhaps difficult for an American to understand that the Japanese, even though they were the aggressors in Asia, believed that the Asian nations would support them in a war against Great Britain and the United States. Events in China and Southeast Asia have since proved that there was, even during the war years, a strong dislike for the Western nations. But the Japanese did not realize, at least immediately, that they, too, were disliked, even hated, by their fellow Asians.

Kishi was highly pleased when, in January, 1943, Tojo inaugurated the new policy with the reversion of Japanese concessions in China to the puppet Nanking government. And he listened approvingly as Tojo told a group of industrialists that Japanese businessmen "should cease to entrench themselves behind a bulwark of special rights and interests" and "should work with the Chinese on a basis of equality." Kishi recognized this as a disguised promise to Chiang Kai-shek that if he came over to Japan's side, China would not be treated as an inferior. But if Tojo was seemingly prepared to compromise his hierarchal principles, Chiang Kai-shek had no intention of compromising his own nationalist aims, especially now that the winds of war were beginning to shift direction.

Chiang's stubbornness was further reinforced by the declaration issued in December, 1942, at the Cairo Conference, where the Chinese leader had talked with Roosevelt and Churchill. It was decided at this meeting that Japan, after its defeat, would be stripped not only of all territories it had seized since 1931, but also of Formosa, the Pescadores, Korea, and the former German islands in the Pacific. This was intended, Kishi and most of his colleagues figured, more as propaganda to keep Chiang Kai-shek happy than as a genuine statement of war aims. Even so, with China now looking forward to the return of its former possessions, particularly Manchuria and Formosa, the attractiveness of Japan's "new China policy," it was clear, had been considerably reduced.

Nor did the establishment by Tojo of a Greater East Asia Ministry that was supposed to give "special consideration" to Southeast Asian interests have much success, Kishi observed. The Ministry's main job was to coordinate, under military supervision, the economic exploitation of the conquered areas on a basis of "reciprocal co-operation." It also promoted carefully controlled "independence" movements in these former European colonies in an effort to make the Japanese conquerors look like liberators. The Ministry urged the subject nations to reject "Western materialism" and embrace a "superior order of culture," which meant, in undisguised terms, the old hierarchal principle.

But these propaganda efforts, which might under other circumstances have had an important effect, were more than offset by the behavior of the Japanese soldiers occupying these nations. Treated with brutality and contempt by their officers, who thought nothing of cursing, slapping, or beating them, and enraged, in turn, by the incomprehensible lack of humility displayed by their "younger brothers," the troops reacted, as after the fall of Nanking, with unbridled savagery. Ironically, Tojo's ideological aims in Asia were defeated largely by the policies of his most reliable pillar of support—the Imperial Army.

But if this failure on the Asian political front was a serious obstacle to the war effort, even graver was the state of Japan's faltering economy, which Kishi found almost impossible to gear to the rising military needs. Early in the war, the economy had been relatively healthy. Japan's armed forces had been able to draw on stocks of munitions and surplus shipping tonnage accumulated in prewar years. Added to this was the loot obtained from conquered nations. But by late 1942, as a result of the Midway disaster, the hard fighting in the Solomons, and the destruction of merchant shipping by Allied submarines, these stocks were seriously depleted. When the services began demanding more ships, planes, equipment, and munitions, industry was unable to meet these demands.

Kishi, trying to remedy this situation, found himself up against an impenetrable barrier of economic disunity, created by the lack of centralized responsibility for the planning and execution of industrial mobilization. The Cabinet Planning Board was supposed to co-ordinate the government's economic policies, but lacked the executive powers necessary to carry out this function. The Prime Minister had trouble persuading the ministries, each of them jealous of its jurisdictional prerogatives, to implement his economic directives, even after getting a special act passed empowering him to force them to obey. The ministries were unable to control the *Zaibatsu,* which still tended to ignore all orders that threatened to reduce their profits. The situation was further complicated by bitter competition on the part of the Army and Navy for priority allocations of most war goods, a struggle that was reflected in strife between the various sectors in which war was being waged. The South Pacific, the Central Pacific, and the China fronts all competed strenuously for the available supplies.

Kishi concentrated on trying to win the co-operation of the *Zaibatsu.* An important step toward industrial consolidation had been taken shortly before Tojo came to power, but on *Zaibatsu* terms. The trusts had formed into massive cartels called Control Associations, each ostensibly embracing a whole industry, which were supposed to be responsible to the Ministry of Commerce and Industry. But in reality an association consisted of only the leading *Zaibatsu* in a particular field (the president of the biggest combine was automatically director), and operated on an almost completely autonomous basis. Controlling the procurement of materials, funds, and labor, these associations were able to prevent the enforcement of any general system of priorities and thereby to devour the smaller, "less efficient" firms that were deprived of the benefits of cartel membership. The *Zaibatsu,* while theoretically operating under government direction, actually dominated all industry through the associations for their own profitable purposes.

Kishi was not opposed to the principle of the Control Association. He was in favor of all forms of industrial consolidation, certain, as he had always been, that efficiency depended to a preponderant degree on the extent to which the big companies could be made bigger and the small firms, fewer. Only through such a process, he thought, could production and distribution systems be improved, and workers, who were in extremely short supply because of military conscription, be used where they were most needed.

In March, 1942, Kishi reported at a meeting of prefectural governors in Tokyo, "Progress is being made with the movement for amalgamation of smaller manufacturers and traders, which is necessary in order to rationalize industry and improve the production and distribution of various materials, and the number of surplus workers resulting from amalgamation will be transferred to industries important for national defense." Shortly afterward, he told a reporter, "Manufacturers without whom the nation could do very well must be reduced in number so that labor can be diverted to other undertakings, where the shortage of manpower is keenly felt."

But while Kishi encouraged the Control Associations, he felt that they had to be placed under government control. Japan could no longer afford an industrial policy of "profits as usual." Determined to press the issue before the nation's economic chaos seriously affected military operations, Kishi encouraged Tojo to obtain from the puppet Diet virtual dictatorial powers over the national economy. The *Zaibatsu* bitterly resisted this threat, reminding the government in no uncertain terms that the war could not be fought except for their production efforts. The government was finally forced to compromise. The Diet, the

Zaibatsu leaders agreed, could grant Tojo supreme authority over the vital industries of iron and steel, coal, light metals, shipping, and aircraft. But in return, seven *Zaibatsu* representatives would be attached to the cabinet in an official advisory capacity with power equivalent to that of a minister without portfolio.

A cabinet adviser's council was appointed in March, 1943, which, according to a government announcement, would "participate in the Premier's conduct of administrative affairs with regard to expansion of wartime production and execution of the wartime economy of the nation." Industry joined the military on the highest level of government leadership. This was a major victory for industry, and was to prove a major defeat for the military. The need to consult with the advisory council completely hamstrung Tojo's efforts to use his new powers for the fulfillment of his, and Kishi's, goal. The opposite effect was actually achieved, with industry increasing its influence over the government. The *Zaibatsu* now could even claim official sanction of its profit-motivated policies.

With economic disorder spreading, complicated by a growing food shortage as farms were shorn of peasants inducted into the military services or into the factories, even the controlled newspapers, Kishi noted, began to complain, if in subtle, understated terms. One paper charged that the government "had not yet made participation in the production effort 100 per cent effective in the nation." Another claimed that while most of the people were suffering from the food shortage, some were earning "extremely large incomes" from war production. Still another said that the government's demands for a more intensified effort had been "very frequently handicapped by the individualistic character of Japan's economic structure . . . and by the resultant competition."

Kishi, no less than the newspapers, realized that his effort to win control of the combines through the concentration of powers in the Prime Minister had failed. He desperately juggled other ideas in his mind, and began drawing up a plan that contained the germs of nearly all of them—a drastic, far-reaching program of industrial reorganization, which, Kishi confidently believed, would have more chance of success than any other measures he had yet proposed. He slaved away day and night on this program, conferring with Tojo, other cabinet members, and fellow economic experts. He was working against time. The nation was in grave danger of losing the war as the result of material shortages.

Kishi offered his first public hint that revolutionary control measures were being worked out in a speech delivered to the Diet in June, 1943, causing a sensation in apprehensive *Zaibatsu* circles. In November, 1943, with the Army and Navy crying for more planes, ships, and equipment, Kishi's plan was announced. His own Ministry of Commerce and Industry, three other ministries, and the Cabinet Planning Board were abolished, and under a Munitions Company Act, a new, powerful Munitions Ministry, which absorbed the bureaus in Kishi's ministry that dealt with heavy industry, was created. The bureaus concerned with consumer goods were transferred to the Ministry of Agriculture, which now became the Ministry of Agriculture and Commerce. Tojo became Minister of Munitions, but Kishi, with the dual titles of Vice-Minister of Munitions and Minister without Portfolio, was given practical control of the new ministry. An official radio broadcast explained that Tojo "would not actually exercise any supervisory powers over Vice-Minister Kishi."

The ministry, Kishi told the press, would mobilize all the resources of Japan for prosecution of the war and control the allocation of raw materials, concentrating in particular on aircraft production. Designated private companies specializing in various phases of war production were to become "munitions companies." The government would determine production schedules and issue orders relating to acquisition, storage, movement of basic materials, improvement of techniques, labor, and other matters. The government could also restrict the designated companies from engaging in other than prescribed operations, control the use of funds, and order amalgamation or dissolution.

In order to encourage companies to accept these obligations, they would be granted special privileges. The government would grant them priorities in the acquisition of materials, capital, and labor, and would guarantee profits, give subsidies, and indemnify losses. Under this compromise plan, Kishi hopefully indicated, maximum industrial unification could be achieved, and the *Zaibatsu* would be guaranteed sufficient benefits to make governmental control worthwhile for them.

The trusts initially balked at the plan, which quite obviously could not work without their co-operation. They were fearful lest the new Ministry of Munitions try to usurp the power of the Control Associations to which they belonged and force them to accept diminished profits. Kishi, in his most persuasive manner, told the industrial leaders that "conditions have greatly changed between the time the Control Associations were established and the present. In particular, we must change

184 KISHI AND JAPAN

our ideas in the light of the enforcement of the Munitions Company Act. The aim of the Control Associations is to utilize fully the knowledge and experience of industry, and, in unity with the government, work for increased production. The mission of the Control Associations has now taken on greater importance, and must not be reduced. . . . The government holds the foregoing view."

Reassured, the industrial leaders concluded that perhaps the Munitions Company Act would be acceptable after all. The Associations themselves had never been able, or willing, to enforce priority controls, so maybe it was just as well to leave this difficult job to the government, which was ready to offer them so many advantages in return for their co-operation. Moreover, the industrial advisers in the cabinet had approved the Act and could always pressure the government to rescind any order that might prove unsatisfactory to the *Zaibatsu*. One of the advisers, Ginjiro Fujiwara, had become a Minister without Portfolio directly under Kishi, thus offering added assurance that the *Zaibatsu* interests would not be ignored. The trusts had come a long way since prewar days when Kishi, Tojo, Hoshino, and company had refused to let the traditional *Zaibatsu* get a foothold in Manchoukuo. And their power was gradually increasing; they were strong enough to be able to gamble on Kishi's plan.

Kishi himself was acceptable as an economic czar to both sides. Industry was impressed with his promise that the "mission of the Control Association . . . must not be reduced," while Tojo admired his determination to unify industry and increase war production at any cost. But Kishi soon learned that it was no easy matter keeping everybody satisfied. He found himself caught in a whirlpool of conflicting interests. He was plagued on one side by the attitudes of the Army and Navy, which, in their frantic race for military supplies, were reluctant to co-operate with the Munitions Ministry. They flatly turned down Kishi's plea that they contribute to the common pool the manufacturing plants and stocks of raw materials they maintained for themselves to supplement what they obtained from the "untrustworthy" *Zaibatsu*. Nor would they permit the ministry to review and adjust their needs to the over-all national production capacity.

Furthermore, Kishi was confronted with the refusal of the *Zaibatsu* to invest in enterprises that were not highly profitable, however important they were to the war effort. Thus, he had to burden the government with the direct management of mines producing rare metals, such as tungsten and molybodenum, because industry could not see a "future" in such ventures. The *Zaibatsu* claimed, for their part, that price controls rendered production in many fields impossible, forcing them to divert a portion of their output to the black market as the only means of breaking even. And they also railed against other regulations, which, they said, reduced rather than increased efficiency.

Kishi sympathized with many of the *Zaibatsu* complaints, but he was frustrated in his efforts to meet them by Tojo's constant interference, despite the Prime Minister's promise to give him a free hand in the implementation of the new economic program. Tojo, grossly exaggerating the regulatory provisions of the Munitions Company Act, insisted that military supervisors be stationed in all factories under the Munitions Ministry's jurisdiction. These supervisors could issue directives, even though they had little or no knowledge of industry. Typical of the results, Kishi angrily observed, was the use of untrained engineers and inferior quality materials in the manufacture of such new electronic products as radar, which was so vital to Japan's defense. "Industry," Kishi told his friend, Nakayasu, "must be placed under less pressure if it is to produce efficiently. What do those soldiers know about what materials, and how much of each, must go into the construction of a particular item?"

To this problem was added a lack of unity even within the Munitions Ministry itself. Fujiwara, the *Zaibatsu* representative, was in charge of iron and steel, while other officials headed land transportation and shipping, each of them operating his department independently despite their mutual dependence on each other.

This industrial chaos* meant continued haphazard war production and material allocation, and these conditions were aggravated by the tremendous toll which Allied submarines took on raw material shipments from Southeast Asia. The submarine attacks resulted not merely in the loss of cargoes, but in a shortage of cargo vessels.

Kishi found himself on the horns of a frightening dilemma. Badly as the new program was progressing, he thought, his experience and persuasive abilities might still be of some use in promoting economic unity.

* Later, when he had left the government, Kishi described to a reporter of the *Mainichi Shimbun* some of the difficulties he had faced in his position as economic czar:

"It often takes two or three months for the Munitions Ministry to reach a decision on an important matter. Then the decision must be discussed at a meeting of the cabinet, which, in turn, issues an order to be executed at various government and industrial levels. Thus, it may take half a year before the decision goes into effect. Even a wise decision is sometimes worthless by the time it is executed, for the situation by then has changed."

He realized that complete failure of his plan could spell military defeat for Japan, a possibility, however dreadful, that had to be considered. But was it fair to Japan, or to himself, to continue trying to perform so vital a job after a reasonable effort had proved fruitless? Perhaps someone else with a fresh approach might succeed where he failed. The decision was a difficult one, for, with Japan's very life at stake, there was little margin left now for an administrative error. He finally concluded that he should resign. Perhaps Fujiwara, as a *Zaibatsu* official himself, might be able to handle the deteriorating situation. At least a new man would be able, with a clear conscience, to make recommendations to achieve the industrial efficiency so desperately needed. Kishi had exhausted his own resources. He had become trapped between the military and the *Zaibatsu,* trying to make a compromise between two groups that would not compromise.

His mind made up, Kishi went to Tojo's office and offered his resignation, suggesting that Fujiwara replace him. The General replied dryly, almost in the tone of a rebuke, "Do you mean that you intend to give up your job when it is only half-done? Do not forget that you are obligated to His Majesty to do your best. You cannot back down now. You must stay with me until the war is won."

Kishi had not expected such strong resistance. He had already done his best and had failed—in no small measure because Tojo himself had obstructed his work. Still, Tojo had entrusted him with more responsibility than he had allowed most of the cabinet ministers. And it would be difficult, even unethical, to oppose the wishes of the man who had, after all, promoted his career. But even more important was Kishi's debt to the Emperor. Perhaps he had not quite done his best yet. After considering all these factors, Kishi told Tojo that he would withdraw his resignation, and, with grave uncertainty, returned to the chaos of his economic battlefield.

This battlefield became the scene of increasingly bitter struggles among government administrators, industrialists, generals, and admirals as news from the military fronts grew worse. Each of these groups blamed the others for the lack of a co-ordinated war effort. The *Zaibatsu* leaders, convinced their companies were being strangled by ever-tightening government controls, began to sabotage war production, not necessarily refusing to produce goods, but not hurrying either. They seldom even tried to meet the time schedules set by government or military authorities. The Army and Navy, violently condemning these "unpatriotic" tactics, dealt less and less with the cartels as they tried to produce almost all their own needs, although they still had to depend on the combines for aircraft.

Competition between the two services for war output reached such absurd lengths that the Army decided to build its own submarines for transporting troops rather than entrust this naval job to the Navy, refusing even to accept technical advice.

Kishi, meanwhile, stood helplessly by while Tojo, on the one hand, continued, in his desperation, to intensify regulation of industry as the military situation worsened, and on the other, proved incapable of controlling the policies of the two quarreling services. Tojo finally succeeded in reinforcing his control over the Army when, in February, 1944, he added the post of Chief of Army Staff to his positions of Prime Minister, War Minister, and Munitions Minister. But the Navy remained practically free of his authority, even though he selected as the Navy Chief of Staff an ardent follower of his, Admiral Shimada, who remained concurrently as Navy Minister. This only increased the difficulties, since most of the admirals resented the appointment of a man whom they considered a puppet of the Army.

Japan's whole war effort began to crumble under the massive external and internal pressures that were rapidly building up. Kishi could see the effect in human terms when he visited the factories. Productivity had been relatively high when the war began, with the workers full of enthusiasm. They had been well clothed and had had plenty of rice, beans, and other staple foods. Though many of them had earned much more money in prewar jobs (they had been conscripted for war work at "soldier's pay" —1.60 yen (forty cents daily for men and one yen (twenty-five cents) daily for women), they had looked forward to victory in war and the era of prosperity that would follow the end of the conflict.

But now, Kishi saw, morale could hardly have been lower. He felt a surge of pity for the workers—mostly young schoolboys and girls—as he watched them on assembly lines, turning out airplane parts, bombs, or grenades, gaunt in appearance, perfunctory and listless in their work. Their eyes, it seemed to Kishi, might have belonged to the dead. These children were working twelve and sixteen-hour shifts, and with food scarce, they were eating mainly a watery soup containing shreds of eggplant. Most of them didn't even have shoes. Under such conditions, it was little wonder that productivity was so low and the accident rate high.

How long could this go on? Kishi asked himself. How many men would have to die, how low would Japan's production have to get, how close to starvation would the nation have to be before some effort would be made to end the war? It was now the spring of 1944. The war had been in progress for almost two and a half years. He recalled how he had calculated before the conflict broke out that Japan could not effectively carry on a major war for more than two years. That deadline was already past. American production strength was reaching its peak, while Japan's was swiftly weakening. Tojo had made a fatal mistake not to offer peace terms to the Allies when the Japanese had been riding high early in the war.

But Tojo still thought that Japan could win permanent control of all that it had gained by inflicting a decisive defeat on the Allied forces. He still believed that American naval forces would overextend themselves, operating too far from their home bases, and that the Japanese could inflict on them enormous and irreparable losses before they came within striking distance of Japan itself. But Kishi was beginning to believe what the Allies had announced at the Cairo Conference—that they would accept only "unconditional surrender"—and if this was their aim, they would inevitably be able to accomplish it if they were willing to continue fighting long enough. Because the day would come when Japanese war production would simply grind to a halt.

Japan, as Kishi now saw it, had one last chance to achieve a peace that might permit it to keep something of what it had gained. The Americans would soon launch an assault on the island of Saipan at the outer edge of Japan's "final" defense perimeter. If Saipan fell, B-29 Superfortresses would be within range of Japan itself, permitting the wholesale destruction of factories and cities. Continued fighting under these conditions would be equivalent to national suicide. But if the enemy failed to take Saipan, rather than face a prolonged war he might settle for peace terms acceptable to Japan.

Tojo, he knew, would not take this view. He would probably prefer to drag all Japan into oblivion rather than surrender. Kishi felt, however, that it was his duty to try to impress the facts of the situation on Tojo. The General would be furious, and might even have him arrested by the *Kempei Tai,* the "legal authority" to which Tojo was entrusting more and more power. Kishi decided that he would have to risk this, if only because no one else close to Tojo would. Tojo had no reliable political advisers. Furthermore, Kishi was equipped, as few other officials were, with the cold economic facts and statistics to back up his argument. It was up to him, Kishi concluded, to persuade Tojo to make a major military stand on Saipan, and seek peace if the battle was lost.

Kishi went to see Tojo. He pleaded for a relaxation of controls on industry as a means of alleviating the situation to some extent. "It is clear that our production will never reach maximum efficiency. But a loosening of regulations may at least remove some of the causes of the present lack of co-operation." But even such concessions, he made it clear, would have little value at this stage of the war unless Japan won the battle of Saipan. "If that battle is lost," he said, "Japan will be wide open to bombing attacks and the nation's factories will be the first targets. Production of any kind will soon be impossible. Therefore, it is evident that a defeat at Saipan will constitute the final blow that Japan can afford to take. Let us try to win at Saipan, but if we are defeated, then we should explore the possibilities of peace."

Tojo thrummed his fingers on his desk. In a calm voice, he replied that there was little possibility of Japan losing Saipan. "We have never been more prepared for a battle. Some of the best troops we have in Manchoukuo have been transferred there. And the Navy is fully prepared to take on the American fleet." Pausing for a moment, he added testily, "In any event, your field is the war economy. Don't poke your nose in the business of the Supreme Command."

Kishi answered without hesitation, "This is not the time to quibble over areas of responsibility. The time has come when we must face the grave question of our country's destiny. I am therefore advising you in my capacity as Vice-Minister of Munitions. It is, indeed, my responsibility to do so. If I am at fault, it is in not having spoken more directly before this."

Kishi got up from his chair, bowed, and walked out.

Several days later, Kishi learned that the Americans had landed on the beaches of Saipan.

CHAPTER X

THE SPIDER AND THE WEB

THE INVASION OF SAIPAN was cynically presented to the public by the Supreme Command as part of a well-calculated program to "trap" the American forces, which would sustain greater losses than the Japanese even, it was implied, if all of the defenders were killed. The Army and Navy tried no less strenuously to withhold the true story of the invasion from the cabinet, arguing that they were directly responsible only to the Emperor. Tojo, in his triple capacity as Prime Minister, War Minister, and Army Chief of Staff, was admitted to Imperial consultations, but the two military organs delivered distorted reports even at these conferences. What Tojo did hear, he was himself reluctant to let his colleagues, or the public, know, for widespread knowledge of the Saipan disaster could have gravely threatened his regime.

Kishi and other government leaders, however, gradually learned details of the calamity from Marquis Kido, who was present at the Imperial consultations, and from military informers who opposed Tojo's rule. And the more the cabinet learned, the greater was the resolution of some of its members, particularly Kishi and Foreign Minister Mamoru Shigemitsu, to get rid of the General as a move toward a negotiated peace. After conferring with influential contacts in all branches of the government, Kishi ascertained that a veritable web of intrigue against Tojo had evolved outside the cabinet, embracing naval leaders, Elder Statesmen, Diet members, and most important of all, Kido. The Marquis, reasoning that an imperfect peace, possibly permitting Japan to keep what it had at the time of Pearl Harbor, was now essential, had his finger in every plot.

The Army and Navy were loath to release the full story of Saipan for more than the conventional reason that it was necessary to keep up public morale. They were afraid and ashamed to admit the fact that, far from proceeding "according to plan," they had made a catastrophic strategic miscalculation based on faulty intelligence. Anticipating an initial attack on Palau Island, the Supreme Command had transferred the main Japanese fleet and land-based air forces to this stronghold in the hope of knocking out the United States Navy with one gigantic blow. As a result, Japan had few ships and planes in the vicinity of Saipan when the American attack was launched, and they were either destroyed or forced to retreat, leaving the Japanese garrison on the island at the mercy of United States naval and air bombardment and marine infantry assaults. The anti-Tojo sentiment that burgeoned after this disaster was by no means softened by the news that sifted through a few days later that the Japanese Combined Fleet, rushing to protect Saipan, had been defeated in the Philippine Sea in a momentous clash with the American navy.

Kishi's worst fears had materialized. The defense line beyond which Japanese forces could not retreat had been broken. B-29's were now within range of the heart of Japan. Tokyo and the other major cities lay helpless before the onslaught of enemy air power. The only conceivable answer was surrender, a limited one if possible. Kishi believed that surrender did not have to mean an end to the Japanese dreams of empire. After all, had not his forefathers survived the defeat at Shimonoseki only to grow stronger from the lesson they had learned?

Fortunately, Kishi thought, he was not alone in wanting to get rid of Tojo. Anti-Tojo sentiment was growing in the military ranks, in circles close to the Emperor, in the Diet, and among the people, who were beginning to ask if "planned" defeats were really victories. Not all of these critics wanted peace; some simply believed that another leader might better prosecute the war.

The press boldly began taking the government to task for its failure to co-ordinate a total war effort. Kishi was startled to read one newspaper report of a meeting held by editors, leaders of the Imperial Rule Assistance Political Association, and former Diet members, which quoted one speaker as saying, "I think there are various ways to arouse the Japanese people, but the most important one is freedom of speech. In the past few years, the people have not been able to say frankly what they think. . . . We can never develop the total power of the people in this way."

But Kishi knew it was too late. Even the "total power of the people" would not be enough now in the face of the Allied juggernaut moving toward Japan. "Tojo has to go," Kishi told his brother, Ichiro. "The situation is hopeless. We have few planes to defend Japan against enemy air attacks, and hardly enough fuel to use these. And after the first wave of major attacks, we will not even have factories in which to build planes."

Meanwhile, the anti-Tojo conspiracy gathered momentum as the realization that the nation was no longer able to defend itself against enemy attack crystallized into growing panic with the first bombings of industrial targets in southern Japan. One of the focal points in this intrigue was the Navy, which had never fully agreed with the Army's "reckless" aggressive policies. It blamed the Saipan and Philippine Sea disasters on Tojo's refusal to give the Navy more air support, and started a whispering campaign against his assistant, Admiral Shimada, who had told other naval officials, "Let's not exaggerate the situation. Saipan is, after all, only another island. Its loss is not critical."

Another leading force in the anti-Tojo plot was the *Jushin,* or council of Elder Statesmen, consisting of former prime ministers and court officials. The influence of the *Jushin* on state policy was comparable to the power that the elders in a family or a village exercised as a matter of right within the Japanese social hierarchy. This influence was wielded through the Emperor—via the Lord Keeper of the Privy Seal, Marquis Kido—who, by tradition, seldom resisted the advice of the *Jushin,* even if it were opposed to that of the government. And this Imperial support was now doubly guaranteed by the fact that Kido, who exerted an even more direct influence on the Emperor, had become a strong anti-Tojoite. Further unity resulted from the fact that some of the leading Elder Statesmen were admirals, which facilitated close co-operation between the Navy and the *Jushin.*

The conspiracy to overthrow Tojo had begun more than a year before, in February, 1943, when Prince Konoye secretly called on Kido and argued that the war be brought to an end while Japan still held a strong bargaining position. In March, Kido, convinced that Konoye was right, expressed this view to the Emperor, who agreed with him. From then on, the *Jushin,* which, in addition to Konoye, included Baron Kiichiro Hiranuma, Admiral Keisuke Okada, and Baron Reijiro Wakatsuki, met secretly at frequent intervals to discuss means of overthrowing Tojo and seeking peace without provoking a bloody military *coup d'état.*

They developed contacts within the government with people like Hisatsune Sakomizu, Okada's son-in-law, who, as a member of the Cabinet Planning Board, was able to keep them well informed regarding Tojo's plans. But they achieved their most important preliminary goal when the former Ambassador to Nanking, Mamoru Shigemitsu, who also wanted peace, replaced Masayuki Tani as Foreign Minister. In May, the *Jushin* approached Prince Takamatsu, a younger brother of the Emperor, and found him willing to head a "peace" government, which, it was hoped, would be accepted by the Army in view of the fact that he was a prince. However, no one was yet ready to test the mood of the Army, particularly of the fanatical Young Officers' group, which was determined that Japan would never surrender. Sharp in the memories of the "peace-makers" was the Young Officers' revolt of 1936 which claimed the lives of so many government leaders. Both Okada and Hiranuma had barely escaped assassination in that uprising.

In the early days of the conspiracy, the *Jushin* and Kido hoped that Japan might still emerge from the war in control of its prewar territories —settling for the independence of the Southeast Asian nations that Japan had occupied. But they were, after Saipan, prepared to make far greater concessions, and their determination to force Tojo out was growing.

Tojo felt the political rope tightening around his throat, but he bitterly and tenaciously clung to power. After the Philippine Sea debacle, the General, anticipating the increased pressure that would be exerted on him, called on Kido and told him in an almost mocking manner that he would resign if a "suitable successor is available." Simultaneously, he encouraged the spreading of new rumors that his departure would mean the spilling of considerable blood. To back up these rumors, the *Kempei Tai* became more active than ever, keeping constant surveillance on everyone suspected of opposition to Tojo, including Kishi, who was never out of the sight of an agent standing across the street or leaning against the stone wall surrounding his house.

Still, the plotting went on. Okada, who hoped to replace Tojo as Prime Minister, smuggled a message through a trusted messenger to Admirals Mitsumasa Yonai and Nobumasa Suetsugu, offering the post of Navy Minister to the former and that of Navy Chief of Staff to the latter, in a new government headed by himself. Although they expressed interest, the two men were reluctant to work with each other due to a deep personal antagonism between them. Finally, an anti-Tojo businessman and naval adviser, Aiichiro Fujiyama,* arranged for a secret meeting of Okada, Yonai, and Suetsugu in his house, and over a bottle of sake, all pledged to work together for Tojo's fall. Okada then met with Hiranuma and they

* Foreign Minister in the Kishi cabinet.

agreed that the *Jushin* should sign a memorandum asking the Emperor to dismiss Tojo. But as rumors of a military coup that would "bathe Tokyo in blood" grew stronger, the will-power of the plotters grew weaker. Their plan hung in suspension.

They decided finally to strike at Tojo from within the cabinet itself. Fujiyama told me that he asked Keita Goto, the Minister of Transportation, to "precipitate some crisis in the government that would force the resignation of the cabinet." But Goto refused. Fujiyama then approached Kishi, who agreed to co-operate despite the risks involved.

At an emergency cabinet meeting, Kishi got up, looked directly at Tojo, and said in a determined voice, "This cabinet must take full responsibility for the conduct of the war."

The implication was clear that the Tojo government, having failed to lead a successful war effort, was duty-bound to resign. Kishi noted with satisfaction the approving looks of some of his colleagues around the conference table, who were pleased that he had assumed the dangerous responsibility of expressing what was in their minds.

"We owe it to His Imperial Majesty and the future of Japan to determine how well we are fulfilling that responsibility."

Tojo now unreservedly regarded Kishi as his enemy. "If the Minister has finished his statement," he replied, "we will continue with the business at hand."

That ended that. Kishi knew better than to continue. Though he felt comforted by the fact that he had given impetus to the movement to depose Tojo by bringing it into the open for the first time, he had also left himself open to arrest, or even assassination.

Tojo hoped that terror would hold his enemies off until he could reconstruct his cabinet on a broader basis, permitting him to remain in power. Unaware that Yonai had already agreed to join a new cabinet, he planned to relieve the pressure of the Navy and the *Jushin* on himself by inviting the Admiral to serve in his government. To counter-balance this selection and keep the Army happy, he planned to add to his cabinet General Nobuyuki Abe, whom he knew supported him. Tojo intended also to bring into the government a member of the Imperial Rule Assistance Political Association to quiet rumblings in the Diet. He would force the resignation of Admiral Shimada, in whom the Navy had no faith, from his twin positions as Navy Minister and Navy Chief of Staff. But before any of these moves could work, Tojo felt, he had to get rid of Kishi, who was now openly trying to overthrow him. Kishi's resignation would not only rid him of a dangerous thorn in his side, but give him a scapegoat on whom to blame the shortages of aircraft, fuel, and other supplies.

As the last Japanese defenders on Saipan fell, Tojo, anxious to implement his plan before this news became public knowledge, sent Hoshino to ask Kishi for his immediate resignation. Kishi was stunned by the suddenness of this demand. "I will think it over and speak with Tojo myself," he replied politely, but with some agitation. When Hoshino had departed, he telephoned Marquis Kido and asked to see him the following day.

The next morning, Kishi arrived at Kido's house as the Marquis was feeding his dogs—several chows and police dogs, each locked in separate cages against the front wall of the sprawling wooden structure. Tumultous barking drowned out the words of greeting between Kido and his guest.

"In these hard times," Kishi said, with a flicker of a smile, "it's a wonder you can feed the dogs."

"Soon," replied Kido, scratching his gray mustache, "we may have to eat the dogs."

The two men entered the house and sat in their stocking feet on embroidered cushions. "You perhaps know why I am here," said Kishi.

"I have a suspicion."

Of course Kido knew, thought Kishi. Kido knew everything. No policy, plan, or plot could succeed without his support, for he was the eyes and ears, and even the brain, of the Emperor. Everybody had to confide in him—the military, the businessmen, the Elder Statesmen—before they could start grinding their axes. Kishi felt at ease with the Marquis. After all, he had worked under him in the early period of his career, and they had spent many evenings together discussing books when they both belonged to the book-reading group of the Ministry of Commerce and Industry in the middle 1920's. He felt he could deal with the situation directly.

"The Prime Minister has asked for my resignation," Kishi said. "I would appreciate your counsel."

"Tojo," Kido replied, "hopes to prolong the cabinet by changing its complexion. But there is a strong tendency among the *Jushin* to favor dissolution. We cannot overlook the opinion of the *Jushin,* or of the public. Moreover, your resignation would probably not save Tojo's cabinet, for I have reason to believe that Admiral Yonai will not accept the General's invitation to join it. And, if this is true, the Prime Minister may not be able to withstand the pressure on him to resign. So, if I were you, I would be hesitant to resign, at least until it is clear how the other proposed cabinet changes work out."

With a serious, troubled expression, Kishi said, "But Kido-san, Tojo is my superior. He is responsible for bringing me into the cabinet in the first place. Is it proper that I defy him?"

Kido looked at Kishi with eyes that, characteristically, seemed to tell more than his words. "Do not forget that though the Prime Minister may advise on cabinet choices, every minister is appointed by His Majesty. However, it is for you, of course, to use your own judgment."

Kishi left, his mind still not made up.

That evening, when he arrived home, he changed from his Western clothes into a comfortable *yukata* (an informal kimono) and, while Yoshiko prepared dinner, went out on the veranda overlooking his walled-in garden. He sank into a low bamboo chair, savoring the magnificent isolation, breathing in, as if gasping for life, the sweet, yet earthy, night air. In the moonlight, he could see the shadowy outline of his dwarfed fir trees, his camellias, with the petals shining like luminous cotton. This was a good place to consider one's problems.

Tojo, by recommending his appointment, had been his benefactor. But the General had done himself a favor as well, for he had needed him, thus, in a sense, canceling the *giri*. At the same time, Kishi asked himself, was not his primary obligation to the Emperor? And had Kido not made it clear that the Emperor would be reluctant to see him resign? Yet it was no easy matter flatly opposing the will of the Prime Minister, who would regard such action as a basic breech of ethics. And there was another consideration, too. Tojo's honor was at stake, for his overthrow at this moment of military retreat would mean for him a grave personal loss of "face," and to avoid this he might stoop to any desperate means. Many officials, military and otherwise, had already been exiled to distant military posts or sent off into front-line positions to certain death.

Only a few months before, the fascist leader, Seigo Nakano, had been "persuaded" by the *Kempei Tai* to commit *hara-kiri*. The *Kempei Tai* had many devices by which it "persuaded"—the small, damp cell in which one could never stand straight, the red-hot poker brands on the forehead, the constant beatings, the thin rope tightened around the neck. . . .

But the personal danger seemed almost remote and inconsequential in the face of the danger that threatened Japan. Tojo was ready to have the nation commit mass *hara-kiri* rather than seek peace with the enemy. Some of his officers were even talking about arming the whole civilian population with bamboo spears in a last frantic effort to fight off the American forces that would inevitably be landing in Japan. They were already spreading the slogan: "A Hundred Million Die Together." But why should the whole country die to save the "face" of its bungling leader? Why should the Emperor have to perish because of the folly of his advisers? The Emperor constituted the spiritual roots of Japan. As long as he remained, the Japanese as a people remained, and victory could one day be salvaged from defeat.

The following day, Kishi called for an appointment with Tojo and went to see him at his official residence, outwardly calm, but uneasy at the thought of the ordeal that lay ahead. He entered the Prime Minister's office and bowed to the straight, sturdy uniformed figure behind the desk. Tojo rose, returned the bow and walked up to greet Kishi, showing him to a cushioned easy chair near the door, then sitting down opposite him on the other side of a little tea table.

"Kishi-san," Tojo started brusquely, "I trust you received my request for your resignation?"

"Yes, I did," replied Kishi. "But before I give you an answer, permit me to ask how you plan to reorganize the cabinet so that you can stay in power?"

"I'm not disposed to answer that right now," Tojo replied haughtily.

Kishi bore in. "It is my understanding that you hope to strengthen the cabinet by including in it Admiral Yonai and General Abe. If you should fail to obtain the services of one or both of these men, would the cabinet then resign *en bloc?*"

"It's not for you to ask questions. I'm a soldier, and when I'm given an order by a superior I obey it unreservedly. That is what you must do."

Kishi said, "I am not a soldier. I am not familiar with military strategy. But I know that in the political sphere, one must consider the results of one's actions before one acts, or the common goal will not be attained. The whole cabinet is responsible for starting the war. We are all responsible for the way the war is going. So if one of us falls, we must all fall. Did you yourself not say when I once tried to resign that I was shirking my responsibility?"

"That has nothing to do with the present!" replied Tojo.

But Kishi shook his head negatively. "I have decided not to resign unless the whole cabinet resigns."

Tojo's face turned livid with astonishment and anger. Clenching his fists on the table to contain himself, he said calmly, "Kishi-san, if you quit, the cabinet could be saved. Regardless of what your views may be, is that not a small request to make of an old friend?"

"My resignation alone would not save the cabinet. If I resigned, taking full responsibility for our supply shortages, would that help you replenish these shortages? Would my departure mean a sudden jump in the production of planes, when we hardly have enough fuel, spare parts, and qualified pilots for the planes we now have? The situation is, in fact, bound to grow worse in the future no matter who is in charge of munitions. Now that Saipan has fallen, more and more of our factories will be bombed. Events point to the need for a completely new emergency cabinet. My sense of responsibility to the Emperor just doesn't allow me to resign meaninglessly when there is no sign that the tide of war would turn in our favor."

Tojo banged his fist on the table, almost upsetting the two cups of tea that had been placed there by a servant girl during the conversation. "You dare defy me?" he shouted. "Do you realize that I can have you arrested? I could easily find a pretext."

Heavy silence followed. As Tojo turned his head away, Kishi knew he had won an initial victory. He had forced Tojo to lose his temper, and therefore "face." Feeling more sure of himself, he replied with calculated calmness:

"Perhaps. But whatever you say or do, *I am determined not to submit my resignation individually.*"

Tojo, trembling with frustration and a sense of humiliation, got up and slowly walked to a nearby window, from which he gazed into infinity. His fingers, locked behind his back, twisted in their embrace, showing the man's inner agony.

"Kishi-san," Tojo said, turning toward him, "we have been friends for a long time—since Manchoukuo. Have you forgotten all that I have done for you? I gave you every kind of co-operation in Manchoukuo. I appointed you Minister of Commerce and Industry. I've helped you. I have never asked anything in return. Now I am asking you to do something for me for the first time. Do you feel no sense of obligation toward me?"

Tojo drew a package of cigarettes from the upper pocket of his tunic, removed one, and lit it. The matchlight revealed a smug sense of confidence on Tojo's face, which appeared to say, "At last I have trapped him."

Kishi replied after a tense pause, "Yes, it is true. We have been friends for a long time. And that is why it is very difficult for me to oppose your wishes. Normally, I certainly would not do so. But these are not normal times. And I must do what I think is best for the country. I could not in good conscience resign when it is my feeling that by doing so I would be helping to perpetuate policies not in the nation's interest."

Finally, after more than two hours of threats, pleadings, and argument, Tojo gave up. As Kishi walked to the door and opened it, he faced Tojo and bowed, but the General turned his back. Kishi, his face pale and his knees shaky, left. His friend, Kan'ichi Nakayasu, who was waiting for him in his car, asked, "Well, how did things go?"

"I've never experienced anything so painful," Kishi said.

"Did you finally give in to him?"

"No," Kishi answered. And he remained silent all the way home.

Tojo was not beaten yet. He decided to request the Emperor, through Kido, to dismiss Kishi from his post. He called on the Marquis at the Palace and formally explained the cabinet changes he would like to see approved by the Emperor. With an air of triumph, he announced that he had dismissed Admiral Shimada and that Admiral Naokuni Nomura, Naval Attaché in Berlin, had agreed the night before to replace him. He hoped that Admiral Yonai and General Abe would also join the cabinet. "And in order to strengthen the Air Force," he added, "Fujiwara shall serve full time as Munitions Minister, and, therefore, we request the retirement of Kishi." Kido was noncommittal. When the General had left, he informed Admiral Okada of Tojo's proposals.

Later that day, the *Jushin,* encouraged by the stand Kishi had taken, met at the home of Baron Hironuma to carry out their long-delayed plan for ending Tojo's rule. Elder Statesmen present in addition to Hiranuma included Prince Konoye, Admiral Okada, Koki Hirota, and the two military leaders Tojo wanted in his cabinet, Admiral Yonai and General Abe.

Yonai was the key figure. Abe was not anti-Tojo and would have agreed to join the cabinet if Yonai did, but the Admiral was known to be distrustful of Tojo. He had been lukewarm about the war from the first, having realized when it began that it had to be won quickly or the Navy wouldn't have the fuel and other supplies to carry on. The Army, he thought, was too recklessly ready to gamble with the future of the nation. In the fall of 1943, he had secretly ordered Rear Admiral Sokichi Takagi of Navy Headquarters to submit to him a thorough analysis of Japan's chances of winning the war. In early 1944, Takagi reported that Japan could not conceivably win the war and should seek peace immediately on the best terms it could get, even if this meant giving up all its overseas possessions. Yonai was now in a position to help move Japan toward this goal.

As the Elder Statesmen sat around a table, Yonai said, "I have been asked several times to join the cabinet. . . . I have no intention of doing so."

"Although the people may be completely out of sympathy with this cabinet," Abe replied, "the situation would become more difficult if it were replaced by a still weaker cabinet."

Hiranuma said, "Whether the cabinet is overthrown or not, or whether the next cabinet will be a weak one or not, is not the point. The point is that we are really concerned about our country, and we must make up our minds to do something."

"Even if I were asked to, I would not join the cabinet," Hirota interjected.

"In order to find our way through the current difficult situation," Okada counseled, "it is necessary to renew the popular mind. All people must rally and co-operate to build a powerful national cabinet which will surge forward unswervingly. A partial reorganization of the cabinet will not be of any use."

All except Abe agreed that Tojo's efforts to reconstruct his cabinet must be frustrated, and this decision was immediately transmitted to Kido, who informed the Emperor of it. Tojo learned the news from a military informer. At the same time he received an even more infuriating report that Kishi was plotting to bring a "fellow Choshu man," Field Marshal Terauchi, Commander of the Southern Area Army based in Singapore, to Tokyo to replace him.* Tojo had deliberately kept Terauchi, one of his most bitter personal enemies, out of the way by giving him a distant command. Being overthrown by this man would be the ultimate humiliation.

In a last desperate effort to retain his power, Tojo resigned his position as Army Chief of Staff after inducing General Yoshijire Umezu, Commander-in-Chief of the Kwantung Army, to take that post. Then he called a cabinet meeting for the following day, July 18, 1944, hoping that his colleagues, appeased by this diminution of his power, would agree to plans for a reorganized cabinet.

The evening before the meeting, Kishi, after consulting with Fujiyama and other anti-Tojo figures, met with Foreign Minister Shigemitsu and Agricultural Minister Uchida to co-ordinate statements they would deliver calling for bloc resignation of the cabinet. This would be the decisive conference, and no detail could be overlooked. Even the timing was important. It was decided that Uchida would speak first, then Shigemitsu, and Kishi last. The next morning, Kishi again conferred with Fujiyama, who told me that he asked, "Are you still prepared to go through with this? You know what might happen to you if Tojo should survive your

---

* Kishi denies having been associated with any plot to replace Tojo with Terauchi.

attack—or even if he should not." Kishi replied that he was ready to take the chance.

Shortly after the conference started, he made a sign to Uchida indicating it was time for him to speak. But Uchida looked away. Kishi then motioned to Shigemitsu, but the Foreign Minister also ignored him, doodling caricatures of some of his colleagues. Kishi realized, with a sense of shock, he says, that he would have to face the malice of Tojo and the *Kempei Tai* alone. He got up and analyzed in detail the deterioration of the nation's economy and the glum prospects of success in the war. As he spoke, Kishi maintains, Uchida and Shigemitsu appeared to be indifferent. Kishi ended his talk by urging that the Tojo cabinet resign *en bloc.*

When few of the cabinet members rallied to Tojo's support, the General, his voice heavy with bitterness, said, "I must ask you all to submit your resignations." Kishi observed Tojo with compassion at this stunning moment of defeat. He noted the heavy rings under his eyes, the sallow complexion, the sagging shoulders. After all the cabinet members had signed a document of resignation, one of Tojo's military aides turned to Kishi and snarled, "You have caused this! You and Kido."

Kishi replied, "It is my view that the resignation of the cabinet is necessary for the good of the country. I have acted in accordance with the dictates of my conscience and the responsibilities of my office. You, a mere staff officer, have no right whatsoever to tell a minister appointed by His Majesty how he should think or act!"

That same day, Tojo, the letter of resignation in his briefcase, proceeded to the Palace to keep an appointment with the Emperor. He was greeted in the elaborately furnished anteroom by Kido.

"Who would you recommend to replace you as Prime Minister?" Kido asked in a manner that suggested he was sorry Tojo saw fit to resign when his services were so badly needed.

The General replied with stinging sarcasm, "I don't think you need my opinion. I am sure the *Jushin* has someone in mind already."

Tojo then entered the Emperor's office, and, after having steered his country toward destruction for two years and nine months, submitted the resignation of his cabinet to His Majesty. On the same day, Imperial General Headquarters belatedly revealed to the public the news of the annihilation of the Saipan garrison, which "victoriously fought to the last man." Radio Tokyo calmly followed up with an explanation of the natural consequences of that "planned" rout. "The American occupation of Saipan brings Japan within the radius of American bombers. But we were well aware of this contingency and have made the necessary preparations."

Tojo grasped desperately at every straw offering some possibility of settling accounts with his foes. At a meeting of the fallen cabinet, which remained in power in a caretaker capacity until a new one could be formed, Tojo got up and read a communiqué which his War Ministry had drafted, violently accusing the *Jushin* and "several members of the cabinet" of having plotted the overthrow of the government. He demanded in a threatening tone that the communiqué be made public. Shigemitsu, who knew that he was one of the "conspirators" referred to, this time rose, and, branding Tojo's charge baseless, asked his colleagues to kill the communiqué. They did so. But the Cabinet Board of Information, under pressure from the Army, belatedly released the communiqué anyway. Tojo received some further measure of consolation from the rejection of Field Marshal Terauchi as his successor. Tojo prevented Terauchi from becoming Prime Minister by advising His Majesty that Terauchi's recall from the war theater at this critical time could have disastrous military consequences.

But Tojo was at last out of power, due in no small degree to Kishi's courage. The last few months had been the most trying of Kishi's life. He had defied the will of a desperate man, who could have ordered his assassination. He had decided that it was in the interest of the nation to seek peace, even though that peace would now be linked with defeat. Defeat was a disgrace, even as victory was glory. But once disgrace became inevitable, continued death and destruction could not reduce its ugliness and was, therefore, however just Japan's cause, without meaning.

CHAPTER XI

❧❧❧

DEATH OF A DREAM

SHORTLY AFTER the fall of the Tojo cabinet, Kishi returned with his family to Tabuse. With his savings and money inherited from his father, who had died a few years before, Kishi could now afford to be idle. He had not been able to relax for a long time. Now, at last, he was relieved of the crushing burden of the war economy and the dispute with Tojo. But Kishi was by no means a free man, for, while Tojo was no longer in power, his army followers, embittered by his fall, had not deserted him. District police agents trailed Kishi wherever he went, questioned him about whom he had seen and what he had discussed, stood by the front door asking the business of everybody who came to visit him. Several times they telephoned him, threatening to kill him for his "treasonable" role in Tojo's overthrow. This constant harassment eliminated any possibility of a real rest. Often at night he dreamed of being arrested, tortured, killed. And he knew that Yoshiko, though never mentioning the matter, lived in even greater dread.

The surveillance was intensified when Kishi began indulging in local political activities, which the *Kempei Tai* was convinced were intended to further discredit the militarists. With a number of friends in Yamaguchi, Kishi organized a district association called the *Bocho Shunju Doshi Kai*. Its announced aim was to assure maintenance of minimum living standards through local economic co-operation, and thus lessen the dependence of the area on bureaucratic and military control from Tokyo, with which communications were becoming increasingly difficult as war pressures grew. But the organization was also intended to solidify support for Kishi in the next Diet election, scheduled for 1946.

Kishi realized that planning for a future election was not altogether realistic, since it was neither likely that the war would last that long nor that Japan would win. Still, a compromise peace might be reached, leaving Japan an unoccupied country, free from enemy domination. In any case, after the feverish activity he had become accustomed to in the past few years, Kishi needed something to keep him busy, however limited the potential political fruitfulness of the new organization. As he traveled from town to town in the prefecture organizing cells, he was never free of the police shadow. Agents even insisted on being present at the meetings. But he was not arrested, probably, he thought, because his high-placed friends in Tokyo had prevailed upon the military police leaders to spare him.

The military influence in Japan, however, was by no means diminishing. The *Jushin* had been able to bring to bear sufficient pressure to topple Tojo, but not to overcome the determination of the Tojoite Army to prosecute the war to the bitter end. After rejecting Terauchi as Prime Minister, the Elder Statesmen considered choosing, as Okada had planned, a naval figure, but finally discarded this idea for fear—which still dominated their every move—that the Army would rebel. As Tojo had come to power on the false theory that he was the only man who could control the extremist elements in the Army, another "moderate" general was now chosen by the *Jushin*.

The new Prime Minister was General Kuniski Koiso, known as the Tiger of Korea because of his military exploits in that country and also because of his catlike face—sharply slanted eyes, flat, broad nose, and thin, pursed lips. (At sake parties he enjoyed the title of Champion Baldhead of Japan.) With the retention of Shigemitsu as Foreign Minister and the choice of Admiral Yonai as Deputy Premier and Navy Minister, the peace group thought it had a government that could finally end the war. Koiso was instructed by the Emperor, on the advice of Kido, to accomplish this "as quickly as possible," but the new Prime Minister, under Army pressure, called on the people to "give their last ounce of energy" to the war effort. But to reduce the influence of the Young Officers' clique on the cabinet, Koiso established a six-man Supreme War Council which met in secret to determine policy.

On every war-or-peace issue, however, it was divided down the middle, with Koiso, Shigemitsu, and Yonai favoring peace, and the War Minister and Army and Navy Chiefs of Staff supporting continued war. Yonai had

Admiral Takagi make a second survey to determine how the Army could be won over, how peace bids could be made to the Allies, and how the public would react to a surrender. Meanwhile, the peace groups tried to win converts to the idea of surrender among the generals as well as the young officers, but the War Minister's refusal to co-operate all but ended this effort.

Friends coming from Tokyo informed Kishi of the increasing tension in the government, about which he was unable to learn from the heavily censored newspapers and radio. The government was riddled with intrigue, but everyone involved was afraid of the Army, and army officials themselves were afraid of each other. The same threats of revenge and assassination that had plagued Kishi now paralyzed the activities of Japan's new leaders.

Kishi was also told that Japan's military position was growing ever more untenable. Guam fell in July, 1944. Ammunition and fuel were running desperately low, with hundreds of planes grounded for lack of gasoline. There was a shortage of experienced pilots. Enemy aircraft and submarines had cut Japan off almost completely from raw material supplies in Southeast Asia.

In September, 1944, Foreign Minister Shigemitsu urged that a special envoy be sent to Moscow in the hope that the Russians would mediate the Pacific War. But the Soviet government discouraged this move by showing no interest. Then the Swedish Ambassador to Tokyo, Widor Bagge, was asked to sound out London through the Swedish government on a proposal whereby Japan would surrender all wartime conquests, including perhaps Manchuria. The British answered that surrender would have to be unconditional, a capitulation that even the peacemakers were not yet ready to accept. In October, Prince Konoye's younger brother, Baron Tadamaro Miyagawa, contacted Chinese secret agents in Shanghai, former acquaintances of Konoye's, who had indicated in correspondence that the Chinese government was willing to discuss peace terms. But this effort, too, broke down.

Konoye himself was one of the most fervent of the peacemakers, fearing not only the physical destruction of his country but the danger of a communist revolution in the wake of defeat. In his obsession with this menace, he formulated a desperate plan to destroy the militarists by setting one faction against another. The Emperor would appoint Konoye Prime Minister and Konoye would select as his war minister one of Tojo's bitterest personal enemies, retired General Jinzaburo Mazaki, who had played a leading role in instigating the Young Officers' revolt of 1936. Mazaki, the

Prince reasoned, would purge the Tojoites and thus clear the way to peace before the communists could take over the country. Winning the support of Shigeru Yoshida, an influential ex-diplomat, who also favored peace, he obtained an audience with the Emperor and presented his proposal in elaborate terms:

"A defeat is a serious stain on our history. However, we can accept it as long as we can maintain our Imperial system. Public opinion in America and Britain, on the whole, does not yet demand a fundamental change in that system. What we have to fear, therefore, is not so much a defeat as a communist revolution which might take place in the event of defeat. Conditions, both internal and external, point to the danger of such a revolution. In the first place, there has been the notable ascendancy of Soviet Russia. In the light of her recent activities in Europe we must assume that she has not abandoned hope of bolshevizing the entire world.

"At home, potentially dangerous factors include the rapid deterioration of living conditions; the increasingly loud voice of labor; the rise of pro-Soviet feelings as enmity against America and Britain mounts; attempts by extremist groups in the Army to achieve radical changes in our internal policies; and the disguised activities of the communists behind both the military and the bureaucrats. A majority of younger officers seem to think that the present form of government is compatible with communism. The communists are influencing them with the theory that even under communism Japan can maintain the Imperial system.

"I have now come to doubt seriously whether the whole series of events from the Manchurian Incident (in 1931) to the present war hasn't been what they have purposely planned. It is a well-known fact that they openly declared the goal of the Manchurian war was to achieve drastic reforms in domestic affairs. Of course, the reform sought by the military may not necessarily be a communist revolution, but the bureaucrats and civilians collaborating with the military definitely intend to bring about such a revolution. In the last few months, the slogan, 'A Hundred Million Die Together,' has become increasingly louder, seemingly among right-wing people, but it has its real basis in the activities of the communists. Under such circumstances, the longer we continue the war, the greater will be the danger of a revolution. We should, therefore, stop the war as soon as possible."

Konoye then offered his proposal that he be appointed Prime Minister so that General Mazaki could be brought into the cabinet.

Whatever effect his appeal may have had on the Emperor, it had little on his adviser, Kido, who had been present during the audience. The Marquis, too, feared the communists—particularly the threat they constituted to the Emperor system. But he did not, nor, for that matter, did

Kishi, believe that the government was heavily infiltrated by pro-communists. And he resented the slur on the name of the "bureaucrats and civilians who collaborated with the military." After all, he had once fallen into this category himself. Kido saw the plan as inevitably producing a bloody incident that could, in the end, engulf himself and the other peace-seekers, thereby defeating its very purpose.

Meanwhile, the Supreme Command decided to play what was probably the last card that could lead, if not to victory, to an "honorable" peace. It would use its entire fleet, or what remained of it, to prevent an American landing on the Philippine island of Leyte, without which Japan would have almost no oil, rubber, or metal ores to keep its sluggish war machine going. The peacemakers approved of this move, figuring they had something to gain whether the battle was won or lost. If Japan won, the Allies would be more willing to discuss a conditional peace. If Japan lost, the Army's hand would be weakened.

Kishi knew from reports on the radio that the battle was pending, but he could hardly believe his ears when several days afterward the report circulated that the Japanese fleet had been victorious. Prime Minister Koiso appeared to confirm this report when he told reporters that the battle of Leyte would irrevocably settle the issue of the war. The wheel of fortune had turned, it seemed, producing the first major Japanese victory since 1942.

But then Kishi learned from a high government official that Japan had, in fact, lost almost its entire fleet. What made this even more unbearable was the information that the Japanese Navy might have won the battle except for a fatal tactical error. The Japanese had divided their fleet into three forces, one in the south, another in the center, and a third, acting as a decoy, in the north. The decoy, as planned, drew Admiral Halsey's main fleet away from Leyte, though at the price of four carriers, two destroyers, and a cruiser. The southern force was all but destroyed by Admiral Kinkaid's fleet. But the center force, while suffering considerable damage, steamed through San Bernardino Strait into Leyte Gulf, and, with the help of *kamikaze* attacks on Admiral Sprague's destroyers that were protecting the beaches, could have wiped out the invading troops streaming ashore from transports—if it had realized that the way was clear. Instead, it had retreated. That was the end of the battle for Japan.

A few weeks later, in November, 1944, Kishi heard news that indicated the war itself was nearing an end. The Americans launched their first heavy bombing attacks on Japan from bases in Saipan, with high altitude daylight raids destroying the aircraft plants in the Tokyo area as

Kishi had warned Tojo they would. But it was on March 9, 1945, that final realization came to the people of Japan that their leaders had not only lost the war, but were leading them to mass suicide.

As Kishi sat with his family at breakfast that morning, listening to the radio, he turned pale as Radio Tokyo reported calmly, as if presenting a standard communiqué, that most of Tokyo had disappeared overnight after a fire-jelly bombing raid by hundreds of low flying B-29's.

"The storm of fire," the announcer said, "swept whole districts. Only here and there the blackened walls of stone buildings remained standing.*
. . . After the first incendiaries fell, clouds formed and were lit up from below with pink light. From them emerged Superfortresses, flying uncannily low. . . . The city was bright as at sunrise. . . . We thought the whole of Tokyo was reduced to ashes."

That night, Kishi learned later, as a result of that one attack on Tokyo, more than 80,000 people were killed, more than 100,000 injured, more than 1,500,000 left homeless, and 270,000 buildings had suddenly vanished, among them his own house. Attacks of similar scope continued to be made on cities throughout Japan. It was no longer necessary to hide from the public such news as the fall of Okinawa in April, 1945, or Germany's surrender in May. These distant events had little meaning for people to whom war had been reduced to a simple matter of personal survival in a world of smoking ruins. Kishi boiled with frustration and anger as he listened to Radio Tokyo try to calm the populace simply by removing the fear of the unknown. "The enemy doubtless will make an offensive against us by combined land, sea and air operations, but this has been taken into account in our plans."

As American bombs kept raining on Tokyo and other Japanese cities, Kishi noted that hints of dissatisfaction with the military leadership on the part of Diet members and other civilian officials were becoming more conspicuous in the newspapers than in past days, veiled though such criticism was. And the dramatic fall of Iwo Jima to the Americans gave the press further courage. When a reporter friend of Kishi's from the *Mainichi Shimbun* visited him—Kishi had got to know him in the few weeks following Tojo's fall when the ex-Minister had rented an office in the Mainichi Building—Kishi offered to contribute an article to the paper in the form of an interview. If *Mainichi* would go along with him, he said, he would, at the risk of retaliation by the military, bluntly advocate reduced military control of the nation.

Mainichi's editors agreed, and the interview was carefully prepared,

---

* Stone was seldom used for building purposes in Japan.

with each word weighed and re-weighed in the light of possible consequences. The theme of the interview was the need for increased civilian
authority in the government, an extremely bold position to take at a time
when the militarists were frantically trying to maintain their authority. But
to minimize the dangers involved, both for Kishi and the newspaper, in
this delicate effort to cultivate the seeds of an antimilitarist popular
movement, he stated that a civilian-led political system was necessary,
not to bring peace, but to carry on the war more effectively—though he
well knew that the leading civilian leaders in Japan, from Kido down,
were struggling to bring the war to a halt and would undoubtedly do so
if they held the reins of government.

"If I had breathed the slightest suggestion that Japan should surrender,
or had even hinted at such a thing by omitting reference to the need to
fight on," Kishi explains, "the article would never have been printed, and
if it had been, both the editors and I would most certainly have suffered as
a result. As it was, we took a very great risk in so openly attacking military authority."

The article, entitled *War Politics,* was published on March 27, 1945.
It read:

"With the bombing of Japanese cities—Tokyo, Nagoya, Osaka,
Kobe, and others—and now with the fall of Iwo Jima, the war has
reached a very grave stage. In view of this situation, the people are
awaiting ever more impatiently the appearance of effective war administration. A *Mainichi* reporter asked Nobusuke Kishi, ex-Minister,
for his opinion on the means of bringing this about.

"Reporter: How do you feel about the loss of Iwo Jima?

"Kishi: Like everybody else, I have been deeply moved. I think that
from this point on we should be more realistic in our political and
economic thinking. The soldiers on Iwo fought to the last drop of blood
in the hope that every added second of effort would give the people
at home more time to prepare themselves for carrying on the war. But
what have we been doing here? As a Japanese, I feel a sense of shame
when I think of the sacrifices of our courageous soldiers. And my heart
is filled with sorrow. However, just being sorry is not enough. The
whole nation, including both military and civilians, must do everything in its power to prove its gratefulness. Our policies have to be
speeded up and executed with great strength and determination.

"Reporter: There seems to be a growing desire by the people to
strengthen national leadership by strengthening the political administration of the war.

"Kishi: In a great war such as we are fighting today, ultimate victory requires the close co-ordination of political administration and war
strategy. From past experience—for example, World War I—it is clear

that victory can only be won under a system in which civilian and military leadership are co-ordinated in the operation of the war. . . . Sometimes political administration must have precedence over military control. Thus, the relationship established in World War I between Marshal Foch and Prime Minister Clemenceau in France was a perfect example of good co-ordination in war. Naturally, when victory or defeat is to be decided on the basis of a short-term battle, political administration must be subordinated to military leadership. . . . However, in a long-term war in which the fighting is carried to the very homeland, the civilians should have great power. To win this war, we must be prepared for a long period of fighting. And I think that only with the strengthening of civilian administration can the war be carried on effectively. This is the only way Japan can win the war.

"Reporter: What is the nature of the political movement that you would like to see formed?

"Kishi: A spirit is growing among the people which is making them stand up and oppose the status quo. This spirit reflects the kind of political movement that should be formed. The people must unite to protect the nation and extricate it from the unprecedented crisis in which it finds itself. No consideration should be given to past experience, dignity, or tradition. The movement must be of a reformative character if it is to save the country. A mere parliamentary party will be meaningless. In other words, the political power of the people must be directly connected with the administration of the war. Today, the people and this administration are separated.

"In view of the urgency of the situation, the development of new strength with which to carry out a long-term war without fear or delay is necessary. This strength cannot be provided by individuals. Only an organization can co-ordinate political power with war administration, one that is based on the political unity of the people. It is clear . . . that such unity cannot be brought about by the government. And it is equally clear that the political leaders themselves cannot bring this about. It should revolve around the leadership of pure-hearted people who wish to unite for a common purpose. There has never been a time when true political unity has been so desperately needed.

"Reporter: I understand the enemy has begun to conduct peace strategy.

"Kishi: I think it is important that the Japanese be ready to continue the fight, while refusing to submit to injustice. If we fell victim to the enemy's strategy and considered making peace, Japan would be in the same position as Germany in World War I. I want to encourage the building up of popular political power in order to carry on this just war and to eliminate whatever hinders this effort. Only the establishment of a people's political organization could achieve the necessary industrial production and military defense. Most of the Diet members, Privy Councilors, and other various so-called political leaders have made no effort to initiate such an organization. Frankly,

I think most of them are reluctant to volunteer but realize that something should be done. Why doesn't somebody propose a plan, and if it is a good one, we will follow. We cannot save the nation by maintaining the status quo. In view of the fact that our soldiers on Iwo Jima all sacrificed their lives to protect the country, we should throw off all inhibitions and act. Otherwise, we cannot call ourselves Japanese subjects."

Kishi, after reading the published article, apprehensively awaited the knock on the door that would mean his arrest. But although the district police re-tightened their surveillance of his activities, nothing more frightening happened. In any event, he thought, the risk had been well worth taking. Perhaps his words would help to awaken the people to the desperate need of freeing themselves from the military yoke, and thus make it easier for the civilian peacemakers to assert their will.

In June, Kishi went to Tokyo to see what damage had been done to his home and to settle other private business. He had to stand up for several nights on a jam-packed train that was balked along the line by scattered wreckage on the tracks and crowds of people desperately trying to squeeze in through doors and windows. They were silent people with worried, haggard, tense faces, many of them the husbands, wives, brothers, and sisters of Tokyoites whose fate, with communications between various parts of Japan now practically cut off, they would not know until they reached the capital. Kishi was thankful that his family was far from any industrial center.

Kishi arrived in Tokyo shortly after a bombing. From radio and newspaper reports of the terrible destruction wreaked upon the city, he knew what to expect, but as he emerged from the partially shattered railroad station, he stopped with the abruptness of a hiker suddenly finding himself at the edge of a precipice that wasn't on the map. He stared incredulously into the scorched desert that sprawled before him like a great black shroud, with concrete chimneys grimly poking from the ashes here and there to form giant tombstones. The scene reminded him of an impressionistic drawing he had once seen, depicting the end of the world. The few people within sight offered an added dimension of realism to this grotesque picture as they wandered aimlessly in the wilderness like the last survivors of civilization, searching for food and the remains of dear ones. Many of these pitiful figures were children, barefoot and ragged, their faces smudged with charcoal and mud, their eyes dazed and distant, accusing in their innocence, as they begged from passing strangers for a few sen with which to buy rice.

Kishi began to sweat in the intense summer heat, which hung, appropriately, like a pall over this landscape of death. He removed his hat and wiped his forehead with a handkerchief, then started walking, hat in hand, toward what had been the heart of Tokyo. Only the charred skeletons of a few large buildings remained. Even the main palace building, behind the moat-surrounded stone wall that still bordered the Imperial grounds, was in ruins. There was little traffic on the streets, many of which were completely blocked with debris. Kishi stared at the tall, gaunt young men gradually clearing away the wreckage under the watchful eyes of rifle-carrying soldiers. They were American prisoners of war, some of the first he had seen. They worked quickly and efficiently, and it seemed to Kishi, almost with a smile on their stubbled faces, as if silently mocking their captors. Had they no sense of humility, or shame, in their disgrace? Did they not know that they were here because they had failed in their missions?

As Kishi walked on, the sultry air grew stagnant with the smell of decaying flesh, emanating from pyres of dead bodies awaiting cremation, corpses with blackened skin, most of them with their clothes burned half off. The body of one woman, whose hair was singed almost to the scalp, lay stomach-down with a little bundle strapped on her back—a dead infant. Blending with the odor of death was the stench of human excrement that filled more than a dozen large wooden "honey buckets" being carried by a passing truck on its way to the suburbs where peasants still needed fertilizer to grow the little food available in Japan these days.

No public transportation appeared to be running, so Kishi got a ride in the front seat of a military truck. As the vehicle weaved and groaned through the wreckage strewn on the road, the driver, an aging soldier with deep, sunken eyes, said in a calm, reflective voice, "There isn't much left of Tokyo, and those of us who are still alive will fight on as long as the Emperor wishes. But what is it all for? The Emperor's advisers are bad men. They advised the Emperor to start the war, and then they told us we were winning. Look how they lied. But now they cannot lie any more for we can see what is happening with our own eyes. I don't mind dying for the Emperor, but I would like to take with me the men who advised him to go to war."

Kishi did not reply, looking straight ahead through the broken windshield. He was afraid to meet the eyes of the driver, just as once, many years before, he had avoided looking into the eyes of Uncle Matsui after he had broken the lid of his uncle's little red teapot.

The driver dropped him near his destination, which, he discovered, had been reduced to an open patch of land containing only charred rubble. His house had vanished. He walked over to a large rock that had once been part of his garden and sat down on it, contemplating the lifelessness of his once magic little realm. Gone were the azaleas and the fir trees and the ferns, and when he breathed in the air, once so fragrant, there was only the stale, carbonic odor of devastation.

Kishi used to love the isolation of his garden, where for brief moments he could free himself from the bonds of reality. Now, as he sat where his garden had been, he was once more engulfed by isolation, but this time, ironically, the isolation, not of a tiny, transient world of freedom, but of a boundless ashen graveyard, horrifying in its truth.

Suddenly Kishi heard a vague buzzing sound in the distance, and his heart skipped a beat as he searched the sky. Several bird-like silhouettes emerged from a low-hanging cloud. They were Zeros. He immediately recognized them; he had once been responsible for producing them. They were heading southwest, apparently toward the bloody battlefields of the Pacific. *Kamikaze* suicide planes, Kishi guessed. A one-way flight that would end, if all went well, in the flaming belly of an enemy warship. Innocent-minded young men with the Emperor's name on their lips carried by a "divine wind," like ephemeral cherry blossoms, toward the eternal embrace of the Sun Goddess. Kishi wondered what they must be thinking as they glided over the great smoldering desert below. Could they die in peace knowing they were to die in vain?

He then saw a soldier leading a group of about twenty boys, from eight to eighteen years of age. A few clumped along in *geta,* but most were barefoot, and their clothes were a tattered combination of ill-fitting army and civilian garments, with some wearing nothing except shorts. In one hand they carried shovels or picks, and in the other, bamboo spears whittled to a sharp point at one end. The group halted in the distance and started digging along the side of the road, obviously training for the day when they would be expected to throw invading American forces back into the sea. They would make a last stand, fighting modern weapons with bamboo spears, as Lord Mori's samurai warriors had done. This was the madness that had fueled the war he had once approved; the madness that had been so painstakingly camouflaged as glory. His mind flashed back to the exhilarating moment when he had signed the resolution of war that was to send Japan rocketing toward its rightful place in the sun. "I should have known," he told himself. "I should have known. What a terrible, unforgivable mistake."

Kishi returned to Tabuse to await the end of the war. His trip to Tokyo had convinced him that it couldn't last much longer, however many *kamikaze* pilots plunged to death or bamboo spears were hurled against steel tanks. By this time Prime Minister Koiso had fallen, unable to withstand the pressure on him as the Americans inched their way toward the homeland, hopping from one island to another. Koiso had satisfied neither the militarists, who wanted a policy of no-surrender-at-any-cost, nor the *Jushin,* who deplored his refusal or inability to make any serious peace moves. The armed services, moreover, were highly embarrassed by his public statement that the outcome of the battle of Leyte would determine that of the war. They could always make defeat look like a strategic withdrawal, but they could not explain away a statement like Koiso's.

At the same time, the Supreme Command was furious with Koiso for having fallen for what was apparently a peace hoax. In March, 1945, he had invited from Shanghai a Chinese named Miao Ping, who professed to be a confidential emissary of Chiang Kai-shek. Miao proposed that in return for Japan's withdrawal from China and abandonment of the Nanking regime, Chiang would prevent the Americans from landing in China and would co-operate with Japan against the communists threatening his country. The "emissary" departed and no further word was ever received.* On April 4th, Koiso resigned.

Kido met with the *Jushin* to choose a successor, and the issue of peace or mass suicide came into final focus. Tojo, now one of the *Jushin,* demanded that his supporter, General Shunroka Hata, be chosen to deal with the invasion of Japan itself, flatly warning that the Army would take over the country if any other choice was made. Kido, however, warned that the people were ready to rebel against the Army, and in the end he forced Tojo to accept the selection of seventy-eight-year-old peace-minded Baron Kantaro Suzuki, a retired admiral and a veteran politician. A major victory over the militarists was achieved. But the Army, as a warning to the new leaders, arrested Yoshida and two other politicians who favored peace, though setting them free after a few weeks' imprisonment.

Suzuki and Foreign Minister Togo, who replaced Shigemitsu in the cabinet after a lengthy absence, pursued a policy aiming at surrender in spite of this attempted intimidation. Shortly before they came to power, Shigemitsu had told Swedish Minister Bagge as he was about to return to Sweden that the military clique was responsible for the war and that the Japanese diplomats had to end it, hinting the desire for Swedish

---

* It was believed that he was merely trying to sound out the Prime Minister and to weaken the Japanese determination to continue the war.

mediation. But the new cabinet banked instead on using Russia as a mediator, unaware that in February, 1945 Stalin had reached an agreement with his allies to attack Japan in August in return for South Sakhalin, the Kurile Islands, and railroad and harbor concessions in Manchuria. In June, to pave the way for Soviet mediation, Japan proposed to the Soviet Ambassador in Tokyo a non-aggression pact between the two countries, but met with indifference. In July, Suzuki ordered the Japanese Ambassador in Moscow to request the Soviet government to receive Prince Konoye, a special envoy from the Emperor, to discuss peace, but the Russians stalled as Stalin and Molotov left for an Allied meeting in Potsdam. The results of this conference reached Japan on July 26th.

Kishi, ill with scarlet fever, listened to the radio next to his bed throughout the day and evening, almost memorizing the peace terms contained in the Potsdam Declaration: unconditional surrender and "removal from authority and influence for all time of those who had deceived and misled the people of Japan into embarking on world conquests"; military occupation of Japan and complete disarmament; destruction of war industries; relinquishment by Japan of all overseas territories; punishment of war criminals and establishment of all human liberties, including freedom of thought, religion, and speech. If these conditions were met, the Allies promised Japan future access to raw materials and participation in world trade, and withdrawal of Allied occupation forces when a "peacefully inclined and responsible" government had been set up "in accordance with the freely expressed will of the Japanese people."

Kishi found these terms harsh. After all, unconditional surrender was the ultimate in humiliation. But he favored immediate acceptance. The Potsdam Declaration actually offered some reason for optimism. The promise of free thought, religion, and speech indicated, if made in sincerity, a surprisingly liberal attitude toward a vanquished people. The Japanese people themselves were now clamoring for these very things. Even more important, the specification that the Japanese would choose their own government seemed to offer hope that the Emperor system would be retained. It was inconceivable that the people would repudiate it. Still, the fact that the Allies had not specifically stated the Emperor's position worried Kishi. He regarded with a painful sense of resignation the notification that war criminals would be punished. Was he not one of them? He had signed the resolution of war. He recalled his visit to Tokyo —the soot-blackened bodies, the woman with the little human bundle strapped to her back, the dazed, hungry children, the boys with the bamboo spears. Someone had to pay for that. But why weigh the merits of the

216 ខ KISHI AND JAPAN

ultimatum? Kishi thought. Japan had no choice. It had to accept the terms while there was still a chance to preserve the roots of the Japanese spirit.

Suzuki, Togo, Kido, and the *Jushin* were of the same opinion, but the militarists, seeing that they were singled out for punishment, still talked of resisting on the beaches of Japan, with all the remaining serviceable planes—about 2,800—to be thrown at the invasion fleet in hourly *kamikaze* attacks, and two-man submarines and individual swimmers serving as torpedos. "Even if we lose a million, or two million, or three million men," argued one general, "the enemy will also lose millions, and then public opinion in America will force the Allies to give us honorable peace terms. Or if we all have to die, that is still better than agreeing to a dishonorable peace. We can never accept unconditional surrender."

Nevertheless, the Supreme War Council did not flatly turn down the Potsdam Declaration, but decided to wait for Russia's leaders to return to Moscow to make a last attempt at soliciting their mediation. As the world waited for Japan's answer, Kishi was shocked to hear a report on the radio that Suzuki had off-handedly stated at a press conference that the "government intended to ignore the Potsdam Declaration."

One week later, on August 6th, Kishi heard Radio Tokyo announce America's reaction. "A new type of bomb had fallen on Hiroshima, causing considerable damage," it said. Not yet realizing, because of the casualness of the announcement, that the world had entered the atomic age, Kishi was far more stricken by the Domei News Agency report three days later, on August 9th, that Russian troops had invaded Manchuria. Stalin and Molotov had delivered their answer to Japan's appeal. News of the dropping of the second atomic bomb on Nagasaki added to the emotional impact of Japan's tortured death wails.

Kishi knew that the end had come, even as Kido saw the Emperor and obtained his immediate agreement that the Potsdam Declaration must be accepted without delay. At ten A.M., the Supreme War Council met and agreed unanimously in principle to accept the Declaration, but the militarists—three of the six Council members, led by War Minister Anami—held out for four conditions: retention of the Emperor system, no Allied occupation, voluntary Japanese withdrawal of armed forces from occupied territory, with the nation disarming and demobilizing itself, and the trial of war criminals by the Japanese government. An emergency meeting of the cabinet followed at which the Home Minister declared he couldn't guarantee internal peace and order unless the Allies agreed to the four

conditions, presenting once more the image of a blood-bath of assassinations.

As a last resort, Kido and the *Jushin* called an Imperial Conference
that night, attended by the six members of the Supreme War Council, the
heads of the General Affairs Bureaus of the Army and Navy, the Chief
Secretary of the Cabinet, the Director of the Planning Board, and the
President of the Privy Council. The proud, defiant men, including Kishi,
who had served in comparable capacities at the Imperial Conference held
in a luxurious Palace chamber four years before to set the nation on the
road to a glorious destiny could hardly have imagined that they, or their
counterparts, would one midnight shabbily meet in an eerily-lit air raid
shelter to writhe in the humiliation of surrender. And writhe they did,
during several hours of debate, until Suzuki finally got up and told the
shocked group of quarreling men, "We've discussed this question for a
long time without reaching a conclusion. The situation is urgent and any
delay in coming to a decision should not be tolerated. I, therefore, propose asking His Imperial Majesty for his own views. His wishes should
settle the issue and the government should follow them."

Thus, with the world finally crashing down upon their heads, the advisers of the Emperor finally agreed that it was time to stand up to the
militarists with the ultimate weapon at their command—the Emperor
himself. In a quivering voice, Hirohito said:

> "I agree with Foreign Minister Togo about acceptance of the Pots-
> dam Declaration. Since the beginning of the Pacific War, there has
> been a great disparity between our calculations and the realities. . . .
> With things in this condition, how can we win even if we have a battle
> in the homeland? If all the citizens should die, we would hardly be able
> to perpetuate the nation. I think that we must decide at this time to
> terminate the war, although it is an unbearable thing. I realize that if
> we terminate the war in this way, it will mean losing the Army, which
> we have had since the time of the Emperor Meiji. However, when I
> think of all the men who have died and the families of the dead, I feel
> as if my heart were broken. In order to open the way to future peace,
> we must bear the unbearable. It is needless to worry about the royal
> family."

A shroud of silence blanketed the room as if the world had suddenly
come to an end. Then Japan's strong men, some of whom would have
seen their children bayoneted by the enemy, if necessary, spontaneously
burst into sobs. Suzuki said, "The Imperial decision has been expressed.
This should be the conclusion of the conference."

Acceptance of the Potsdam terms was unanimously endorsed at a cabinet meeting—provided the Emperor's position remained unchanged. This decision was then transmitted through the Swiss government to the United States, China, Britain, and the U.S.S.R. The American reply, refusing any commitment regarding the Emperor, was heard over the San Francisco radio in the early hours of August 12th, and once again Japan's leaders found themselves hopelessly divided on the question of peace. At another emergency Imperial Conference on August 14th, the Emperor stood up and told the militarists with unprecedented directness:

"It seems to me that there is no other opinion to support your stand. I shall explain mine. I hope all of you will agree. The American answer seems acceptable to me."

The Emperor then instructed Prime Minister Suzuki to draft an Imperial Rescript ending the war, returning to his chambers with Kido to prepare a recording announcing the decision to the people.

That evening, the Japan Broadcasting Corporation sent several technicians to the Palace to make the recording, which the Emperor, in his nervousness, took two hours to complete. But even as Kido locked up the disc in a palace vault, thousands of young officers, led by a group of rebellious majors and lieutenant colonels, poured from their barracks to prevent the broadcast and kill those who had advised the Emperor to make it. The anticipated coup that had for so long frozen Kido and the *Jushin* into inaction was materializing. Even the Emperor himself could not yet bring the military diehards around. The officers and their men, crying for revenge, burned down the homes of Suzuki and Hiranuma. Kido's house was occupied, and he only escaped alive because, failing to recognize him, the soldiers refused him entry. Gratefully, he dashed back to the Palace and hid himself, with the Minister of the Imperial Household, in the air raid shelter in which history had been made.

Shooting the chief of the Imperial Guards for his failure to join in the rebellion, the rebels searched the Palace for Kido, while others took over Radio Tokyo nearby. They tried to broadcast, but were frustrated by an air raid alarm during which all communications were, ironically, cut by the Army. At daybreak, the military police finally arrived and recaptured the building, after which Radio Tokyo went on the air and calmly announced that the Emperor would speak at noon. Lacking co-ordination and decisiveness, the rebel movement began to break up, and ended, at the command of General Seiji Tanaka, chief of the Eastern Army, with five of the rebel leaders falling to their knees on the Imperial plaza and disemboweling themselves. General Tanaka joined them in death shortly afterward.

On August 15, 1945, Kishi, as he lay in bed recovering from his illness, Yoshiko kneeling beside him, listened to the low, hesitant voice of
the Emperor proclaim in oblique Imperial language the death of a dream:

". . . Despite the best that has been done by everyone, the war
situation has developed not necessarily to Japan's advantage, while
the general trends of the world have all turned against her interest.
Moreover, the enemy has begun to employ a new and most cruel bomb,
the power of which to do damage is, indeed, incalculable, taking the
toll of many innocent lives. Should we continue to fight, it would not
only result in an ultimate collapse and obliteration of the Japanese
nation, but also it would lead to the total extinction of human civilization. . . . This is the reason why we have ordered the acceptance of
the provisions of the joint declaration of the Powers. . . . Beware
most strictly of any outbursts of emotion that may engender needless
complications, and of any fraternal contention and strife that may
create confusion, lead you astray, and cause you to lose the confidence
of the world. . . . Let the entire nation continue as one family from
generation to generation, ever firm in its faith in the imperishableness
of its divine land, and mindful of its heavy burden of responsibilities,
and the long road before it. Unite your total strength to be devoted to
the construction of the future. . . ."

Yoshiko turned to Kishi and said in a choked voice, "At last, Nobusuke, *peace*."

Kishi nodded. He knew what she was thinking, something that must
have been tormenting her for a long time. He was a "war criminal," and
soon they would come for him. He lay quietly with his eyes shut.

Kishi had recovered from his illness by the time the first small group
of Americans landed at Atsugi Airdrome on August 28, 1945. With his
family around him, he waited expectantly for word of his fate, listening
to the radio and discussing with his neighbors every step in the implementation of the surrender. He could imagine the sorrow in the heart of
Shigemitsu (who had become Foreign Minister again in the royal cabinet
formed immediately after the Emperor's broadcast) as he hobbled on
one leg,* decorously, and incongruously, dressed in top hat, striped pants,
and cutaway. A man on crutches, armed with nothing except dignity, he
seemed a symbol of his nation as he was brought to the table on the
deck of the *U.S.S. Missouri* to formalize the extinction of the great Japanese dream.

As Kishi listened to a description of the historic ceremony over the
radio, he was overwhelmed with the realization of what Japan had tried

* Shigemitsu had lost a leg during the same 1932 Shanghai Incident in which
General Ueda, Kishi's pre-war military boss in Manchoukuo, lost his.

to accomplish by going to war. Lined up on the deck of the *Missouri* were representatives of the United States, Great Britain, the Soviet Union, and an endless list of smaller countries. Japan, an island nation of eighty million people, about half the population of the United States alone, a nation almost without resources, which less than eighty years before had been an isolated feudal state without a single modern industry, had attacked all these countries and had expected to win! He felt pride that his nation had been able to do as well as it had done under the circumstances, but simultaneously, an overpowering sense of guilt for having helped to commit his people, so innocent, to a war which Japan could never have won. He had so carefully avoided all his life any competition in which the odds were against him, yet he had dared to gamble the future of his country against astronomical odds.

A deep, unfamiliar voice now boomed forth in English, interrupted at intervals by a Japanese translation. It was the voice of a man who was now even more powerful than the Emperor—Allied Supreme Commander General Douglas MacArthur. Kishi listened intently, his heart thumping, for from the victor's first words to the conquered he might be able to sift some suggestion of Japan's—and his own—future.

". . . It is my earnest hope and, indeed, the hope of all mankind, that from this solemn occasion a better world shall emerge out of the blood and carnage of the past—a world founded upon faith and understanding—a world dedicated to the dignity of man and the fulfillment of his most cherished wish—for freedom, tolerance, and justice. . . ."

Freedom, tolerance, justice . . . were these the words of a conqueror? However good had been Japan's intentions, were these the words with which Japan had greeted the people of the nations it had conquered? Japan was now helpless. The victor could treat the vanquished as it pleased. Was this how it pleased? Certainly there was great dignity in that voice, and it seemed to ring with sincerity. Of course, only time would tell whether actions would implement the words or whether the words were hollow, intended only as a deceptive means of winning Japanese cooperation.

Kishi's first favorable impression of the conqueror did little to calm his concern about the possible behavior of the occupying soldiers. Kishi recalled the trip he had made to the United States in 1926. He found some solace in recollections of the kindness of the people he had met. But he remembered, too, the racial prejudice he had encountered. And men usually became different beings when they put on uniforms and occupied other countries. Many of his own people had turned into beasts when they had been turned loose, free of inhibitions, in foreign lands, lands they were supposed to protect and guide. The military had tried to keep this from the people, but too many haphazardly censored letters from soldiers at the front had revealed the atrocities that had occurred. Kishi wasn't clear about the reasons for them, but perhaps brutality was a natural reaction on the part of all conquering soldiers. If so, Japan could be in for an era of terror even worse than that which had passed.

Less than two weeks after the surrender ceremonies on the *Missouri,* Kishi read in the newspaper that Tojo had been thwarted in an attempt to kill himself. As police were about to arrest him in his Tokyo home, he shot himself in the chest, but American army doctors, ironically, had saved his life. Tojo had lost "face" again, using a pistol on himself rather than the traditional dagger—and failing to die at that. Kishi felt a strange surge of pity for him.

But Tojo's effort to take his life also stimulated another reaction in him. Was it not proper that he himself commit *hara-kiri?* While he debated this question, a messenger delivered a telegram from Shiina. "Americans aren't likely to convict and execute you so advise don't do anything rash."

It was good to know that an old friend hadn't forgotten him, but the matter could not be based simply on whether or not he would be hanged. It could not even hinge entirely on the criterion of family honor. It had to be considered in the light of what was best for Japan. If he permitted himself to be tried before the court of world opinion, he could perhaps be of some service by presenting his country's cause in true perspective. Japan had made an enormous tactical mistake in going to war, but he still believed that the decision had been justified in principle. Certainly arrogant militarists like Tojo would never be able to convince the world of the true nature of the causes of the war, of Japan's sincere and good intentions. Only men like himself, men more adaptable to reality, could do this, and thereby salvage something of Japan's future.

Kishi decided to solicit the opinions of his relatives and friends. It was only natural that he should discuss a question of such import with them. His family's honor was involved. Thus, with almost the same calm that he would have displayed in calling a meeting to discuss some minor local problem, he summoned more than a score of people to help him decide whether he should live or die.

As they sat on cushions sipping sake, one neighbor volunteered, "You are a good friend, Kishi-san, and that is why I think I can speak frankly. We are all men of Choshu here, the descendants of Lord Mori. Whatever the circumstances, we are still samurai. Could you imagine one of Lord Mori's retainers giving himself up alive to the enemy?"

There was silence for a time. Kishi began to feel that they had decided his fate. "Do you speak for everyone present?" he asked.

But then—Kan'ichi Nakayasu spoke out. "I don't see the sense in your committing suicide. It would be far more honorable to speak to the Americans and tell them the truth as you see it, why we had to go to war."

Again there was silence.

Kan'ichi Nakayasu turned from Kishi to the others present. "It is not as if we were led into a war which we did not want and did not believe in. The whole Japanese nation is responsible. And should we therefore all commit suicide? Or ask this man to sacrifice himself for our equal guilt?"

There were murmurs of approval. "I feel that the present circumstances require Nobusuke Kishi to appear before the court. If then this court decides to execute him, he can think about taking his life."

This seemed to turn the tide, and only a few of the men continued to argue that Kishi should not permit himself the dishonor of being taken prisoner. Kishi remained silent, feeling that he should not influence the men. He had in his heart a growing desire to live, and he was entirely willing, even anxious, to meet the men who would determine his guilt and his punishment. Yet, he would consider seriously the advice of the assembled group, whatever it was.

While the discussion was in progress, an official from the prefectural office appeared and handed Kishi a notice ordering him to report to the American forces in Yokohama on September 17th. Local police would come to the house for him and accompany him to the train. This news and the courtesy with which it was delivered, and the indication that Kishi was to travel, not as a criminal, but as a man who was being asked to keep an appointment, had a strong effect on the men present. Most soon agreed that Kishi should report to Yokohama and that he should stand trial. In the midst of the conversation, a plump middle-aged woman, dressed in an old sweater and ragged trousers, common attire in these days of hardship, entered the house. She was a local Shinto mystic, known as the Goddess of the Dancing Religion, an eccentric who claimed, quite unreasonably, 500,000 followers. Seating herself next to Kishi, whom she had known since childhood, she said with great animation, "Kishi-san, I will save you. You should not commit *hara-kiri* nor turn yourself over to the Americans."

"Go away, old woman," said one of the guests.

"I will hide and protect you," she said, ignoring the remark. "In a few years, Japan will need you and you will be called back as a hero. Meanwhile, I shall be your custodian. I will hide you where the foreigners can never find you or bring harm to you."

Someone else said mockingly, "If you were younger, old woman, I might let you hide me. But you are too old to keep a man."

The Goddess, trying to recover her authority, said, "Let us all pray for Kishi-san that he may emerge from this trouble in happiness and good health."

For several minutes, the guests—and Kishi himself—chanted Shinto prayers,* pausing occasionally to swallow down a cup of sake. Finally, Kishi's secretary lost control of himself. "This is childish nonsense," he said. "Kishi-san's very future is at stake, and here we are letting an old fool of a woman tell us what to do. The place for prayer is before the holy altar, not in an atmosphere such as this." "You will drop dead within a year," said the Goddess.**

"She meant no harm," Kishi declared. "I respect her good intentions. To hide or to be hidden, it is not my way, but it is only her way of saying that I should live. And so I shall. I have reached a decision. I am going to report to the Americans."

The house was quiet the morning of Kishi's departure. Each member of the family, wife, daughter, foster mother, and son—Nobukazu had returned home after the war from Kyoto where he had been attending college—remained in his or her own room to weep alone, for none would be seen doing so in the presence of the others, and particularly before Kishi. Kishi entered his son's room shortly before he was to leave and said, laying his hand on the youth's shoulder, "Nobukazu, do you remember those two Chinese proverbs I once taught you? I've written them out—in my best calligraphy—so that you can pin them on the wall and read them whenever you feel that the world has turned against you."

The boy took the paper which Kishi handed him and looked at the proverbs.

A man does not get angry with passion, but with reason.

No goal is beyond attainment if a man is sincere.

"I shall remember them always," Nobukazu said.

Later in the morning, Nakayasu came to say goodbye, and Kishi told him, "My friend, as you know, I may never come back. Please look in

---

* Followers of the Dancing Religion often pray while shuffling around, hands outstretched, in a kind of sleep-walking trance.
** Kishi's secretary dropped dead within a year.

on my family when you can. The land can be worked and food grown. Also, the trees can be chopped down. They should bring in a good price as there will be little fuel this winter."

The police escort finally arrived and the family, together with many friends, walked slowly, silently, through the front gate to the waiting military truck. All of them bowed to him and he returned the gesture. Then, briefly pressing his wife's hand in his own as his eyes met hers for the first time that day, he climbed into the front seat of the truck. Everybody smiled as the vehicle pulled away. It was important that one smiled on a last goodbye.

CHAPTER XII

❧

THE NAKED AT MIDNIGHT

10 A.M.
September 17, 1945

Dear Yoshiko:

. . . I had a brief rest at Katsunoi, then my train arrived—it was an hour late—and I was literally thrust into it through a window. All the way to Tokyo the train was so crowded that I could hardly move. It arrived at Ofuna at 10:30 last night and I took a tram to Kamakura, staying there overnight. I had a very sound sleep and feel quite fresh now. . . . I shall leave for Yokohama after lunch today and then [presumably will be taken to Sugamo Prison]. . . . Have faith in God and make an invocation to Him. During my absence, I want members of the family to keep in good spirits and help each other, with mother as head of the household; and no grumbling or womanish ways are to be permitted. Please tell mother to take good care of herself. And encourage Nobukazu and Yoko to become part of a strong generation.

Nobusuke

Kishi, fatigue and tension reflected in his thin, ashen face, first saw Sugamo Prison from the rear of an American military truck. As the vehicle turned down a side-street from the congested traffic of western Tokyo, the squat, gray, three-story structure, resembling a giant concrete hand, with six long cell-blocks extending like fingers from the main prison building, stood ominously etched against a lead-gray afternoon sky.

The truck, filled with nearly a dozen suspected war criminals, pulled up

225

to a large wooden-framed barbed-wire gate, over which arched a wooden sign with the roughly painted words, "Sugamo Prison." Two American soldiers, wearing white helmets and bands marked with the letters "MP" around their arms, opened the gate after another had checked the driver's papers. The vehicle then entered the barbed-wire-enclosed seventeen-acre prison compound, and the gate slammed shut with a shuddering echo of finality that sounded to Kishi like a thunderous hand-clap announcing the end of a Shinto prayer. The truck sped through several hundred yards of mud wasteland, then entered an inner compound that was surrounded by a twenty-foot-high stone wall, and stopped in front of the headquarters building. The prisoners awkwardly piled out with their baggage, Kishi carrying a small leather suitcase and a bundle wrapped in straw matting. They followed an M.P. in single file into a large bare reception room.

In a few minutes, a Japanese inmate dressed in old American army fatigues entered carrying a trayful of small white bowls of steaming rice, which he silently distributed, together with chopsticks, to each of the newcomers. Kishi, who felt too tired to eat, watched his comrades, some of whom were once high military officers, diplomats, and big businessmen, with dismay as they scooped the rice into their mouths with the gluttonous air of men consuming their last meal.

After the bowls had been collected and removed, an American army intern entered, accompanied by a Japanese interpreter who barked, "Remove your clothes." The prisoners glanced at each other briefly in embarrassment, and Kishi noted for the first time the tragi-comic appearance of the group, some dressed in homburgs and black diplomatic overcoats, others in Japanese army fatigues and ragged civilian clothing. He himself wore an old gray suit, a shirt with a frayed unstarched collar, and a white panama hat, though it was autumn. When the prisoners had taken off their clothes, they lined up in front of the intern, who examined them, took their blood pressure, and gave them shots. A soldier distributed fatigues to the new inmates, taking away the clothes they had been wearing, as well as their baggage, for inspection.

Kishi and his companions then followed an M.P. through a door leading to one of the long cell-blocks which were lined on both sides with cells occupied by earlier arrivals. They were finally halted, and the guards led them to individual cells, each about three yards square with a *tatami* floor, a steel door with a peep-hole and a large, barred, unbreakable glass window, a small section of which could be opened slightly. In one corner was a cylinder-shaped toilet, which, when covered, served as a chair, and under the window was a washbowl with a board over it for use as a desk or table.

Exhausted from the long trip, Kishi removed his fatigues, spread out a *futon* that lay folded in a corner, and collapsed on it, using his shoes, wrapped in a towel, as a pillow. But just as he was about to fall asleep, an American dressed in white smock and trousers entered with a DDT-gun and, ordering him to get up, sprayed him thoroughly. Kishi, though realizing this was a routine hygienic practice, was nevertheless repulsed by its implication. The prisoners, he thought, were probably a lot cleaner than the men who sprayed them. He had never known a Japanese infested with bugs.

When the American in the white uniform had gone, he lay down again, this time under the covers, but now too unnerved to sleep, he watched the bright quarter moon that sent in a stream of light through the barred window, imagining it as a huge mocking smile from heaven. Before the surrender, this prison had been occupied by thieves, rapists, murderers. Now he, Nobusuke Kishi, top student in his class, builder of Manchuria, designer of Japan's war economy, had been placed in a cell intended for common criminals. The sum total of all his achievements, of his life, was this three-square-yard prison cell. Thank God Moyo was not alive to see this nightmarish ending to her dreams for him. . . . Finally he drifted off to sleep.

At six A.M., he opened his eyes and stared into the expressionless face of a young G.I. guard who was bending down and shaking him. "Time to get up," the soldier said. "Sweep up the cell as soon as you get dressed." Kishi, shivering in the cold autumn air, crawled from bed and hurriedly put on his fatigues, his mind still numb as he swept the matting. At six thirty a guard opened the door and Kishi stepped out, lining up with the other prisoners in his cell-block in the corridor, where breakfast was ladled out from large aluminum pots by a K.P. team that included two Japanese generals and two privates. Kishi wondered what agonizing thoughts ran through the minds of the generals as they worked alongside men who were once at the opposite end of the social and military hierarchy, but he could tell nothing from their faces, which were utterly devoid of expression, with eyes lowered so as not to meet the gaze, sometimes bitingly ironic, of those being served. Once through the line, Kishi returned to his cell to consume his small portions of rice porridge, soybeans, and green tea.

After breakfast, the prisoners, on their hands and knees, scrubbed the corridor with brushes and soap powder, while cold air sweeping through the passage froze them to the bone and numbed their hands. But despite his own discomfort, Kishi was disturbed most of all by the sight of several elderly prisoners panting and shaking in their misery as they dragged themselves along, trying to do their assigned work. He felt a vague aching in his heart. At a time when they should have been enjoying the honor and respect that society would normally owe them, they were paying off a debt to society.

When an American officer walked by, Kishi got to his feet and said, "Lieutenant, may I ask a favor?"

The officer, a handsome young man with crew cut, stopped and turned toward him. "What is it?" he asked.

"These old men," Kishi said in halting English, "could they be excused from this work? They can't stand the cold and hard work like the younger prisoners."

The lieutenant looked around. "Okay, that guy, that one and . . . that one, can go back to their cells," he said, pointing to the designated prisoners. Then he continued on his way.

As Kishi helped one of the three older men to his feet, he said, "Some of these Americans seem quite human. A kind man, that officer."

The old prisoner replied casually, "He's the executioner."

The personal possessions of the prisoners, having been inspected, were returned to them, and became a favorite topic of discussion. What each had brought reflected to some degree his attitude toward the future. Kishi had blankets, one pair of shoes, clothes to last him for several months— long enough, he figured, to serve through his trial. Then, if he were to be hanged, he wouldn't need anything anyway, and if he were to remain in prison for an extended period, he would certainly be provided with the necessary things.

Conversation on this and other subjects was possible mainly during the daily hour-long walk the prisoners took around the courtyard under the watchful eyes of several M.P.'s. Many of the inmates would not talk about their past lives while inside the building. Outside there was no danger of hidden microphones. Kishi, however, seldom spoke even during these strolls, which were taken in double-file, but he enjoyed listening to the others talk. He heard Admiral Sankichi Takahashi say to his partner, Ryoichi Sasakawa, an extreme right-wing nationalist politician, "Sasakawa-san, what on earth are you going to do with the pile of things in your cell? You hardly have enough room left for yourself."

"You think it is too much?" Sasakawa, a stocky man with a round, animated face, replied. "I don't think it's enough. We'll probably be here at least two years. . . ."

"Two years!" exclaimed the admiral. "Never!"

"Well, how long do you think we'll be here, Takahashi-san?"

"Oh, a few months."

"Are you serious? You are certainly optimistic. We'll probably be here at least two years just waiting for sentence to be passed. So naturally I want to be as comfortable as possible."

How useless to argue, thought Kishi, over a future so unpredictable.

Prison life, despite the handicaps, offered some small pleasures. Twice weekly, the prisoners took steaming baths in the group bathtub. Moreover, they were supplied with newspapers and periodicals, which permitted them to keep track of time and the Occupation, and they could receive books, pens, pencils, paper, and other such items from their families and friends. Eventually, as the prison population grew, Kishi and his fellow inmates found themselves with cell partners, with whom they played cards, chess, and *go,* usually for cigarettes, high stakes considering that each prisoner received only five daily.

The prisoners were surprised when told that they would be permitted to celebrate *Kigen-setsu,* or Empire Day, the anniversary of the divine founding of Japan, the very symbol of the nationalism that had resulted in their downfall. Kishi, who was delighted at this unexpected leniency on the part of the conqueror, almost agreed with one inmate who commented, "The United States is a wonderful country. It is truly democratic and civilized."

And so on the eve of *Kigen-setsu,* laughter and song and *Kimigayo,* the Japanese national anthem, rang out through the prison, punctuated by unbridled shouts of *"banzai! banzai!"* as the prisoners gathered in the corridor to revive for a few hours a dream that was dead:

> *May the dynasty endure a thousand,*
> *Yea, eight thousand years.*
> *Until the time when the grains of sand*
> *Changed to rocks, are clothed in moss.*

Sasakawa, seated on the floor next to Kishi, told him in a voice broken with emotion, "I'd be willing to worship the Americans as gods if they released us right now."

But suddenly, the conquerors tightened the rules and life became more difficult. The reason for this lay in the suicide of Germany's Hermann Goering just before he was to be hanged. The Occupation authorities, to make sure that no other war criminals would succeed in such an effort, banned most gifts, including writing utensils, permitting each prisoner to keep only one small pencil. In order to make use of every bit of his pencil, Kishi left it in water overnight so that the wood would soften and could be easily split away from the lead, which he manipulated with a sheath of paper.

Goering's suicide meant also that prisoners, despite the bitter cold, were not permitted to pull their blankets over their heads at night. Kishi tried to obey this rule, but in his sleep he automatically slid down under the covers to form a cocoon of warmth with his breath, only to be awakened each time by the guard constantly looking into his cell.

But the cruelest hardship of all was the inspection for suicide instruments the prisoners had to endure each morning in the nude, this degrading ritual taking place in the freezing corridor. Their bodies nearly turned blue with cold, but this was a minor discomfort compared to the psychological horror they underwent. Nudity in the communal bathroom was one thing. Many times in the past Kishi had gone bathing in bathrooms swarming with members of the opposite sex, but this was quite natural and took place in an atmosphere of cleanliness and good health. Besides, everyone had a certain degree of privacy by proxy, since people simply ignored the nudity of their fellows.

But now the prisoners stood in line as they might for a military inspection, the only difference being that they were unclothed. Kishi, like the others, agonized in humiliation. He recalled the similar agony he had undergone when, as a boy of four, he had been carried to his great-grandfather's house in a net hung from the end of a pole, while people laughed at him. Now, he felt like laughing himself, partly as a reaction to his utter embarrassment, but also because of the grotesque nature of this revelation of human flesh and values.

There they stood, stark naked together—generals, diplomats, ministers, sergeants, privates; the mighty, the arrogant and the humble, from every strata in the Japanese social hierarchy. There were no uniforms or medals to distinguish their ranks. All were equal in their bareness. The top general and the lowest private could be told apart only by the degree of abasement reflected in their eyes.

An American soldier walked slowly down the line stopping to examine a bony admiral here, a paunchy bureaucrat there, utterly indifferent. The prisoners tried desperately to maintain some semblance of "face," pretending to ignore each other. But there was no posture they could assume that would uphold their dignity, though most of them self-consciously crossed their arms as if hoping to reduce the area of exposure. If any of the men had possessed suicide weapons, Kishi guessed, they would probably have been used during these inspections.

The physical hardships which the prisoners were subjected to, however, were light compared to what Allied prisoners of war had undergone, and even to what ordinary Japanese criminals suffered in other prisons. Moreover, the war criminals were consuming about 2400 calories of food daily, as against 1900 for the average free Japanese. Most prisoners, nevertheless, complained bitterly—especially during their daily strolls in the courtyard.

"The food isn't fit for dogs," said a disgruntled colonel, adding, though he knew the Japanese government was responsible for feeding them, "The Americans would like to see us starve."

"We shall freeze to death," said a former cabinet minister. "Where are the famous American steam heaters?"

"I can stand the food and the cold," a straight-backed admiral retorted, "but to pick up cigarette butts after these uncouth Americans is enough to make one wish one were dead."

Kishi felt contempt for such men. It seemed to him that Japan's defeat had destroyed that honor and dignity which was kindred to the Japanese spirit. He seldom complained, accepting his fate without a whimper. His acceptance of the present circumstances made him a kind of hero in the eyes of his fellow inmates, who were secretly ashamed of their own wretched attitudes. They marveled at his ability to experience imprisonment without malice or rancor.

Kishi's attitude of dignity and calm resignation was reinforced when the Occupation authorities announced they would not arrest or try the Emperor as a war criminal. The possibility that they might had been one of his biggest worries. He had felt deep sorrow when he had read the Imperial Rescript issued on New Year's Day, 1946, three months after he had entered Sugamo, in which the Emperor renounced his "divinity" and the legend of Japan's divine origin.

The renunciation of his own godliness, probably done under pressure from Occupation headquarters, he guessed, actually had little significance, for the Japanese had always considered him a mortal anyway. But it did come as a shock to many that he wasn't descended from the Sun Goddess. Kishi, of course, had never, at least in his adult years, believed the theory of divinity literally himself, any more than many Westerners, including some of the most religious, take literally every word in the Old or New Testaments. Even so, it had represented a spiritual symbol to him, and even more important, a powerful factor in the unification of Japan. But the Emperor's New Year's statement had greatly weakened the Emperor system, and was perhaps meant to be, he had feared, the first step toward its complete elimination, which would leave the people utterly without spiritual roots.

However, now that the Emperor was to escape prosecution, the nation would keep the source of future strength. The traditional structure, even if considerably modified, would be retained, and it was this respect for the Emperor which promised that Japan in the future would have a stable government and the loyalty of the people. Only in this way would Japan be able to escape the horrors of revolution and civil war which countries like France, Russia, and the United States had undergone. "Now that I know the Emperor is safe," he told several fellow inmates, "I could die in the morning a happy man."

Kishi was far more anxious about his family's plight than his own, as he learned from the newspapers of the difficult living conditions outside the prison. There was a shortage of everything, particularly of food, and his family in Tabuse had no money even to hire workers to cultivate the land. He was greatly relieved when he received a letter from his wife indicating that their relatives and neighbors were pitching in and working the land. At the same time, wealthy friends like Kan'ichi Nakayasu and Aiichiro Fujiyama were helping financially. No one was starving.

Kishi sometimes wrote to the family about his prison hardships, but expressed more concern about the situation at home. In one letter to his wife, he said:

> "The intense cold has caused my ear-lobes to become frostbitten and this is often painful. It is particularly painful and itchy in bed. I haven't had this—or chapped hands—since childhood. It reminds me of the chilblains that Yone and Masayo (their maids) have on their hands. However, we are supplied with oil ointment, which I find a big help. The food situation here isn't too good. This causes me concern about the food problem outside. . . . I am most appreciative of the kindnesses shown the family by our relatives, friends, and neighbors in these difficult days. It is important that all of us should co-operate with each other. If we do things with sincerity of the heart, God will surely keep and protect us."

In another letter to Yoshiko, he wrote nostalgically:

> "Writing letters makes my thoughts of home grow stronger and I wonder about the welfare of my mother, wife and daughter. May the land of Fresh Rice-Ears enjoy good rice crops this fall. The past days are like a dream, and how distant seem the days ahead!"

Kishi began to consider the future of his children, whose chances for marriage into good families he feared might be hurt by his imprisonment. He was particularly uneasy about his daughter. He read every day in the newspapers about girls who turned to streetwalking to supplement their families' meager incomes; and many, even from the best families, worked as cabaret hostesses.

His concern grew after watching a Japanese movie—films were shown once a month in the courtyard—about postwar immorality, a tragedy that was driven home still further when a fellow inmate sobbingly confided to him that economic circumstances had forced his daughter to serve American soldiers. Yoko, of course, was of stronger fiber. She could be trusted. Still, as a father, Kishi worried. His letters to her—and to his son—were often philosophical essays. He wrote Yoko once:

"Young people must achieve true self-realization and, with genuine passion, try to cultivate their faculties and use them. Life has no meaning unless one achieves self-knowledge and realization. One only hurts his dignity by receiving from, and fawning upon, others. One must exert his own efforts and cultivate his own ability. At the same time, one must discard from his mind every selfish motive in doing so. I am counting on you and your generation because I truly believe that the naïveté of youth will permit you to do this. Take good care of yourself. Show this letter to Nobukazu when you have read it.

Father"

It was a memorable moment for Kishi when his family came to see him in Sugamo for the first time, permission being granted the relatives and friends of prisoners to visit them once a month for thirty minutes. Kishi smiled through the beard he had grown as he entered the visitors' room and saw his wife, daughter, and son on the other side of a fine wire barrier that, at first, made them difficult to recognize.

"My dear Yoshiko. And Yoko and Nobukazu. It is so good to see you. I never thought I would see you again."

"It is wonderful to see you, too," said Yoshiko, dabbing at her eyes with a small white handkerchief. "How are they treating you? Are you getting enough to eat?"

Kishi smiled. "Enough to stay healthy. We always get just a little less food than we want. That is very good for the stomach."

He silently surveyed his family. Yoshiko, with eyes lowered, said, "I know you must be ashamed of us, dressed as we are in these old, rather unsightly kimonos. I didn't want you to see us like this."

Kishi replied, "This is not the time for looking smart, Yoshiko." He turned to his son and said, "You have grown into a handsome young man. Are you working now?"

"Yes, father. Nakayasu-san offered me a secretarial job with his company. I earn five hundred yen a month."

Kishi's eyes bulged in amazement. "Five hundred yen a month!" he exclaimed. "Why that's almost as much as I made as a minister. I can hardly wait to tell my friends."

Nobukazu reddened. "It's not as good as you think, father. You see, five hundred yen since the war is very little—barely enough to live on."

Kishi, seeing that he had embarrassed his son, said, "Don't worry. One day you will be making the salary of a minister."

He turned to his wife, "Isn't it time, Yoshiko, that we find a suitable wife for Nobukazu? Perhaps you can obtain the daughter of one of our good friends in Yamaguchi or Tokyo. Send me pictures of any likely prospects."

Yoshiko assured him that she would. Kishi then focused his attention on his daughter. The radiance of her fine aristocratic beauty warmed his heart as he gazed at her. "You, Yoko, are still very young and have time. But one day you shall have the finest husband in the land."

Smiling, she replied, "Oh, father, we want you at home. When will they let you go?"

"I don't know. I must still be tried." He added vaguely, "Don't worry, God will protect us all."

As an M.P. came over indicating that the time was up, Kishi gave his family a parting look. The three visitors bowed deeply and left.

The visit of his family gave Kishi new spirit. He was encouraged more than ever to make the best of prison life. Though forbidden to have a needle and thread, he mended his clothes with a fishbone pierced at one end with a nail he had found in the courtyard, and the thread of an unraveled towel. For amusement, he made Japanese teacups from orange rind left over from breakfast, using a sliver of glass which he had also picked up in the compound to cut the rind into the required shape, then drying the skin until it stiffened into a sturdy cup.

Kishi indulged in intellectual pleasures, too. Besides gorging himself with books, mostly oriental classics (reading matter was among the gifts still permitted), he learned how to write Chinese poetry. After his release from prison, he explained, "Chinese poetry expresses the true feelings of the prisoner. Whether a Japanese is educated or not, whether he is talented or not, he writes poems before he goes to the scaffold. And whether it is good or not, the poem always moves him."

His pride in Japanese sensitivity led to a rather contemptuous appraisal of American culture, at least as reflected in the G.I. He felt that Americans were a people without taste or appreciation, a mechanical-minded people who were absorbed in the efficiencies and trivial comforts of a mechanical civilization. One night, a guard entered his cell to make sure his head was outside the covers and found him writing in bed by moonlight.

"What are you doing?" the G.I. asked.

"I'm writing a poem."

"You're what?"

"I'm writing a poem."

"Well, I'll be. . . ." exclaimed the guard. "A poem. You are about to be hanged—and you're writing a poem. Well, I must give credit to you Japs. You sure have guts. I couldn't write a poem even if I was in love."

Kishi stopped writing and put the pencil and paper away. How had Japan ever suffered defeat at the hands of such people? he asked himself. It was as incongruous as to discover that the scribblings of fools had superseded the wisdom of the ancients.

Kishi wrote most of his poems for his wife, recalling the sweetness and warmth of home life, expressing the tenderness he felt toward their children. He did not consider himself a poet, but found in writing poems a solace and escape from loneliness.

I dreamt last night of sipping green tea with my family after growing tired of reading in the long autumn night.

Four years ago I gathered mushrooms with my wife and daughter in the hills near home, and as the season approaches again, I wonder if the mushrooms are sprouting anew.

The coming of autumn brings recollections of my daughter and other children gathering chestnuts every day in the woods near home.

Kishi scrawled one poem on the bare white wall of his cell, feeling considerable comfort each time he gazed at it:

Insignificant being though I am, I shall leave my name to posterity.

Once, he received from a friend, who was trying to nourish his morale, a poem that read:

As precious as life is the worthy name, which will not fade for a million years.

Kishi replied:

My wish is to explain for posterity the just war that is known by a different name.

Yes, the war had been just, even if, at the same time, wretched. Kishi knew he deserved to be punished with the others for his share of the responsibility, for the mammoth tactical error that had been made. Millions of Japanese had been killed and left homeless—and all in vain. But somehow he would make the world understand that Japan, at the time of decision, had seen no alternative to war. He would explain with the proper humility, yet with unswerving conviction, how Japan's traditional economic ties with China, so vital to his country's existence, had been threatened by the growth of a Chinese nationalism as powerful as Japan's but without its idealism; how the United States had failed to understand what this threat meant to Japan and had itself endangered the country's life with an economic blockade. Japan's leaders should have known that war was not the answer, but reason simply was unable to overcome the tremendous emotional pressures exerted on them. If only the world had recognized Japan's good, indeed godly, intentions, however erroneous had been its ultimate resort to war.

Was Japan, because of a single miscalculation, to be forever deprived of the status it deserved among the nations? He anxiously sought clues to this question in the newspapers. Sitting cross-legged in his cell, he devoured every column, every word in the Japanese and English-language press, as well as in *Time, Life, Newsweek,* and other American publications.

He was grateful for one thing, anyway. General MacArthur was not carrying out a policy of vengeance. His regime not only agreed to retain the Imperial system, but seemed genuinely interested in Japan's reconstruction. Nevertheless, Kishi was worried about how this was being accomplished. MacArthur was trying to push through a new constitution that would restrict the powers of the Emperor and make the cabinet responsible to parliament. It looked as if the General wanted to remake Japan into another United States, to destroy the unique traditions and values that made Japan great, and put in their stead an imitation democracy.

Democracy! Certainly it could be useful—if fitted into the Japanese pattern of life. Prince Ito, friend of his great-grandfather, had understood this when he composed the Meiji Constitution, creating a system of representative government and a Bill of Rights to safeguard the rights of the individual and of property. But sovereignty resided in the person of the Emperor. That was Japanese democracy. As the newspapers had quoted a Japanese leader that very morning, "The government of the new Japan must have a democratic form which respects the will of the people. In our country, from olden days the Emperor has made his will the will of the people. This is the spirit of Emperor Meiji's Constitution and the democratic government of the future."

But what was MacArthur trying to do? To transfer sovereignty to the people. This would only mean disorder, anarchy, a breakdown of the Japanese social order, Kishi thought. It was not that he lacked respect for the will of the people. After all, he had run for parliamentary election in 1941 after he had been selected Minister of Commerce and Industry— when no other minister would chance losing such an election. He had done so because he thought the people should have the chance to approve or disapprove of him. He had done so because he knew that the support of the people was essential to effective government.

But democracy could be carried too far. The discipline of Japanese society—the key to the nation's greatness—could only be maintained if the people remained responsible to the Emperor. Already the effects of too much democracy had been felt. Family ties had loosened; daughters walked the streets and aged parents were neglected. Children were abandoning the Japanese classics for those ridiculous American comic strips, and in *Life* magazine, he had seen a shocking picture of Japanese boys and girls walking hand-in-hand in the park. What was happening to the rich, rock-hard character of Japan, the tight national fabric in which each thread had been so firmly woven?

Even more disturbing were the gains being registered by the communists, who were winning control of the new labor unions, infiltrating parliament, working to end the Imperial system—though discreetly playing down this part of their program. On May Day (1946) tens of thousands of people carrying red flags had, under communist direction, invaded the Imperial Palace grounds to protest against the food shortage—as if the Reds cared whether all of Japan starved! And the people were falling for their false slogans.

MacArthur, shackled by his promises of free speech and assembly, had not lifted a finger to slow the communists down—not until almost a year later, in February, 1947, when they planned to stage a general strike, which might have resulted in a communist seizure of the government had it not been banned at the last minute. It took a long time for MacArthur to realize that the communists were abusing the privileges he had granted the Japanese people. Perhaps now, Kishi hoped, the Reds might lose some popular support—now that the people finally understood that the Americans were opposed to communism. Many of them had probably thought MacArthur supported the Red movement. After all, both claimed that they wanted "democratic" reforms, such as elimination of the *Zaibatsu* and redistribution of the land to the peasants. One of the most effective communist weapons was to use democratic slogans to confuse the people.

Kishi realized communism had an appeal of its own to the Japanese, that it fed on more than American tolerance and the hunger and misery prevailing in the country. The Reds were dedicated and dynamic, constantly waving flags and shouting hollow promises, the same tactics that, for a far nobler purpose, had turned Japanese soldiers in the war into bitter-end fighters. During this time of turbulence and disillusionment, it was not surprising that this fanaticism could easily be diverted into ultra-revolutionary channels.

Moreover, the collectivism preached by the communists was far easier for the Japanese web society to understand than was the unorderly individualism of the Americans, constituting a factor that fit in neatly with the philosophies of both liberal and conservative elements. The liberals, revisionist by nature, were attracted by the communist *theory* of collectivism, which promised to eliminate all social distinctions between people through the establishment of a classless society. The conservatives were drawn, to some extent, by the communist system as it was actually practiced, with the accent on hierarchy, though hierarchy based on political rather than social considerations. Some traditionalists could visualize, incredibly enough, communism within the framework of the Imperial system. The Reds were playing it smart indeed, telling the revisionists that communism offered "each according to his needs," and the Imperialists that it promised "each according to his ability."

On the surface, communism was an imposing doctrine to many Japanese. But it would be disastrous, Kishi knew, if the Reds came to power. For no matter what they promised, they would inevitably destroy the Emperor system, the very soul of the Japanese nation. They would also do away with private industry, taking over the *Zaibatsu* they were now campaigning against and all other Japanese firms. Kishi smiled as he recalled how his political enemies had called him a "communist" before the war because he had favored a "planned" economy.

Furthermore, a communist government would naturally be subservient to Moscow, and this would mean the permanent subjugation of Japan.

Kishi would have little love for Russia even if it weren't communist. But he distrusted far more a communist Russia, which wanted, as the Czar never had, actual political control of Japan.

This was not all. He also despised the communists because . . . because he was Japanese. And he was sure that other Japanese would eventually feel the same once they saw through the propaganda camouflage. Aside from their disagreeable policies, the Reds, he had learned from meeting them before the war, simply weren't gentlemen. They ignored the niceties of Japanese life. They were loud, crude, impolite. They did not bother to bow correctly, nor to smile in order to hide a heavy heart. They were insensitive people who did not know *giri*. These were the scoundrels to whom MacArthur, at least until recently, had given a free hand.

Kishi often discussed political questions with Jusoh Miwa, his liberal-minded friend. "I favor giving sovereignty to the people," Miwa told him on one of his visits. "It is the only way to guarantee against another Tojo coming to power and again offering disastrous advice to the Emperor."

"But Japan needs strong leaders to keep its unified character," Kishi replied. "I disapproved of Tojo and helped to force his fall, but he was a man comparable to a hundred men. His weakness was that he had too many military advisers and almost no one who could give him political advice."

"You see where such leaders have led Japan," Miwa said. "The Japanese people must have more freedom in the future, not more unity."

"Freedom is a relative term," interrupted Kishi. "It could mean anarchy."

"Tell me," said Miwa, "are you happy in prison? Many people outside are nearly starving. They envy you prisoners. You don't have to worry about where your next meal is coming from. You don't have to pay rent. You get free baths, haircuts, medical treatment. You're not really so badly off. But I'll bet you would change places with any homeless vagabond if you had the opportunity."

After a moment, Kishi replied, "I suppose you're right."

"You see, freedom, however you define it, means quite a bit to you," Miwa said, smiling. "And freedom is something we would never have if sovereignty were not given the people."

An M.P. standing nearby started moving toward them. Kishi's friend whispered, "Our time is up. Be careful what you say about the government after this. If he heard what you said, things could go bad for you at the trial." Pausing, he added with some concern, "How do we know that this wire netting separating us isn't recording our every word?"

"I'll speak as I wish and I don't care who knows my views," said Kishi firmly.

Miwa laughed. "You're getting to sound like a real democrat."

When he returned to his cell, Kishi lay on the *tatami,* his head resting on his hands, and, in some confusion, contemplated his conversation with Miwa. Why had he defended Tojo? Why did he still remain loyal to the man and system of government which had brought disaster to Japan? All that he could summon to support his view was the feeling that Japan's ancient and honorable heritage was now being threatened. Neither communism, Russian-style, nor democracy, American-style, were capable of filling the nation's spiritual vacuum. What, indeed, was freedom? he asked himself. Had he ever really experienced it? Would he even recognize it if he possessed it? In a sense, was not life itself, with its binding obligations, like a huge prison? . . . He fell off to sleep and dreamed of his childhood. He went fishing again for eels with Uncle Matsui and he carved sheets of pounded rice into round little cakes that felt soft and spongy in his hands . . .

In May, 1946, the trial of twenty-eight major Japanese war criminals for "crimes against peace, war crimes, and crimes against humanity" began before an eleven-nation International Military Tribunal for the Far East. Kishi had seen little of Tojo, the principal defendant, in Sugamo, as the two were assigned to different cell-blocks, but he had caught glimpses of him during the morning strolls in the courtyard and at the occasional social gatherings that were permitted. Once, Tojo agreed to carve his name in one of Kishi's orange-rind teacups. But he usually tried to avoid his wartime subordinate, who had so "ungratefully" helped to unseat him from power. Kishi believed that Tojo and all his top cohorts would be hanged in short order, and that the remaining important war criminals—himself included—were faced with the prospect of following them to the gallows shortly afterward.

The trial, however, dragged on for months on end as Allied defense counsels used every legal trick to defend the war criminals, who were given free rein to propagandize the cause of Japan. Kishi read Tojo's testimony carefully. He admired his courage in taking full responsibility for Japan's defeat, if not for the war itself. Tojo said:

"I believe firmly and contend to the last that it was a war of self-defense, and in no manner a violation of presently acknowledged international law. As to the other question, the responsibility for defeat,

I feel that it devolves upon myself as Premier. The responsibility, in that sense, I am not only willing but sincerely desire to accept fully."

If Kishi could sympathize with Tojo's moral view of the war, he considered the General's statements in court too blunt, too inadequately explained, showing little or no regret. Tojo obviously cared less about clearing Japan's name in the eyes of the world than about clearing his own in the eyes of the people he had led to ruin. He was still as clumsy as ever in the handling of delicate matters.

Kishi was astonished when, after nine months of confused testimony, only seven of the twenty-eight accused, including Tojo, were condemned to death. Kido, Hoshino, and even Admiral Shimada, who had directed the attack on Pearl Harbor, got off with sentences of life imprisonment. Togo was given twenty, and Shigemitsu only seven, years. Kishi, for the first time, felt that he had a good chance of avoiding the noose himself, for certainly his guilt was less than that of the men who were to be hanged.

He was deeply impressed by the painstaking efforts of the Allies to conduct a fair trial. No Japanese court would have offered the defendant such ample opportunity to present his case and been so ready to give him the benefit of the doubt, at least under the wartime regime, and he felt a sense of shame that he and his fellow prisoners had at first so distrusted the American attorneys representing them. He had agreed with one friend who had said, "I'm afraid that our American lawyers, being here in Japan for the first time, will interest themselves far more in the sights of the country than in our cases."

But now Kishi and all the prisoners were convinced that these attorneys were doing their utmost in the "search for the truth." Sasakawa said, "These wonderful men are like one's very conscience. We Japanese have the *Bushido* code of chivalry, but the Americans obviously have a brand of chivalry, too."

Optimism now pervaded Sugamo Prison, but Kishi refused to jump to conclusions and continued living from day to day, still leaving his future in the hands of fate. Nevertheless, he waited anxiously for his trial to come up. Meanwhile, other prisoners—mostly war criminals accused of individual atrocities—were tried, and some hanged, all secretly in a corner of the prison compound. As the condemned were kept in a special death-house, the other inmates could only surmise that a hanging had taken place from rumors circulated by prisoner K.P.'s, who were careful to note the amount of food prepared each day. As the food diminished, so did the confidence of many of the prisoners still to be tried.

The rules at Sugamo were gradually relaxed again to permit more prisoner gatherings and entertainment. Inmates could now visit each other's
cells during specified periods of the day, using this time to play games
or exchange nostalgic family recollections. About once a month, a party
was held in the corridor, at which songs were sung and traditional Japanese plays enacted by the inmates, who fashioned costumes and props
out of newspapers.

The prisoners also formed a relief association to assist the families of
war criminals living in destitution, telephoning friends to ask them for
contributions to the fund. Requests made to Diet members for relief
measures eventually resulted in the passage of three relief bills. The
prisoners optimistically established classes in radio repair, barbering, and
massaging to prepare themselves to make a living when—and if—they
were released. Since a masseur, to practice, had to have a license granted
only after passage of a national examination, the prisoners got the Welfare Ministry to designate the prison school as an authorized training
institution.

"Prison has prepared me to do many things," Kishi told his wife. "As
a 'big shot,' I never did any menial labor myself. I always gave such work
to underlings. Now I understand how hard, and sometimes painful, such
tasks can be. I have a better sense of values. With the experience I've
gained in prison—from scrubbing floors to doing my own laundry—I'll
always be able to make a living."

Kishi and the other older prisoners spent part of their leisure advising
younger inmates on personal matters, counseling them on everything from
property rights to family matters. It was only Japanese, they thought, for
the elders to help younger people solve their problems. Kishi was surprised, and disappointed, to learn that many of these problems concerned
the failure of wives to stand behind their prisoner husbands. It was not
uncommon for a wife to demand a divorce, and, under the liberal social
laws recently passed, she could obtain one. She would often simply explain that she no longer wanted her husband because he had committed
war atrocities, the usual crime of which the younger prisoners were accused. Japanese women, Kishi thought, were forgetting their deepest
obligations. Of course, he could understand the wife's viewpoint, however much he disapproved of it. Her husband shared the responsibility
for the catastrophe that had befallen Japan, and so he was now regarded
as an unscrupulous man in the eyes of many disillusioned people. Thus,
if she had already been unsatisfied with her marriage, she had what

seemed like a good excuse to leave him, and she was encouraged by the new divorce law.

But this excuse, Kishi believed, was hardly a valid one, for, odious as her husband's crimes may have been, he was not basically responsible for them. He was, in most cases, a soldier and therefore he had acted under the orders, or the encouragement, of his superiors. The generals were the guilty ones, not the privates who, while in uniform, did not, and could not, act with free will. In any event, a man's actions in war, however abominable, did not justify his wife's abandonment of her marital obligations to him. On the contrary, it was her duty to comfort and support him at this time of great difficulty.

Kishi was thankful that his family and friends had not forsaken him. They understood that he had made an honest mistake when he had signed the resolution of war, believing that this decision was in Japan's best interest. He had not deliberately violated *giri* to his family name—any more than had the common soldier.

As if substantiating the firmness of his family ties, a letter arrived from Yoshiko informing him that she had found an excellent match for their son: Nakako Tanabe, a daughter of an old friend of the family from Yamaguchi. Enclosed was a picture of the girl. If he approved, Yoshiko wrote, the wedding would take place without delay. Kishi looked at the photo. A fine, elegant girl, he thought, and of excellent family. Yoshiko had done a good job. He gave his blessing in a poem:

For three years have I missed the family gatherings, but now our son's bride shall bring joy to us all.

Yes, he concluded, he was indeed a lucky man.

Kishi could excuse the mistaken behavior of subordinates supposedly reflecting the will of their superiors. He could also excuse the behavior of these superiors if stemming from fundamentally moral intentions. But he was contemptuous of men who proved themselves morally unworthy of the place they had occupied in life, for in claiming a place not meant for them, they had cheated the community. And this contempt extended to a large number of his fellow inmates. As their bodies were stripped of gaudy uniforms and striped trousers, so, it seemed to Kishi, were their souls stripped of spirit, pride, and courage. He listened to some of them whine and complain without pause, watched others go about their duties like dazed, beaten animals. At mealtime, he saw a few ex-generals and cabinet officials served larger portions of food than the other inmates because they had bribed the cooks with cigarettes. He observed once-proud officers

selfishly shoulder their way to the front of the mess-line instead of waiting
their turns. It was not surprising, he thought, that many of these men
were charged with cruelty to war prisoners.

Kishi was especially ashamed to have once associated with a former
cabinet minister who became the laughing-stock of the prison because of
his indecent efforts to conceal food. In view of Japan's food shortage and
the black market resulting from it, a strictly-enforced Sugamo regulation
prohibited prisoners from retaining any part of their food rations not
consumed. One day the inmates were served an extra portion of mackerel
pike, a "common people's" fish which few of Japan's former leaders had
ever eaten, but which in these days of shortage seemed fit for an Emperor.

The statesman in question decided to keep this additional ration, either
to eat it later or for black-market purposes, wrapping up the fish in an
old newspaper and hiding it under his blankets. But hardly had it been
concealed when a cell inspection began. The ex-Minister, who had coolly
helped to determine world-shaking policies only a short time before, became so desperate, so afraid, that he tried to flush the fish down the toilet.
But, to his chagrin, the fish obstinately refused to go down the drain, and
to make matters worse, water started overflowing the bowl, even as he
heard the inspector's footsteps approaching. He frantically rolled up a
sleeve and extended his arm into the toilet, literally pushing the reluctant
fish into the drain, succeeding in this desperate endeavor just as the inspector opened his cell door. The indignity of the scene had thoroughly
revolted Kishi. He had contempt for a former cabinet member who would
hoard food and then react with such panic.

A former military commander in the Philippines was also despised by
Kishi. This general would never smoke his ration of cigarettes, but saved
them for the day of his release, when he planned to dispose of them on the
black market. However, his cellmate, another general, found the hiding
place where he stored these cigarettes and secretly smoked every one of
them. When the dispossessed prisoner discovered this, he almost suffered
a stroke. Although Kishi could not respect either of the men, he sensed
that a kind of justice had resulted.

Kishi also regarded with disdain a top wartime politician whose reputation for valor had been spotless before he entered Sugamo. But now, instead of facing his fate with the courage expected of him, he tried a devious
means of escaping it, falsely claiming that he suffered from tuberculosis
in the hope of being released. Though an X-ray was taken of his chest,
he somehow convinced himself that the doctors would believe him and

packed his things the morning after the examination to be ready to leave the moment his release orders were issued, even bidding his friends goodbye. The orders failed to come through that day, but he remained optimistic, explaining to his companions that it was Saturday, and no Americans worked on Saturday. On Monday morning he was ready to go again. As it turned out, nearly everyone in the prison was released before this man.

Equally repugnant to Kishi were the wretched bathing manners of some of the prisoners. There is something of a spiritual nature about taking a bath in Japan, an occasion when men traditionally lay aside their worldly troubles and relax mind and body. Any breach of bathing etiquette is virtually equivalent to sacrilege. Yet, when bath-time came, generals and politicians raced to the bathroom like unmannered children, many not even bothering to put on their sandals. And when they got there, they fought over the few safety razors available for shaving at the wash-bowls. Even in the bathtub, a waist-deep pool large enough for several bathers, the conduct of some of the men was shocking. One prisoner dared to soap himself in it, something unheard of in Japan, where all washing is done outside the tub, which is used only for warming and soaking.

Such crude behavior might be tolerated in a common soldier, but not in men of rank and breeding. It made Kishi wonder if the Japanese had been as strong and united in spirit, purpose, and dedication as he had believed. Had the moral fiber of the Japanese community been broken by defeat? Had the Japanese lost their status as a civilized people?

Kishi told his son, "There's one thing I'm learning about in Sugamo— human nature. I've seen men for the first time stripped of convention and pretense, and when I think of some of the people who have led Japan, I'm disgusted. We cannot blame this on the Americans. They may not understand our customs, and they may inadvertently force us to violate certain of our manners, but they have not brought upon us this disgrace. My son, there is nothing worse than to see civilized men turn into animals."

Such men, unlike Kishi, had not been able to weather the sudden crack-up of their orderly, hierarchal world. No longer held in place by their bonds with society, completely cut off from the community they had led, they found themselves drifting in a moral void, just as had the captured soldiers who had disobeyed them by living. They were no longer concerned with personal or family reputation. They had no conception of the rules in this strange, new world without perspective, where generals and privates ladled out soup side by side. And thus did men who had once been powerful and able enough to shake the world suddenly turn into pumpkins at the stroke of Japan's midnight.

Few prisoners were able to survive completely the rigid moral test of Sugamo, and those who did were among the first ones Kishi, and most of his fellow inmates, had expected to crack. They had believed that the military, with their rigorous disciplinary training, would stand up best to the prison hardships, followed by the civilian extreme rightists who would not compromise on the thesis of Imperial infallibility. The weakest groups, he had thought, would be the businessmen and the nobility, who, knowing only luxury and comfort, would find it impossible to adjust to prison life.

The opposite proved true. Businessmen such as Gisuke Aikawa, Koichiro Ishiwara, and Shozo Murata constantly displayed good spirits, offering words of hope to the others, refusing to become discouraged whatever the news or the circumstances. For their world had actually been least affected by defeat. They had from the first been uneasy about the war, on the one hand realizing more clearly than most people the economic potentialities behind the Western war machine, and on the other, fearing the ascendancy of the military, with whom they were traditionally at odds. Now, if they ever got out of prison alive, they could start rebuilding, even if within a new, unfamiliar world. As for Kishi, he too had had certain reservations from the beginning about the war, and since Saipan he had been convinced of its futility. Thus, he had had many months to condition himself to the defeat he knew was inevitable. In addition, his extraordinarily cool and philosophical nature gave him the necessary strength to withstand prison life.

But for the military, the defeat meant that they were, to all intents and purposes, dead. And even the fact that they were physically living was inwardly painful to them, for as soldiers they should have had the courage to commit *hara-kiri*. Even Tojo had compromised with his principles, trying—and failing—to take the easy way out by pulling a trigger rather than ripping his belly open as tradition required. This group had been trained to endure hardships, to die gloriously in war without a second thought, but it had not been trained to live in defeat.

Prince Nashimoto, former Grand Marshal of the Imperial Army, and the only member of the Imperial family to be arrested or imprisoned, proved to be one of the few "militarists" with moral staying power. He cleaned toilets and served K.P. duty with the quiet unperturbed dignity with which he had once led military parades. "I must set a good example," he told Kishi with a smile. "After all, I'm here as the representative of the Imperial Household."

Kishi compared the weakness and pettiness of most of his fellow inmates with the qualities displayed by their American attorneys. The United States, as the victor in the war, owed nothing to the vanquished. It was free to take its pound of flesh, and American—and world—public opinion would probably approve. Yet the Americans, even if they did not really understand Japan, were trying their utmost to be fair. They were, in fact, exhibiting some of the very ideals of conduct that were supposed to constitute *Bushido*—justice, benevolence, politeness, sincerity, honor, courage—though they had nothing to gain in terms of personal glory in the eyes of the community to which they belonged.

But what of Japan? Even when it had all of East Asia under its wing, it had not lived up to the *Bushido* code. Did not the daily testimony at the trials reflect the extent to which this code had been violated—murder, rape, atrocities beyond imagination, committed against people whom the Japanese had professed to consider as their "younger brothers?" It was not difficult to guess how Japan would have acted if it had won the war and had occupied America, with which it had no racial or sentimental ties whatsoever.

Stirred by these thoughts, Kishi began reading more books dealing with Western democratic theory, including the complete text of the American Constitution. Sometimes when the moon was bright, he would continue reading long after the electric lights had been turned off. There were so many questions that needed answering. Occasionally he discussed them with his fellow prisoners, but more often he dwelled upon them in solitude.

Originally, he had thought America's victory was just a matter of material superiority. But now he began to doubt that machines alone had been responsible for the success of the Americans. Certainly in some of the jungle fighting this could not have been so. It had been man against man, and the Americans—many of them seemingly uncultured and shallow—had matched or bettered the spiritually powerful Japanese. They must have been fortified with some strong inner spirit, too—a spirit, perhaps, which he did not understand. He would study their philosophy more carefully and objectively than he had before. Maybe there was, indeed, something that Japan could borrow from American thought, as it had borrowed from Chinese philosophy in the distant past. Perhaps the Meiji leaders had erred in importing Western machines without investigating the environment in which they had been developed.

These thoughts led to other disturbing questions. If Japan had lost a battle of the spirit, perhaps, after all, it did not deserve the place in the sun it sought. On the other hand, could it be true that the loss of one battle, however great in scope, repudiated the whole spiritual and philosophical foundation on which Japan had judged its history and based its future?

He thought of Great-grandfather Sato, the personification of Choshu glory. Had he been living a hollow dream? He visioned his samurai mother kneeling at the altar of Hachiman Shrine. Had she, too, been wrong? And Ikki Kita, and Dr. Uesugi—had these brilliant minds so greatly erred? If it were true that all had built their world on a base of sand, then the war perhaps was more than a tactical blunder. For unless motivated by spiritual objectives of a higher order, was not war intrinsically evil, whoever won it? One thing was certainly clear. Japan in the future would have to use peaceful means to attain its ends, and such means appeared more characteristic of democratic than of totalitarian philosophy.

American-style democracy, Kishi knew, was rooted in the thesis, "All men are created equal." The fundamental political strength of the United States was based on the principle of equality. This system was perhaps good for America. But could it be applied to Japan? The traditional Japanese way of life was founded on social stratification, each family constituting a society within the greater society of the state, and each individual fitting into his proper place on both levels. The state was, in fact, one large family, headed by the father of all Japanese, the Emperor. For Japan, this had always been the natural way of life, and it was, it seemed to Kishi, unfortunate that the other countries of Asia could not appreciate the value of such a family system on an international scale.

He remembered that a Japanese philosopher had once written:

> "The equality and freedom which Japan considers, and moreover tries to realize, is the true equality and freedom resting on just principles of nature. That is to say, by the recognition of man's inequality, each individual is given his appropriate place. Human beings, who to begin with are unequal, are thus enabled to avoid the misfortunes arising from this inequality, and each person is permitted to fully manifest his talents and ability."

Kishi firmly believed that this was a much sounder appraisal of the human condition than the American doctrine. It was false to say that "all men are created equal." Still, was the Japanese philosophy really incompatible with that of America? When the United States spoke of "equality," it quite obviously did not mean that all men are equal in terms of ability, but simply that all men have the right to equal opportunity. This principle was, to be sure, unknown in pre-Meiji feudal Japan, when every individual was born into a particular caste and bound for life by the special social laws governing it. But since the Meiji Restoration, the Japanese people had, to a considerable extent, enjoyed equality of opportunity to develop themselves as their abilities permitted. Any child with superior intelligence could take the entrance examinations to middle school, high school, and university. True, few children of peasant and worker families could afford such schooling, but there was no rule against their advancement.

This thought revived in Kishi's mind memories of the agony he had undergone at examination time at each stage of his school life. The cruel competitive spirit among the students, the sword of family honor hanging over his head, the terrible tensions, followed by indescribable relief when he discovered that he had passed the examinations. He had been very fortunate. But how miserable had been his companions—more than 80 per cent of the applicants in some cases—who, having failed, had humiliated their families. They had had to be satisfied with a lower niche in the social hierarchy. But were modern Japanese really able to accept, as their ancestors had done under the feudal system, their "proper place" in society?

It seemed clear that they were not. Of course, no one would openly say so. However, after dealing with bureaucrats for so long, from clerks to ministers, he knew how restless and dissatisfied they were; how unhappy and frustrated his own father had been. And Kishi himself had always sought to advance his career more swiftly than called for under the rules of seniority. Perhaps there was something in the argument voiced by "liberals" that Japan's social structure had to be revamped to fit into the twentieth century. Kishi thought of the Americans he had been able to observe, particularly the G.I. prison guards. Uncultured as they were, there was something admirable about them. They seemed so calm, so unperturbed by the trials of daily life. The Japanese, on the other hand, never seemed to relax, except during special periods when a person was permitted to forget the world of *giri,* as at geisha parties. Perhaps that was one reason why Japan took itself and its dream so seriously, and why it had rushed so insanely into war.

Might it be possible, he wondered, to incorporate the unity of the Japanese social organization, loosened sufficiently to absorb the pressures of the modern tempo, into a democratic political structure? Would this not draw into harmony the best of two worlds?

While Kishi groped with the elusive concepts of democratic theory, he had less trouble understanding the concrete manifestations of democracy reported daily in the press. MacArthur was pushing through one reform after another. A Japanese Bill of Rights guaranteeing the basic freedoms was decreed and the Home Ministry, which had operated a ruthless centralized police force, was abolished. A United States-type constitution was reluctantly accepted by the Diet, restricting the powers of the Emperor, who became but a symbol of state, making the cabinet responsible to the Diet, forbidding the rebirth of the disbanded military, and removing from political power the peerage, which was to exist only through the present generation. Land reform measures were passed, permitting three million tenant farmers to obtain possession of five million acres of land. Labor unions sprang up, with membership gradually rising to six million. The *Zaibatsu* family combines, with their concentrated economic power, were broken, although not entirely destroyed.

Kishi was opposed to a number of these reforms, but his opposition was directed more at their form and degree than at their substance. He was not convinced of the wisdom of such drastic revision of the Constitution, though he began to realize the importance of giving the people ultimate power. The document might have been more palatable if it had been written within an indigenous philosophical framework. The wording and presentation were thoroughly Western in character, giving no quarter at all to the spiritual traditions of Japan. The preamble started out, "We, the Japanese people . . ." But the Japanese people had played no role in drawing up the document or approving it. This had also been true of the Meiji Constitution, which had used the name of the Emperor as its authority. But the Emperor had represented the people and so, in a sense, this constitution had been their own. The new model was a thoroughly foreign creation with no native roots whatsoever. Could any nation live by such a code?

Kishi was also concerned about the complete freedom given labor unions, which, he feared, would become the tools of the communists and other leftists. And he wasn't at all sure that the partial breakup of the *Zaibatsu* was wise, particularly at a time when Japan's economy needed the strengthening that only industrial consolidation could offer.

Still, these objections to the MacArthur reforms were relative, not absolute. In any event, Kishi concluded, no new constitutional rules could basically change Japan's character, nor for that matter, the character of any nation. And the Americans had been able to put into the new Constitution certain necessary reforms which Japanese politicians could never have done. These reforms might later be used to eliminate some of the obvious flaws in Japan's national fabric.

By early 1948, Kishi noted that the steamroller of reform was slowing down. The reason for this could be found in the newspaper headlines—the Berlin Blockade, the North Atlantic Treaty Organization, the Marshall Plan, Mao Tse-tung's conquest of China. The cold war was blazing. The world had largely divided into two armed camps, one led by the Soviet Union, the other by the United States. Washington no longer had time to remake Japan. It wanted to *save* Japan. If communist aggression continued, it was feared, South Korea, and then Japan, would be swallowed up in the Red tide.

At the same time, the United States suddenly realized that Japan could be a big help in pushing back this tide in Asia. Political and ideological considerations in this country had to give way to more pragmatic policies. Economic reconstruction on the speediest basis possible—even if it meant a halt to the decentralization of industry—would have to be given priority. The United States even favored granting complete independence to Japan, but this was impracticable at the time because of Russian opposition to an American-proposed peace treaty, which would have provided for continued stationing of United States troops in Japan. Instead, Washington drew up a plan for maintaining occupation forces in Japan, while allowing the country almost complete autonomy.

As part of this whirlwind effort to woo rather than reform Japan, the International Military Tribunal for the Far East advised Washington in December, 1948, to authorize the release of nineteen leading war criminals, among them Nobusuke Kishi. Kishi heard the news while playing *go* with Ryoichi Sasakawa in the latter's cell. Someone dashed in and, excitedly pointing to an afternoon newspaper, cried: "Look! Here on the front page. Nineteen of us have been recommended to Washington for release—without trial. Both of you are on the list."

Sasakawa grabbed the newspaper, mumbling to himself as he read. His forefinger halted at his own name. "By God, that's right," he exclaimed. "Kishi-san, we're going to be free men."

Kishi, without expression, looked up momentarily, then down again, as he moved a disc on the playing board. "You owe me another cigarette," he said calmly.

"A cigarette!" replied Sasakawa. "Soon we'll be able to buy cigarettes in any store. Maybe even American cigarettes. Aren't you excited?"

"Of course it's good news," Kishi said. "But it's a bit frightening, too. In a way, even more frightening than the idea of being hanged. For death, after all, is the quick, natural way of atoning for mistakes. And once one has conditioned himself to dying, it is really not so difficult. But I'm not sure whether I'm ready to face the world again."

Sasakawa replied, "But there are still many things you have to look forward to. . . . Your wife, your children, your grandchildren. . . . Do you know the first thing I'm going to do when I get out of here?— stuff myself with *fugu*. In a way, you know, we're like *fugu*.* Now that we've been expertly cleaned, people might like us. But whether they do or not, I'm going to enjoy life from now on."

"You are very optimistic, Sasakawa-san. . . . I'm over fifty now. I've lived my life, and this new chance to live again is, in a sense, like an un- expected bonus. I don't know whether it will be possible to win back the respect of the people, but I shall do my best to make up for the wrongs I have committed in the past. Prison, I think, has better prepared me to serve my country than any school I ever attended." Kishi paused. "It will be strange living in the new Japan. We can no longer be truly independent, even when the American soldiers leave. The way things are going, we've got to join either the Russian or the American bloc to stay alive. And Japan's interest, it seems to me, can best be served through continued co-operation with the United States."

Ryoichi Sasakawa laughed. "Always politics, Kishi-san. You live and breathe politics."

"Yes," said Kishi, sighing. "I suppose I am made that way."

"Then let me warn you," said Sasakawa. "If you choose to co-operate with the United States, you may not be so lucky as you were this time."

Kishi frowned. "I don't understand."

"Well, you should consider carefully that Russia and America may eventually be at war. If Russia wins, those of us who join the United States will probably be hanged. But if America wins, those who sided with Russia will probably get off pretty lightly—as experience has indicated. So perhaps it would be safer to line up with Russia."

Kishi shook his head negatively. "I would rather hang than leave the road open to communism. American-style democracy has its short- comings, but it is likely to best serve Japan's interests. Also, don't forget that the Americans have set for us a pretty good example in moral be- havior. They have been kind to us in our humiliation and have given us a lesson in how to be civilized. I feel therefore that we should entrust the future of Japan, if it must be entrusted to some outside force, to the

---

* The *fugu* is a poisonous fish that can cause death unless it has been expertly cleaned.

nation that has treated us in so dignified a way. I do not even favor neutrality. It would be disastrous for Japan to remain neutral against a force as hostile and aggressive as communism is. And since we no longer have Manchuria as a breakwater against the communist tide, we have all the more reason to throw in our lot with America."

Kishi returned to his own cell and wrote a poem to his wife:

The hearsay that good news is very near stirs my mind nowadays.

An answer came soon, two days before Christmas—a visit by the whole family. This time, in addition to his wife, daughter, and son, a shy, pretty girl he didn't know stood behind the wire barrier.

"Father," Nobukazu said, with some embarrassment, "this is Nakako, my wife. We were very sad that you were not able to attend our wedding."

The girl bowed and Kishi responded with a smile. "Welcome into the family. Yoshiko has done well, finding so lovely a daughter-in-law for us."

He asked Nobukazu, "How is your job going?"

"Not bad," his son replied. "I am now earning 2500 yen monthly. This is still far below the salary of a minister, I'm afraid."

"Is it true," Yoshiko asked, "that you will be released any day now?"

"I've heard many rumors," Kishi answered. "We'll just have to wait."

"Has there been any change in the routine, any sign that might indicate . . . ?"

"Well, last night they cut my hair and it wasn't my day for it. And this morning I was told to put my things in order. But that doesn't prove anything, of course. . . ."

The next morning, December 24, 1948, three years and three months after entering Sugamo, Nobusuke Kishi, shabbily clad in the khaki uniform, peaked service cap, and brown boots of a Japanese private, his worn, bearded face radiating suppressed exuberance, climbed with his baggage into a jeep, which a G.I. driver drove to the barbed-wire gate of the prison. Kishi showed his release papers to a guard and entered the great new world that was giving him a chance to repay the incalculable debt he owed it.

CHAPTER XIII

❧❦❧

THE NEW DEMOCRATS

THE JAPAN that stretched before Kishi's eyes as he sat beside the G.I. driver in the jeep had an unreal quality to it—like the glittering new world a blind man might see on suddenly regaining his sight. He recalled the drive through Tokyo in the truck that had taken him to Sugamo more than three years before—the charred ruins on all sides, the miserable, hungry, ill-clad people, the shattered, empty stores, the gloom of defeat that wrapped itself around the city like a blanket smothering a child.

There seemed to be no sign of gloom now as a cold winter sun caught Tokyo in its bright glare. New modern shops and department stores, some in the process of construction, stood where there had been wreckage. Through their doors poured throngs of last-minute Christmas shoppers, most of them dressed in gaily colored Western clothes and carrying decoratively wrapped packages. Each ripple of laughter, bark of an automobile horn, and whistle of a traffic policeman that accompanied this bustling urban scene was as soothing to Kishi's ear as the wail of a plucked *koto* string. There were other things that surprised him, too. Japanese girls walking arm in arm with American soldiers, newly built movie houses showing Wild West pictures, huge flickering neon-lit signs extending from virtually every shop and perched atop nearly every building.

So these were the sights and sounds of postwar Japan. He was excited by this strange, chaotic world. But his excitement was mixed with some discomfort as people looked at him curiously, with a touch of disdain, it seemed. The sight of his crumpled army uniform, the symbol of a bitter memory, jangled, he was well aware, a delicate public nerve.

The jeep finally arrived at Kishi's destination—the Prime Minister's official residence. He had arranged with his brother, Eisaku Sato, who had quit the bureaucracy after the war to enter politics and was now the Chief Secretary of the Cabinet, to meet there following a cabinet meeting. Kishi got out of the jeep, thanked the American driver, and went to the back door of the house, ashamed to call at the front in his shabby condition. He rang the bell and a maid opened the door, staring at him as if he were a beggar. "What do you want?" she asked.

"I am Nobusuke Kishi, brother of the Chief Secretary." The woman called a uniformed guard to the door, who, recognizing Kishi, apologized for the maid's behavior and led him into the parlor. His brother entered. The two men, too embarrassed to show their emotion, shook hands in silence. Finally, Eisaku said, "Congratulations." Then several of Kishi's closest friends, including Shiina and his old secretary, Takeshi Akimoto, joined them, greeting the bearded visitor warmly. "I've got to return to the cabinet meeting," Sato said. "Meanwhile, I suggest you shave and change clothes and we'll meet later for lunch." Within an hour, Kishi emerged from the guest bathroom feeling and looking like a different man—bathed, clean-shaven, and neatly dressed in a new suit that Akimoto had brought with him.

Kishi and his friends then went to a nearby restaurant, where the guest of honor ordered *toro sashimi,* sliced raw tuna. As the waitress, a pretty kimono-clad girl, left, Kishi said, "It's pleasant to be served by a young girl again after all those fat generals who served us in prison." He added when the laughter of his friends subsided, "I had erotic dreams quite often—and at my age, too."

Eisaku walked in and the group talked and laughed and exchanged jokes; it was like old times, as if nothing had changed. Kishi spoke only briefly of his life in Sugamo. "The most important thing that happened to me in prison was that I got to understand the real essence of human nature, particularly my own character. It is difficult for a man to evaluate himself while he is enjoying prosperity, fame, and power. But when he is deprived of these things and finds himself in great difficulty and adversity, he begins to realize what he really is and he will better know how to direct his life."

He paused, then said, almost incredulously, "Strange, isn't it? We're all democrats now."

That evening, Christmas Eve, scores of Kishi's old acquaintances, friends, and relatives—including his son, Nobukazu, who was working in Tokyo—gathered at Sato's home to welcome him back. With sake and beer flowing freely, they talked nostalgically of the past. They talked with mixed hope and cynicism of the present and future—the economic hardships, MacArthur's policies, the confused political scene, the prospects for independence.

The highlight of the evening was a telephone call from Aiichiro Fujiyama, who offered him a job with his company. "His kindness moved me so much that I felt like crying," says Kishi. Having been a suspected war criminal, he was barred from working for the government, and therefore had planned to go into private business. But he hadn't expected to find a good position easily. The public was still bitter toward those who had led them to war. Any company that hired war criminals was jeopardizing its reputation. But Fujiyama had not forgotten him. Kishi accepted the offer gratefully.

Kishi and his son took a train to Tabuse the next morning, and were met by their family and friends. Riding through the town in the automobile of a neighbor, Kishi re-experienced the joys of his youth. New Year's was approaching, and women and their helpers were busy as they had always been, pounding rice outside their houses. He gazed fondly at the rice fields and the meadows where he and his friends used to fly dragon-shaped kites and the river where he had so often gone fishing with Uncle Matsui.

His eyes watered when he glimpsed the Sato house, its brown wood as solid and indestructible as the memories of childhood within it. It was deserted now. Great twisting vines clutched at its walls. Moyo and Hidesuke were gone. The Sato children were scattered everywhere. Kishi recalled the feverish activity that had once gripped the Sato home at this time of year. He could still hear the hissing of the steam in the brewery where his father's helpers had converted rice into sake, the day-long banter of women hired to bake *mochi*.

He turned to Yoshiko, who was sitting next to him and asked with a smile, "Do you think mother will let me cut rice-cakes for the holiday?"

"If you promise not to eat all of the cakes yourself like you used to."

Kishi remained in Tabuse for about a month, going for long walks in the hills, fishing with his boyhood companions, getting fat on the cooking of his foster mother and wife, living the poems he had written in prison. But once he was thoroughly rested, Kishi became impatient to begin his new life. With his family, he went to Tokyo to live with Eisaku and his wife Hiroko—the daughter of Uncle Matsui*—until he would be able to build his own house.

Kishi did not want for career opportunities. Fujiyama appointed him as an executive in his Nitto Chemical Company. Shiina and other friends, including a well-known politician, Kenya Ino, formed the Toyo Pulp Company and selected him as chairman of the board. Kishi did little actual work for these firms, but the use of his name was of value to them when it came, for example, to obtaining bank loans. Though Kishi was just out of prison, most people in the business and banking world who knew him were convinced that he would soon rise to the top again —either in business or in politics. Their generosity, however, stemmed not only from the belief that he was a good risk, but from the fact that most of them had received favors from him in the past. They were bound by *giri* to repay him.

Despite the business opportunities open to him, Kishi had no intention of remaining indefinitely in the commercial world. Driven by the same desire for public recognition and idealistic sense of mission that had carried him to the top of the wartime political hierarchy, he was now determined to become involved in the postwar political struggle. But his idealism, while still intense, was no longer tinged with arrogance and authoritarianism. "I could be a successful businessman," he told his brother, Eisaku, "But this is not what I want. I feel I should play a stronger part in the reconstruction of Japan. As soon as I'm depurged I'm going into politics."

Though still barred from political activity, he began planning a new political career in conjunction with some of his fellow purgees. His closest collaborator was another ex-bureaucrat, Hideyuki Miyoshi, whom he had known since pre-Manchoukuo days. When Kishi had been jailed as a suspected war criminal, Miyoshi, who had been purged from politics but had escaped imprisonment, often visited him at Sugamo. Kishi, in his gratefulness, had sent his friend a poem:

> *In a world that changes*
> *For either good or bad,*
> *The only thing that will never change*
> *Is a true friendship.*

* Eisaku had been adopted as a prospective husband for Hiroko.

Miyoshi's regard for Kishi was reflected in his efforts to help Kishi regain political influence after his release from Sugamo. As soon as Kishi was freed, Miyoshi started lining up support for his friend among such important politicians as Kenya Ino and Hisatada Hirono, and businessmen like Tatsunosuke Takasaki.

He stressed that Kishi was uniquely qualified for a top political position and enjoyed a tactical advantage in that his brother, Eisaku, was on familiar terms with Prime Minister Shigeru Yoshida. Kenya Ino, though politically ambitious himself, agreed to back Kishi when the time was ripe and, in the meantime, have him elected to the chairmanship of the Toyo Pulp Company, which Ino partially controlled.

Miyoshi's promotional campaign began in earnest in the fall of 1951 when he and several other followers of Kishi, including Kentaro Ayabe, Eiji Arima, Yoshiaki Iko, Yuki Takechi, and Kunio Morishita, were depurged, making them eligible to enter politics. Under Miyoshi's leadership and in secret consultation with Kishi himself, who was still forbidden to engage in political activities, they formed an organization called the New Japan Political and Economic Research Association. On the surface, this was only a discussion group which sponsored lectures on reconstruction problems by scholars and business people. But the central, if unstated, purpose of the association was to lay the groundwork for a political organization that would give former purgees a chance to participate in politics and to infiltrate the influential positions in the established parties which were being held by men jealous of their jobs.

Headquarters was established in a midtown office building known as the Kojunsha—the same building in which Takeshi Akimoto, Kishi's former secretary, managed a private company, the Kizan-sha. It was thus easy for Kishi to maintain contact with the organization, and be able to offer the alibi to the Security Police, which investigated him several times, that he was visiting Akimoto. Kishi and the other leaders of the group also met once a week in the offices of the Toyo Seikan Company, where President Takasaki treated them to bowls of eel and rice.

Japanese independence was near, and as Kishi's depurging was anticipated, the association decided the time was propitious to convert itself into a more active political group to be called the Japan Reconstruction Federation. Kishi and the others agreed that the new organization would be considerably strengthened if Mamoru Shigemitsu, the wartime Foreign Minister, could be persuaded to accept the presidency.

For Shigemitsu, who was expected to be depurged about the same time as Kishi, had a large personal following and probably more prestige than any of the wartime leaders. He enjoyed the exalted status of a senior statesman; he was, to a large extent, free of the stigma attached to many of his former colleagues, having actually been opposed to the war from the beginning.

The political spectrum was a welter of splinter groups, and none, Kishi thought, really represented a large segment of the people. On the far left was the Communist Party, which was still strong, having won about ten per cent of the votes in the January, 1949, election. But the communists were gradually losing strength due, as he had foreseen in prison, to the violent and abominably rude tactics they employed to achieve their ends. They had allegedly murdered the president of the railway system in a labor dispute and had used Japanese prisoners returning from the Soviet Union for propaganda purposes, corralling them as they disembarked from repatriation ships, and forcing them to participate in Red rallies without even giving them a chance to be welcomed back by their long-suffering families.

The people were at last beginning to see the communists in their true light. The Reds were digging their own grave, confirming with their every move the incompatability of communism with the traditional Japanese concepts of social orderliness. Nevertheless, the party still was a political menace—particularly with neighboring China and North Korea in communist hands. Peking had already posed a threat to Japan by signing, in February, 1950, a treaty with the Soviet Union for the purpose of preventing "the rebirth of Japanese imperialism." The danger of the spreading communism influence would grow if the United Nations didn't win the war that had broken out in Korea in June, 1950.

Unfortunately, the communists received considerable support from the left-wing elements of the Socialist Party, who were always apologizing for the aggressive policies of Moscow and Peking. The right-wing socialists refused to have any truck with the Reds, but with the monolithic Japan Federation of Trade Unions (Sohyo) supporting the leftists, the moderates could do little to counteract the pro-communist tendency. The left-wing socialist group also appealed to those who backed many communist policies but could not accept the revolutionary and un-Japanese tactics of the Communist Party itself. This socialist faction seemed to promise a peaceful means of obtaining revolutionary results.

The conservatives, while still in control of the government, were leaving themselves wide open for possible leftist gains in the future, a danger of no small magnitude considering that a Socialist premier had held office, if for a rather brief term, in 1948. The conservatives were divided into three groups—the misnamed Progressive Party, powerful Bukichi Miki's Japan Liberal Party, and Prime Minister Shigeru Yoshida's ruling Liberal Party. All had a single central goal—power for power's sake. Within the Liberal Party itself, which enjoyed a small Diet majority, Yoshida was resented by many members for his starched-collar, authoritarian ways. And he was being condemned by the public because of his close identification with Occupation policies.

Curiously, Yoshida also benefited from these policies insofar as they concerned measures taken to strengthen the Japanese economy. As the result of American-instituted economic reforms, and financial aid, the budget had been balanced for the first time since 1931, industry had been rationalized to a large extent, and production had significantly increased. The reforms, which, Kishi noted with interest, were accomplished through free enterprise rather than planning methods, offered even greater dividends when the Korean war broke out. As the base for the United Nations Forces, Japan contributed more than five hundred million dollars worth of supplies to the war effort. A rise in trade added to the industrial boom. Textile plants turned out more than half of what they sold in their best prewar days. Coal output had increased by more than six times since 1945. Electric power exceeded its previous high by more than 50 per cent. As prosperity spread, the people were willing to go along with the government in power, despite the fact that what vigor it possessed sprang largely from American policies and money.

Kishi stood on the left fringe of the conservative bloc, not too distant from the right-wing socialists. This seemed natural. Democratic conservatism was the obvious counterpart in the new Japan to the blinding dictatorial traditionalism on which he had been fed in pre-war days, while many aspects of the national socialism he had once championed were supported by the right-wing socialists. Whereas Kishi had previously considered himself a kind of bridge between totalitarian brands of conservatism and socialism, he now thought of himself as a link between democratic versions of these same two political camps.

The political aims Kishi would foster were cut out for him. In the midst of the corruption, self-interest, and virtual anarchy plaguing the nation, he would preach the doctrine of unity, a unity which could only be found, he would tell the people, in a disciplined reformist movement of moderates drawn from all parties, including conservatives and socialists.

Kishi had once before supported a mass movement—the Imperial Rule Assistance Political Association of the Tojo era. He had supported that movement because he had been disgusted by the political ills that had afflicted Japan in the 1920's and early 1930's. He was no less repulsed by the similar ills that now beset the country, and was convinced that the solution lay in a "spiritual mobilization" effort, appealing mainly to youth, but this time within the framework of a democratic, rather than totalitarian, system. In an article published in the Japanese magazine, *Nippon Shuho,* shortly after he was depurged, Kishi wrote:

"The ideal of party politics is the conduct of affairs of state by two big parties pitted against each other, as in Britain or the United States. My desire is to see here in Japan two big parties—conservatives and reformists—rival each other, taking the middle-of-the-road course to assure the greatest happiness to the greatest number, which is the ultimate goal of democratic government. As for myself, I have little interest in the conservative parties. What I am most anxious to see is the birth of a national reformist party embracing the reformist elements of all parties. . . . At the same time, to protect farming villages and manufacturing plants against the vandalism and ideological aggression of the communists and to uphold democracy, we must rely on the united efforts of young people burning with a desire to rebuild their country."

The time for Kishi's entry into the political arena finally arrived with the negotiations that took place in the fall of 1950 for a Japanese peace treaty, which would automatically nullify the political purge. The United States was anxious to conclude such a treaty, and so there promised to be few of the customary diplomatic difficulties and delays. Fully occupied with the Korean War, the Americans had been turning over an increasing number of its Occupation responsibilities to the Japanese government anyway. The granting of independence would, it was hoped, rally the Japanese people to the Free World cause. Under foreign rule, they were, in general, apathetic toward the Korean situation and skeptical about American promises to permit Japan full opportunity to develop its trade. When a treaty arrangement was finally reached, providing for independence but the continued stationing of American troops in Japan under a Mutual Security Treaty and Administrative Agreement, the new Japan Political and Economic Research Association announced its conversion into the Japan Reconstruction Federation, to be led by Shigemitsu and Kishi as soon as they were depurged.

Kishi was immediately besieged by reporters. When asked if he expected a public reaction against war criminals and depurgees playing an important role in Japan's postwar politics, he replied:

"As far as I am concerned, I buried my past during my imprisonment in Sugamo. My association with the Tojo cabinet may be held against me, but in my own mind I feel certain that I am now qualified to participate actively in the rehabilitation of Japan. I only want the chance to prove this to the people."

Although independence day was set for April 29, 1952, American and Japanese leaders agreed that Kishi and several other purgees would be depurged in advance of this date—on April 18th. As this day neared, Kishi, calculating that it was now safe to involve himself openly in politics, offered Japan a hint of his future tactical plans when he sharply criticized Yoshida's economic policies and his inability to unite the conservatives. Yoshida, infuriated, avenged this outburst by removing Kishi from the list of persons to be depurged before independence day.

Kishi immediately turned this move to his political advantage, telling the press cannily:

"I'm not at all surprised by Yoshida's action. He has the same insolent, dictatorial attitude toward the general public. The people are actually embarrassed by him. But can authoritarianism be applied in a democracy? The answer is obviously 'no.' The first principle of democracy is to decide on matters after consultation and talks. Consultations may take a lot of time, but they are, it seems to me, the first requisite for democratic politics. . . . The people, it is quite evident, are not overwhelmed by the fact that Japan is about to regain its independence. This is because Yoshida has never tried to explain to the general public in simple words the importance of the peace treaty. Thus, the popular belief is that Japan, despite the signing of any treaty, will still not be independent in the true sense of the word. It is questionable, indeed, whether the Prime Minister *will* assume a frank and courageous attitude toward America."

Kishi's speech was reproduced and given an important position in all newspapers. He had pleaded the cause of "democracy" on the one hand, of "true independence" on the other. Before he had even entered the political scene officially, his name had made headlines, a situation that hardly eased the animosity of crusty, imperious Prime Minister Yoshida toward him.

Yoshida had never been overly fond of Kishi, to whom he was distantly related by marriage. (Hiroshi, the eldest son of Kishi's uncle,

Yosaku, with whom the young Nobusuke had stayed while going to Yamaguchi Middle School, was married to Yoshida's eldest daughter, Sakurako.) He deplored Kishi's record of collaboration with the military, feeling that this proved Kishi could not be trusted. Yoshida's own record, however, was not spotless. As Japanese Consul-General in Mukden in the late 1920's, he had helped pave the way for the military seizure of Manchuria in 1931. When Manchurian war lord Chang Tso-lin refused to lease land to the Japanese, Yoshida had warned him that Japan would, if necessary, assume ownership. He had also told the Chinese civil governor that anti-Japanese movements in the area, such as the collection of duties on Japanese goods, had to cease, and he had prohibited the construction of railroads that would compete with the South Manchurian Railway Company.

But in the 1930's, Yoshida had allied himself with Elder Statesmen, capitalists, and other "moderates" who hoped to prevent the military from taking complete control of the government. This resulted in an Army veto in 1936 of his appointment as Foreign Minister. Furthermore, as Ambassador to Great Britain from 1936 to 1939, he developed a warm feeling toward the West, and he tried, until the Second World War started, to promote Anglo-Japanese friendship. After Pearl Harbor, while most Japanese rejoiced, Yoshida smuggled a letter to American Ambassador Joseph C. Grew, who was interned, expressing regret that war had broken out. Later, at about the time Kishi began opposing Tojo, Yoshida plotted with Prince Konoye against the General and was jailed for three months toward the end of the war.

The relationship between Yoshida and Kishi was aggravated not only by past political differences, but by a deep conflict in personality. Both were ambitious and of authoritarian nature. This nature was in both cases adjustable to the requirements of a democratic system, but in making this adjustment, the two men presented a sharp contrast.

Yoshida once told Kishi, "A good Prime Minister must permit democratic elections. But when the elections are over, he must assert his full authority." Yoshida lived up to this maxim. He was blunt and uncompromising with his foes and often displayed toward them a most un-Japanese impoliteness, once causing a furor in the Diet by referring to a Socialist opponent as a "fool." Many politicians, moreover, would not forgive Yoshida for having flagrantly ignored giri to a very popular figure, Ichiro Hatoyama. He had become Prime Minister in 1946 after Hatoyama, founder of the Liberal Party, had been purged by General

MacArthur as he was about to take over the post. Hatoyama supported Yoshida as his replacement on the understanding that Yoshida would relinquish his power when the purge period was over. But in 1951, when Hatoyama was free to enter politics, Yoshida refused to honor the agreement.

Kishi, on the other hand, is a warm and genial man, and is often more solicitous in his dealings with his foes than with his friends, hoping thereby to reduce the resistance to policies he advocates. He is capable, when necessary, of using forceful measures to get his way. But he usually resorts to such tactics only after all effort at persuasion has failed.

Independence day finally came, and Kishi, automatically depurged, formally joined the Japan Reconstruction Federation. For some time, the rumor had persisted that Shigemitsu had changed earlier plans to accept the presidency of the organization to become president of the Progressive Party instead. But Shigemitsu assured the leaders of the new group the day before the inaugural meeting that he still intended to lead the Federation. Nevertheless, two days later, Shigemitsu, perhaps because he realized the Federation wanted his name rather than his leadership, agreed to become president of the Progressive Party.

Kishi and Miyoshi were furious. At the last minute, they were left without the man on whom they had depended to bring to their organization the support of a large, ready-made bloc of followers. Shigemitsu had, in Kishi's opinion, betrayed him again—just as he had when he had backed down on his agreement to denounce Tojo at the final meeting of the Tojo cabinet. Without a single member of stature comparable to that of Shigemitsu, the Japan Reconstruction Federation, its leaders knew, was being launched under highly disadvantageous circumstances.

Shigemitsu, Kishi believed, had done a disservice not only to the Federation, but to himself. As head of a new organization, he would be able to go much further than as the chief of an established party. The people would be given a chance to get used to re-accepting the leadership of a wartime minister. He would be in the political limelight, but at the same time not glaringly so. Instead, Shigemitsu had chosen to jump too far too fast. He had ignored the old Japanese proverb, "A nail that sticks out is hammered." When the Progressives were beaten soundly in the first national election held after Shigemitsu took over the reins of the party, Kishi commented:

"The poor showing of the Progressives has lowered him in public estimation. A man is at his best when his real value is shrouded in mist. If he had been patient a little longer and remained in mist, he would have served as a useful personage in the reorganization of the political world."

Kishi himself had wanted to remain in mist as the man behind Shigemitsu, for he had not yet the seniority or prestige required to warrant his assumption of direct leadership of his organization. But left little choice, he had himself elected President, with Miyoshi assuming the post of Chief Director. In addition to regular directors, a number of special advisers, not all of them members, were chosen, including Aiichiro Fujiyama, Kenya Ino, and Matutaro Shoriki, publisher of the influential newspaper, *Yomiuri Shimbun,* and a Sugamo veteran.

The organization made public a five-point program which called for policies that would:

"1) strongly appeal to the nation 'by giving it the sense of embarking on a new era';
2) prevent the infiltration of communism, foster true independence, and build a peaceful and democratic country;
3) tighten economic relations with other Asian countries and the United States;
4) facilitate development of agricultural and fishery industries, improve the condition of small and medium enterprises, and 'promote the welfare and happiness of the workers;
5) permit revision of the Constitution and rearrangement of the national structure 'in line with Japan's new status as an independent nation.' "

Kishi had considerable difficulty getting the item on constitutional revision approved by many of his colleagues, since the principal aim of this provision was to permit rearmament, which was expressly forbidden by the Constitution. These men feared the leftists would charge that the organization's real goal was the revival of militarism. But Kishi won his point with the argument that this measure was necessary to protect Japan from communism. "Now that we recognize the necessity of revising the Constitution," he said, "we should be courageous enough to explain this need to the people."

Kishi also disagreed with some of the party leaders, including Miyoshi, regarding the main political goal of the organization. Anxious to run in the Diet elections that were to be held in January, 1953, they wanted the Federation to be a conventional political party with the usual electoral aims. But Kishi insisted that its central purpose should be to "promote a national patriotic movement" that would engulf people, mainly youth, from every rank of society and walk of life—a kind of mass mobilization of the democratic spirit.

"The greatest defect of politics today," he told his colleagues, "is that young men have lost their faith. Under such conditions, they will increasingly turn toward the communists or the fascists. Our movement will help them to understand the advantages of democratic government." If members of the Federation wanted to run in the coming election, he said, he would not stand in their way, but the organization could not be geared at this time simply to winning Diet seats. "Of what value would a dozen or so seats be, anyway?" he asked. He personally did not intend to run for office. "It is more important for the nation that I create this national movement than that I run for election."

But if this was Kishi the idealist speaking, Kishi the realist had more practical motives for his stand. He would have preferred that his organization steer entirely clear of the elections because a severe defeat—and after Shigemitsu's "betrayal" this could not be dismissed as a possibility —would probably signal its death. As for himself, having only recently emerged from prison, he might well lose an election at this juncture, impairing his whole future.

There was another factor; his brother, Eisaku, a member of Yoshida's Liberal Party, planned to run for election in Yamaguchi Prefecture, the same province where Kishi believed he could himself, because of the Sato tradition, make the best race. Of course, both might win, but if one lost—and inwardly Kishi feared that he would—the loser would be deeply hurt. It was not easy losing a popularity contest to one's brother. The best thing for him to do, Kishi decided, was to wait until people forgot the past. For the present, he would build up a popular following on the foundation of political anarchy that was gradually eating away public morale. Things looked so unstable now that there would probably be another election not long after the one scheduled, and then perhaps he would be ready to take the plunge.

Miyoshi, meanwhile, gathered considerable funds for the electoral campaign, contributed in large part by executives of firms that Kishi had helped during the war, such as the Yawata and Fuji Iron Manufacturing companies and Nippon Kokan. Kishi himself, reconciled to the fact that his organization would enter the election, embarked on a three-month tour of the country to publicize his movement, gather additional campaign funds, and set up branch offices in Yamaguchi, Totori, Ehime, Kochi, Kagoshima, and Fukuoka. But he insisted in his speeches that the Federation would never become an "ordinary political party." He was embarrassed, indeed, when, after making this very pronouncement before an Osaka audience, he learned that his colleagues in Tokyo had applied to the government for recognition as an "ordinary political party."

Kishi's reaction, however, was characteristically realistic. Most members of his party, out of office since the war, were too politically hungry to restrain. They were willing to risk all for immediate satisfaction. There was little Kishi could do about it, and so, with resignation, he continued his campaigning with undiminished enthusiasm. He called for the establishment of Federation cells in every town and village, warned of the communist threat, and demanded that the Constitution, particularly the provisions forbidding rearmament, be revised so that Japan could attain "true independence." While he was touring, an article he wrote for the magazine *Nippon Shuho* summed up many of the ideas he expressed in his speeches:

"I am afraid it will take Japan at least thirty years to become independent, in reality as well as in name, and thereby be entitled to rejoin the community of nations as a respectable member. It is up to the Japanese people as a whole, but especially the youth of the country, to put forth every effort for the reconstruction of their country.

"In order to regain real independence we must consider the national defense problem before anything else. The rearmament question is very much in the news and has given rise to much discussion. Some are in favor of rearmament, but there are a great many who are against it. There are three opposition factors:

"1) The fair sex is, as a rule, opposed to rearmament. In particular, this is the case with women who lost their husbands, brothers, or sons in the war, and who are being compelled to live a miserable life because both state and community have failed not only to give them adequate aid, but have even shown a tendency to hold them in contempt. To them war is anathema.

"2) The youth of the country are most likely to be affected by rearmament in the event it is realized. It is only to be expected that they should raise objections. They are afraid that they may be utilized as human bullets; that they may be sent to the firing front in Korea.

"3) Dissatisfied with the pension policies of the government, wounded ex-soldiers in white middies are making a pathetic appeal, in the streets and in trains, for assistance from the general public—a factor which has intensified hatred of war.

"The mistake common to these lines of argument against rearmament is the hasty conclusion that rearmament means war. It is true that without armament there would be no war in which arms are used, but then, that would not necessarily eliminate aggression. The history of war is replete with instances in which the disturbance of the balance of power engendered aggression. It is like volcanic eruptions taking place in weak spots in the earth's crust. If all the nations in the world were to renounce war, all would be well. If Japan is alone in renouncing war, however, she will not be able to prevent others from invading her land. If, on the other hand, Japan could defend herself, there would be no further need of keeping United States garrison forces in Japan.

"Personally, I do not like the prefix 're' in the word 'rearmament.' For it smacks of a return to militarism. Now that Japan has regained its independence, if nominally, it must eliminate the necessity of keeping foreign troops here for protection of the nation against aggression. Japan should be strong enough to defend herself. This is the right and obligation of an independent nation. That the Japanese nation seems to prefer relying, as long as possible, on the protection of the United States, is proof enough that this country, conditioned by Occupation policies, has lost its sense of self-reliance, and that the spirit of independence she once had has been paralyzed."

Kishi made it clear that he favored revision not only of the constitutional article pertaining to rearmament, but of the Constitution in general. He was still convinced that it should be rewritten more in conformity with national tradition and in the Japanese manner of expression, although without diluting the democratic freedoms provided for by the MacArthur-created document. He wrote:

"Now that the Occupation has ended, our Constitution will have to be restudied on a new basis and be amended in pursuance of the will of the entire people. Since our Constitution is our fundamental law, which should be adhered to by the whole country, it must be a reflection of the will and wishes of the Japanese people. It is my belief that our Constitution should be revised as soon as possible."

Kishi's logic, especially concerning the rearmament issue, made a strong impression on those who listened to his speeches, and business people in particular contributed to his cause. His views appeared to be even more valid after communist-led riots at the Imperial Plaza in Tokyo on May Day, 1952, injured many innocent people. This event brought back, with a sense of horror, memories of the "February 26th Incident" and other prewar military uprisings. The communists, as a result, hit a postwar low in popularity. Conversely, contributions to Kishi's movement increased. But Kishi discovered that he had a long road to travel to obtain national support for his program. In the small towns, few people knew of him or his organization. At one village meeting, a local dignitary introduced him with the wrong first name. And it was in these same areas that the traditional parties were well entrenched. Kishi was not overly optimistic about the Federation's chances in the election.

The Yoshida cabinet resigned in August, and the election was finally held. Kishi's worries proved to be far from unfounded. On election day, as he sat in the small, rather shabby headquarters office of his party, surrounded by other party officials, he listened with a sinking heart to monotonously consistent radio reports of Federation defeats . . . Eiji Arima, Naotake Tuzaki, Toshikazu Fuke, Go Sato, Naotake Hamada, Ikei Shizeki, Masso Taki . . . and even Miyoshi. Only one member—Yuki Takechi—won in his constituency, while hardly a score of candidates succeeded who supported the Federation to some degree but ran under the banner of other parties. Kishi was particularly disappointed over Miyoshi's failure. He was not only a close friend, but in his view, the very "backbone" of the organization. It was a good thing that he personally had not entered the election, Kishi thought, for he, too, almost certainly would have lost.

He had, unfortunately, calculated correctly. The time had not been ripe for his organization to start competing for votes. If his colleagues had listened to him and kept the movement aloof from the election it would have grown in strength and stature and been in a position to make a good showing in the future. As it was, it had hardly had the opportunity to get off the ground and spread its true message. It had been accepted as just another political party, little different from the others. Moreover, the fact that he and many other leading members had been war criminals and purgees was still too fresh in the public's mind. There was also another factor. Perhaps the idea of a mass movement frightened the people, reminding them of the Imperial Rule Assistance Political Association with its dictatorial effort at spiritual mobilization. Maybe the people didn't want to be mobilized—even for democracy and peace. "It may be," he told reporters, "that we're a little behind the times."

One thing was certain, Kishi knew. The Japan Reconstruction Federation was dead. But he personally had been spared by virtue of the fact that he had not been a candidate. To remain politically alive he now had to join one of the established parties. And, since Yoshida's Liberal Party had won the election, if with a bare majority, its relatively strong position, and the moderate tenor of its policies, seemed to offer him the best opportunity for a comeback. This party was still deeply split. Perhaps he was the man to unify it. He could, in fact, use the Liberal Party as a rallying point for a reorganization of all conservatives. He might be able to achieve, through inside maneuvering, what he had failed to accomplish from the outside.

As a result of the defeat of the Japan Reconstruction Federation, Kishi narrowed the scope of his unification dream, scrapping plans for an organization that would embrace reform-minded people of all political shades. He decided to join the strictly conservative camp. What reform and unification he could now achieve, it was clear, would have to be limited to this group. The most logical two-party system, he now felt, would pit conservatives against socialists, who were equally disunified. The socialists had split into Right-Wing and Left-Wing Socialist parties after independence because of the strong tendency of the latter to flirt with the communists. Kishi told a reporter of the *Yomiuri Weekly:*

> "The conservatives and socialists should form united parties and draw a clear-cut line between themselves and the Communist Party on the one hand and the extreme rightists on the other. But the conservatives should not exclude persons with progressive ideas and the progressive party should not be composed solely of radical socialists. Though the Labor and Conservative parties in England have a history of long and hard hostilities, they never have completely opposite views on diplomacy or national defense or economic policies. The same is true of the Democratic and Republican parties in America. Japan should follow this pattern. Though the progressive and conservative parties may have different viewpoints, the members should have friends in the opposing party whom they can trust. In considering our politics of the future, I am of the opinion that we must have a wide range of acquaintances in both parties and then have gentlemanly disputes over policies."

His adventure with the Japan Reconstruction Federation may not have hurt him at all, Kishi reflected as he laid plans for "invading" the Liberal Party. He was now a prominent postwar political figure. If he had tried to join one of the old parties at the outset, he would have been lost in the shuffle of aspiring leaders. There was, of course, one hitch —Yoshida. He wondered whether this sour, unforgiving old man could be persuaded to let him enter *his* party.

Kishi called on his brother, Eisaku, who had won a Liberal seat in the election and was on intimate terms with Yoshida. He explained to him his desire to join the party and asked him to speak to the Prime Minister about it. Sato did so, but Yoshida angrily rejected the proposal. Kishi did not give up. His colleagues in the defunct Japan Reconstruction Federation wined and dined influential Liberal leaders, dropping hints of the considerable financial support behind Kishi which could be channeled into party coffers. Pressure on Yoshida finally grew irresistible and he agreed to discuss the matter with Kishi.

At a meeting between the two men arranged by Sato, Yoshida, though reluctant, coldly granted Kishi's request for party membership. But, it was decided, Kishi would first be sent as a personal envoy of the Prime Minister to West Germany to study its reconstruction program. His admission to the Party would take place while he was abroad, making it appear, to save Yoshida "face," that the Prime Minister was acting of his own free will.

Although the occasion for the trip to Germany was politically contrived, Kishi had long hoped to make such a journey. "In the confusion of postwar Japan," he told a reporter, "I feel that I must look at the country from abroad if I am to see the forest from the trees. And since Germany suffered much the same fate as Japan, this is the logical country from which to look." A comparison of the reconstruction problems and progress of the two countries, he was sure, would provide him with a better perspective of the situation in Japan, helping him to determine the political and economic course Japan should follow.

After an elaborate send-off party held in Tokyo's Imperial Hotel, Kishi, in February, 1953, embarked on his first trip to the West in more than twenty years. In 1930, he had also gone to Germany to study its development progress. What he had learned then had helped to strengthen the economy of Japan's totalitarian system. The information he would gather now, he hoped, would be used to hasten Japan's reconstruction as a democratic state.

Kishi visited every important city in West Germany, as well as West Berlin, touring factories and speaking with old business friends and government leaders. During a visit with Dr. Hjalmar Schacht at his office in Bonn—the former Nazi was now a lawyer and economic adviser —Kishi told him that, like the Germans, the Japanese were making every possible effort to rehabilitate their national economy. As for himself, he added, "I am going to try to do my part in building up Japan regardless of the obstacles."

Schacht replied that this was a wise attitude. "Though we may be targets of the world's hatred, let us never cease trying our best to bring prosperity to our homelands."

But Kishi, despite his show of pride, was inwardly envious of West

272 ಲ KISHI AND JAPAN

Germany's progress. It was rebuilding its industry far more swiftly than his country. In a radio interview after his return to Japan, he reported:

"In Japan, one can see many foreign cars in the streets and many nice new buildings, but reconstruction, in reality, has been carried out only in form. Basically speaking, our feet are not yet off the ground. The situation is quite different in Germany. The ruins of Berlin still exist, but all industries are in full operation.

"The Siemens factory in West Berlin is a good example. This plant was almost completely demolished during the war, and what little equipment was left, down to the toilet plumbing, was taken away by the Russians. Yet the Germans have rebuilt it—and history should record how they did this in large red letters. About eighty workers who had long served in the factory got together and searched for machinery among the ruins. They repaired what they found and built a barracks to serve as a factory building. That was how the new plant was begun. . . ."

The spirit of free Germany was reflected in the close co-operation between management and labor, which offered a sharp contrast, he thought, with the industrial strife in Japan. Kishi said:

"One is greatly impressed by the fact that every German . . . businessman and worker is bursting with confidence and giving everything he has to the reconstruction of his country. There are no labor struggles. Business and industrial management are making the workers feel that they are working not so much for individual employers as for the nation. On the other hand, in Japan everybody thinks only of himself. We do not look at things on the basis of national interest or the people's future. And that goes for both the capitalists and the workers."

Kishi was also impressed by the high moral level of West German officialdom, which seemed all the more honest in the light of the corrupt practices he viewed as common in Japan.

"Marshall Plan funds are being spent very wisely. A chart is kept showing how every bit of American aid is used. I asked if this wasn't supposed to be a secret and was told that it may be in France but not in Germany. 'We are not ashamed to show the chart to anybody,' I was told."

With equal enthusiasm, Kishi praised West Germany's political stability.

"As an election is scheduled for September, I asked people from all classes about the outlook and almost everybody agreed that although [Chancellor Konrad] Adenauer's party may lose a few seats, there won't be much change. If West Germany changed its basic policies, they said, reconstruction would be hampered and the people would suffer. Adenauer has the support of people from all classes, including many of the workers. For though his government is supposed to be conservative, it has an extensive social welfare and workers' housing program. As for rearmament, there is considerable opposition from women, workers, and young people to this, but on the whole, those who understand the communist aims feel that rearmament is inevitable."

Kishi also saw in the character of Adenauer's Germany the embers of a reawakening nationalism, which aroused a similar glow in himself, unpleasantly accentuating in his mind the meekness and docility of the Japanese in the wake of defeat.

"One reason for the Germans' unity of purpose and action is, no doubt, their undiluted sense of national pride. They have no feeling of inferiority as the result of their defeat in the war, as many Japanese seem to have. I was even told that our two countries would determine the world's destiny—Germany in the West and Japan in the East— and that we must, therefore, overcome all difficulties confronting us."

Reminded of his own caustic appraisal of some aspects of American culture, he added:

"The Germans say they have little respect for American culture and do not like many of the Americans, but that they do not show their anti-Americanism because they need America's aid to reconstruct the country. The Germans have mature minds. They are adults. . . . Of course, as Germany has been defeated many times in the past and after each defeat has reconstructed itself, the people don't feel so deeply about being beaten. On the other hand, Japan was defeated in the last war for the first time in its three thousand-year history, so it is natural that we should be more dejected and timid. Moreover, General MacArthur's policies helped to foster an inferior feeling. But now that foreign countries are beginning to accept us as equals, this feeling should be eliminated . . ."

While Kishi was still touring Germany, he received a telegram that the Liberal Party government had fallen and that a new election would be held shortly. The crisis had been precipitated by the withdrawal of Ichiro Hatoyama from the party and the formation of another splinter party under him. This news caught Kishi by surprise. He had long prophesied that political instability would continue without a powerful and concerted drive to bring unity and order to Japan. But he had not expected so short a life for the new government or he never would have left the country. After viewing at first hand the political, economic, and psychological stability that underlay West Germany's reconstruction program, he was more disgusted than ever at the inability of his own countrymen to run a responsible government—and at a time when the Korean conflict and the cold war, complicated by the sudden death of Stalin, were aggravating world tensions. Perhaps now, with Yoshida's influence at a low ebb, he could make headway with his political and economic plans as a member of the Liberal Party.

Kishi flew back to Japan immediately, determined to take advantage of this opportunity. Hardly had he stepped out of his plane at Tokyo's Haneda Airport when he began his campaign. He told friends and newsmen who turned out to greet him, "Stalin has died; the world finds itself in one of the most difficult and delicate situations since the war. And yet, at such a grave moment, the Diet is dissolved—as the result of purely emotional and selfish motives having nothing in common with the will or lives of the people. In my opinion, this is stupid. Although I am now a member of the Liberal Party, as I have said many times, I do not fully approve of its policies. I will try my best to improve them."

Kishi added forcefully, with words that echoed back to his war-planning days, "The Liberal Party must cast off its old skin. Politics cannot be limited to the smooth management of personnel affairs. Policy should be the guiding line of a nation. In Japan, we must work out a new policy with more emphasis laid on the development of trade and manufacturing. Moreover, these plans must not be of the 'let-alone' type, but, instead, should be carefully worked out—like the Russian five-year plans."

Japan needed, he seemed to say, a kind of national socialism washed in the purifying substance of democracy—a mixture of political liberty, free enterprise, and socialist planning. When a reporter asked him how he intended to put his program into effect, he replied with blunt pragmatism, "What controls politics is power, and power lies in money. Only a powerful man, able to put his enemy to rout, can make a leader. I must be powerful enough to achieve the unification of the conservatives to permit the implementation of necessary political and economic policies." Kishi implied that he had many rich people behind him.

He decided to run for the House of Representatives, the lower house of the Diet, in Yamaguchi Prefecture. He immediately won the support, financial and vocal, of such prominent and diverse figures as Aiichiro Fujiyama, Kiyoshi Sugiya (Director of the Economics Department, University of Weseda), Ichiro Tamaga (novelist), Fusao Hayashi (novelist-critic), Keishichi Ishiguro (judo expert and humorist) and Tsusai Sugaware (essayist). Within five days of his return from abroad, he was actively campaigning. The time was now ripe, he believed, for his candidacy. The last campaign had given him prominence. Now he had the advantage of membership in Japan's largest party, as well as that deriving from the fact that this party seemed hopelessly split, while he was the champion of unification.

Kishi entered the electoral race in Yamaguchi, even though he knew he would be splitting votes with his brother, reducing Eisaku's chances for re-election. *Giri* had to give way to the practical need for political reformation and the psychological necessity of proving to himself and the world that he was back in the good graces of his community.

He plunged into his electoral campaign with drive and aggressiveness. He spoke in dozens of meeting halls and from trucks that blared his speeches over loudspeakers. He wrote pungent articles in campaign pamphlets and local newspapers. He appeared on numerous radio programs. These tactics were similar to those he had employed when he last ran for office—in 1942, shortly after Pearl Harbor. He recalled how thrilled he had been when he had won. Now he realized what a shallow victory that had been. He had wanted to believe that the community had voted for him because he was Nobusuke Kishi, but in reality, it had voted for him because he was the candidate of the war-makers, and the war-makers were popular in those days.

In this democratic era, the situation was different. He was running against several candidates who had a fair chance to defeat him. The fact that he had been an associate of the military dictators was a black mark against him—one that the Socialist candidates, in particular, were quick to magnify in their electoral speeches. If he won under these circumstances, the victory would be a real one. It would mean that he had been forgiven for his past mistakes and that a new political life lay ahead. He fought like a man fighting for his life.

Kishi promised the people at one rally:

"I will sacrifice myself in the cause of democratic government in Japan. The unbearably ugly struggle for power among the existing political parties, which we all can observe so clearly, must be ended as soon as possible. Otherwise, the public might lose confidence in, or even deny the practicability of, party politics, thus playing into the hands of the extremists. Democratic government in Japan would be nipped in the bud and the terrible autocracy we once knew would engulf us again. I cannot close my eyes to this situation. I pledge myself to fight the kind of government we have today, which is nothing but selfish plots and political backstage dealings that ignore the wish and will of the people."

In another talk, Kishi said:

"Japan cannot be reconstructed as long as it is flooded with small parties eternally struggling for power. Indispensable for a truly democratic government is the two-party system—a liberalistic conservative party and a moderate progressive party. Moreover, they must not oppose each other for reasons of self-interest. Opposition should merely concern matters of policy, and even in this context, the two parties should go hand in hand on many of the main issues. However, judging from the present political state in Japan, it appears that the conservative parties alone, when unified and regulated, can stabilize the political situation and improve the life of the people."

At still another meeting, Kishi maintained:

"Independent Japan can be defended only through close co-operation with the defense plans of the other free nations. However, we cannot rush into a defense build-up. Our defensive strength can only be increased gradually as our economy is reconstructed."

Partly because of these passionate, relentlessly uncompromising pleas, partly because of his family background, Kishi won a seat in the Diet by a large margin. Eisaku also won, putting his conscience at ease. The fear that his own entry into the race might reduce his brother's chance of winning had not proved justified, though a bitter contest was waged between those who campaigned for the two brothers. Kishi did not care to think what an ugly situation might have resulted if he had won while his brother lost. In *Shukan Asahi* magazine, he wrote, "I am very friendly with my brother. We have a proper amount of understanding for each other's political actions. What troubles us most is that we are from the same electoral district."

The night of his victory, Kishi set off on an exhausting tour by plane, train, and automobile to campaign for several old friends—and important creditors—who were running in various parts of the country for the House of Councilors, the upper chamber of the Diet. This election was held a few days after the lower house contest, and Kishi, on the strength of his triumph, was in a position to repay *giri* to men who had helped him, including Shinji Yoshino, his boss in prewar days, and Gisuke Aikawa, who had worked with him in Manchuria. Kishi displayed the same boundless energy and untiring efforts that he had made in his own behalf—and all the candidates whom he supported won.

His political rebirth had been accomplished. And this time he had the sanction of the people. He had won by democratic process the same office that he had once obtained under a totalitarian regime.

CHAPTER XIV

THE LAST LAP

K ISHI NOW CHANNELED all his energies toward accomplishment of his next objective—consolidation of the conservative parties. Such unity, he believed, was a prerequisite for political stability and prosperity, without which, as the election had indicated, Japan might surrender to the leftists, and even abandon its efforts to develop democratic government. The Liberal Party had won the most seats, but, together with the other conservative groups, had lost a considerable number to the leftist bloc, which included the left and right wing Socialists, the pro-communist Farmer-Labor Party, and the communists. This threat of a leftist surge to power came, moreover, at a time when Japan was supposed to assume new obligations under the Mutual Security Treaty with the United States. Japan had promised the United States to increase its own defense budget on the condition that America would enlarge its contribution to the Japanese military build-up, but it didn't have the funds to carry out its end of the bargain.

The division of the conservatives into several parties, and the parties into numerous factions, was irrational, Kishi thought, having little to do with differences of substance. Essentially, all the conservative groups agreed on major issues—co-operation with the United States, amendment of the Constitution, a fundamentally free enterprise economy. But they were divided on the basis of personalities. Japan was still suffering from the effects of its feudalistic inheritance. As the old samurai had fought furiously and endlessly to enhance the power of *daimyo* and clan, the modern politicians coagulated into factions behind the most influential individuals as dictated by self-interest, *giri,* or a common provincial heritage. Kishi realized that the factionalism within the parties could only be eliminated gradually, as the people grew used to voting for candidates on the basis of ability and policy considerations rather than family name or tradition. But, he thought, there was no legitimate reason why several parties, which were artificial factional groupings, could not be united if they were ideologically compatible.

Soon after the election, Kishi told a group of his own personal followers that "the conservative parties must at all costs reach a firm agreement to co-operate with each other before the nomination of a prime minister. A coalition cabinet of the conservative parties is essential if we are to have a stable government."

Miyoshi and others argued that this solution was too "idealistic," but Kishi replied sternly, "Our ideal is to unify the conservative parties. That may be impossible for the moment. But it is not impossible to move gradually toward that ideal. We must start somewhere—and soon." He added, "We Liberals must be prepared to make concessions to our fellow conservatives. We must not insist that Yoshida be returned as prime minister if this issue is a stumbling-block to unity. We must be realistic."

Kishi was displaying his usual political astuteness. He was ready to offer a concession he was only too glad to make. Yoshida's ouster, a prerequisite for his advancement to a top role in the Liberal Party, would hardly have saddened him. True, Yoshida had approved his entry into the party, and he owed him something for this. But on the other hand, the Prime Minister had only agreed to this under considerable pressure. Moreover, with the nation in the throes of anarchy, individuals had to be sacrificed if necessary for the good of the community.

Kishi tried to arrange a meeting between Yoshida and Shigemitsu, the Progressive Party president, in the hope that they would agree on a common policy. He appealed to the Prime Minister through his brother, Sato, who was now Secretary-General of the Liberal Party, while Miyoshi and other Kishi followers tried to convince Shigemitsu of the wisdom of such a meeting. Yoshida was finally persuaded to call on Shigemitsu at the latter's residence. He promised to consult with the Progressives on all policy matters. Nevertheless, Shigemitsu, who had hopes of becoming prime minister himself, refused to join in a coalition government, though he agreed to be a "co-operative oppositionist." Kishi, while failing to bring about the thaw of coalition, had managed, at least, to chip the ice.

Kishi then considered moving in a new direction. He could pave the way toward unity, if not through coalition, through the formation of a new party that would embrace members of all existing conservative groups except the Yoshida diehards, who would eventually be forced to join the united opposition. He hesitated to take this step, however, remembering the fate of another movement he had tried to inaugurate—the Japan Reconstruction Federation. His influence was far greater now, of course, but he was still, relatively speaking, a political newcomer. In addition, there was the delicate problem of Kishi's younger brother, who would be placed in an embarrassing position, particularly in view of Sato's role in persuading the Prime Minister to accept Kishi into the Liberal Party.

But Kishi finally decided that Yoshida, for the good of the country (and for Kishi's good, as well), had to be sacrificed. As in the case of his abandonment of Tojo a decade before, this was no time for faint heart. Conservative unity could never be achieved, Kishi was convinced, as long as Yoshida, whose stubborn, arrogant personality so deeply riled opposition conservatives, remained in power. Kishi called a meeting of anti-Yoshida conservatives and bluntly told them that it was necessary to initiate a new movement to "stabilize the political situation." He proposed that a committee be set up to study possible changes in the Constitution, which would gradually develop into a new party. And when the issue of constitutional revision was raised in the Diet, Kishi and his followers pressed successfully for the establishment of such a committee.

Yoshida, who now greatly feared Kishi, selected him as chairman of the group, hoping to keep him out of his political hair by diverting his attention to the constitutional question. Yoshida played into the hands of his tormentor, who craftily used committee meetings to discuss ways of realizing a political reorganization. Compounding the irony was the fact that Yoshida had selected Kishi for the committee on the recommendation of Sato, who had also hoped to sidetrack his brother's anti-Yoshida activities.

As Kishi's movement began to take form, it became evident even to some of Yoshida's strongest "supporters" that they could ignore it only at the risk of being left out of Japan's future political picture entirely. Two leading factions in the Liberal Party, one led by Taketora Ogata, a close associate of Yoshida's, and the other by Tanzan Ishibashi, met with the Kishi group and agreed that another conservative party should be formed, creating a New Party Promotion Council. Soon afterward, all the conservative parties set up special negotiating committees to work out plans for a new party.

But no sooner had Kishi's maneuvers begun to bear fruit than the fruit withered on the vine—at least temporarily. For the pro-Yoshida Liberals joined in the movement *en masse* and insisted that the president of the new party be elected by popular vote, calculating that the anti-Yoshida politicians would never chance the possibility that Yoshida's long reign as Prime Minister would influence the people to select him as head of the new organization. With the anti-Yoshida elements, as expected, fearful of such an eventuality and the pro-Yoshida representatives—led by Kishi's brother—sabotaging all efforts at conciliation, negotiations fell through.

Kishi would not accept defeat. He would not let the movement die. In collaboration with Ishibashi and a Progressive Party leader, Hitoshi Ashida, he converted the New Party Promotion Council into a Council for the Preparation of the Organization of a New Party to work out actual party policies and sponsor political meetings throughout Japan to popularize the movement. Kishi, who assumed the post of Secretary-General of the new council, embarked on an all-out anti-Yoshida campaign in an attempt to isolate the Prime Minister's followers and force the resignation of the government, which would, he thought, clear the way for the prospective new party to take over power. Before a cheering crowd in Nakanoshima Public Hall in Osaka, Kishi candidly stated:

> "We have no intention of supporting Yoshida in the presidential election of the new party, which, we believe, must be entirely different from any conservative party ever formed in Japan. One of the aims of the new party is to achieve stability in the Diet. Another is to institute a system of planned economy to replace the haphazard economic policies of the Liberal Party. The leaders of our party, therefore, must be fresh and full of vigor. They must be capable of developing the party into a great popular movement."

Kishi had brought his movement out of the smoke-filled room into the airy public meeting hall for the first time.

Yoshida's followers, alarmed by this open revolt, lured a number of Progressives away from the new party group with glittering promises of patronage and political concessions. Many remaining Kishi backers, fearful of being left out on a "new party" limb, also had second thoughts, which were strengthened when Yoshida hinted to Ashida shortly before the Prime Minister left on a trip to the United States and Europe that he would retire from office on his return to Japan. Why form another party—a precarious political experiment at best—they asked, if Yoshida intended to resign in any event? Kishi saw his budding movement slowly disintegrate, as had his previous ones, failing to convince many of his followers that Yoshida's hint was simply a ruse intended for that purpose.

Kishi had other troubles, too. Secretary-General Kenzo Matsumura of the Progressive Party, fearing that he and other Progressive leaders would be given only minor positions in the proposed new party, tried to remove Kishi from leadership of the movement. He secretly arranged a meeting between Progressive President Shigemitsu and Hatoyama, leader of the largest anti-Yoshida faction in the Liberal Party, to discuss this possibility. But Kishi, learning of this conspiracy, told Hatoyama, "If you wish to initiate such action against me, go right ahead. But I will never follow you. I shall simply establish another party in opposition to yours as well as to Yoshida's." Kishi was invited to the conference, which, instead of "dumping" him, confirmed his leadership of the new party movement.

He continued to find himself confronted by obstacles. He called a meeting of the Council for the Preparation of the Organization of a New Party and advocated broadening the membership. But Yoshida's followers applied *en masse* to join the party, threatening to inundate, as they had done before, the new political grouping. Kishi, infuriated, told Hayato Ikeda, who had replaced Sato as Secretary-General of the Liberal Party, that "those opposing the spirit of the movement will not automatically be admitted to the Council. We will screen everyone carefully."

Despite Kishi's screening efforts, many pro-Yoshida politicians managed to join the Council. But undiscouraged by the potential danger posed by this fifth column, he scheduled a meeting of the General Assembly of the Council, which consisted of delegates from all over Japan, to elect a Representative Committee for the purpose of converting the organization into a full-fledged party.

He then turned to the problem of selecting a candidate for the presidency of the party, who would probably be the next Prime Minister. Himself? The thought was inviting, but the moment was not yet right for such a jump. The people now accepted him as a national leader, but they might balk at his assumption of the top job. Not enough time had elapsed since his depurging. He could not afford to risk failure. Besides, he was still in his fifties, and there were many members senior to him who would resent his open leadership. He could, however, still pull the strings of national policy to a large extent from behind the scenes, as Japanese leaders had done for thousands of years. After considerable discussion with his colleagues, he decided that Hatoyama, a likable, good-natured, highly flexible politician, would be the best candidate. He would probably be willing to follow Kishi's advice more easily than most other important members of the movement.

But many Council officials feared, as they had previously, that Yoshida who, as Prime Minister, still wielded a good deal of influence in the country, might possibly win the presidency in a popular vote, or in any case, that his supporters might capture the majority of seats in the Representative Committee. To calm such apprehension, Kishi told reporters, "The President will be elected democratically by popular vote, and it is, therefore, evident that we cannot deny Yoshida the right to be a candidate. But it is also evident that neither Yoshida nor any of his close associates can win. The opposition conservative parties will oppose them, and even in the Liberal Party itself the anti-Yoshida trend is strong."

Meanwhile, Kishi urged his friends in the financial world to further strengthen the confidence of the anti-Yoshida Council members by throwing their support more fully behind the new party. Under the prodding of these men, the Japan Federation of Employers Association for the first time openly expressed its dissatisfaction with the Yoshida government. "The stabilization of the political situation," it said in a statement, "is of the greatest importance. It must be achieved at any cost. However, a fresh and strong new government leader is required for the task."

Kishi then tried to split the Yoshida bloc itself by wooing powerful Taketora Ogata. Asking for his support, Kishi revealed to him that he would press for the election of Hatoyama. But Hatoyama was a sick man, he said, and would have to be replaced before too long. It was only natural that when this time came Ogata would be the logical man to succeed him. Shigemitsu? He would lose influence when the new party was established and the Progressive Party went out of existence. As for himself, Kishi explained, he was too young to be prime minister. He promised Ogata his support.

Ogata conferred with other pro-Yoshida leaders, and the group replied that Kishi could only win their co-operation if Yoshida were selected a member of the Representative Committee, or at least, if Hatoyama's candidacy for president of the party were withdrawn. Kishi indignantly answered, "The Liberal Party is not yet dissolved. It is quite unreasonable to expect the head of an existing party to be included in the Representative Committee of another party."

This new setback only solidified Kishi's determination to push through his plans. The time for a showdown with Yoshida had come. Kishi outlined his strategy with his lieutenants shortly before the General Assembly of the Council met. When the Assembly finally opened, this strategy was revealed within a minute, the amount of time the meeting lasted. As soon as the proceedings started, Kishi got up from his seat and motioned, "I propose that the Representative Committee be composed of the following five members—Kanemitsu, Ashida, Ishibashi, Kishi, and Hatoyama." Kanemitsu, Chairman of the General Assembly, responded in a single breath, "Is there any objection? No? Then I declare Kishi-san's motion adopted. The Assembly is hereby adjourned."

All delegates departed except those favorable to Yoshida, who, in their surprise and frustration, accused Kishi of making a mockery of democracy.

Shortly afterward, Kishi, as well as Ishibashi, were expelled from the Liberal Party for having "repeatedly violated and ignored party decisions." Party leaders had refrained from taking such action previously for fear that followers of the two men would also quit the party, but now they had to oust them to redeem "face." They lost, as they had calculated, about forty members, who overnight switched to the new organization. With the pro-Yoshida opposition now crushed, the new Democratic Party, ostensibly led by President Hatoyama, but to a large degree controlled by Kishi, who had himself elected to the strategic post of Secretary-General, was finally established on November 24, 1953.

Just as he had planned, Kishi, smashing every barrier in his path, had organized a party embracing all conservatives other than the pro-Yoshida faction of the Liberal Party. The latter still controlled 185 Diet seats compared to the Democrats' 125. But it was evident from the reaction of the press, economic circles, and public opinion polls that the new party, offering fresh leadership and lacking the taint of having operated under the Americans during the Occupation, was the conservative party of the future. To underscore their independent attitude toward America, Kishi and the other leading Democrats advocated "normalization" of relations with the Soviet Union, which hadn't yet signed a peace treaty or re-established diplomatic ties with Japan. The Yoshida group was wary about taking such a step at the height of the cold war, but there were few real policy differences between the two parties. The Yoshida followers, the Democrats figured, would sooner or later have to join them on Democratic terms or die in isolation. Kishi, against enormous odds, had taken a giant step toward his coveted goal of conservative unification.

The Democratic Party laid plans for forcing a government resignation in partnership, for the sake of expediency, with the two socialist parties— the three groups now commanded a majority in the Diet. The Liberal Party, cornered, split on the tactics it should adopt. Yoshida and some of his followers favored waiting for the inevitable vote of non-confidence, then dissolving the Diet and gambling on survival in a new election, though Yoshida decided that he would retire from political life regardless of the outcome. But Ogata, who was slated to replace Yoshida as Liberal leader, sensed that the party would be severely defeated in an election and advocated immediate resignation of the government, and union with the Democrats. Otherwise, he feared, the Liberals, if they did suffer an electoral setback, would be forced to join the Democrats in the end, anyway, and under far less advantageous conditions.

Finally, Yoshida, under tremendous pressure from the Ogata faction, called for the resignation of his cabinet. But before the Liberals could broach the question of conservative union, the Democrats, with Kishi leading the negotiations, concluded an arrangement with the Socialists whereby the latter would support a Democratic-led government in return for the promise that a general election would be held shortly after the new party came to power.

Kishi had at first held out against such an accord. He was disturbed by the idea of collaboration with socialist groups that included many pro-communists, and he feared that such co-operation would unnecessarily alienate many Liberals, roughening the road to conservative amalgamation. But his colleagues argued that the proposed agreement would permit the Democrats to bargain with the Liberals from a position of maximum strength. The Liberals would certainly lose influence in an election, while the Democrats were likely to win control of the government. Kishi had considered this matter from the long-range point of view, but his fellow politicians were primarily motivated by hunger for immediate power.

Unable to resist the pressure, Kishi conceded. Hatoyama then met with Right-Wing Socialist President Kawakami and Left-Wing Socialist President Suzuki, and the three men signed the accord. On December 9, 1954, Hatoyama, with the support of the Socialists, was chosen Prime Minister, defeating Ogata, the Liberal Party candidate. Kishi was now in a position to pull the strings attached to the highest official post in the land.

His first job as one of the most important men behind the Prime Minister was to help in the selection of a cabinet. He decided to remain outside the cabinet himself so that he could more advantageously deal with the problem of uniting with the Liberals, though his friends argued that a cabinet job would put him in a better position to succeed Hatoyama eventually as Prime Minister. He told a reporter, "We may have succeeded in forming a new conservative party, but our work has not ended; we have gone only halfway toward our goal."

With Kishi and other Democratic leaders stumping the country calling for restoration of diplomatic relations with Russia—a popular stand in this post-Occupation period—and "clean politics," a "Hatoyama boom" soon thundered through the nation. This was the time, they felt, for a test of strength. An election was held in January, 1955, and the Democrats won 185 seats out of a total of 467. The Liberal Party could boast of only 112 seats as compared to its previous 180. But as Kishi had prophesied, the Democrats lacked the majority necessary to lead a stable government.

Kishi himself was one of the winning candidates, easily retaining his Diet seat. As a result of his victory, with its indication of a brighter political future, the "Kishi faction" increased in number from about ten to thirty, giving him an even greater influence within his party.

He wasted no time utilizing his new prestige. Many of his colleagues favored establishment of a purely Democratic cabinet on the same co-operative basis with the Socialists that existed before the election. But on Kishi's insistence, the Democrats abandoned the Socialists and arranged a working relationship with the Liberals, which, Kishi hoped, would pave the way to union.

Kishi, ironically, suffered a setback at the hands of his brother. The Liberals had promised Kishi that they would support Bukichi Miki, a senior politician and formerly head of the small Japan Liberal Party, who had become the most influential member of the Democratic Party apart from Kishi himself, for the presidency of the Diet. But instead, Sato, still an important figure in the Liberal Party, engineered a deal with the Socialists that gave the post to a Liberal. Kishi, because of his brother's action, lost "face," which resulted in a considerable cooling of his relations with Miki and his followers.

The Democratic Party found the political going extremely difficult as a minority ruling group. Kishi approached his brother and other leading Liberals time after time with compromise proposals, but without success. The party also failed to win the co-operation of the Socialists, though it supported socialist demands for the conclusion of a peace treaty with Russia and trade with Communist China. The Socialists were especially irked by the government's efforts, which, they charged, constituted a continuation of Yoshida's kow-towing to America, to strengthen Japan's self-defense forces as required by an agreement with the United States and to amend the Constitution to permit conversion of these forces into a full-fledged military establishment.

Finally, some measure of co-operation with the Liberals was achieved on the question of the national budget. The Democrats proposed a figure of several billion yen, a modest one in line with campaign promises.

But the Liberals demanded a forty-three billion yen increase to finance their pet domestic projects. A compromise was reached calling for a twenty-five billion yen augmentation. Kishi reluctantly approved of this breaking of the party's public pledge for the sake of what he considered a more important principle.

"We don't think it was a good thing," he told the press, "for the Democratic Party to compromise with the Liberal Party on the question of the budget after our promises to the people. But we have given way to some degree in the hope that this move might lead to a union of the two parties."

While Kishi concentrated mainly on fostering unity among the conservatives, relations between Japan and the United States grew somewhat strained as the result of his party's effort to establish itself in the public eye as entirely independent of American policy. Hatoyama, in particular, was carried away by the tremendous applause he received whenever he called for the "normalization" of relations with Russia and trade with Red China.

Communist influence in Japan had, in fact, greatly receded since the May Day riots of 1952, but the bulk of the Japanese people, however much repelled by communism, wanted a peace treaty and diplomatic relations with the Soviet Union as a manifestation of Japan's final restoration to the community of nations. Moreover, they imagined China as potentially the same huge market for Japanese goods it had been before the war. It was still Japan's natural trading partner. But the Japanese also supported these measures because they enjoyed following policies that obviously disturbed Washington. They were offered their first opportunity to feel and savor the independence they had never really taken seriously in the several years since the San Francisco peace treaty.

But the government's program to make the people take independence seriously was beginning to stimulate considerable friction with the United States. Japan, Kishi and other Democratic strategists believed, could not afford to alienate America too strongly. It needed American economic and technical aid to build up its industries, American markets for its goods, particularly textiles, American agreement, mostly for political reasons, to revise the Security Treaty making Japan an equal partner. From the long-range point of view, Japan needed America as ultimate protection against the Red tide that had already flooded the Asian mainland. Kishi and his fellow rulers realized full well that in the era of the cold war, Japan, as a relatively small nation, had to cling to one of the two great power blocs, whatever pretense they had to make about "true independence." Kishi, when asked on a radio program for his opinion on "neutralism," replied,

"In present international circumstances, I don't think there is any room for 'neutralism' to exist."

Japan stressed two foreign policy lines—"independence" and rejection of "neutralism." It was still possible, Kishi thought, to enjoy a reasonable degree of independence without having to be on the neutralist fence. Propaganda was angled to fit the audience. There was emphasis on "independence" at home, and on cold war partnership abroad. The Japanese people, however, grew impatient. They wanted their government to convert its nationalist promises into action. Violence was already brewing under the instigation of the leftists. Japanese farmers formed human chains to prevent a government survey for a fifty-acre expansion of the American air base at Sunakawa, and residents in the Mount Fuji area bitterly protested against artillery practice by American forces stationed in the region. On the other hand, some American officials began to fear that the Japanese government, in its attempt to woo the public, might be clearing the way toward neutralist, or even anti-American, policies.

The government hastily decided that it might be possible to satisfy, at least to some extent, both the Japanese people and the Americans by sending a delegation to Washington. It could then explain to the United States Japan's true domestic and international political intentions, while perhaps winning concessions, such as a revision of the Security Treaty, to please the people at home.

Shigemitsu, who was once again Foreign Minister, was named as the top Japanese representative, largely because of the importance of his post. Few of the government leaders believed him forceful or articulate enough to be able to wring concessions from America or clear the air regarding Japan's cold war orientation. Bukichi Miki and Hatoyama therefore asked Kishi, who possessed the very talents for persuasion lacking in Shigemitsu, to accompany the Foreign Minister. But he hedged at first. He had long been anxious to visit the United States, which he had not seen since pre-war days, but he had hoped to go under different circumstances—as a private citizen free to mix with the people and study their "way of life." He would certainly not be free on this short, concentrated government mission. And he did not relish the idea of being, in a sense, Shigemitsu's "aide," when actually he wielded far more power in Japan than the Foreign Minister. In any event, there was too much chance of the trip ending in failure, he thought, and he didn't want to be associated with an unsuccessful venture.

But under pressure, particularly from Hatoyama, Kishi used this opportunity to do some hard bargaining for the cause of conservative unity.

As Hatoyama, fearful that his power would be threatened by such unity, was hampering Kishi's efforts toward this end, Kishi agreed to go to America if the Prime Minister promised to campaign for consolidation in a joint speaking tour of Democratic and Liberal leaders he was trying to arrange. Hatoyama accepted and Kishi prepared to leave for the United States, figuring that the trip might at least serve the interests of political unification.

He arrived in Washington on August 26, 1955, and participated with Shigemitsu in conferences with Secretary of State John Foster Dulles, members of Congress, and other high American officials. Shigemitsu tried to set the keynote for the meetings when he told reporters, "We think it is now time to wash out any trace of the unfortunate war. We must go forward constructively toward a posture of complete independence."

But it did not take Kishi long to conclude that the Americans were not in a bargaining mood. They politely refused to risk revision of the Security Treaty at this time in view of the many potential dangers in the Far East and the slow pace of Japan's self-defense force build-up. And while the Americans did not question Shigemitsu's pro-West attitude, they recognized that his position in the Democratic Party was shaky. Further, they feared that Hatoyama's motives in calling for "normalization" of relations with Russia were tinged with neutralism. For the time being, there would be no change in the treaty, nor any reduction in the number of American bases or troops stationed in Japan.

The trip offered few political trophies for the Japanese people, but it did establish conditions for a better working relationship between the two countries. Kishi impressed American officials with his explanation of Japan's policies in regard to Russia and Red China, which the Americans did not protest too strongly, and the efforts being made to unify the conservatives in order to establish a strong, stable government capable of fending off the challenge of the socialist "neutralists" and communists.

After several frantically busy days in Washington, Kishi returned to Japan. He had mixed feelings about the mission. Charitably speaking, it had been only a limited success. But he was glad, after all, that he had gone. He had had the opportunity to meet some of America's leaders and learn at first hand their attitudes toward Japan, and to clarify for them Japanese policy and opinion. And he had registered a personal triumph as well. *Newsweek* magazine had described him as a man of "direct action and decision" who, "unlike most Japanese, moves swiftly and boldly." His career would by no means suffer from the experience. But more important, he was now better qualified to help steer his country's policies.

Kishi reported to Hatoyama that the trip confirmed, in his opinion, that Japan must in the future consider its domestic policies from an international point of view. The nation could not improve relations with the United States, he said, unless it were able to stabilize its domestic political situation, which meant conservative unification.

The need for unity grew clearer for an increasing number of conservatives as they observed with alarm that the two Socialist parties, which had also been painfully plodding toward consolidation, were nearing their goal. When Socialist union was finally achieved, Kishi and his fellow conservatives shuddered with the realization that the combined Socialist Party had more seats in the Diet than either of the conservative parties individually. Kishi approved of the Socialist amalgamation in principle, for a two-party system had been his goal from the start, but it was the timing that disconcerted him. The Socialists had consolidated their forces in advance of the conservatives. No less worried and anxious for conservative unity were the businessmen, who were not unaware that the power of the Socialists was rooted mainly in the support of the labor unions, which were, to a large extent, led by communist sympathizers.

Some of the most powerful of these businessmen, most of them belonging to the fishery, fertilizer, and mining industries, were (and still are) strong supporters of Ichiro Kono, the Minister of Agriculture and forestry. Kono had rocketed from obscurity into a highly influential position, not only because of this financial backing, but, to some degree, because Hatoyama owed him considerable *giri* accumulated in prewar days and therefore felt obligated to confer with him. Kono was a master at weighing down his associates with *on,* and then squeezing them at the opportune time. He enjoyed one of his biggest political boosts before the war when a leading political figure became involved in a scandal over a woman. Kono had the matter hushed up with cash out of his own pocket, and became an important creditor of this politician.

Such methods of operation have not made this heavy-set man with a chubby face and small, shifty eyes highly popular among his colleagues. But because of the political and financial strings he manipulated, Kishi, desperate to achieve conservative unity while the political iron was hot, co-operated closely with him at the risk of antagonizing the anti-Kono elements. The stage was now set for the final move toward unification.

Kishi and Miki met with Ogata and Banboku Ono of the Liberal Party in a series of conferences, while Hatoyama, as he had promised Kishi, participated in a joint speaking tour with Ogata calling for union. The only question remaining was the leadership of the projected new party. The

Democrats insisted that Hatoyama be President and continue as Prime Minister, while the Liberals argued that the matter should be decided by a vote of all members of the two conservative factions. The four-man conference finally reached a compromise whereby Hatoyama would remain Prime Minister and Ogata would be party President. This agreement was ratified by a joint "preparatory association" of the two parties, and on November 15, 1955, the Liberal-Democratic Party was born. The new organization was now the majority party in the House of Representatives and held the largest number of seats in the House of Councilors.

Kishi, who became Secretary-General of the party, told a group of his followers who gathered at the old Democratic Party headquarters to congratulate him:

> "The birth of the Liberal-Democratic Party means, on the one hand, the establishment of a democratic political structure based on the two-party system, and on the other hand, the concentration of political power sufficient to permit implementation of uncompromising reconstruction policies. This political structure will permit stable and honest administration of the Diet, which will be operated in accordance with the sound rules of democracy. Under this new system, parliamentary government will be protected from the threat of dictatorship—rightist or leftist. But the Liberal-Democratic Party, to justify its designation as a party of all the people and prevent the return of fascism, must turn to the left to some extent. For example, we must expand social security and institute economic measures to attain full employment. At the same time, the Socialist Party should move toward the right to prevent the growth of communism. Now that we have a two-party system, we must exert every possible effort to develop it along moderate, democratic lines.
>
> "As for our reconstruction policies, one must be the revision of our Constitution, especially the part that forbids the establishment of defense forces. We must also promote economic relations with the Asian countries and maintain close friendship with the United States, Great Britain and other free nations. We must build up our economy by means of planning and raise our moral standards through reform of our educational system."

When Kishi finished his talk, the small audience cheered and ran over to shake his hand. But he was saddened by the absence of his closest associate, Hideyuki Miyoshi, who was in the hospital with an incurable disease. Kishi, against Miyoshi's will, tried to persuade Hatoyama and other party leaders to agree to his friend's appointment as Minister of Home Affairs in the new government, despite the fact that Miyoshi would probably never be able to exercise actively the functions of the post. The bestowal of such an honor would help, however little, to repay his friend,

Kishi thought, for all that he had done in helping to re-establish him as a leading political figure. But this effort on Miyoshi's behalf failed. When Miyoshi died in February, 1956, Kishi said, "I owe the position I hold today to Miyoshi-san."

Japan, for the first time since the war, had the basis for a stable, democratic government capable of carrying out effective reconstruction policies. Now Kishi set his sights on another goal. The nation had a workable political system, but it also required expert and imaginative leadership, leadership, which to be truly democratic, had to be asserted by those openly in power. Yoshida had retired. Hatoyama could not fill the bill. Kishi knew that he could. At the proper moment, he would emerge from the political shadows to become Prime Minister.

But this moment seemed distant. Ogata, as the President of the party, was slated to replace Hatoyama as Prime Minister in the near future. And even among the former Democrats, Kishi's influence was limited. Bukichi Miki was his senior and there was no assurance that he would back him for the premiership even after Ogata's term. Suddenly, Kishi found his plans for the future telescoped almost into the present. Ogata died within two months after the merger. A few months later, Miki died. Kishi stood virtually alone at the top of the party hierarchy, adding most of Miki's personal followers to his own. And Hatoyama was a very sick man.

Kishi soon discovered that stable, democratic government stemmed not so much from the form of parliamentary system as from the spirit in which it was operated. His first lesson came when the Liberal-Democratic Party, riding on an absolute majority in the House of Representatives, pushed through, under his guidance, a number of bills without benefit of adequate debate or negotiation with the Socialist minority. As a result of these steamroller tactics, many bills, including some of a bi-partisan nature, were blocked by a vengeful opposition in the House of Councilors, in which the conservatives lacked a majority. Even the conservatives in the upper chamber resented the tactics of their counterparts in the lower house, fearing their effect on the party's popularity.

Particularly bitter was a wasteful two-months' struggle, led by Kishi, for passage of a new electoral law which would increase the number of seats in the Diet by dividing some of the large electoral districts into two sections, each entitled to a representative. As the areas involved were in conservative territory, the Socialists—backed by public opinion—strongly opposed the measure. But the bill was forced through the lower house before finally dying in an upper-chamber pigeonhole.

The atmosphere became so inflamed that on one occasion, during discussion of a conservative bill to exclude members of the communist-infiltrated Japan Teachers' Union from all boards of education, several Socialists in the upper house rushed at their conservative foes with fists flying. Only the intervention of a swarm of policemen was able to quell the near-riot that ensued. The presence of about five hundred policemen in the Diet building reflected the fact that Kishi and his colleagues had expected such violence. Kishi told the press after the incident, "Originally, I thought we should let the Socialist Party fight our bills with violence and then wait for public opinion to determine who was wrong. However, as members of the party in power, we decided that it was our responsibility to keep order, while continuing to press for passage of measures we consider necessary for the good of Japan."

Kishi appeared willing to risk the breakdown of the two-party system of parliamentary government he had brought into existence through the use of tactics inviting violence and police action for what he considered the "good of Japan." While the Socialists proved themselves hardly more sensitive to the requirements of parliamentary procedure, Kishi, it was clear, also needed more experience in conducting government based on the supreme tolerance of opposition demanded under a genuinely democratic system.

Kishi and his party tasted the fruit of their tactlessness in the upper house election of July, 1955, in which half the seats of the chamber were at stake. The Liberal-Democrats ended up with about the same number of seats they controlled before the election while the Socialists increased their number by twelve. The Socialists were thus assured of more than one-third of the seats in the house, enough to prevent the revision of the Constitution as demanded by the conservatives. Kishi told newspapermen:

"As the Socialist Party has succeeded in obtaining one-third of the seats, which was its primary aim in the election, it goes without saying that the goddess of victory has beamed upon the Socialists this time. I, for one, believe very firmly that we should make every effort to shift our administrative procedures and policies to permit us to turn the tide of our fortunes. We must realize that while the conservative forces have been consolidated, the Socialist Party is growing stronger and has the power, at least potentially, to prevent the execution of one-sided conservative policies."

Kishi had been burned in Japan's first experiment in two-party democracy, but recognition of his errors showed a capacity to grow.

He had to grow quickly, for with the deaths of Ogata and Miki, his responsibilities multiplied. One of the main problems facing Japan was the issue of relations with Russia, which was rapidly coming to a head.

Russo-Japanese discussions on a peace treaty and the restoration of diplomatic ties had been held on and off since the summer of 1955, but with no results. Finally, in May, 1956, Ichiro Kono went to Moscow and concluded a fishery agreement with the Soviet government lifting Russian restrictions on Japanese use of the northern seas between Siberia and Japan. Kono, hoping to take full advantage of Russia's sudden display of reasonableness, urged the government to open fresh negotiations with Moscow for "normalization" of relations between the two countries. Though Hatoyama, for political reasons, heartily agreed with Kono and was ready to reach an accord at almost any cost, many members of his party were equally determined that Russia would have to agree to the return of several islands Russia held as war prizes before a treaty would be possible. And Moscow had flatly turned down this condition, and showed no sign of willingness to give in.

With the "peace-at-any-price" advocates pitted against the supporters of a "get-tough" policy, led by the Yoshida group, the Liberal-Democratic Party was in danger of disintegration. Kishi found himself between these two extremes. He wanted an early peace settlement, for this would give Hatoyama, who was under increasing pressure from party leaders to resign as his health deteriorated and his ineptitude grew, the "face-saving" opportunity to withdraw in glory. This, Kishi thought, would open the way for his own ascension to the premiership. But at the same time, Japan's interests required further compromise on the part of the Russians. Some solution to this dilemma would have to be found if the party was not to be ripped apart.

Kishi formulated his strategy. He obtained agreement of both factions in his party to a proposal to send Foreign Minister Shigemitsu to Moscow to negotiate personally with the Russians. This represented no small victory for Kishi, for the Hatoyama group thought Shigemitsu was too inflexibly opposed to Russian terms, while Yoshida's followers were against any delegation making the trip. When the Shigemitsu mission failed, Hatoyama, increasingly impatient for a grandstand triumph before his political fade-out, was highly receptive to the advice of some of his advisers, including Kono, that he go himself to Moscow for a "summit meeting" with Russia's Khrushchev and Bulganin. Kishi was at first only lukewarm to this idea, fearing that another failure would hurt the party's prestige and make it difficult for Hatoyama to resign without losing "face."

But the pressures generated in favor of the meeting grew as the public clamored for it, Hatoyama strained at the leash, and the Russian government hinted its readiness to re-open the territorial question. Kishi, more-

over, saw merit in the argument that if Hatoyama did not go, the party
might split apart anyway, whereas, if he went and succeeded in his mission, even to a limited degree, history might conform to Kishi's plans.

Kishi had only to convince the Yoshida group that Hatoyama should
go. When he failed to do so, he resorted to the tactics he had employed
in forming the old Democratic Party, isolating the Yoshida faction by
persuading the rest of his party that the conference was necessary to save
conservative unity. "I will not compromise with the Yoshida faction," he
announced. "Nor do I intend to persuade it to follow our course. As the
Secretary-General of our party, I think Prime Minister Hatoyama should
go to Moscow and negotiate a settlement."

Hatoyama and his advisers left on the delicate mission in October,
1956, and, miraculously enough, reached an agreement with Khrushchev
and Bulganin. The negotiators agreed that the state of war between Japan
and Russia should be ended and diplomatic relations established. The
settlement had been achieved through the simple expediency of post-
poning consideration of a formal peace treaty, which would include final
disposition of the Japanese islands held by Russia, for an indefinite period.
Hatoyama, furthermore, drew a promise from Moscow that it would return at least the Habomai and Shikotan Islands upon conclusion of a
treaty. He could thus go back home with the plum of renewed relations
with the Soviet Union, while having left the way open, at least theoretically, for Japan to get back its islands some time in the future. The trip
had, in political terms, proved profitable indeed. The Liberal-Democratic
Party drew the cheers of the public, and even the Socialists had to approve
of the conference results. Hatoyama was now ready to resign in a burst
of glory, and Kishi was set to replace him.

But though Kishi's plans had worked to perfection up to this point, he
found new obstacles threatening them on Hatoyama's triumphant return
to Japan. He had expected the Prime Minister to designate him as his
successor before resigning. But instead, Hatoyama, having convinced himself in the midst of the applause that he, and not Kishi, was the true
savior of the party, exhibited his "independence" by leaving it to the
party to elect a new President, who would automatically become Prime
Minister.

There was an immediate scramble for power among those opposing
Kishi. Members of the old Liberal Party, centered around the Yoshida
faction, threw their support behind Mitujiro Ishii, a key Liberal, despite
efforts by Eisaku Sato to head off this movement against his brother. And
other conservatives got behind Tanzan Ishibashi, who, with Kishi, had

been one of the founders of the Democratic Party. Kishi's close association with the unpopular Kono was no small factor in the mushrooming
of this opposition. The selection of Kishi as party President—a majority
vote by party delegates was necessary for victory—was now by no means
certain.

Kishi began to worry in earnest when his two opponents joined in a
"stop Kishi" campaign, denouncing him to the public as unfit for the
job because of his support of Tojo during the war. In every speech, they
dug up bits of his past, asking their listeners how they could trust such
a man in the nation's highest political office. And Kishi, on the defensive,
could only reply that the past was dead and gone. But he wasn't sure
whether the people believed him.

On election eve, he was unable to sleep as a thousand thoughts vied
for his restless attention. He could still visualize the little flower girl who
had approached him on the street some days before, bundled up in black
coat and knitted bonnet, and asked him to buy a bouquet. Recognizing
him, she had added with frightening seriousness, "If you don't buy my
flowers you will drop dead." Kishi had smiled and bought the bouquet,
and now he wondered in a rare moment of mystic fantasy, if fear of
sudden political death had not prompted him to make the purchase.

Through an open window across the room, Kishi could see the dim,
misty outline of a quarter moon, the same kind of moon, he reflected, that
had mocked him that night almost a dozen years before when he had first
entered Sugamo. Many things had happened since that night. Could he
possibly have dreamed then that he would one day be a free man, much
less a contender for the premiership? Yet he had condensed almost a
whole new lifetime into the space of a dozen years. He was but a pace
away from his coveted goal. A pace? It seemed, the more he thought about
it, like a mile, 10,000 miles. His fear grew that he would fail. He was glad
he had bought the flowers from the little girl.

The next morning, in the auditorium of the Sankei Building in downtown Tokyo, several hundred delegates of the Liberal-Democratic Party
gathered to select a new party President. Ballots were distributed and the
delegates filed past a ballot box that lay on a table on the platform at the
front of the hall casting their vote. Kishi, who sat on the platform together with other party officers, watched each delegate as he dropped his
ballot into the box, as if trying to determine from his expression whom
he was voting for. Finally, when all the votes were in, the ballots were
counted by a special committee and one of its members announced the
results: Ishibashi—151, Ishii—137, Kishi—223.

Kishi had received the biggest vote, but failed to carry a majority. Another vote would have to be taken to choose between the two strongest candidates—Kishi and Ishibashi. The delegates filed past the ballot box again, and by this time the tension in Kishi had dissipated into a kind of nervous lethargy. Once more the ballots were counted and the outcome announced to a silent, taut audience: Kishi—251, Ishibashi—258. Most of Ishii's followers had thrown their vote to Ishibashi, who was the new President of the party and next Prime Minister of Japan. As cheers echoed through the hall, Kishi suddenly felt numb, his face a pale, expressionless mask. Recovering in a moment, he got up from his chair and walked over to Ishibashi, who was surrounded by his followers. He smiled, his eyes glittering, and while newspaper photographers and movie cameramen snapped and ground away, he shook hands with the winner and congratulated him.

Kishi's narrow defeat was one of the severest blows he had ever received. It was infinitesimal in significance compared to the defeat he— and all other Japanese—had suffered in the war. But as he had shared that catastrophe with his fellows, it had not greatly disturbed his personal ego. Somehow collective defeat, however terrible the consequences, was, at least in the early stage of shock, easier to accept than an individual setback. Only seven votes. So close. Yet, he had lost, and he might never again have the opportunity to attain the heights of that elusive peak so tantalizingly out of reach. It was ironic; he had won almost every personal contest—from chess to politics—that he had ever entered, only to lose the biggest game of all.

Kishi now had to make a fateful decision. He had far more followers than Ishibashi, who had won the election with the temporary support of a number of factions. If he remained behind the scenes and pulled enough wires he might still be able to force Ishibashi's resignation eventually, as he had arranged Hatoyama's. And many of his backers urged him to do this, especially after Ishibashi selected some of Kishi's strongest antagonists for cabinet positions, including Hayato Ikeda, an uncompromising disciple of Yoshida, who was given the key job of Finance Minister.

But Kishi decided against such tactics. He had felt justified in pressing for the elimination of Hatoyama in the light of the latter's incompetence, due to advanced age and illness. But Ishibashi was something else again. He was a stronger leader, even if less able and imaginative than himself. It was, therefore, his duty to co-operate with the victor despite personal political differences for the good of the party and the country—particularly with the faction-ridden conservatives still in danger of splitting apart on almost any controversial issue. And as Ishibashi could never be managed from backstage as Hatoyama had been, he could only make his influence felt through open co-operation on the cabinet level.

Kishi thus accepted an offer by Ishibashi to be Foreign Minister. Not only was this the second highest post in the cabinet, giving him considerable opportunity to direct government and party policy, but he would be able to build up his international prestige. He would also be in the best possible position to strengthen Japan's relations with America and do away with the lingering hatred still felt toward Japan by Southeast Asia, foreign policy goals on which pivoted Japan's future prosperity. Kishi once again was the pragmatic idealist.

He took his new job almost more seriously than was appreciated by some of his fellow government members. At cabinet meetings, he would bombard the plump, jolly Prime Minister with detailed questions about foreign policy and point to innumerable items that needed to be studied. His colleagues were not used to this kind of direct questioning and scientific approach to policies. It was hardly in the Japanese tradition for a man in such high place to concern himself with "details" that would better be left to subordinate bureaucrats. Perhaps Kishi was still a petty bureaucrat at heart, they thought. Such attention to the "insignificant" could not help but blur his view of the over-all picture, to which a minister was supposed to confine himself. Furthermore, when a new minister was being briefed on policy by the Prime Minister, his duty was simply to listen, not risk embarrassing his superior by asking questions he might not be able to answer.

While Kishi prepared himself for the job of Foreign Minister, the whole political picture started changing. Ishibashi fell ill and was unable to attend the opening of the new Diet session on January 30, 1957. The Prime Minister's keynote address was then postponed until February 4th. But when it became clear that Ishibashi would still be too ill to attend, leaders of the Liberal-Democratic Party called an emergency party meeting at which it was decided that an acting prime minister would be appointed. Kishi's name immediately came to the fore. Some members opposed his selection, but most of them, taking into account Kishi's power and the dramatically small figure by which he had lost the election, agreed that he was the logical choice, if only for the sake of maintaining a semblance of party unity. This view was shared by Ishibashi himself.

Kishi, who was now definitely established as the heir to the premiership, accepted the honor with a mixed sense of humility and delight. He had an unprecedented opportunity to draw the various factions of the party closer together. At a press conference, Kishi, now heavily indebted to his superior, said, "The main policies of the Ishibashi cabinet shall remain unchanged. Ishibashi-san has selected me as Acting Prime Minister in the firm belief that I will support them, and I intend to do so. I can assure you that the government will not attempt to conduct two kinds of diplomacy nor to reshuffle the cabinet in the absence of the Prime Minister. I have no intention of imposing my will through what would amount to a coup d'état."

Kishi then delivered two speeches in the Diet, the keynote address as Acting Prime Minister and a foreign policy speech as Foreign Minister. In the former, he called mainly for the restoration of discipline in the Diet, and "positive economic measures" to achieve higher living standards and full employment, including expansion of Japan's economic structure, increased trade, and more social security.

In his foreign policy talk, Kishi stressed his long-held view that domestic policies must be geared to international diplomacy. He added:

"As we wish to make Japan a truly democratic and peace-loving nation, it is only natural that co-operation with the Free World should be the basic principle of Japanese foreign policy. . . . There need be no fear that Japan-United States relations will cool off as the result of Japan's restoration of diplomatic relations with the U.S.S.R. The United States and Japan have mutual interests and aims in the political, economic, and military fields. To tighten these relations even further and make them everlasting, generosity, good will, and sincere, frank talks between our two countries are essential.

". . . At the same time, the improvement of Japan's position in the United Nations, in international society, depends on our success in strengthening friendly ties with our brother Asian nations, mainly through 'economic diplomacy.' To secure such ties, we must settle, first of all, the reparations issues and contribute to the welfare of Asia. We should draw up concrete aid plans for this purpose. I wish to visit these countries at a proper time to make them see our eagerness to help them in any way we can.

". . . As for our relations with the communist countries, they will be handled practically, not ideologically. Each problem will be studied separately in accordance with the best interests of Japan. As Japan is economically interdependent with Communist China, we must take proper measures, while co-operating with the Free World, that will lead toward the easing of the embargo against China and toward the expansion of Japan's China trade. There are many outstanding issues between the U.S.S.R. and Japan, including the signing of a peace treaty, fishing, the repatriation issue, the draft of a Japan-Soviet commercial pact. But they will be solved one by one."

When Kishi finished speaking, he remained at the rostrum to answer questions from the opposition. If he had rattled his party colleagues with his sharp questioning at cabinet meetings, he startled his political foes with his polite but unusually frank and direct answers. He offered no vagaries and left little room for rebuttal to his clear and thorough expositions. One observer commented, "Listening to his explanations or replies is like eating the *table d'hôte* meal from the *hors d'oeuvres* to the dessert, everything being served without a hitch." Kishi had given an impressive opening performance.

Meanwhile, Ishibashi was not getting any better. The matchstick structure of the Liberal-Democratic Party trembled as political cross-winds rustled through it. Some party leaders thought Kishi should remain simply Acting Prime Minister no matter how long Ishibashi remained ill, while others wanted to make him Vice-Premier. Kishi's personal followers pressed for the resignation of the whole Ishibashi cabinet to clear the way for an entirely new government, with Kishi as full-time Prime Minister. The Socialist Party, though hardly sympathetic toward Kishi, demanded Ishibashi's resignation as a means of promoting discord among the conservatives, warning that it would not approve passage of the 1957 budget in the absence of a legitimate Prime Minister.

Many of Kishi's political foes, conservatives and Socialists, fully expected him to make a move to force the resignation of the Cabinet and then take over the government himself. After all, they argued, had he not turned against Ichizo Kobayashi, his superior in the Ministry of Commerce and Industry in pre-war days, and against General Tojo during the war? Why would he not "betray" his present superior, Ishibashi, particularly when he was faced with so few barriers? And he would have a good excuse, too; the government couldn't continue operating without a Prime Minister.

But his friends knew that the ease with which he could "betray" Ishibashi was one of the reasons why he would not do it. When a child, he would always fight older boys. Victory then was much sweeter. By the same token, he had fought Kobayashi and Tojo from disadvantageous positions—and over matters of principle. But now it was Ishibashi who was in the weaker position. Kishi would not take advantage of the Prime Minister, especially after the latter had supported him as his substitute, and when there were no important differences between them. But not only *giri* was involved. A reckless move would be politically unwise. He would simply antagonize a large segment of the party and further split the organization. And this would be defeating his own ends, for his central aim was to solidify the party. Therefore, as his followers intensified pressure on him to make his move, Kishi urged them not to take any "short-sighted action."

The tension reached a peak when Ishibashi's doctors, after giving him a thorough medical examination, advised that he continue to rest for at least another two months. The same day, a letter from Ishibashi arrived at party headquarters. Opening it, Kishi read:

"I am very sorry to have troubled you so much with my unexpected illness. I do not know how to thank you for your efforts to set my mind at ease. But as the doctors have advised me to take another two-months' rest, I feel that I must resign from the premiership. . . . My resolution to do so is firm and unchangeable. . . ."

Kishi and other party leaders met at midnight in the Prime Minister's official residence to discuss the situation and decided that the government would resign *en bloc* and that Kishi would be nominated as the next Prime Minister. Kishi, outwardly calm, but turbulent with emotion under the cool surface, arrived home at two A.M. on February 23, 1957, to find a cheering throng of friends and followers waiting for him in front of the house. Smiling, he wordlessly made his way through the crowd, entered, and headed upstairs toward his room. A secretary rushed up after him and suggested that he come down and make a short speech. "Please ask everyone to leave," Kishi replied sharply. "This is a time for reflection, not for rejoicing." Presently, Yoshiko came down and told the secretary, "My husband hopes you will understand. He is a bit nervous. After all," she added with a note of carefully contained pride, "he is to be the next Prime Minister."

Later in the day, Kishi sent word to Ishibashi that he would follow his policies and retain his cabinet choices, though he was under tremendous pressure from his followers to get rid of at least some of them. On being named Prime Minister, Kishi kept his word to Ishibashi, thereby taking over a conservative party that had never been more united behind its leader.

A powerful blend of ambition, unyielding will, sincerity of purpose, political acumen, and phenomenal luck had borne fruit. Kishi had finally realized his dream and, curiously, the dream of Moyo, though she never would have understood the new Japan. He had reached the top, and under conditions that favored his remaining there for a long period. But even more important, he was now in a position to repay the people his enormous wartime debt by leading them along the right path to the sun.

CHAPTER XV

REPAYMENT OF A DEBT

K ISHI TOOK OVER the reins of power at a crucial juncture in Japanese history. In the dozen years since the end of the war, which had left Japan in ruins, its economy prostrate and its people dazed and de-moralized, the nation, with American help, had accomplished a miracle of reconstruction. The basic rehabilitation had been achieved under Yoshida during and immediately after the Occupation, and by the time he resigned, industry had been entirely resurrected. Tokyo, Osaka, and other bombed cities had been rebuilt, with housing capacities surging beyond pre-war levels. Workers were earning more than ever before, and farmers were beginning to reap the advantages of their liberation from farm tenancy.

The ascension to power of Hatoyama in 1954 opened a new phase. His government represented the first postwar leadership untainted by Occupation ties with the American conquerors. Under Hatoyama, Japan, experiencing a slump after the Korean war windfall, paused to consoli-date its enormous gains. And with Kishi playing no small role behind the scenes, it began laying the groundwork for long-range economic prosperity, political stability, and restoration of its international prestige and influence. A five-year economic development plan was drawn up based on a predicted increase in the gross national product of five per cent annually. By the end of 1957, the plan was being adjusted to meet an actual rise of eight per cent.

A two-party system came into being, largely due to Kishi's efforts. Diplomatic relations were established with the Soviet Union, trade ties, with Communist China. The United States was tendered friendly but clear notice that Japan would henceforth expect to be treated as a sovereign equal.

When Kishi stepped into the premiership on February 27, 1957, the time had come for Japan to advance toward its long-range goals. These goals did not basically differ from those he had sought as a member of the Tojo cabinet. At that time, too, he had dreamed of a strong, prosperous Japan run by a stable government capable of winning for the country the international recognition it deserved. But if the objectives were the same, Kishi, with the crusading fervor of the convert, was determined that this time they would be accomplished within a peaceful, democratic ideological framework.

In his inaugural speech before both houses of the Diet, Kishi stressed:

"The operation of the Diet must be conducted in accordance with the spirit of democracy so that the people's trust in party politics and the existing political parties will grow. I believe that truly democratic politics must be based on the understanding and the support of the whole nation. I therefore pledge myself to be a true representative of the people in my efforts to further the (aims) of the nation . . ."

Since these words were spoken, Japan has furthered its aims to a greater degree than the Prime Minister himself had thought possible. Kishi and his people, by channeling the energy, will-power, and agressiveness that once made them a military scourge into pacific constructive pursuits, have produced the greatest prosperity in Japan's history. In 1959, industrial production was almost double, industrial investment and national income triple, the prewar peak. Japan, moreover, has won in peaceful competition world markets that are absorbing Japanese goods three times the value of products exported when the country exploited captive markets in China and other occupied Asian areas. Japanese trade, technical, and investment missions are knocking on doors in the remotest corners of Southeast Asia, the Middle East, Africa, and South America. On a recent trip around the world, I met a Japanese oil technician on his way to Saudi Arabia, a Japanese iron ore mining excutive en route to India, a Japanese electrical salesman in Nigeria, and I visited a Japanese trade exhibition in Ethiopia.

This picture of vigor, enthusiasm, and optimism is reflected in Japan's soaring living standards. The summer visitor to a top-grade geisha house need no longer depend on the traditional paper fan for relief from the heat; the house will probably be air-conditioned. His meal is likely to be fresher and better cooked than ever before; the seaweed-wrapped morsels of raw fish will come out of a refrigerator, the steaming rice from an automatic rice cooker. His entertainment will be varied; when he tires of watching the geishas perform the delicate movements of the Kabuki dance, he can turn on television in the next matted room and wonder at a Japanese Elvis Presley spasmodically swinging his hips—or he himself can rock-and-roll with the geishas to juke-box records.

The benefits of comfortable modern living are evident everywhere. The Japanese people, able to save one-sixth of a per capita income 20 per cent higher than in prewar days, are spending 40 per cent more money on consumer items, including many luxuries. In 1950, modern appliances were virtually unknown in Japan. Today, demand for many such items exceeds supply. Of Tokyo households at the end of 1959, about 50 per cent had washing machines; 50 per cent, television sets; 20 per cent, refrigerators; 25 per cent, electric rice cookers; 15 per cent, vacuum cleaners; 40 per cent, electric fans. Almost every Japanese home is equipped with a radio and electric iron. Such products have, in the ten-year span, reduced the amount of time the average urban housewife devotes to housework from thirteen to nine hours daily.

These statistics mirror the drastic change in the living conditions of the Japanese worker since prewar days. The high consumption level of the worker is, in fact, virtually supporting the Japanese economy. There is, to be sure, a significant disparity between the living standards of the 60 per cent who work for small, inefficient manufacturing enterprises and the 40 per cent who are employed by larger companies. Nevertheless, the average worker's family spends only about 40 per cent of its income on food, permitting it to indulge in many luxury consumer goods. The average Japanese worker manages, at the same time, to save more than 12 per cent of his income.

True, his salary is still extremely low by Western standards—the unskilled laborer earns about $45 a month—but this does not represent a true comparison of real wages. For one thing, it is estimated that the yen equivalent of the dollar will buy in Japan about twice the amount of goods that could be purchased in the United States. Also, the basic needs of most Japanese are much simpler than those of Westerners. They require little or no furniture for their homes. And their staple diet consists mainly of rice, fish, and vegetables, which can be purchased very cheaply in Japan. An important part of their daily needs are provided—at least by the large concerns—in the form of paternalistic benefits.

The 10,000 workers employed at the huge Hitachi Works in the town of Hitachi, about 100 miles from Tokyo, are representative of Japan's industrial employees. This plant, which produces boilers, turbines, rectifiers, condensers, rolling mill equipment, nuclear reactor equipment, and other heavy industrial items, is one of twenty factories composing Hitachi, Ltd. Before the breakup of the *Zaibatsu,* Hitachi was associated with the great Nissan combine that helped to industrialize Manchuria.

Jiro Suzuki, a husky square-faced thirty-five-year-old foundry worker, has been employed at Hitachi Works since 1939, when he was recruited by the company after graduation from middle school. Wearing goggles, black boots, a long-sleeved canvas apron and hood that covers a blue peaked cap on which is sewed a yellow Hitachi insignia, Suzuki makes molds for melted iron from pressed foundry sand. He operates a huge Japanese-made machine, called the "Sandslinger," an automatic high pressure compressor. Though it compresses the sand almost twice as fast as the hand air compressor he used previously, his job today is essentially the same as it was when he started working for Hitachi for $18 monthly. He now earns $63 a month, plus about $16 in overtime pay.

Younger men employed in the same capacity but without his seniority may be making as little as $25 monthly. Suzuki actually gets a higher salary than most workers with the same seniority, for one-third of his wages is determined on an incentive, or productivity, basis, and another one-third according to the quality of his work, considerations that could make a difference of about 20 per cent between the pay of the worst and the best worker. Suzuki is far above average in both categories. In addition, he is given summer and Christmas bonuses equivalent to about five months' salary, and a small family allowance equal to about .5 per cent of his wages.

Furthermore, Suzuki can purchase most of his needs, from electrical appliances to food and clothing, at the company store, where prices are 20 per cent under the normal retail level. He is entitled to twenty days vacation a year, which he takes with his family at a company-owned mountain resort in Nasu, northeast of Tokyo, where he is charged only $1 a night including food, or at one of the thirty odd hotels around the country with which Hitachi has 20 per cent discount arrangements.

The company also provides Suzuki and his co-workers with entertainment facilities. He can play a game of *go* or buy an inexpensive meal in the company clubhouse. He can indulge in a glass of beer in the company bar, either on a bar-stool or in a matted booth. There is also a well-equipped gymnasium where Suzuki, who used to be *sumo* champion of Hitachi, Ltd., can still work out. He can also watch his company team play soccer and baseball against competing firms. If Suzuki or any member of his family falls ill, they can be assured of excellent medical treatment in the modern company hospital, which has three hundred and fifty beds and a staff of thirty-one doctors and one hundred nurses, with one hundred more undergoing training. Suzuki spends about .5 per cent of his monthly pay on medical insurance, the company contributing an equal sum.

Suzuki lives in a small wooden tatami-floored house on the company premises, which he rents for only $1.25 a month. The house is crowded. He and his wife, Hanako, a slim, attractive woman, have four children, aged two to eleven, all boys. Although it is not uncommon for a family of this size, even in the middle class, to live in such a small house Suzuki plans to build another wing to the house, at his own expense. In the main room of the house, the family keeps warm at a table that stands over a *hibachi* pit containing an electric heater. In the other room, a small desk fills a corner. A wardrobe and a cabinet where *futon* are kept, each covered with white cloth, lines one side of the room, and a chest of drawers occupies another corner. On the wall over the desk is a color wedding picture of Crown Prince Akihito and Princess Michiko in full traditional costume. ("Akihito is a man of the people," says Suzuki.)

In the small kitchen, lit with a hanging naked light bulb, there is a sink with cold running water, a two-burner portable gas stove, and, on a shelf, a new automatic electric rice cooker. Pots and pans are piled up in a large bamboo basket, and two small baskets for draining rice hang on the wall. The bathroom next door has a wooden bathtub with a built-in stove for the burning of coal. Cords of wood are piled up in a corner for starting a fire. The bathroom also features a late model washing machine.

After a dinner of fish, rice, vegetables and tea, Suzuki's wife, dressed in a kimono, usually remains at the table by the *hibachi* reading to her two younger children. The nine- and eleven-year-old boys, dressed in the black, brass-buttoned uniform of the schoolboy, will probably be studying, one at the table, the other at the desk—though sometimes they hide a Japanese comic book in a history or arithmetic book so that Father Suzuki will not notice that they are neglecting their homework.

Suzuki considers this a serious matter, for he wants his boys to go to college and become engineers. "I only hope I'll be able to save up enough money to pay for their educations." With good times having increased his purchasing power about 20 per cent in the last four years, Suzuki has, for the first time in his life, been able to save a substantial part of his salary. To date, he has put away about $335.

The Suzukis plan their budget carefully. They spend monthly, in addition to the small sum for their rent, about $55 for food, $5 for clothes, and $5 for entertainment, which includes magazines, movies, and radio tax. He could afford a television set, Suzuki says, but he is afraid it would keep the children from their studies. The cash purchase of such items as a bicycle, which his wife uses to go shopping (he walks to work), further depletes the pocketbook.

His union dues amount to $1 a month. Suzuki is an active member of his moderately socialistic union, an affiliate of the independent All-Japan Electrical Workers Union, which comprises about 120,000 workers. He is by no means unaware that the union has helped to obtain a five to six per cent yearly increase in wages. He also sentimentally recollects that he met Hanako, a former Hitachi employee, at a union meeting. The company lost a worker and he gained a wife.

Even a newly recruited worker at Hitachi is able to live comfortably and still save part of his salary. Masatoshi Sekine, a nineteen-year-old mechanical inspector of thermal power, just out of high school, earns only $24 a month, but he nevertheless saves 10 per cent of this. A handsome youth with eyes that squint behind thick glasses, Sekine, a bachelor, lives in one of the company dormitories, sharing a matted room with another worker. He pays monthly $1.50 for the room, and $8 for meals served in the large cafeteria, where a typical dinner might include fried sausage, cabbage, mashed potatoes, soybean soup, rice, and tea. He spends about $2.50 a month for clothes, and $1.25 for movies and other entertainment. He usually prefers to watch television in the recreation hall, read technical books in the library, or listen to his collection of classical Western records in his room. In the near future, Sekine intends to take the entrance examination of the Hitachi Technical Institute operated by the company. Graduation from this school, whose curriculum is equivalent to two years of college, would make him an engineer.

Not all of Hitachi's workers are as well off or as secure as Suzuki and Sekine. About 3,500 of them are "temporary workers," who are a safety valve, so that the firm can lay off a portion of its personnel in case of bad times. No regular workers, except in very unusual cases, can be dismissed, due partly to paternalistic tradition and partly to the power of the labor union. (Conversely, almost no employee will quit before forced retirement at fifty-five, due to company loyalty, the reluctance to lose seniority, and the difficulty in switching to another job.) These temporary workers receive wages similar to those paid the regular employees, but are not entitled to any fringe benefits, except bonuses. Usually young and unskilled—the average is twenty years old as compared to thirty-four for the "regular"—they have an opportunity to become permanent employees after one year if they pass an examination, and about 40 per cent do so.

Aside from company benefits, the workers have, for the first time, begun to benefit from modern state-directed social welfare measures. Japan's first minimum wage bill was passed by the Diet in 1959. Although it has been criticized as lukewarm—the employers themselves are expected to work out agreements concerning minimum wages and only in exceptional cases can the government recommend or impose wage rates—this legislation is an important initial step in an unexplored field. Old-age pension and national health insurance systems embracing the entire population for the first time have also been inaugurated.

Hardly less spectacular than Japan's urban economic progress has been its agrarian revolution. While Communist China offers the image of an oppressed communal farm society, Japanese farmers are providing the politically uncommitted nations of Asia with an impressive example of what peasants can accomplish under a free enterprise system.

One such farmer is Yasuzo Sekine,* who lives in Furuya, a typical little Japanese farm town of eight hundred and thirty households, about twenty miles from Tokyo. The bareness of the matted living room in Sekine's thatch-roofed, wooden house is accentuated by the presence of two items: a seventeen-inch television set and a bamboo-framed certificate on the wall honoring Sekine for his record rice yield in 1958. These two proudly displayed possessions reflect the remarkable changes that have come over Furuya since three million Japanese families were liberated from farm tenancy by the Occupation. The TV set symbolizes the growing prosperity of Japan's farmers, 40 per cent of the population, and the certificate, awarded by the mayor of Furuya, explains how they achieved this well-being.

"Things sure have changed," says the assistant director of the Furuya agricultural co-operative. "The first thing a girl asks today when a farm boy proposes to her is, 'Have you got a tractor?' "

Sekine and his fellows have boosted Japan's total agricultural produc-

* The names Sekine and Suzuki are very common in Japan, accounting for their multiple use in this chapter.

tion by 35 per cent since 1952. They have made Japan almost self-suffi-cient in rice, the mainstay of the Japanese diet, producing five bumper crops in a row, all purchased by the government under a generous price support program, paying them $80 per ton. They have also registered unprecedented wheat yields.

Sekine, whose family is among the 60 per cent in Furuya who became landowners under the agrarian reform program, owns only 1.5 acres of land—hardly more than a "backyard" in American terms, but an aver-age-size farm in overcrowded Japan. The land reform law limited a farmer's holding to three acres, except in the few cases in which a land-owner could show that he personally had worked more land than that. The division of Sekine's farm into fifteen tiny scattered patches reflects the fact that he had worked as a tenant for many landowners. For his labor in the landless years, he received less than 50 per cent of the yield of each patch, payment that amounted to a bare subsistence.

"We were hungry in bad crop years," says Farmer Sekine, a chunky man with a kind, friendly face. "Sometimes the landlords would take pity on us and let us keep more of our yield than our contract called for. But it's terrible for a man to have to depend on the good heart of his landlord to stay alive."

One of Sekine's landlords was Shintaro Kishino, a slightly built, wrin-kled-faced man who, oddly enough, is now director of the village co-operative. Sekine was one of about one hundred tenant farmers who worked Kishino's eighteen acres of land. Under the reform program, Kishino was forced to turn over all but three acres of his land to Se-kine and his other tenants for a twenty-year government bond, while Sekine was given twenty-four years to repay the government. As things turned out, inflation erased the value of Kishino's bond and permitted Sekine to discharge his debt within five years. Today, the once powerful landlord is content to work for Sekine and his other former tenants, whose incomes are only slightly less than his own.

Sekine, profiting indeed from his new role as a landholder, earns a gross income of more than $2400 a year, netting about $900 after operating expenses and taxes. Dressed in cotton jacket, brown corduroy trousers with patched knees, and black rubber boots, he painstakingly exacts from his sparse earth each year one hundred bushels of rice, which the government buys for $640, and one hundred bushels of wheat and barley that bring in $280. He also produces eight hundred pounds of cocoons selling for $420, and his two hundred hens lay eggs valued at $1100 His earnings are little, of course, by American standards, but an Emperor's ransom in terms of traditional Japanese rural income.

Sekine is able to save almost 30 per cent of his net earnings, for his living expenses, though higher than ever before, amount to little more than $600 a year. He spends much of this on clothes for his family, which includes six children, three boys and three girls, aged four to seventeen. And he also devotes considerable sums to entertainment. Before the war, the Sekines limited themselves to occasional visits with the neighbors, and during the Occupation they found square dancing, taught them by American officials, an inexpensive diversion. But now they can afford to pay the bus fare to Tokyo to see a stage show or spend an hour or so in a coffee shop listening to American juke-box music. They also take in a local movie once or twice a month.

About half of Sekine's living expenses go for food. His family is eating more nourishing meals than ever before. The main dish is rice mixed with barley. Rice is a relative luxury for Sekine and his fellow farmers. "When I was a boy," says Sekine, "almost all we ever ate was barley. We couldn't afford to eat rice when the profit from every grain meant something."

Curiously, the urban population is, on the contrary, consuming less and less rice. In any event, this staple commodity is rationed on a monthly basis of fifteen days' supply per person. Rationing is still considered necessary, for despite Japan's near self-sufficiency in rice, many farmers illegally withhold part of their crop from the government to dispose of it on the black market. But though even black market rice is cheaper than wheat products, the Japanese—both farmers and urbanites—are consuming increasing quantities of the latter. Wheat now constitutes about 16 per cent of the Japanese diet as compared to 6 per cent before the war. The Sekine children are treated to an afternoon snack of biscuits filled with fruit jam, and bread is included in their school lunches, paid for by papa but provided under a Ministry of Education program. Sekine strongly favors this program, for he knows from reading government pamphlets that wheat products are good for his children's health. But ironically, he, like most Japanese farmers, is not prepared yet to reduce his wheat acreage, as the government is urging, to permit the import of cheaper wheat from abroad, though the present high cost of wheat foods limits consumption by his family.

Sekine is investing a large share of his income in the improvement of his farm, one reason why he won the certificate for the highest rice yield in the community last year. With Japanese ingenuity, he is able to rotate crops on his minuscule 1.5 acre farm. Most of his land consists of rice paddy on which he grows two crops annually. His smaller patches of "upland," or dry, soil, support two wheat and barley crops a year, in spring and fall, a "dry" rice crop in summer, and small mulberry and soybean crops. The yields of all these items have greatly increased—wheat production has doubled—as the result of a water drainage project being undertaken for forty families by the Local Land Improvement Association, which is partly subsidized by the government. Sekine contributed $90 as well as labor to the project. He has also constructed a $1400 warehouse for his produce, a small building in which to raise silkworms, and chicken huts for his new and highly lucrative poultry business.

At the same time, Sekine has adopted new farming techniques taught him by the Occupation-spawned Farm Extension Service, which tells him about the latest research, conducted at new experimental stations, and the use of fertilizers, insecticides, and weed-killers. He has learned how to increase his rice income through controlled cultivation in nursery beds, spreading oil paper or plastic sheets over his beds to reduce the cold. Thus, he can start seeding in April instead of June, and begin harvesting before the destructive typhoons strike in September, while the government pays him a bonus for early delivery. Furthermore, overlapping with the wheat planting season is avoided, an important consideration, for a delay of two weeks means a 30 per cent drop in the wheat yield.

The Extension Service has taught some of Sekine's neighbors how to grow new crops. For example, Tokijiro Suzuki is now cultivating mushrooms under controlled temperature conditions in large dirt-filled wooden bins set up in a little concrete house specially built for the purpose. The mushrooms—two crops a year—are sold to a cannery and exported to the United States, earning yearly $550 for Suzuki. With the help of the Extension Service, Suzuki has also built a well in his dry land area and is pumping up water to provide more paddy land.

Sekine is devoting part of his income to the improvement of his house, which has been in the family for five generations. He is proud to show visitors the new innovations he has introduced. Returning from his fields on a brand-new motorcycle, which permits him to travel swiftly from one patch of land to another, Sekine greets his guest with a deep bow. Then he leads him through his front yard to the house, built of rotting, white-painted wood turned an insipid gray by the elements. He pushes the front door, which creaks open on rusty hinges, and, walking over to a porcelain sink, proudly turns on the faucet to show that he now has running water—something new. He also points smilingly to a dusty telephone just installed.

"We were going to buy a washing machine," says Mrs. Sekine, who, like most Japanese peasant women, wears a long-sleeved white apron, loose cotton knickers, and, when she is outside, tight-fitting rubber boots with canvas tops. "But we decided to get a television set first because the children were always over at the neighbors' watching theirs. We couldn't get them home for dinner."

In the last year, the Sekines have added a second floor to the house where several of the children sleep. It is also a convenient place to dry *mochi* on large throw mats in the winter. Sekine is thinking of building a complete new house eventually, something like the one his neighbor, Suzuki, has constructed. The Suzuki house is the attraction of the neighborhood, costing $2800 in cash. A four-room tile-roofed structure, it contrasts sharply with Suzuki's old thatch-roofed home, which is now used as a barn. It is made with the fine oak grown on his own land and has paper walls decorated with charcoal landscape sketches.

Sekine also considered purchasing a hand-tractor like the one belonging to another neighbor, Izaemon Arai, but he decided against this, for his land requires considerable non-chemical fertilizer, and it is therefore economically practical for him to use his draft cow for plowing. Farmers Sekine and Arai like to compare their latest acquisitions. Sekine takes his friend for a ride on his motorcycle and Arai reciprocates by giving him a spin in his three-wheel truck. Often they talk while Arai, a small man with a thin, strong face, sits outside his house on a mat and makes bamboo brooms, which he sells in the local market. The job, one of many handicrafts Japanese peasants engage in to augment their incomes, consists of tying several short, slender bamboo stems to the end of a long bamboo pole with wisteria vine.

Sekine's life is closely bound up with Furuya farm co-operative, which has greatly facilitated the rise in his living standards since the Occupation. It markets his products, sells him farm tools and equipment, as well as consumer items ranging from overalls to electrical appliances, provides him with credit for such purchases (though he almost always pays cash), and banks his earnings. The Ministry of Agriculture deposits payment for his rice crop, and his wheat and barley crop as well (he is free to sell these two crops, but not his rice on the open market if he so desires) in his savings account, which he draws upon according to need. The co-operative also polishes his rice and barley, mills his flour, and produces soya sauce from his soybeans. Sekine, like his fellows, has a $30 investment in the co-operative. The project, though now operating profitably under Kishini's drection, was a losing proposition when it was first inaugurated. Completely unfamiliar with business procedures, the farmers were easy prey for crooked brokers who sold them non-existent fertilizer and farm tools for cash in advance.

If Sekine is satisfied with the present, he is somewhat concerned about the future. For one thing, the limitation on individual farm acreage has placed an automatic ceiling on his income, however greatly it has increased up to now. But even more important to him, only the family of his eldest son will be able to make a comfortable living from what little land he has. His two other sons will probably have to move to the city, as most younger sons are doing today, and find work in factories—a fate, Sekine feels, that should befall no boy born and bred on a farm.

The fact that his second and third sons will have to give up farm life underscores Japan's basic economic difficulty—overpopulation in relation to resources. But it also suggests a possible long-term answer to this problem. With the large-scale absorption of peasants into an expanding industrial structure, more land will remain to fewer farmers. On the other hand, some agricultural experts point out, increased industrialization might actually aggravate the present situation. Many farmers, hungry for immediate financial gain, are, even today, selling their land to business interests for conversion into factory and other non-agricultural sites. About fifteen thousand acres of farmland are vanishing each year, a trend which, if maintained, could cancel the advantages of a smaller farm population.

But despite difficulties on the horizon, peasants like Sekine have found at least a temporary solution to the farm problem. By working and reworking with the latest methods every square inch of their tiny strips of earth, they have managed to rise within a decade from grinding poverty to relative prosperity.

The rapid rise of living standards in the cities and on the farms reflects the tremendous production surge of Japan's industry. Rebuilt and modernized by the time Kishi became premier, the nation's factories have been, since his ascension to power, competing with or outproducing the other nations of the world in many items. At the end of 1959, Japan ranked first in ships and fishery hauls, second in rayon, synthetic textiles, and motorcycles, third in cotton textiles, nitrogen fertilizers, sulphuric acid, and medicines and drugs, fourth in cement, fifth in paper, lumber, pulp, power generation, and cotton spinning facilities, sixth in steel, and crude iron, seventh in coal. It had the sixth largest merchant marine fleet and ranked eighth as a consumer of electric power and petroleum. Further, new industries, such as electronics, aeronautics, petrochemicals, synthetic resin and atomic energy, have registered extraordinary progress.

This astonishing rate of industrialization has been accomplished under an economy that is far from unregulated, but nevertheless much more liberal than the pre-war economy. Japan's five-year plan under Kishi, whose economic past was so intimately enmeshed in "controls" and "planning," has simply served as a useful vehicle to guide the government in drawing up economic policies. No effort is made to implement it. In fact, the planners have not yet displayed the optimism that would be justified. The five-year plan inaugurated in 1958, which called for a 6.5 per cent average annual growth, must be revised upward to provide for an actual 7.6 per cent expansion. Kishi ordered his economic experts to study the possibilities of working out a plan for the doubling of the national income within ten years.

But while industry operates with little concern for official plans, it is still dependent on the government in many ways. Government loans and subsidies, coupled with the control of money by the Bank of Japan, have in no small measure fostered the nation's extremely high industrial investment rate, which almost equals that of West Germany, France, and Britain. The government regulates rice prices and rations this staple commodity to make such regulation easier. It controls foreign exchange allocations to prevent luxury imports and unnecessary purchases of technical know-how from abroad, though it is gradually loosening its import restrictions and has approved the payment of almost $40 million a year, mostly to the United States, for foreign royalties and engineering assistance. The government often exerts pressure on over-productive companies, particularly textile concerns, to cut down their output. And occasionally it finances the development of new industries, such as synthetic rubber, as it has done since Meiji times. But, in general, the tendency is toward liberalization. "In earlier days," says one economic observer, "Kishi's job was to plan for totalitarianism and war. But he realizes that much less planning and regulation are needed when democracy and peace are the nation's goals."

The planning and regulating which the government does engage in usually has the approval of industry. Industry even participates in the formulation of policy, for few decisions of economic import are reached without lengthy discussions between government officials and representatives of the industrial associations. But these associations, or cartels, which number more than two hundred, have little in common with those that Kishi had nurtured, under the Tojo administration, for purposes of war. The latter had been completely under the thumb of the giant *Zaibatsu,* which, as Kishi ruefully discovered, had the power to force the government to act in their selfish personal interests. The present associations have rigidly limited advisory powers, and, composed of many companies of all sizes, function in the interest of a whole particular branch of industry. They still fix export prices, with government approval, but even many Western experts believe this is necessary to some extent to prevent unreasonable competition from unreliable, fly-by-night firms that hurt legitimate Japanese companies, as well as Japan's reputation abroad.

The tendency toward industrial unification is also mirrored in the actual reamalgamation of *Zaibatsu* segments that were established as independent, and, in the eyes of Kishi and many Japanese, unreasonably small and uneconomic units during the Occupation. But the new combines, too, differ from their old counterparts.

A revealing comparison can be made between the pre-Occupation Mitsui *Zaibatsu* and the largest portion of it now operating as a single unit, the Mitsui Trading Company. The old trust was controlled through a holding company by a single family, the Mitsuis, who owned almost all the stock. Investors in the new firm number more than three million people. The pre-war giant embraced companies involved in almost every industrial activity. The present one is almost entirely a trading company, and handles only 10 per cent of Japan's foreign trade as compared to 25 per cent before the war. True, there is still something of an *esprit de corps* among former Mitsui employees, and this residual sense of loyalty has led to close co-operation with ex-Mitsui companies in other fields. But such co-operation exists only when it is consistent with good business. The relatively weak Mitsui Bank has been a less important creditor of the Mitsui Trading Company than the Mitsubishi Bank, which was part of the competing Mitsubishi *Zaibatsu.*

Even if the *Zaibatsu* were to attempt to attain their former control of industry, the question of who would lead a thoroughly reinstituted *Zaibatsu* could not easily be answered. Baron Hachiroyemon Mitsui was the feudal lord of the trust in bygone days and his power was unchallengeable. Today, his lieutenants head individual enterprises of their own and are not anxious to take orders from a new over-all feudal chieftain for the sake of a tradition that is more a nostalgic memory than a practical business arrangement.

President Yasutaro Niizeki of the Mitsui Trading Company, an ardent supporter of Kishi, was only a junior director in the Mitsui empire when it was dissolved. With $400 borrowed from the Mitsubishi Bank, the origin of Mitsubishi's standing as a creditor of the company, Niizeki re-activated a tiny segment of the Mitsui Trading Company, and, with amazing business agility, absorbed within a decade fourteen other detached Mitsui companies. Today he directs a firm that sells yearly about $1.3 billion worth of metal products, chemicals, textiles, machinery, cement, lumber, and other items. He has little desire to play second-fiddle again to any other Mitsui executive.

Conversely, Niizeki, whose tough, dynamic manner belies his talent for painting pictures of flower arrangements, would be a strange successor to Baron Mitsui, even if he could achieve the latter's former exalted position. Mitsui (who with no further ambitions, lives quietly in retirement), was a man of infinite wealth and regal tastes. Niizeki owns only about 1 per cent of the stock in his company and earns a salary of $600 a month, half of which goes for taxes. He can live comfortably, if modestly—about in the style of Nobusuke Kishi—because he is entitled to bonuses, virtually free housing, the use of a company car, and other fringe benefits. He also has an extremely generous expense account which permits him, among other things, to entertain business associates at expensive geisha parties. But Niizeki is by no means a rich man, either by American or Japanese standards. He is a solid pillar of the middle class. In fact, the heads of most of Japan's largest companies are little more than salaried managers. With few exceptions, only the owners of small or medium-size firms (for example, Foreign Minister Fujiyama) control all or most of their companies' stock, and such concerns are too limited in size to pose a monopolistic threat. Thus, quite apart from the previously mentioned distinctions between the old *Zaibatsu* and the new, Niizeki and most of his fellow businessmen are by no means comparable to the industrial *daimyo* who only recently passed into oblivion.

Even so, if the present trend toward industrial co-operation and amalgamation is carried too far, they could spell danger for Japan's postwar free enterprise system. Up to now, however, such practices appear to have increased the stability of Japanese industry as a whole, and to have stimulated the production of high-quality goods, without substantially hurting small legitimate enterprises.

Rising world demand has made possible Japan's present industrial boom. Exports in 1959 rocketed to more than $3 billion, the highest figure in Japanese history. For the first time since the war, exports exceed imports. Significantly, 30 per cent of these exports went to the United States in 1959, as compared to 24 per cent in 1958. At the same time, trade with Asia dropped to second place, totaling 24 per cent, as against 28 per cent the year before. These statistics indicate only too well the increasing dependence of Japan on the United States for continued prosperity.

In reorienting its main trade routes westward, Japanese industry, with Kishi's encouragement, has geared its policies to winning American customers on a permanent basis. The label *Made in Japan* no longer means cheap, shoddy goods as in prewar days, but quality textiles, cameras, transistor radios, toys, chinaware, sewing machines, binoculars, pearls, motor scooters, and electric fans. These and other products are of original design, too. Japanese trade associations severely condemn manufacturers who have not yet discarded the pre-war habit of copying foreign designs. A sign of the times was a recent case in which an Italian firm was accused by the Japanese of reproducing a Japanese designed transistor radio. In protest, a government official said, almost with pride that the occasion for such a statement had arisen, "We consider this a most immoral act!"

The Japanese transistor radio is a good example of the high-quality merchandise that is flowing from Japan today. One firm, the Sony Corporation, actually leads the United States in transistor application, though it received a license from an American company to produce transistorized items only in 1952. Led by dynamic young executives in their thirties and forties, the company has turned out the smallest transistor radio in the world and the first direct-viewing transistor television set, and may be the first concern to apply the tunnel diode, a tiny basic circuit component, originally reported, incidentally, by a Japanese scientist in 1958, to radio and TV. "Our prices may not favor us in the United States," one company director told me, "but we believe Americans will buy our products because they are more advanced than anything produced in the United States."

If trade with the United States will remain the principal source of Japanese well-being for an indefinite period, Kishi is convinced that in the long run Japan's closest economic ties must be with its Asian neighbors, its natural trading partners. A major element of his foreign and economic policy is the cultivation of closer relations with these countries. But the obstacles are great. Not the least formidable is the psychological barrier. Still lacking complete trust in the motives of Japan, the Southeast Asian nations are wary about tightening their economic ties with that country. There are also practical difficulties. These poverty-ridden nations have not the purchasing power to import on a large scale. Furthermore, most Southeast Asian countries have little else to sell but rice—high priced at that—while Japan is now almost self-sufficient in this commodity.

Kishi's administration helped to resolve the psychological problem through the conclusion of war reparations agreements with Burma, the Philippines, Indonesia, and South Viet-Nam. These accords will cost Japan more than $1 billion in goods and services over a period of five to twenty years. In addition, Japan has agreed to "facilitate" $700 million in private loans and other investments in the four recipient countries. It doesn't take long for the visitor to these countries to observe the effects of the reparations program. He is likely to travel from the western tip of Java to neighboring Bali, two of the exotic islands of Indonesia, in a brand-new Japanese vessel. He will see a paper mill, constructed with Japanese materials, going up outside Manila. He will observe a huge Japanese-built and Japanese-equipped hydro-electric dam being carved out of the wilderness of Balu Chaung, on the road to Mandalay.

Kishi, to a very considerable extent, is personally responsible for the easing of Japan's strained relations with the Southeast Asian nations. Nothing has impressed them more than the penitent, humble, yet dignified attitude he exhibited during his two good-will trips in 1957 to Burma, India, Pakistan, Ceylon, Malaya, Singapore, Hong Kong, Thailand, Formosa, the Philippines, Indonesia, South Viet-Nam, Australia, and New Zealand. In May, 1957, before leaving on his initial trip, the first ever made by a Japanese prime minister to these countries, Kishi told the Diet:

"I have long wished to visit the countries of Southeast Asia, with which I am anxious to promote and strengthen Japan's friendly relations. Japan, as a nation of Asia, is closely linked to these countries geographically, historically and culturally. Without peace and prosperity in Asia, there is no hope of prosperity for Japan. The establishment of amicable and neighborly relations between Japan and the nations of Asia is the keynote of my Government's foreign policy."

In the countries Japan had occupied during the war, Kishi apologized for the wrongs done them. In those that were allied with the Western powers, he stressed that Japan was on the side of the Free World in the cold war. And in all the nations he visited, he underscored Japan's determination to work for world peace through close co-operation with the United Nations, and asked for their support of a Japanese appeal sent to the United States, Great Britain, and the Soviet Union for the immediate suspension of nuclear tests.

Kishi also discussed trade possibilities, reparations payments, and offered proposals for economic co-operation between Japan and Southeast Asia. He suggested the establishment of Asian technical training centers which would provide the under-developed Asian nations with Japanese technicians and know-how for the development of their industry. All of the host countries showed considerable interest in this idea, and though plans for such centers have not materialized yet, Japanese technical aid on a less centralized basis is being rendered.

Japan's neighbors also exhibited interest in a blueprint for an Asian Development Fund, which appeared to be a fairly logical method of facilitating co-operation among the free nations of Asia in the promotion of their development programs. Under this plan, the Southeast Asian countries, Japan and the Western powers, but mainly the United States, would set up a fund which would increase annually, starting with $500 million the first year, for the general economic development of the Asian members and to stabilize the prices of basic agricultural products produced by them.

But after a second look at this program, the Asian leaders failed to show enthusiasm. Neutralist nations like India, Ceylon, and Burma feared such a project would tie them too closely to the United States. And nearly all saw in this casually suggested plan the reflection of a previous and unforgotten Japanese program for inter-Asian co-operation: the Greater East Asian Co-Prosperity Sphere. Some were particularly suspicious of provision for a $100 million re-discount plan which would benefit Asian countries in a position to export capital goods. It was clear that under the program, Japan, as the only highly industrialized country in Asia, would be the chief supplier of products to the underdeveloped countries, as it had been when these countries were captive markets.

True, the management concepts involved in the old and new programs were diametrically opposite. The wartime organization was rooted in the theory of hierarchy, with Japan at the top of the pyramid, while the new fund would be managed by a board of directors composed of one representative of each member nation, each with an equal vote. Even so, the Southeast Asian countries were not prepared, so soon after their wartime experience, to bind themselves as closely to Japan as the plan obviously intended. During Kishi's visit in the Philippines, the *Manila Times,* in an editorial entitled, "There's a Catch in It," conceded that the development fund had some "irresistibly attractive features." It said:

"In effect, the scheme would make it possible for countries like Japan to sell a bigger volume of capital goods under a financing system which would be attractive to both manufacturer and buyer. But the capital goods source will logically be Japan and definitely not the Philippines, nor even India, where virtually all capital goods that the Indians can turn out will be absorbed by the demands of India's Five-Year Plan. The reaction from at least one official of the National Economic Council has been described as 'favorable.' We doubt if it would remain so once the various built-in booby traps of the proposal are exposed to public view."

Southeast Asian judgment in general was not as harsh as this, but it soon grew apparent that Kishi's proposal was being considered with reserve. Nor did the Prime Minister receive encouragement from the United States, which was more interested in distributing aid in bilateral arrangements than through an organization in which its voice would be no louder than that of any other single nation associated with the fund. But many economic observers believe that Kishi's idea is basically a sound one, and though proposed prematurely, will, perhaps with some modifications, eventually be accepted as the most logical and efficient way of promoting the development of Southeast Asia. First, however, the nations of this area will have to be further convinced that the imperialistic spirit of the Greater East Asian Co-Prosperity Sphere has been erased from the new proposal.

The very fact that all the host countries showed at least some interest in the fund offered an indication of the impact of Kishi's mission. Kishi, of course, was accorded the most friendly receptions in the countries that Japan had not occupied during the war. In India, Prime Minister Nehru told him that "throughout my life, I have had a very vivid admiration for Japan, despite some differences in policy." In Ceylon, the influential *Daily News* hailed Japan as being "in the vanguard of Asian progress and a model for Asians." In Pakistan, the *Morning News* said that "to an underdeveloped country like Pakistan, Japan could prove a tremendous asset."

Even in territories that had felt the tread of the Japanese military boot, Kishi made an impression. The Singapore *Sunday Standard* declared that his plans for mutual co-operation have "caused a significant setback to Russia's and Red China's plans for extending their grip into Southeast Asia. The Asian leaders lost little time in showing preference for friendly Asian get-togethers under Japanese leadership to bowing to communist pressure." The pro-government *New Times* of Burma said "Japan's emergence as an independent power in Asia following her surrender has been watched with growing admiration by all nations, particularly by the newly freed Asian nations who look to Japan for much guidance and help in developing their own national resources. Japan can play a prominent role in building Asian solidarity."

In Malaya, Prime Minister Tengku Abdul Rahman told Kishi: "It is my hope that the friendship between Japan and Malaya, strengthened by this visit, will be an ever-lasting one." Laotian Premier Prince Souvannaphouma said that Kishi's visit "would mark the tightening of friendship ties which have for a long time united our two countries." In Cambodia, huge crowds lined flag-bedecked streets to cheer Kishi, and wreaths of flowers were presented to him by young girls in national costume.

Kishi experienced his most dramatic moments in the Philippines, one of the most cruelly treated of all the nations Japan had occupied. He was braced for unpleasant incidents. But though he received a generally cool reception, Foreign Secretary Felixberto Serrano welcomed him warmly. The close proximity of Japan and the Philippines and their mutual practice of democracy, he said, made closer relations between the two countries imperative. "A sea of hatred has been swept away by this realization."

Kishi will never forget his visit to a government institution for orphans and waifs where he passed through flower-decorated arches on which were scrawled, "Welcome Premier Kishi" and *"Mabuhay, Mabuhay,"* meaning "Long live, long live!" As children in native dress crowded around him and kissed his hand in the old Filipino custom of showing respect for one's elders, Kishi, deeply moved, took five hundred pesos ($250) from his pocket and donated the sum to the institution. Later, in the shadow of a monument marking a site where hundreds of Filipinos had been burned alive in a building set afire by Japanese soldiers, Kishi said, "I look with shame on the misery we inflicted upon your people and it brings me a deep sense of sorrow. . . . I was received with open arms and am leaving with a warm spot in my heart."

Kishi's journey of penitence was also highlighted in Australia, which harbored an abiding hatred of Japan. His visit had been bitterly opposed by many Australians, and the announcement that he would lay a wreath at the National War Memorial in Canberra drew a storm of popular protest. A member of parliament asked, "Would any wreath laid by a Japanese honor the memory of thousands of Australian men and women butchered and murdered by the Japanese and starved to death in prison camps?" When Kishi did lay the wreath, an Australian war veteran dramatically hurled photostatic copies of Austrialian charges against Japanese war criminals at the war memorial. Ignoring such gestures, Kishi plunged into trade talks with government leaders, and went to the zoo where photographers snapped him feeding gum leaves to koala bears and bread to kangaroos. By the time he left Australia, a leader of the diehard anti-Japanese Returned Servicemen's League commented, with startling realism, "There must be thought of forgiveness eventually. This hatred cannot be carried on indefinitely. We need their trade and their assistance in time of war."

On Kishi's return to Japan, following one of the most difficult and most humbling pilgrimages ever voluntarily undertaken by a national leader, he could say, without exaggeration, that the mission had been a success. Kishi had grown in stature as a man and a leader. And Japan, as a nation, had grown with him. As a direct result of his foresight and courage, the icy relations existing between Japan and its Free Asian neighbors had begun to thaw.

Today, Japan is teaching a large number of Southeast Asian technicians the intricacies of modern industrial and agricultural methods, and fostering exploitation of the resources of its wartime dependencies. It is doing so for the same reasons that Kishi toured Southeast Asia, partly as a matter of conscience, partly as a matter of practical business diplomacy. By contributing to the economic build-up of these countries, Japan is helping them to increase their purchasing power, meaning, in Japanese terms, their ability to import more goods from Japan.

Under America's International Cooperation Administration (ICA) "third country" training program, Japan is providing facilities and teachers. In addition, Japan is contributing almost two million dollars a year to a Colombo Plan technical training project under which more than 200 Japanese experts have been sent to Asian nations and many Asian trainees are studying in Japan. Other Japanese technicians have been dispatched to Southeast Asia under a United Nations technical aid program. The Diet is expected to pass a bill in 1960 establishing a corporation to manage funds to be used for economic development of the area. This program, it is hoped, will lead to a joint Japanese-American aid effort. Kishi feels that this kind of co-operative effort conducted on a project by project basis will gradually eliminate remaining fear of Japanese economic domination and perhaps grow into something like his grandiose Asian Development Fund in the future.

Meanwhile, Japanese companies have in the last few years embarked on a large number of private "joint ventures" with governments and firms in Southeast Asia as well as in other parts of the world. The most important of these partnership arrangements calls for the Japan Iron and Steel Association and the government-owned State Trading Corporation of India to develop jointly the iron ore resources of Rourkela in southeast India, using American aid funds. Significantly, when the mines are developed India will export to Japan two million tons of iron ore annually in return for Japanese products.

Japan is also moving gradually into the Middle East, South America and Africa. It shook the oil world in 1957 when it concluded agreements with Saudi Arabia and Kuwait granting a new Japanese firm, the Arabian Oil Company, a forty-four-year concession to search for and exploit oil. Each of the two Arab countries would receive 56 per cent of the profits that might be earned in their respective territories—oil has already been struck in Kuwait—as compared to the 50 per cent American and British firms are paying under their own Arab oil contracts. Also, large Japanese-Brazilian joint companies will exploit iron deposits in Minas Gerais, and construct and operate a shipyard in Rio de Janeiro. In Africa, Japanese iron and steel mining interests are negotiating for the exploitation of Rhodesian chrome and British East African iron and copper deposits.

Japan's efforts to increase its commercial ties abroad led Kishi, in the summer of 1959, to test his reputation as a highly effective good-will ambassador on a trade-seeking tour of Western Europe and Latin America. That his reputation was already well established was underlined, shortly before he arrived in Britain, traditionally a bitter competitor of Japan for trade in Southeast Asia, in an editorial that appeared in the British *Daily Mail:*

"Why is he coming? Mr. Kishi is, in fact, coming here to talk trade —trade with Britain but more particularly trade with Britain's traditional markets in Southeast Asia. The five-foot-four inch Prime Minister is Japan's most untiring commercial traveller. In his two and a half years in office he has stumped a great deal of the world selling Japan, and where Mr. Kishi has been, trade has followed. That is why Mr. Kishi's brand of good-will is going to affect us all. Whatever comes of his talks here we need not fear they will result in a flood of cheap toys and cotton goods. Mr. Kishi's Japan, like Great Britain, an export-or-die nation, is turning out high quality exports these days and will do anything to avert the dangers of dislocating foreign markets through floods of cheap goods. Business considerations apart, practical politics demand that Japan should be allowed to enter or reenter traditional British markets in Southeast Asia. Mr. Kishi, you see, is not coming to London to ask 'please may we come into your markets?' Rather, he is coming to seek approval for what he is doing and agreement for expansion. Otherwise, of course, there is always China."

Kishi lived up to his reputation in Britain. He asked for increased trade and explained that Japan had, indeed, to "export or die," but that his country would seek to expand its markets only by legitimate means. His honesty and frankness helped to break down much of the distrust of Japan that had existed. In West Germany, when asked by reporters about the low prices of Japanese exports, he replied, "There are various reasons for these low prices, some healthy and some unhealthy . . . sharp competition and low wages are unhealthy. We will improve this situation."

Kishi did not return from the trip with any concrete trophies, nor had he expected to do so. But he succeeded in laying the foundation for improved trade relations with many of the countries he visited. And in Brazil, he also increased prospects of an early pact providing for new Japanese immigration to that country.

The new postwar Japanese influence, quietly but effectively spreading to the remotest areas of the world, is not confined to economic penetration. Japan's diplomatic and political influence, once exerted through threat and aggression, is now being used in the form of a peaceful, even a moral, force, both in the forums of the United Nations and in bilateral relations between Japan and other countries. This new international stature has been attained, in considerable measure, through Japan's entry into the United Nations in December, 1956, only a few months before Kishi assumed power, and its selection to the Security Council for the two-year period from January, 1958 to December, 1959.

But Kishi himself has played a strong personal role in winning for Japan this world respect. His two "missions of apology" to Southeast Asia in 1957, and his tours of Europe and South America were invaluable. His visit to the United States in 1957 convinced Washington that the sincerity, frankness, and dignity he displayed reflected the personality of the new Japan, which could no longer be dealt with as an American subsidiary. This wise conclusion led to a second visit by the Prime Minister in January, 1960, during which he signed a revised United States-Japan Security Treaty legally recognizing Japan as an equal partner.

Kishi received tremendous assistance from Aiichiro Fujiyama, his Foreign Minister and long-time friend. *Giri* was no doubt a factor in the selection of Fujiyama to the position he took over in July, 1957. But the Prime Minister also had other reasons for picking him, and then retaining his services through two drastic cabinet reshuffles. In Kishi's view, Fujiyama has a practical mind, yet a streak of idealism and moralistic sense not too often found in businessmen. Kishi thought this was a healthy combination of qualities for a Foreign Minister to have, particularly one burdened with the difficult job of lifting an outlaw nation to a high level of international prestige and respectability.

Fujiyama, a handsome, white-maned man who has the gentle look of the professor he had wanted to be in his youth, offers this revealing description of himself: "Thick lines and fine lines, strong lines, weak lines, and beautiful lines, my self-portrait is made up of numerous lines of contradictions. Sometimes, from the bottom of my heart, I come all out for justice, and then at other times I self-composedly let my actions trample down justice. Outwardly I seem gentle and sweet and entirely devoid of waywardness, but in reality I am easy to quarrel. I hate company and love solitude, but then, all of a sudden, I start cutting capers in the crowd . . . I cry over *shinpa* (school drama) tragedies and then again I am so cold-hearted that I am unapproachable to others."

When Kishi became Prime Minister and offered Fujiyama his present cabinet position, many of the latter's friends advised him against acceptance. But after Kishi told him, "I would be at a loss if you refused," Fujiyama decided to accept the post. To free himself from other responsibilities, he resigned from one hundred and twenty company and organizational offices, including the presidencies of the Japan and Tokyo chambers of commerce and industry. Kishi and Fujiyama constituted an effective team in their conduct of foreign affairs. As a farsighted businessman, Fujiyama was an excellent complement of Kishi, the former government economist, in the pursuance of what has been referred to as "economic diplomacy."

"It would be an advantage to Japan in the long run," Fujiyama said on assuming office "to assist in the economic development of the Afro-Asian nations even though there may be no immediate profit involved in the project. This is what I mean by the morals of economic diplomacy. Such an attitude on Japan's part would go a long way toward alleviating suspicion that Japan is once again plotting, as in the days of the militarists. And the Afro-Asian group of nations will readily accept Japan's offer of economic co-operation without skepticism."

This prophecy is gradually proving correct, but an even greater Kishi-Fujiyama triumph is the respect they earned for Japan in the councils of the U.N. During his trip to the United States in June, 1957, Kishi said in a world-wide broadcast from U.N. headquarters:

"The United Nations is a monumental accomplishment of man in his pursuit of peace. It is the hope of the world for the elimination of international injustices and inequalities, for the outlawing of war and for the banishment of fear and want.

"I hope under the auspices of the United Nations a sweeping disarmament program will be carried through, which should go a long way
to relieve world tensions.

"I hope, in particular, to see a speedy conclusion of an international
agreement on the banning of nuclear tests with a view to protecting
the human race from irremediable harm.

"And I hope that nuclear energy will be devoted solely to peaceful
purposes promoting world prosperity and progress.

"In spite of the swift march of civilization and the revolutionary advance of science and technology, the world contains vast areas where
prevail appalling poverty and indescribable misery. Peace is impossible
without social and economic progress in these areas.

"It is most gratifying that the United Nations is carrying out many
splendid programs of assistance, which, I hope, will be further ampli-
fied. Let me say that Japan is doing and will do all in her power to support these programs."

Kishi was not exaggerating. Japan's proposal in the Security Council for
the withdrawal of American and British troops from the Middle East during the 1958 troubles is considered by many international observers as
the move that led to a solution of that crisis. A Japanese representative
was selected chairman of a U.N. investigation team sent to Laos in late
1959 to prepare a report on the fighting going on between government and
communist troops. Japan occupies a seat in the executive council of almost every special United Nations agency. Its representatives have been
active members of committees on human rights and on the status of
women. And it has sent technicians abroad under the U.N. program for
technical aid to underdeveloped countries.

But Japan, with Hiroshima and Nagasaki still sharp in its memory, has
been especially active in the field of atomic energy for peaceful uses. It
is the only country so far to have committed itself to purchase uranium
—three tons—through the International Atomic Energy Agency. And
it has been one of the most vociferous advocates of the banning of nuclear
bomb tests. Since 1958 Japan has cosponsored three resolutions in the
U.N. General Assembly calling for the suspension of such tests.

Japan has a deep sense of dependence on the U.N. for the maintenance
of its security and prosperity. One of Kishi's principal objections to the
original United States-Japan Security Treaty was the omission of any
mention of the United Nations due to the fact that Japan was not a U.N.
member at the time the pact was signed. The new treaty, government
officials point out, is based on the United Nations Charter and emphasizes co-operation and settlement of any international dispute without
resort to arms. Japan hopes eventually to entrust its defense entirely to the

U.N. But until this organization is able to guarantee its security, Kishi says, Japan will permit American troops based on its soil to be used anywhere in the world in any operation sponsored by the United Nations. It will, however, only approve a United States military operation not under U.N. auspices if Japan's security is directly involved. The Socialist Party, for its part, says the new treaty makes Japan part of a military bloc, in violation of U.N. collective security concepts. It would put its trust entirely in the U.N.'s powers to maintain peace, even though these powers are limited.

Conclusion of the new Security Treaty was actually one of the greatest achievements of the Kishi regime. The treaty is a tangible symbol of the re-emergence of Japan as an independent world power, a sovereign and equal partner of the United States within the Free World defense system. As Kishi told me, "This is the first time since the war that the Japanese people have been able to exercise their free will in determining Japan's foreign policy orientation. This point can't be stressed too much."

Kishi opened the way to this new formal relationship with the United States when he visited here in 1957. On this trip, he was as relaxed in a sport shirt as he was tense in tails. Wearing a New York Yankee cap, Kishi, a Yankee fan, threw out the first ball at a New York-Chicago White Sox baseball game. In Washington, he played golf with America's most famous golfer, President Eisenhower. As Kishi was about to tee off, the President told him, "We want to see one of your finest Japanese drives." The Prime Minister obliged with a respectable 170-yard offering down the middle, and the two leaders diplomatically ended the game with identical scores.

But Kishi had not come to the United States simply to play golf or watch baseball. He tried to persuade the President and the late Secretary of State, John Foster Dulles, to eliminate whatever remained of the conqueror's hold on the conquered. He asked that all United States ground forces be evacuated from the country; that many of the facilities then being used by United States forces be returned to the Japanese; that Japan be granted jurisdiction over criminal cases involving American soldiers and Japanese nationals if the scene of the alleged crime was not on American-controlled premises; that the eighty-odd war criminals still under confinement be released; that Okinawa and the Bonin Islands, held by America since the war, be returned to Japan; and that a new Mutual Security Treaty be drawn up with Japan as an equal partner of the United States.

Washington demurred on the matter of Okinawa and the Bonin Islands because of the strategic need to maintain American bases there. Japan, however, has since received some satisfaction from the agreement by the United States Congress to compensate the Bonin residents for the use of their land. The Japanese have also been appeased by the decision of the military authorities in Okinawa to pay compensation for land being used on a monthly rental basis rather than in lump sums as they previously had done, to the horror of Japanese and Okinawans who feared they would never get their land back.

Kishi's other requests have been met almost without reservation. There are no United States ground troops in Japan. Hundreds of facilities have been turned back to the Japanese. Even the Air Force units stationed in Japan are kept in areas distant from the big cities so that their presence will not be conspicuous. In the celebrated case of Private William Girard, who killed a Japanese woman on a firing range, jurisdiction was granted to a Japanese court, which gave the accused a suspended sentence. Sugamo Prison has been cleared of war criminals. Final attestation to the success of Kishi's trip lies in the conclusion of the new Mutual Security Treaty.

The revised pact is of greater psychological than practical importance. From a practical point of view, it merely formalizes—for at least ten years—a relationship between Japan and the United States that has existed since the Korean War. The old treaty, signed in 1951, at the time Japan was granted its independence, permitted the United States to use this country as a base for military operations without any conditions attached. However, in recent years America has made it clear that it would not embark on military ventures unless it had the full co-operation of Japan. "If we hadn't made this clear," says one American official, "we probably would have been forced out of Japan long ago."

In theory, even under the new treaty the United States could conceivably use Japan as a base for any military operation it deemed necessary, regardless of the Japanese view. For although the revised pact requires that "prior consultations" be held between the two countries before the United States forces in Japan can be sent on combat missions, or even before nuclear weapons can be brought into the country, there is no provision in the document that specifically requires the United States to abide by a possible Japanese denial of permission, despite President Eisenhower's assurances that the United States would not act against Japan's wishes. Japan thus has no legal veto power over American proposals. Japanese opponents of the treaty have centered much of their criticism on this point, maintaining that refusal to grant Japan veto power "proves"

328 &⤳ KISHI AND JAPAN

that the United States intends to use the country as a base for aggressive activities which could drag Japan into war. The more valid explanation that the United States Congress would be reluctant to approve any treaty with veto strings attached makes little impression on many Japanese.

Kishi, however, is not worried. "The treaty," he told me, "is based on mutual understanding between our two countries. I am sure that if we said 'no' to some American proposal, the United States would understand that we had good reason to say 'no' and respect our wishes."

Indeed, the United States would have little choice. Failure to abide by Japanese decisions, or devious efforts to get around them, would inevitably create an atmosphere in Japan that would not only make continued American operations there impossible, but could result in the ascension to power of the neutralist Socialists. Thus, new treaty, old treaty, or no treaty at all, the United States will effectively be able to use Japan as a military base only so long as it acts in accordance with Japanese wishes.

But however restricted the use of Japanese bases may be, the advantages of having them under almost any conditions are great. Japan is of unique strategic importance in Asia. It is separated from the mainland by a large, protective body of water, yet is within short flying range of both Red China and the Soviet Union (a factor which, the leftists say, could work to Japan's detriment as well as to its advantage). It offers the United States Air Force excellent airfields, scattered throughout the country, from which air attacks could be launched, if necessary, and the United States Navy its best Asian port facilities in Yokosuka. It is, also, the only highly industrialized country in Asia, giving the United States forces an invaluable on-the-spot source of supplies. If the communists took control of Japan, the United States would be severely handicapped in protecting the rest of Free Asia.

Japan, too, gains enormously from the new treaty. It not only verifies Japan's position as an independent nation, but no less important, grants advantages to Japan that few mutual defense pacts, NATO is not one, have ever offered to a signatory. The United States guarantees to help defend Japan if it should be attacked by a third country, but Japan is not obliged to come to our aid in the event the United States or its bases outside of Japan are attacked. Kishi was able to win this advantage, ironically, by pointing to a constitution drawn up by General MacArthur which expressly forbids the use of Japanese forces for other than internal police purposes.

The treaty is also economically advantageous to Japan. American military procurements and spending add up to almost $500 million a year, which make it possible for Japan to maintain a favorable dollar balance. The new pact, moreover, does not require, as did the previous one, that Japan contribute to the cost of maintaining the United States bases, representing a saving of $30 million annually. At the same time, with American troops available to assure Japan's security, the nation has to devote only a minute percentage of its budget to defense purposes.

Kishi has, in his few years in office, gone a long way toward accomplishment of the goals he set for his country. Japan has never been more prosperous, or more respected by the world. And the Japanese people can continue bettering their lives, knowing—though many may not fully realize the psychological importance of this knowledge—that their security is guaranteed no less completely than that of the American people.

CHAPTER XVI

❧❦❧

THE COST OF FREEDOM

THE SUCCESS of Kishi and his people in building a new Japan overnight must be viewed, to be fully appreciated, in the light of the
enormous obstacles blocking their path. Economically, Japan is burdened
with one of the most serious overpopulation problems in the world.
Socially, the sudden disintegration of the nation's tight, stratified web
structure has in no small measure destroyed ethical and spiritual traditions for which no adequate replacements have been found. Politically
and ideologically, a strong leftist minority, supported by the Communist
powers, threatens Japan's fledgling democracy. These basic difficulties
are closely related and often complement and aggravate each other. They
represent formidable barriers to progress, however great has been the
progress so far.

To find concrete evidence of overpopulation, one need only stroll
through Tokyo. Two-thirds destroyed in the war, this city has been
completely rebuilt, and has far more homes and factories today than
before its destruction. But it still cannot build fast enough to keep up
with its swiftly expanding population. Already the largest city in the
world, with about 8.5 million people, it is growing at the rate of 400,000
a year, including 300,000 migrants from the provinces who, unneeded
on Japan's intensively cultivated farms, hope to find work in factories
that cannot possibly absorb them all. The bulk of these migrants live
in a dark, ugly world fringed by a neon glow that loudly proclaims

330

Tokyo a city of gay heart. Behind the glittering façade, which invites luckier Tokyoites to see a Marilyn Monroe movie or a Kabuki play, to buy an electric washing machine or a wooden bathtub with built-in heater, to feast on a thick New York-cut steak or on a pot of *sukiyaki,* the newcomers live in shanty-villages made of corrugated iron, wooden planks, and oil cans, under bridges, on park benches, and in railroad stations.

No less revealing is the melancholy that dwells in the eyes of the angelic-faced young prostitute just arrived from the country as she idles nervously on a Ginza street corner; in the blank expressions of teen-aged girls squatting on a matted floor, mechanically assembling toy airplanes marked "U.S. Navy" which are destined to reach the hands of American children; in the dusk-gray portrait of a woman, baby strapped on back, heating a bowl of rice on the deck of a cargo-laden house-barge anchored for the night on the Sumida River; in the pensive expression of an unemployed young man sitting in a coffee shop listening to scratched recordings of Bach or Beethoven; in the feeble beckoning of old shoe-shine women lined up on their knees outside Yurokucho Station, shivering in the cold.

The dreariness of this picture might appear to contradict the image of a Japan enjoying the greatest prosperity in its history. But there is no conflict. Though Japan has achieved a virtual miracle of economic growth, the fact remains that its living standards are low compared to Western levels, and hardly commensurate with the nation's ranking as one of the world's great industrial powers. The trouble is that the meager natural wealth of Japan, which can boast of adequate amounts of rainfall and second-grade coal only, must be divided among too many people, leaving an insufficient share for each. The four fragile islands of Japan together comprise an area smaller than California, and only 16 per cent is arable due to mountainous terrain. Yet, they are today teeming with 93 million people, well over half the population of the whole vast, rich United States. This enormous figure is expected to increase until 1985, when it will reach a peak of 105 million, after which a gradual decline is anticipated.

Actually, the birth rate has been decreasing since 1951, and is now only 15 per 1000 people, lower than the rates in such Western countries as Denmark, Switzerland, and France. But the main factor behind this fall has been artificially induced abortions which are legal in Japan but cannot be considered a long-range solution to the population problem. Such abortions in 1959 totaled more than one million, or almost 80 per cent of the number of children born. The extent to which this method of birth control is accepted morally, and as a practical measure, is reflected in a pamphlet published by the Japan Family Planning Association. The publication states that "the reduction of the birth rate in Japan, though dependent mainly upon artificial abortions, is evidence that Japan's cultural level is higher than that of other Asian countries, which do not even resort to abortions."

The government is meeting some success introducing modern birth-control techniques in Japan. It sponsors a birth control program under which medical consultants travel from village to village, offering information on contraception at meetings held in schools, halls, or private homes. Private organizations subsidized by the government distribute contraceptive devices among the poor. Labor unions have their own consultants. But while this birth-control campaign may popularize to some extent the use of contraceptives, its only effect will be to remove the hazards to health resulting from abortions. It is not likely to influence greatly the present moderate birth rate.

The fact is that neither abortions nor other forms of birth control can solve the great population difficulties that Japan will face in the coming years. The nation's labor force, which even now, at 45 million, is far in excess of what can be efficiently absorbed, is expected to increase by a million annually for the next five years, and will expand to about 53 million by 1985—during a period in which progress in automation will greatly reduce the need for human labor.

Government authorities have been trying to alleviate this situation through emigration, but has met with little success. Since 1952, only about 10,000 Japanese have moved abroad, mostly to South America. Under an arrangement with Brazil, obtained by Kishi when he visited Rio de Janeiro in 1959, that country is supposed to absorb 100,000 by 1962. But hardly more than 2000 Japanese left for Brazil in 1959. Most countries today prefer Japanese immigrants, not as hired help, but as self-sustaining enterprisers. However, most Japanese who are interested in emigrating do not have the necessary capital.

Nor do plans to foster migration to the northern island of Hokkaido, the only sparsely populated part of Japan, offer much encouragement. Because of the extremely cold winters in this area, which are comparable to those in the neighboring Siberia, not many people want to move there, and in any case, because of adverse natural conditions, Hokkaido can support few more settlers. The improvement of ports and harbors and the construction of several new industries will permit the absorption of little more than 5 per cent of the population of the other islands.

The one realistic long-term way of dealing with the population question, Kishi believes, is to expand the Japanese economy at a rate sufficient to absorb the increasing pressure expected in the next fifteen years, in other words, to assure everybody of a job. This is why Kishi encouraged ever greater investment, even during slumps, and ordered an investigation of the possibilities of doubling the national income within ten years. Such a feat would not greatly enhance the salaries and living standards of each individual Japanese, but it would provide more employment. The root of Kishi's plan is to foster the rapid growth of the chemical industry and export industries such as toys, transistor radios, and textiles, which require a great deal of hand labor rather than large capital. This plan, of course, is dependent on an ever broadening export volume, especially to the United States, as well as on greater consumer demand at home.

Though the population has increased every year, less than a million people of working age were totally unemployed at the end of 1959, with an additional 1.5 million hired on a part-time basis. One reason for this surprisingly modest unemployment problem lies in the virtual refusal of most Japanese to remain without work. If jobs are not available, they will, with extraordinary resourcefulness, create them. One small community in Tokyo is living testimony to this uncontainable spirit. The 150 people residing in this wood and corrugated iron shanty-town several years ago started collecting old tin cans and newspapers, which they sold to metal and paper concerns. Today, they operate a thriving business, and are building themselves a whole new village.

There is another explanation, too, for Japan's ability to keep unemployment to a minimum—the preservation within a large sector of industry of Japan's old feudal social organization, based on paternalism. Most companies are staffed with far more personnel than is required for efficient operation. Offices and factories are the most crowded in the world, and there is considerable duplication of work. But except under highly unusual circumstances, no one is fired, though all non-executives must resign at the age of fifty-five to permit the employment of youths out of school. After that, they must either find jobs with small concerns, usually at much lower pay, or be supported by their children.

Since the war, the breakdown of Japan's feudal structure has probably been slower in the industrial sphere than in any other sector of national life. And whatever the cost of feudal inefficiency, it is considered by the

Japanese—as well as many Western experts—necessary until the economy can absorb the entire working force on a fully rationalized basis.

But the cost is high. True, Japan has been able in recent years to produce high quality goods at marketable, in some cases, barely competitive prices (Japanese prices, it may not generally be realized, are today more often too high than too low) because of the availability of relatively cheap labor and the inventiveness and drive of Japanese business leaders like those of the Sony Corporation. But excessive paternalism has created, and is continuing in considerable measure to nurture, a worker who is often as unimaginative as he is dedicated and technically able. Like the soldiers of old Japan, he is conditioned to follow the orders of his superiors with no questions asked.

"Once these Japanese learn what to do, they do it as well or better than Americans," an American technical adviser to a Japanese aircraft firm building United States jet planes told me. "But the trouble is that they tend to obey their superiors blindly. So if we make a mistake in our instructions, it'll never be questioned. They'll go right ahead and carry out the orders. And that's a pretty dangerous situation, particularly when you're building planes."

American engineers who directed construction of the recently completed Sakuma Dam, the largest construction job ever undertaken in Japan, can confirm this appraisal of the Japanese worker. When they requested replacement of several tunnel mucking machine blades that had worn thin, they received new ones promptly—with teeth meticulously filed down just like those of the discarded blades.

The Americans met with other frustrations, too. Japanese engineers responded to repeated requests for trained mechanics to maintain expensive machinery by appointing unskilled workers to the jobs and issuing them armbands marked "expert." On one occasion, Japanese technicians jeopardized the security of the whole project by letting a watchman sleep. If they had awakened him, they explained, he would have lost "face." Workers had a good excuse for being sleepy. Instead of working three eight-hour shifts around the clock, they worked two twelve-hour shifts, two men to a shift, who took turns dozing off. Thus, four overtired workers were used on each job instead of three fresh ones for the simple purpose of giving more men work to do.

The Japanese college-trained industrial supervisor sometimes exhibits as little initiative and imagination in his work as those under him. One reason is that almost no one works his way up from the bottom in

Japan. If one lacks higher education, he starts at the bottom and stays pretty close to the bottom, however much ability he may display. If he has been to college, he starts as a supervisor and rises in the company hierarchy on a seniority basis, however little ability he may display. Rare is the university man who would stoop to manual labor, even for demonstration purposes. If the answer to any particular production or engineering problem is not contained in some book, it often will not be found. For the supervisor usually has not the basic experience to work it out for himself. Nor will he always avail himself of opportunities to expand his practical knowledge. Japanese supervisors seldom attended briefing sessions on new techniques held by the Americans at Sakuma, fearing they would lose "face" before their subordinates by admitting they had something to learn.

Inefficiency is, needless to say, even greater in the small factory or workshop. Although these smaller concerns constitute more than 90 per cent of the plants in Japan, they produce only 40 per cent of the goods. In the United States, such establishments would be forced out of business by the competition from the larger ones. But in Japan, they can remain alive because instead of competing with the giants, they complement them. They produce traditional Japanese hand-manufactured items such as wooden bathtubs and pottery, or hold sub-contracts to produce parts for the big firms, an arrangement that the latter find quite expedient and profitable.

A typical small factory is the Matsumura Company, which uses crude tools to turn out electrical parts such as wires and fuses. The plant is a barn-like wooden structure in the middle of a field on the outskirts of Tokyo. It is so poor that it can afford to deliver its goods only by bicycle. Working conditions are extremely poor. Lighting is bad, the hours are long, and wages range from $20 to $35 a month. Such firms often produce inferior parts to the detriment of the quality of the finished product. Feudalism penetrates so deeply that an employee will not marry in many cases without the boss's approval.

Kishi and his government colleagues, for altruistic as well as humanistic purposes, are reluctant to root out these tiny industrial anachronisms. Despite the social and economic problems they present, they are keeping a large proportion of Japan's workers, who could not be absorbed by the big concerns, occupied. The specter of unemployment requires the retention of feudalistic practices.

Such practices explain why Japanese productivity is many times lower than in American factories. Efforts are being made to narrow this gap, particularly through the Japan Productivity Center, which sends businessmen to the United States to study industrial organization and brings American industrial experts to Japan to offer on-the-spot advice. The managing director of Tokyo's Seika Shoe Company, using a modern American shoe plant as a model, has increased production speed 20 per cent simply by rearranging placement of his sewing machines to lose less time between processes of manufacture. But substantial improvement of Japan's total industrial productivity will only be possible when the reduction of population pressure will permit the elimination of the feudal concepts that prevent the workers from being used with maximum economy and efficiency.

Persistent remnants of feudalism exist in other strata of Japan's social structure, but with less justification. Family relationships are complicated, illogical, and unsatisfactory. Although many young people are choosing their own mates since the war, the fact that such a choice is still subject to ultimate veto by the parents has been a source of considerable unhappiness, and even tragedy. Most young lovers will sever their relationship rather than marry without the approval of their parents. Some wait years before getting married, hoping that the reluctant elders will eventually change their minds. Doubt, suspicion and unrest are the result of these confused and conflicting family concepts.

Many couples let their elders have the final say so that they will not be disinherited by the reluctant parents if their orders are disobeyed. Particularly in the case of middle- and upper-class families, economic security is hard to achieve without family money and connections. A more important factor is the continuing, if weakened, hold of *ko* on most young people. They might disobey their parents today in many ways, but marriage is, to an important degree, still a family affair. The extent to which this is true is reflected almost daily in newspaper announcements of double suicides.

One of the most dramatic death pacts in recent years, involved Princess Eisei Aishinkakura, the half-Japanese niece of Emperor Pu-yi who had ruled the puppet state of Manchoukuo as Emperor Kang Teh, and a university classmate, Takemichi Okubo. When the parents of both objected to their seeing each other, they ran away, leaving a note that they intended to commit suicide. In a radio broadcast, the distraught mother of the girl pleaded, "All is forgiven—you can marry." But it was too late. Police combing a wooded hillside on the Izu peninsula found the nineteen-year-old princess, her head resting on the left arm of her lover. An old Japanese army pistol was in Okubo's right hand, bullet holes in both their temples. Eisei was wearing a gold engagement ring, and on the ground nearby was found, in traditional fashion, locks of their hair and clippings of their fingernails wrapped neatly in tissue paper— mementoes of another era.

Love is not the only reason for self-destruction in Japan, which has one of the highest suicide rates in the world. Suicides are particularly common among the unemployed, and among students who fail examinations. In one case, three sisters all killed themselves as an expression of loyalty to their mother when their father began having an affair with another woman. A feudalistic means was thus used to protest a violation of the modern, and still largely unaccepted, concept of male faithfulness. Many suicides are committed for no particular reason at all—simply discontent with life in general. They are symptomatic of the spiritual emptiness that pervades Kishi's Japan. It is not only the retention of feudal restrictions, but the premature lifting of such restrictions that is at the root of Japan's present social difficulties.

In the United States and Western Europe many young people belong to a "lost" generation. In Japan, such a generation also exists, and is much larger and more genuine than any to be found in the West. The word "lost" in that country connotes not simply apathy, restlessness, and social dissatisfaction, but a deep confusion and basic lack of understanding of the new environment that has enveloped the nation.

Before V-J Day, the Japanese youth found himself under tremendous stress as he relinquished his childhood freedom to take his place in the great, almost inflexible, social mold with its rigid values. But because the adjustment was so difficult, and in many cases, impossible, the individual was all the more relentless in his effort to fit into the mold. Japan's surrender left him a moral and spiritual invalid. He found himself floundering without a standard of values by which to live. With the Emperor suddenly reduced to mortal rank, Japan's divine past dissolved like a dream. State Shinto was destroyed as a concept, and Shinto as a religion without nationalist connotations became almost meaningless or, at the most, together with Buddhism, a mere social convention. The United States poured political, technical, and cultural innovations into the country, but it could not export the spiritual values of the Americans who had created them.

Democracy offered the Japanese the freedom to believe in anything they wished. But they also needed a belief. Today's Japanese youth, though never subjected, as were their parents, to the shock of the nation's sudden release from its social strait jacket, are entering an incomprehensible world, a world that cannot be explained to them by their family, by their national history or by their traditions. While their parents still retain elements of the discipline imposed on them by their former values, many young people are growing up without even this crutch to help them cope with the problems of a modern society inherited from a conqueror of completely alien political and cultural background. The Japanese people, especially the youth, resemble full grown trees that must still grow roots.

Actually, the great majority of Japanese have been able to find a certain amount of satisfaction and happiness even in a world without strong spiritual values. Professor Tadao Umezawa of Osaka University recently said:

"The function of religion is to give each individual the basic principle to deal with problems in his daily life. Then, what has happened to the Japanese people without religion? They have managed to live somehow. In their case, there is no basic, permanent principle. Yet, there is a certain flexible principle. It is a very temporal down-to-earth rationalism. Deep in the minds of today's Japanese there lies dormant a very realistic, as well as instinctive, philosophy. Modern Japanese are very realistic people, with no parallel in the world. We threw away religion and gave ourselves to practical philosophy. Japan has been able to acquire science and technology in such a short time because of this realism. And with a practical philosophy we will be able to deal with our daily lives. [But is this enough?] Unless each person has within himself the spirit to deny reality and to step beyond reality, there is danger that he will totter when pressure becomes too great. Therefore, democracy cannot be strong if the people lack spiritual power."

The lack of "spiritual power" is even now taking a certain toll in Japan. This country, for example, has been plagued since the war with a juvenile delinquency problem that never existed previously. About 50,000 young men and women were arrested in 1959 for murder, rape, theft, intimidation and numerous other crimes. More than five-hundred juvenile gangs prowl Tokyo's narrow back streets. Some of them, like their New York counterparts, have adopted mysterious names, such as the Black Dragon Association, though there has been no inter-gang violence as in America.

Shintaro Ishihara, who, at twenty-eight, is a successful author, movie star, composer, and actor, describes in his sensational best-seller, *Taiyo-no-Kisetsu* (Season of the Sun), with relentless realism the lack of scruples and inhibitions of the zoot-suit and suede-shoe-wearing cult of *Taiyo-*

zoku. These Japanese youth might be superficially comparable to American "beatniks" who sit around coffee houses cursing and hating the world. The *Taiyozoku,* however, neither curse nor hate. They are utterly indifferent and devoid of sentiment, believing simply and only in self-gratification. Their cynicism and attitude of abandonment stem not from economic factors—most of them come from well-off families—but from an absence of ethical values. The hero of Ishihara's novel is a high-school student, ruthless, vain, and lustful, whose most satisfying experience is to batter fellow students into unconsciousness in the school gymnasium while his girl friends cheer him on. He has an affair with one of these girls and she makes the mistake of confessing her love for him. Viewing the girl as a commercial commodity, he callously sells her to his elder brother for $14. She becomes pregnant and dies following an abortion. The hero, far from remorseful, attends her funeral and smashes the girl's picture, attached, in the Japanese custom, to the coffin, saying "How stupid of you to die!" Although Ishihara's novel involves only a fringe of today's younger generation, it is nevertheless a revealing commentary on the rootlessness of Japanese youth.

A particularly tragic aspect of the youth problem stems from the postwar "liberation" of women. Despite the obvious virtues of this emancipation movement, serious social aberrations have resulted from an unbridled feminine rush for freedom. Many young women in small towns and rural areas, unable to find suitable husbands through their families in a Japan suffering as a result of the war from a severe male shortage, have migrated into the cities to enjoy the advantages of the new social order and perhaps find spouses on their own. But in many cases, they have been unable to get jobs or to live on those they can get, particularly if they have a family to support back home. With even qualified men hard put to find satisfactory positions, there is little demand for young, inexperienced girls just out of school. The wage scale for women is extremely low, with office jobs rarely paying more than $28 a month. Frequently, these girls, frustrated by the hard economic facts of life, have chosen other ways of making a living. Many, falling easy prey to pimps or potential customers they have met in bars or on the street, have turned to prostitution. This ancient trade in flesh has always existed in Japan, as in most countries of the world, but until the Occupation it was of a limited, containable nature. Most of the prostitutes were in debtor's bondage, placed in brothels by impoverished tenant farm families. Few girls voluntarily broke away from the security of their homes for a life of prostitution.

The situation, however, has not been comparable in postwar years.

Some of the girls are still unfortunate family pawns, but the great bulk have drifted into the lantern-lit back streets on their own accord. In 1956, at the time an Anti-Prostitution Law was passed, legally banning the practice for the first time in Japanese history, an estimated 134,000 women were plying their trade, half of them brothel inmates, half streetwalkers. Japan had the dubious distinction of leading the world in this activity, with about ten times as many prostitutes as could be found in France, the number two country.

Since the passage of the law, it is unclear whether clandestine prostitution is less extensive. There are some hopeful signs of improvement. About forty former prostitutes are now operating a chicken farm on the outskirts of Tokyo, while others are gardening or learning such professions as dressmaking in more than sixty rehabilitation centers throughout the country. However, these centers, where girls are sent only on a voluntary basis, can accommodate a total of less than 3,000, and not even this many have applied for entry.

Police estimate that between 40 and 70 per cent of the prostitutes who went out of business when the Anti-Prostitution Law came into effect have returned to their old profession, often under the influence of ruthless pimps. The colorful brothels lining the narrow, twisting streets of the ancient Yoshiwara red-light district in Tokyo have supposedly been turned into legitimate restaurants and bars, but many of the girls who once worked in these establishments as registered prostitutes are still catering to old customers in the unlikely roles of waitresses.

The chance to "get rich quick" has not lost its attraction for younger girls who had not been prostitutes previously. Seventy per cent of those arrested since the vice ban have been newcomers. Perhaps even more revealing of Japan's moral and economic climate is the fact that about 30 per cent have been part-time or "amateur" prostitutes. One young woman picked up in Tokyo explained she was trying to make money for her wedding.

Many other girls seeking their way in a world offering them only a bare subsistence work as bar or cabaret hostesses. Japan probably contains more bars and cabarets per unit of population than any other country in the world. These establishments are meant, unlike those in the West, almost exclusively for men, who drop in not only for a drink but to enjoy the company of the hostesses. The girls talk and joke with the customers, pour their drinks, fawn upon them, and in general make them forget the day's drudgery. Since the war, tens of thousands of young women, including college graduates, former airline stewardesses, and some of the most beautiful women in Japan, have assumed this role of the modern geisha.

Most top Japanese executives and government officials frequent geisha restaurants, but people of lesser rank who are not entitled to such high-priced entertainment on the expense account can occasionally enjoy themselves at the less expensive cabarets. With their hostess companions beside them, they sit on chairs instead of on *tatami,* drink bourbon or scotch instead of sake, discuss American movies instead of Kabuki, and listen to the guitar instead of the *samisen.*

Hiromi-san, who is twenty-six, has been a hostess for five years, yet her pretty, oval face reflects the innocence of a schoolgirl who has never been out at night. That is, except for the sophisticated bun into which she rolls her long jet-black hair, and the slight use of mascara over her large, almond-shaped eyes. (Her eyes appear rounder since she had an operation, costing eight dollars, that gave her lids in the Western fashion.) She is only five-foot-three, but looks taller because of the slimness of her figure, particularly when she wears a kimono. Her Western cocktail dresses, on the other hand, have swooping necklines calculated to accentuate her ample breasts.

Hiromi-san works in a small cabaret in the Ginza district of Tokyo, one of forty-three in the same block. The entrance is inconspicuous, with only a small neon sign advertising the name of the club. The establishment caters mainly to a steady, loyal clientele of businessmen with charge accounts. The larger cabarets, garish with lights and huge pictures of scantily-clad girls, draw the transients.

Hiromi-san comes from a family of high social standing which she left behind in Osaka. On graduation from high school, where she finished fourth in her class, she took an office job, but it paid only $25 a month. Finally, she decided to seek a career as a model or movie actress. She went to Tokyo, and found herself among thousands of ambitious girls seeking the same careers. Rather than go home to her old life, she went to work as a cabaret hostess until the kind of job she wanted came along. It has not come yet.

Like most hostesses, Hiromi-san despises her work. She cannot psychologically adapt herself to her job. Yet she is chained to it by the money she can earn, for she makes as much as $250 a month, entirely on tips, charging $2.50 an hour for her company. Some hostesses are out-and-out prostitutes. But many others, particularly younger women working in the better cabarets intended strictly for Japanese clientele (foreigners are usually more demanding of the girls) manage to retain their virtue. Hiromi-san resisted all advances for about two years before finally surrendering to the pressures of her profession. She is now the part-time mistress of one of her customers, a wealthy married man who lives out of town but wants her available when he is in Tokyo.

Hiromi-san will probably remain single, for Japanese men, while they like to frequent these girls, rarely marry them. In any event, it would be difficult indeed for Hiromi-san to get along on the income of the average Japanese man after earning large sums as a hostess. "Now that I know what money is," she says rather pathetically, "my dreams of happiness are over."

Hostesses like Hiromi-san are creating no small problem for the traditional geisha. There are still about 26,000 geisha in Japan, but the number is dropping every year. Geisha parties, because they are so expensive, have always been almost exclusively within the province of top business executives and government officials. But even these "privileged" few are beginning to favor modern night life. The average geisha today is forty-two years old. As geisha are judged mainly on their accomplishments as conversationalists, dancers, singers, and *samisen* players, rather than on their sex appeal, this is still an acceptable age. But there will be few replacements for these women in the future. The Labor Standards Law now makes it impossible for girls between the ages of seven and sixteen to become apprentice geisha, or *hangyoku,* which literally means "half-rate." Equally significant, with the decline in popularity of the geisha, few girls today wish to enter the profession when, as hostesses, they don't have to undergo the rigorous "cultural" training a geisha needs.*

The shallowness of the life that has brought unhappiness to Hiromi-san and many Japanese since the war has begun to produce a spiritual reac-

---

* Geisha are divided into Classes A, B, and C in accordance with their accomplishments. Class A makes about $250 a month, equal to Hiromi-san's earnings. Geisha charges, called *hanadai* (flower prices) virtually require the services of an accountant to calculate. There is a *jikanbana* (hourly flower), an *asabana* (morning flower), an *atobana* (afterward flower), an *akashibana* (overnight flower), a *tachibana* (standing flower), an *aisatsubana* (greeting flower), an *enkaibana* (party flower), and several others. These charges do not include entertainment or food and drink served at parties, which, together with the geisha's service flowers, might amount to $60 or $80 per customer. But if the income of the Class A geisha is considerable, her expenses are similarly so, adding up to more than $180 a month, including $40 for room and board, $40 for flowers used in flower arrangement, $25 for "social" purposes, $22 for hair-dressing, $20 in fees for her instructresses, $17 for personal needs, and $14 for taxes. In addition, the geisha must buy her own kimono, *samisen,* and other paraphernalia. As a result of this heavy burden, geisha locals—many geisha, in tune with the times, are unionized—have recently gone on strike, demanding that the geisha restaurants substantially increase their service charges.

tion. Longing to fill the void within them with some kind of faith, some form of moral discipline, a considerable number have exhibited a renewed interest in religion. More than five hundred new religious creeds have sprung up in the last few years, many of them bogus.* Police arrested the propagators of one movement, called the *Yamagishi-Kai,* which drew peasant followers by promising to show them the way to produce "one million chickens." About one hundred and fifty families were persuaded to sell their homes, their fields, and their forests to donate money to this society. Forming a community of their own on the *Yamagishi-Kai* farm, the dispossessed peasants attended classes which taught them that "men and chickens are one entity," and "if the human beings raising the chickens become better people, the chickens will become better chickens." Many other such strange religions have attracted gullible people who permit themselves to be stripped of all their possessions in the hope of finding spiritual salvation.

Even Judaism, which has never sought followers, has begun to make converts in Japan. Abram Kotsugji, a descendant of Shinto priests, was, at the age of sixty, circumcised in Israel in 1959 and became a Jew. He now intends to found a Jewish mission in Japan. Kotsugji, when a child, purchased a Bible in a second-hand book store and entered a Christian mission where he studied Hebrew and adopted the Presbyterian faith. Later he wrote a Hebrew grammar and tutored Prince Mikasa, youngest brother of the Emperor. After the war, Kotsugji, like most Japanese, found himself in a spiritual vacuity. "I stopped practicing Christianity because I found the Trinity doctrine unreasonable," he says. "I abhorred Buddhism because it is a skeptical religion, without a central idea or purpose. I could not return to Shintoism's immaturity, its inadequate guide for living."

Still, most of the religious groups gaining ground in Japan today are offshoots of Shintoism and Buddhism. The 1946 Constitution stipulates that "No religious organization shall receive any privileges from the State, nor exercise any political authority." But Shintoist leaders are now demanding official recognition of the special relationship of the Ise Grand Shrines to the Emperor. If the latter is the symbol of state, they argue, then the shrines are public entities, deserving state protection. This argument is perhaps the natural outcome of the present nebulous position of the Emperor in regard to Shinto. He can neither dissociate himself com-

* Christianity, with its alien absolute values, has not been able to profit from this religious "boom." Less than 1 per cent of the population is Christian.

pletely from the faith—Prince Akihito was married in accordance with strict Shinto procedure—nor can he actively associate himself with it.

Kishi's Liberal-Democratic Party has formed a special committee which is studying the legal possibility of granting state aid to the Ise Shrines. Meanwhile, a Society for the Aid of the *Jingu Kogakkan*—a prewar state-operated college to train young men for Shinto priesthood which was abolished during the Occupation—has been formed, with former Prime Minister Yoshida as president, and Kishi's successor to the premiership, Hayato Ikeda, as vice-president. This religious society, which ultimately hopes to raise $1.4 million, plans to reopen the college in 1961.

At the inaugural meeting of the group held in July 1959, Yoshida explained its purpose:

> "It is necessary to revive Shinto to make it serve as a moral basis for the people, not yet familiar with democracy. It is a source of great concern for me that the people's mind today is confused and communism is infiltrating it. I am happy that such an organization as this has now been brought into being as the first step toward combating communism."

An even more startling revival is being made by Buddhist sects. This is significant in view of the fact that the Japanese have always regarded Buddhism passively, especially since the Meiji era when this religion was discredited as the handmaiden of Tokugawa oppression. It has had no direct or intimate relationship to the people. Buddhist priests perform mysterious rites in the temple, but outsiders cannot participate, except as is often cynically pointed out, at their funerals. Yet many people are turning toward this religion as a possible answer to their spiritual needs.

One militant sect, the *Soka Gakkai,* has elected all nine of its candidates to the House of Councilors. It is now the fourth biggest force in the upper house, claiming membership of more than one million families. It has won support from intellectuals, small enterprisers, and workers, infiltrating even leftist organizations. Communists condemn it as fascistic and mourn that "a potential for a political, revolutionary fervor has been diverted into reactionary religious channels." Prime Minister Kishi honored the organization with his attendance at the funeral of one of its leaders, "bowing," according to one newspaper, "to two million votes behind the altar."

Soka Gakkai, or the Value Creating Academic Society, was founded in 1930 but had little success until recent years because of its intolerance toward other religions and its militant methods of proselytizing. The sect claims that all religions other than its orthodox version of Nichiren

Shoshu, the teachings of Nichiren,* a thirteenth century Buddhist saint, are evil. It seeks to establish its creed as the national religion of Japan.

What alarms many Japanese about the *Soka Gakkai* is the strong military flavor of its organization, particularly among young people, fanatical with their sudden discovery of new values. In the House of Councilors election in June, 1959, some were arrested for violating the election law in their avid proselytizing efforts. They campaigned from door to door, wrote letters, stopped passers-by on the street to solicit votes. Sometimes they would threaten: "Vote for our candidates or you will be visited by misfortune."

Takashi Koizumi, fifty-year-old director of *Soka Gakkai,* says, "Our purpose is to purify this world through the propagation of the teaching of Nichiren Shoshu. Twenty years from now, we will occupy the majority of the Diet seats and establish Nichiren Shoshu as the national religion of Japan and construct a national altar atop Mount Fuji. This is the sole and ultimate purpose of our association."

Some Japanese see reason for concern about the future of democracy in the fact that so many people are prepared to place the nation's destiny in the hands of fanatical religious sects. Kishi, however, was quite willing to maintain friendly relations with the *Soka Gakkai,* whose support he welcomed as long as it did not interfere with his policies. He does not consider this sect a serious long-term political phenomenon, but a temporary manifestation of the restlessness of the times. He is far more concerned by the direct threat to parliamentary democracy posed by organizations propagating extremist political ideologies.

---

* Nichiren attacked the political and religious leaders of his day as dishonest and preached absolute faith in Buddha's teachings on the "way of purification." According to legend, Nichiren predicted a Mongolian invasion, and was sentenced to death by the Shogunate as an "obnoxious agitator." But the executioner, as he was about to behead Nichiren, was struck by a thunderbolt. The Shogunate, fearful of the "anger of the heaven," spared him.

CHAPTER XVII

❧❦❧

THE EXTREMIST THREAT

Kishi wrote in an "appeal to youth" published in the *Mainichi Shimbun* in April, 1957:

"Ten years after the end of the war I rejoice in the wonderful progress of democracy, but on the other hand, I cannot help feeling a certain apprehension. The fundamental principle of democracy lies in respect for the individual; freedom of speech, thought, and religion; freedom of political association and election; and politics based on the parliamentary system. It is clear from this that democracy is incompatible with fascist and communist despotism. Our people, as a result of many years of despotic rule, lack the tradition of freedom and have the habit of compliance. Consequently, we cannot say there is no danger of our country falling back on the easy solution of despotism, of either the rightist or the leftist variety."

In July, 1959, 2,200 representatives from nineteen organizations filled Tokyo's Hibiya Public Hall for the largest convention of rightists held since wartime days when militarists harangued the people against the United States. This time, ironically, the rally was intended to express opposition to leftist efforts to prevent conclusion of the revised United States-Japan Mutual Security Treaty, which the rightists realized, would give Japan a maximum of independence while guaranteeing its defense against communism—until they themselves could return to power.

In August, 1959, members of three rightist organizations—*Dai Nippon*

Seisant (Great Japan Creation Party), *Gokoku Seinen Tai* (National Protection Youth Corps), and *Dai Nippon Aikokuto* (Great Japan Patriotic Party)—violently demonstrated in Hiroshima on the eve of its atom-bombing anniversary against delegates attending a World Conference Against Nuclear Weapons because it was leftist-sponsored. Jumping out of trucks and jeeps, they attacked the delegates with their fists, spitting curses, while a chartered plane scattered propaganda leaflets over the city.

In March, 1959, while the Emperor and Empress were attending a memorial service for unknown soldiers killed in the war, a member of the ultra-rightist *Seichu Hokoku* (True Loyalty Patriotic Corps) was arrested while trying to submit an appeal to the Sovereign demanding that "false" charges of treason against the twenty-two officers who took part in the "February 26th" incident in 1936 be withdrawn.

More than a hundred rightist societies with over a thousand branch organizations, but with a total membership of only about 65,000, participated in over five hundred demonstrations in 1959. Significantly, two hundred members, compared to twenty-two in the previous year, were arrested. The nationalists arouse bitter memories among many of their countrymen as they militantly parade through the streets to the beat of drums—the Great Japan Ultra-Nationalist Party with Sun-Flag-decorated scarfs around their heads, the Sun-Flag Youth Corps in dark-blue uniforms with the sun insignia on their sleeves, the Protect the Fatherland Party in standard aloha shirts.

Such rightist groups are composed mainly of youths hungering, like their counterparts in the leftist and fanatic religious organizations, for moral roots. Only instead of growing new ones, they are trying to bring to life those that were destroyed. The leaders are often unreconstructed nationalists of wartime vintage. Bin Akao, who heads the Great Japan Patriotic Party, is probably the most vociferous of the rightist chiefs. Akao, a tall, bald man with small, cynical eyes, has a way of getting into the headlines. In February, 1959, while protesting in an audience with Foreign Minister Fujiyama a government decision to permit voluntary repatriation of Koreans in Japan to North Korea, Akao knocked the Minister down and spat at him. In January 1960, Tokyo police confiscated 1500 red, black, and white swastika posters found in Akao's house, matching those plastered on the homes of noted leftists. The posters, however, were not believed to have anti-semitic significance, but to have been intended as a warning to communists and socialists. Akao explained his support of the revised United States-Japan Mutual Security Treaty in these opportunistic terms: "We are using American power. What's wrong with it? Look at Stalin! He himself used Allied power during the war."

But despite this renewed activity, the difficulties rightists like Bin Akao face are formidable indeed. The Japanese people, bitterly disillusioned by the militarists during the war, want no truck now with men of similar ilk. Moreover, most Japanese, including the rightists themselves, realize that Japan must be dependent at this time on either the United States or the Soviet Union for its well-being and security. Since the United States is a preferable ally, a rightist government in Japan, after America's previous experience with one, would obviously not be conducive to the closest relations between the two countries. Further, the rightist groups, in most cases, lack unity and common purpose, a confusion that is evident in their very number. They can achieve co-ordination on specific issues such as anti-communism and the Mutual Security Treaty, but, in general, their policies and views are divergent. All favor a return to the past, but each emphasizes a different aspect of this past. The most reactionary and unrealistic of them insist that sovereignty be removed from the people and returned to the Emperor. Many stress the strengthening of Japan as a nation. Some want the revival of national socialism, or something akin to it, while others merely ask for a "spiritual cleansing of the nation" without clarifying what they mean or how this would be accomplished.

The lack of a central source of financial support also prevents unity. The individual groups are apparently backed by their own special contributors who wish to use the rightists to counter leftist moves. Organizations doing relatively well are not anxious to pool their financial resources with other groups. Most important of all, the rightists, bereft of the Emperor's "divine" stamp of approval, have neither the prestige, the authority, nor an hysterical doctrine like *Hakko Ichiu* to weld together their various groups, much less the entire nation. This situation differs considerably from that in West Germany, where new manifestations of Nazi thinking are in evidence. Nazism, as a purely *secular* philosophy, has a far greater chance of taking root in Germany than its equivalent, linked so intimately to a discredited spiritual concept, has of regaining ground in Japan.

Even so, the rightist threat could become dangerous. If the leftists grow in power, it is likely that the rightists will also become stronger and more influential. Fully aware that they have little or no chance of returning to leadership in the near future, the rightists are, in general, co-operating with the government for the time being and concentrating on the neutralization of leftist policies. One nationalist leader, Takeshi Nakamura, revealingly pointed out, "In pre-war days conditions were such that assassination of one key man could change the political trend. Now, such terroristic assassinations have no meaning. The time for us to come to the aid of the country is when a communist revolution is really near. When that time comes, we must sacrifice our lives to prevent the revolution. Until then, we will reserve and nurture our strength."

Kishi, as he indicated in his appeal to youth, has little use for those who would repeat the mistake that he himself made twenty years ago, and he is somewhat embarrassed by rightist support of many of his policies. Nonetheless, he realizes that the rightists have neither widespread public backing nor the organization to constitute an immediate menace. On the other hand, the leftists have both, and are backed by the great communist powers lying just across the Sea of Japan.

Russia and Communist China won a major cold war propaganda victory in June, 1960, when leftist riots they helped to foment forced Kishi to cancel a good-will visit to Japan by President Eisenhower. The visit was originally announced—as part of the celebration commemorating the centennial of United States-Japan diplomatic relations—in January, 1960, when Kishi went to Washington to sign the Mutual Security Treaty. The President was to stop in Japan on his way home from his scheduled trip to Russia, and Crown Prince Akihito and Princess Michiko were to return the visit a few months later.

But when Premier Khrushchev brusquely withdrew Russia's invitation to Eisenhower, and Kishi pushed through the lower house of parliament ratification of the Security Treaty, Japanese leftists, fearing the trip to Japan would bolster Kishi's stock, demanded that the Premier cancel it. Both Kishi and American officials refused to do so, even after White House Press Secretary James Hagerty and other United States representatives, paving the way for the presidential visit, were mobbed by leftists at the airport on their arrival in Japan and forced to fly into Tokyo by helicopter.

A few days before Eisenhower was to arrive, however, nearly 12,000 leftist students stormed the Diet in the most violent riot to date, and Kishi finally canceled the visit, admitting that he was unable to guarantee the President's safety. Kishi then sat out the continuing riots and demonstrations until final ratification of the Security Treaty took place (under Japanese law, a treaty is automatically ratified thirty days after lower house ratification unless the upper house votes on it before the period is up). But in winning the greatest policy victory of his career, he suffered his worst personal defeat.

Why had he been unable to control the actions of a violent but tiny minority? There were a number of contributing factors. He was plagued by the irresponsibility of a conservative but anti-Kishi press that tacitly encouraged the leftists to resort to violence—much as the prewar press helped spur rightist violence—criticizing the rioters only after the damage had been done. Further, Kishi lacked the support of many key conservatives who, in their hunger for power, also joined the leftists in condemning him. On the other hand, Moscow and Peking openly called for violence, and, it is believed, partially "financed" the rioters, paying many about $1.50 a day for their services.

But probably the most important factor was the inability of the Japanese police to cope with the trouble-makers under Japan's inadequate police laws, which, ironically, were framed by the American occupation forces with a view toward preventing the emergence of a new *Kempei Tai*. The police were helpless to take preventive measures against mob action.

When violence actually broke out, Kishi had the power to use a certain amount of force, and in almost any other country the government would have employed this power. But Kishi hesitated. The fact that he did throws a revealing light on him. No doubt Kishi realized that memories of Tojo's police brutality still lingered in Japan and that strong action might be resented by an unreasonably pacifistic public. But he also knew that to back down in the face of such violence was certain to hurt him politically. Under the circumstances, he would have had little to lose by resorting to harsh police or military measures.

Yet, Kishi, who had once supported Tojo's authoritarian policies and who has never lacked personal ambition, decided to commit what looked like political *hara-kiri* rather than chance large-scale bloodshed, even for morally justified ends. Many people might question his judgment in this case. But few can deny that it reflected an important change in his political and personal values. Unfortunately, the decision also handed the communist bloc its most important victory in Japan since the war, though the resort to guns or bayonets might have played into its hands to an even greater extent.

In few free nations is the influence of Marxism, particularly among intellectuals, more pronounced than in Japan. But this tendency has developed not so much from the artificial persuasion of communist propaganda as from a positive search for a system of values. As a result, Japanese leftists have not followed the traditional communist line, at least since the communists discredited themselves in the May Day riots of 1952. This is reflected in the fact that the Communist Party won less than two per cent of the votes in the upper house elections held in June 1959. The Japanese Marxists are willing to co-operate with communism on an international level, and some are willing to do business with the domestic party for the sake of political expediency, but nearly all consider as "un-Japanese" the communist way of doing things, and are not intellectual slaves of Moscow and Peking like Red-tinged groups in other nations.

Lacking the discipline of the orthodox communists, the leftists in Japan are divided into many ideological factions and sub-factions, ranging from neo-Trotskyite to laborite in the British style—each with its own theory on how Marxism can best be adapted to the Japanese national personality. In this respect, the leftists have not lost their "Japaneseness." Like their venturesome forefathers, who were radicals in their own way, the leftists wish to import many of the principles that their counterparts in other countries are following, but they insist on being selective. They do not want to swallow whole Moscow-fashioned communism, any more than they are willing to absorb the Free World's teachings indiscriminately. Most would probably keep the essentials of parliamentary government inherited from the United States, while drawing upon the ideological substance of the communists. In foreign policy, they would be neutralist. They think, however unrealistically, that Japan, despite its tremendous strategic and material value, can sit out the Cold War. Not only do they want all American troops withdrawn, but propose that Japan's Self-Defense Forces be converted into a non-military "engineering and disaster relief corps," leaving the country entirely defenseless. Japan, they say, with incredible naïveté, should depend for its security on the United Nations and an agreement to be reached between Japan, the United States, the Soviet Union, and Communist China, guaranteeing regional peace.

This extreme pacifistic approach to world problems is, strange as it may seem, one of the main sources of leftist popular strength. Probably no country in the world is as pacifist minded today as Japan, which has not yet fully recovered from the shattering disillusionment of the war. Japan is no doubt the only nation today where the expression, "peace at any price," is commonly heard. It is not unlikely that a large number of Japanese, including many strong anti-communists, would prefer to see a Red government in Japan than to fight another war. By the same token, almost all leftists, however doctrinaire they may be, however completely they accept the other teachings of Marx, flatly repudiate his argument that violent revolution is necessary to take control of the government.

This revulsion toward militarism is one reason why many Japanese, including some conservatives, are opposed to the new United States-Japan Mutual Security Treaty.* And such pacifism explains the government's reluctance to expand the Japanese armed forces faster than the snail's pace at which they are being enlarged today. The government is devoting only a minute percentage of the national budget to defense. The Ground Self-Defense Force has 170,000 men, 80,000 less than the number who composed the Imperial Army of 1931. The Maritime Self-Defense Force operates ships totaling 100,000 tons, and the Air Self-Defense Force consists of nearly 1000 planes, mostly T-33 jet trainers and F-86 Superjets, and about 28,000 airmen. This military strength is estimated by Japanese officials to be about half of the minimum required if Japan is to play an effective role in its own defense. It is pointed out, moreover, that the ground forces lack the latest equipment, that the majority of planes are trainers, and that many of the ships are obsolete.

Plans are underway, however, to improve this situation. Production of the F-104C-J Starfighter jet will soon start in Japan, Sidewinder air-to-air guided missiles are being imported, and the establishment of a guided missile corps trained to handle short-range ground-to-air missiles with nuclear warheads is contemplated, though the warheads would not be stored in Japan. The very possibility that atomic weapons might be brought into the country chills most Japanese.

The government has to proceed slowly in conditioning the people to accept the new "self-defense" forces.**

Complicating matters is the leftist-supported MacArthur Constitution, which specifically bans the build-up of armed forces. This was pointedly illustrated by an incident that took place on the high seas early in 1959, involving a landing support transport of the Maritime Self-Defense Force. A Dutch liner saluted the Japanese vessel as the ships passed each other, but the latter failed to return the salute. When the captain of the liner later asked a Japanese naval official why the transport had shown such lack of sea etiquette, the Japanese, while acknowledging that it was nor-

* It also helps to explain the large number of participants in some leftist-led demonstrations, the great majority of whom are non-violent.

** The Premier refrained from using the "self-defense" forces even to break up the worst leftist riots for fear of adverse public reaction. But in an extreme emergency, these forces, which depend for their existence on the conservatives, would undoubtedly back up the government. Thus, they constitute an ultimate safeguard against revolution.

mal for a commercial vessel and a warship to salute each other, explained that there were "lingering doubts about the status of the Self-Defense Forces." The commanding officer of the transport apologized to the Dutch captain, but it was still unclear whether the Japanese vessel, officially referred to as a "self-defense" ship, was a warship and should be saluted.

The logical thing to do would be to amend the Constitution to permit the open formation of genuine armed forces, but this is impossible in view of the fact that a two-thirds majority vote in the Diet would be necessary, and the Socialists control over one-third of the seats. Kishi had to handle the question of defense with the utmost discretion to maintain the façade of constitutionality.

So strongly anti-militaristic are the Japanese that members of the nation's armed forces almost never wear their uniforms off-duty for fear of being ridiculed and losing "face." They must put up with such remarks as "tax thieves!" and, if they happen to be sitting in a public conveyance, with demands to give up their seats to civilians. Some wives will not even walk beside their husbands if they are in uniform. "The only time I have taken pride in being a naval officer since joining the service in 1957," a member of the Maritime Self-Defense Force told me, "was when my ship went on a training cruise to Hawaii. People of Japanese origin swarmed all over us, invited us to dinner, threw parties for us. I felt as if I had returned home."

The most fanatical leftists can be found among the students, and are, in fact, the student leaders. They head a 280,000-member student organization called the *Zengakuren,* the All Japan Federation of Student Autonomy Councils. These young zealots have helped to give the impression to the world that Japan is a hotbed of communists ready to overturn the government. Their boldness set some kind of record in December, 1959, when, spearheading a wild anti-Security Treaty demonstration in front of the Diet, they and 3000 of their supporters stormed the Diet Building and urinated en masse against its steel doors. They made further headlines the morning of Kishi's departure for the United States, when they rioted in the airport restaurant while waiting for him to arrive. Kishi was forced to leave on his mission via the back streets of Tokyo to avoid being attacked by his people. Finally, they directed the riots that led to the cancellation of President Eisenhower's visit.

Despite their penchant for making headlines, those who participated in these instances of violence, and those who approved of their actions, constitute only a fractional element of the leftist movement, and, indeed, of the *Zengakuren* itself. Police estimate that only about 2000 members

of this student organization are communists, and another 3000, fellow
travellers. The hard core of leadership considers itself Trotskyite in nature
and scorns the Moscow-oriented Reds for preaching such nonsense as co-
existence. "There was a time once," says a Tokyo University professor,
"when we used to say to Communist Party leaders that we should try to
talk things out, instead of resorting to force. But these days that is what
the Communist Party is trying to tell *Zengakuren* leaders."

Prior to the Communist Party switch in policy in 1955 from violence
and iron-fisted tactics to a soft, wooing approach to the people, the
Zengakuren chiefs, most of them party members themselves, worked hand
in hand with the party. But following this shift in the communist line, the
majority of student leaders defied their party elders, stressing violence and
frenzied demonstrations, and were finally ousted from the party in June
1958. Although there are still some party members in the central executive
committee of the *Zengakuren,* most of the student leaders will have nothing to do with the traditional communists. These student troublemakers
by no means constitute a significant menace to parliamentary government.
Most of them, while caught in a revolutionary fervor, have no clear idea
what they want or what revolution would accomplish. Some think that
Trotskyism can somehow be adapted to parliamentary government, but
that, in any case, exploitation of the people by the capitalists and a reactionary government must be brought to an end.

Fusao Hayashi, a popular novelist and former leftist, pointed out after
one big demonstration, "What they did was simply a piece of disgraceful
horseplay that ignored not only the principles of revolution, but the elementary rules that govern any sport. They have been playing at revolution
in a country where the conditions simply do not exist for revolution . . .
this is just a piece of horse opera indulged in by a lot of spoiled brats. It
has nothing whatever to do with revolutionary action in the real sense."

With almost all newspapers, regardless of political color, spouting similar ridicule, and most socialist groups disassociating themselves from the
Zengakuren demonstrations, this organization has managed to discredit
itself no less completely than the Communist Party did on May Day, 1952.
Moreover, the great bulk of members, most of whom join the organization
automatically upon enrolling in a university, have also indicated in informal polls their opposition to the violent policies and tactics of their
leaders. The actions of these leaders are thus significant only in that they
are a manifestation of the deep anxiety and restlessness that plague Japanese youth today.

Kazuo Hiroashi, a thin, tousled-haired student in anthropology at

Tokyo University, who comes from a well-to-do family, as do most of the *Zengakuren* leaders, was one of the young men who participated in the Diet demonstration. He told me:

"Yes, I took part and I even urinated against the door of the building. It is something I shall never forget. I feel degraded. Why did I do it? I hadn't intended to get involved in any violence. I volunteered to go when our leaders called a conference of students and suggested that we take part in a demonstration. They didn't indicate that we would march on the Diet, they just said that we would turn out for a peaceful demonstration. And since I feel that the Security Treaty will lead us to war, I thought it was a perfectly legitimate thing to do.

"I, together with many other students, got off the subway at the Diet Building station and walked up to the street. Many policemen were standing there and tried to stop us, but we got past them and assembled about a block away. We then started filing toward the Diet Building carrying our banners, and I still thought it would be a peaceful demonstration. But as we passed between trucks full of policemen they jumped down and began hitting us with their sticks. We started running toward the Diet in a wild scramble, while our leaders cried, 'On to the Diet compound!' and 'Revolution!' We got inside the compound and simply walked to the main gate of the Diet. Our leaders had worked us up into such a frenzy that, quite illogically, we thought we were suddenly leading a real revolution. They had unmasked their true intentions. They had planned violence all along. And we were carried along with the excitement, as they had foreseen.

"I deplore their methods. They are Trotskyites and have little in common with most of the other students. Still, I can understand their motives. As a democratic socialist, I am for parliamentary government, but the fact is that the Diet does not truly represent the people. In the first place, the Liberal-Democrats buy many of their votes with money, jobs, and favors, and in the second place, the roots of democracy have not grown very deeply yet, and so the people, because of tradition and a feeling of obligation to the present leaders, continue to vote for them, even though many actually would prefer to vote for the socialists. That is the terrible contradiction. Our leaders think violence will awaken the people to the situation, to the rottenness of the present Diet. Their intentions are good, even if their tactics are wrong."

"If most students think as you do," I asked him, "why don't they elect moderate leaders?"

"Because most of us are too interested in our studies to have much time to devote to *Zengakuren*, while the extremists are interested mainly in this organization and therefore are willing to spend as much time as necessary working for it. Also, as the leaders are known to be extreme leftists, no moderates are willing to risk being labeled as communists by trying to become one of them. In short, we are cowards."

"What kind of government would you like to see established?"

"I, and I believe most of the students, want a clean, new type of government which will eliminate exploitation, do away with the greed for profits, and abrogate military alliances that might drag us into war. As for myself, I want peace at *any* price. Kishi probably means well, and maybe he has changed since the war, but he is of the old school and a friend of the capitalists. We want something new, an ideal, something like the communists have, but without the dictatorship and oppression."

"What do you plan to do after graduation?"

Kazuo Hirohashi smiled, rubbing his narrow, tense face with his fingers, his eyes lowered in embarrassment.

"I'm going into business with my father. It's the natural thing to do. I can't avoid it. I'll probably become a Liberal-Democrat like my father and vote for Kishi and his bunch. That's the system. That's the trap. Materialism and tradition stamp out all our ideals in the end, and we find ourselves left with nothing that counts."

Kazuo Hirohashi and his fellows are following in the Japanese student tradition—expressing their cynicism, restlessness, and frustration through wild, emotional demonstrations much as did students in Kishi's college days. Their action represents, in a sense, a last uninhibited fling at freedom before entry into the tightly-regulated and restrictive adult world of *giri*. The bonds of *giri* are much looser now, it is true, but this has not reduced the tensions gripping the Japanese student. On the contrary, his effort to reconcile the conflicting demands made upon him by the traditionalism that still dominates his home and the modern political and social concepts he learns about in school is in many cases even more nerve-shattering than was the attempt of the pre-war youth to fit himself into a social straitjacket.

Furthermore, the competition for admittance into the universities, particularly the "name" institutions, is actually more intense and terrifying than in Kishi's youth because larger numbers of families can afford to send their children to college. Job competition after graduation is also greater due to the rising population problem, with many students settling for positions not nearly commensurate with their abilities or ambitions. Moreover, Kishi and his classmates, having come mostly from families of high social standing, had stronger and more helpful "connections" than do most of today's students, who come largely from average families with little influence. And "connections" still mean at least as much as ability in the landing of a good job in Japan.

Kazuo Hirohashi and many other young Japanese have embraced leftism as an inspirational anchor, not accidentally or through individual discovery, but only after considerable prior political conditioning. Kazuo has been influenced in his thinking to no small degree by his pre-college education, just as Nobusuke Kishi had been, if in the other direction, in his school days. For a very large segment of Japan's school teachers are leftist. This is the result of a deliberate program to infiltrate the school system pursued by the communists and other leftists since the war.

Almost 90 per cent, or 500,000, of Japan's teachers are members of the Japan Teachers' Union, which is led by extreme leftists in alliance with the far left General Council of Japan Labor Unions, commonly called *Sohyo*. Japanese officials estimate that only about five per cent of the members are actually pro-communist, while slightly more than 50 per cent are moderately socialistic. But whatever the degree of leftist orientation, most teachers militantly follow the politically inspired orders of the JTU.

In 1958, stirred to a frenzy by this organization, they demonstrated or protested almost to a man against a Kishi government decision to establish an "efficiency rating" system for teachers to raise teaching standards and root out incompetents. The teachers and their supporters figured, perhaps not unreasonably, that such a system could be used to sift out instructors on a political basis. They walked out of classrooms, went on strike, marched on the Diet, and in some cases, even held school board representatives prisoners in their offices. Neglected students throughout the country were not unimpressed with the struggle their teachers were waging against the authority of the government.

This struggle is blueprinted in a JTU pamphlet designed to indoctrinate new members. It calls "the capitalist class and Government of Japan" the "enemies of democracy and peace," and goes on to say that "our teachers' union is an organization which stands at the forefront of the struggle. Imagine each teacher closely tied, through his fifty pupils, to the working class which constitutes 90 per cent of the entire population! Is it not a picture which is enormously encouraging and gloriously resplendent? . . . We are to fight on the side of these workers against the tyrannical propertied class of Japan." Another JTU document, the "Teachers' Code of Ethics," states that "the realization of socialism is the historical task imposed on the teacher. It is the duty of the teacher to foster young people who would help realize such a society."

Many teachers, according to students, seem to be taking this advice quite literally. Unlike in West Germany, where teachers tend to ignore the Hitlerian period, Japanese instructors, it is believed, generally make clear that the militarists were guilty of no little evil, though current textbooks state the historical facts without making judgment. But many instructors also subtly suggest the corollary that the present government actually represents little more than a camouflaged extension of the wartime militarist regime with hopes of going to war again under the United States-Japan Mutual Security Treaty. Further, they describe the Soviet Union and Communist China in glowing terms, often assigning homework on life in these communist countries.

The government is doing what it can to reduce the influence of the JTU. It has made all boards of education, which, since the Occupation, had been elective bodies easily packed by leftist organizations, appointive by the mayor or prefectural governor. Other measures include the tightening of government control on the editing and publication of school textbooks and the introduction of a "morals" course, which is designed to teach character building and good citizenship rather than the blind nationalism that marked the pre-war "morals" course.

But a far more potent counter-force to the leftist influence in school is the conservative influence at home, particularly in the rural regions. Parents in one village, angered by the political propaganda being fed their children by local leftist teachers, locked the instructors in their homes by boarding up their doors. Country teachers on the whole, however, do not pose too significant a problem, as many of them are also small landowners who do not take the advice of the JTU seriously, even though they are members. And it may be true that most urban teachers as well are not pro-communist. But as in the case of the *Zengakuren,* the rank and file of the JTU tend to accept the leadership of the militant leftists, lacking the democratic spirit and tradition required for effective rebellion.

Though *Zengakuren* may be the most vociferous and certainly the most extreme element in Japan's leftist movement, *Sohyo,* the spirit behind the JTU, is far more dangerous to Japan and the democratic form of government. This labor federation was established in 1950 as an anti-communist organ after Japan's first big post-war union, *Sanbetsu,* came under the control of Red leaders and indulged in such irresponsible activities as the effort to stage a general strike in 1947, which failed to come off when General MacArthur banned it. But communists soon infiltrated *Sohyo* as well, and today, though only about ten per cent of its leaders are believed communists or fellow-travellers, the policy of the organization is to co-operate with the Communist Party in elections, demonstrations against such common taboos as the Security Treaty, and on other occasions when collaboration might be mutually beneficial.

Sohyo, which concerns itself more with the pursuance of long-range political aims than economic benefits for its members (though, like other unions, it has obtained many such benefits since the war), is steeped in a unique ideological confusion. On the one hand, most of the leaders, the same people who established *Sohyo* as an anti-communist union, still have little use for communism, largely because it is "un-Japanese." As Secretary-General Akira Iwai says, "The Communist Party has a history of having once carried out irresponsible agitation and strike guidance in the labor union movement led by its unique international strategy. We cannot fail to have the suspicion that the pacifist movements, cultural movements, and all other movements in which the Japan Communist Party has taken an initiative, might have been launched for ulterior Communist Party purposes. Isn't it necessary for them to assess more properly the neutral policy to be followed under the conditions prevailing in Japan?"

At the same time, Iwai and other *Sohyo* chiefs, who lead 3.5 million Japanese workers, maintain that they can reconcile two irreconcilable concepts: the Marxist doctrine of the need for a class war, and the democratic idea of a parliamentary political system. The result of such unrealistic thinking has been a completely contradictory policy platform which even Japan's greatest scholars have not been able to decipher. The confusion was climaxed when Professor Itsuro Sakisaka, a left-wing theorist, wrote a magazine article in December, 1958, criticizing the Socialist Party as "rightist Fabian" and urging that it become a "new [peacefully] revolutionary political party dedicated to the working class" rather than a "national party." *Sohyo* attempted to clarify this criticism of the Socialist Party:

"We are opposed to the theory of two large parties, each making concessions to the other, and to the theory that the Socialist Party should be a national party. The so-called theory of two large parties argues for the establishment of common ground with the conservative party by bringing the Socialist Party to the right, and for the smooth transfer of political power between the two. There is an extreme cleavage between the life of the laborers, farmers, small enterprisers, and unemployed masses who are the base of the Socialist Party, however, and the capitalist class which is the base of the Liberal-Democratic Party, and the two parties can therefore never find common ground.

"The Liberal-Democratic Party is a class party which pursues only the profit of large-scale capital. A choice must be made between the interests of the rich and the interests of those who work, and there can be no 'national party' which manages to cover both. We believe that we can gain a majority only by faithfully taking up the demands of the farmers, small enterprisers and unemployed workers who are not now voting for the Socialist Party.

"We support parliamentary politics and the policy of establishing a socialist society by peaceful means. It is not proper to the nature of parliamentary politics, however, merely to assent, as at present, to a decision by the majority, on the grounds that 'what the Liberal-Democratic Party says is law.' *Sohyo* has until now supported the Socialist Party because the political line set out in the party platform looks toward a peaceful revolution based upon the development of parliamentary politics tied firmly to mass movements, and because the basis for the party's existence is sought in the toiling masses, with the workers at their center.

"The most important condition for the strengthening and development of this sort of Socialist Party is the progressive emergence of countless activists in shop and factory, firmly tied in everyday life to the laboring masses. And we believe that if the matter is one of revolution by peaceful means, the achievement of a socialist society is not to be expected unless the party becomes yet more actively a class party."

From this statement, it might be gathered that a parliamentary system is desirable, but that the Socialists must engage in uncompromising class warfare with the conservatives, while being free from the obligation of obeying laws passed by a government led by the majority party if this party happens to be conservative. On the other hand, peaceful revolution is advocated, but "smooth transfer of political power between the two" parties is frowned upon, apparently meaning that peaceful revolution would not be permitted once the socialists were in and the conservatives were out. It can only be concluded from these contradictions that *Sohyo,* if it realizes what it really wants, favors the establishment of a dictatorship of the proletariat, although perhaps one less rigid and oppressive than the Communist Party would set up.

When Western socialists visit Japan, they are shocked by some of the meaningless theorizing of the non-communist leftists. It reminds them of the kind of radical talk that was popular in Europe and the United States in the 1920's, when there was considerable meat to the argument that the capitalists were exploiting the workers. But with labor conditions in Japan, as in the Western nations, improving almost daily, such thinking, modern socialists say, is completely divorced from reality.

The most logical explanation why *Sohyo* is so far behind the times is that Japanese labor unions were virtually non-existent after their brief venture into democracy in the 1920's. Thus, when modern full-scale labor unions were suddenly, and superficially, imposed on Japanese society by the Occupation, their leaders had no political or social values to guide them, except those they remembered from an era long past. Nevertheless, *Sohyo*'s leaders are extremely intelligent and able men. Secretary-General Iwai, a thirty-eight-year-old ex-railroad worker, is as shrewd politically as he is naïve ideologically. He is far more concerned, in fact, with increasing *Sohyo*'s political influence in parliamentary councils than with theoretical matters of ideology. Considering the fact that *Sohyo* virtually dictates the policies of the Socialist Party, this friendly, rather soft-spoken man with a flat nose and huge jaws has by no means been unsuccessful. Iwai, many observers think, would favor tolerance if the Socialists ever got into power.

However, his co-leader, *Sohyo* President Kaoru Ohta, is far more to be feared. Ohta, a chemical engineer who used to work for management, representing the latter in the formation of a company labor union when General MacArthur ordered that unions be established, switched over to the labor side of the table and has been a fiery advocate of "peaceful" class war ever since. Ohta, a good speaker with great mass appeal, is more interested in the intellectual aspects of Marxism than in the practical and political means of running the union and enhancing its power. A far more uncompromising man than Iwai, it is believed he might very well try to set up a leftist dictatorship if he had the opportunity.

Iwai and Ohta, in their drive for power, are confronted by an obstacle within their own organization that is at least as frustrating as that constituted by the entrenched capitalists. Most workers in big Japanese firms are unionized, and the majority are members of *Sohyo,* but they do not exhibit an enthusiasm toward their unions in any way comparable to that which can be found in Western countries. Many workers doubt that they owe greater loyalty to their union than to their bosses, who have traditionally been their protectors and their providers, and to whom they still bow in respect. The workers, while receiving paternalistic benefits from their company, are not at all certain that collective bargaining will yield them any greater benefits. In any event, with the idea of a united proletariat still in its infancy in Japan, most workers are concerned only with conditions that exist within their own firm. Ideological and political questions are of little interest to them.

Because of these factors, it has been virtually impossible for the *Sohyo* leaders to make much headway with their "peaceful revolution." A general strike is doomed to failure for lack of widespread compliance. Even localized strikes usually fizzle out before management is too hard pressed. The latter, hoping to stave off further trouble in the future, often makes important economic concessions. But from *Sohyo*'s point of view, as its central aim is political rather than economic, this does not represent success. Meanwhile, pro-communist elements in *Sohyo* have been growing in influence. Ironically, while the apathy of most workers toward their unions hurts the anti-communist *Sohyo* leaders, it helps the Reds. For if the rank and file did take an active interest in their organizations, they would probably demand a purge of the communists.

Actually, an important split in *Sohyo* took place several years ago because of its far leftist tendencies, just as *Sohyo* itself had been born of an anti-communist rebellion. The rebels formed a new labor organization called the All-Japan Trade Union Congress, or as it is popularly known, *Zenro*. Though it boasts only about 800,000 members, it is expected to grow as *Sohyo* continues moving toward the left, particularly now that it is associated with a political organ of its own, the Democratic Socialist Party, which was formed in January, 1959 from dissidents in the Socialist Party.

Zenro is led by forty-one-year-old Secretary-General Haruo Wada, a handsome ex-seaman, who lacks the engaging personality of *Sohyo*'s Iwai, but makes up for this with brilliant administrative skill. He is primarily interested in winning increased economic benefits from management, with whom he thinks the workers should maintain co-operative relations. He considers the *Sohyo* leaders completely unrealistic and avoids even being in the same room with them for fear of exploding in anger at their "naiveté." Deeply distrustful of the communists, he favors close relations with the Free World, though he opposes the Mutual Security Treaty on the grounds that it infringes on Japan's sovereignty.

As both *Sohyo* and *Zenro* sprang into being overnight as full-blown organizations, neither knows much about organizing new unions, concentrating instead on the "cannibalization" of each other's locals. During a *Sohyo*-led strike that took place in late 1958, largely for political reasons, at the Oji Paper Company in Hokkaido, some of the strikers locked their employers in their office. Others, highly indignant at this lack of respect for their superiors, formed an independent union with the help of *Zenro* agents. This second union co-operated with the management, and operations were resumed. Within six months, this new group became the majority union. *Sohyo* took another beating recently when several regional and local chapters of the 300,000-member National Railway Workers Union revolted and also formed an independent union, which may join *Zenro* soon. *Sohyo*, meanwhile, is planning to break *Zenro*'s hold on the textile workers.

Sohyo's political power is channeled through the Socialist Party, which, it is often said, is little more than an appendage of this labor union. The party is dependent on *Sohyo* for an important share of its votes, and for the bulk of its financial support (though a significant percentage of this support comes, curiously enough, from big business as a kind of "guarantee" in case the party comes to power). Since early 1959, the Socialist Party has exhibited a gradual leftward tendency in line with the labor union's orientation. This was the main reason for the rebellion of the right-wing faction and its subsequent formation of a new party, allied with *Zenro.*

The Socialist Party that remains has by no means attained unity in its leftism since this split. Members are still hopelessly divided. A number, following the *Sohyo* line without reservation,* insist that no concession at all be made to the principle of a "people's" party. Others propose moderation if for no other reason than to win enough votes to obtain a parliamentary majority, after which the question of ideological aim could be settled on a more partisan basis. The party controls only about one-third of the Diet at present, and appears doomed to remain at this percentage level unless it can win over a substantial number of middle-of-the roaders.

Paradoxically, the movement of the Socialist Party to the left could be indirectly responsible for a strengthening of parliamentary democracy in Japan. For as a result of this movement the new Democratic Socialist Party has emerged. Though his own party may lose votes to it, Kishi told me, "The establishment of this new party may be one of the most important political events since the war. This may be a wonderful opportunity to reinforce our democratic structure." What Kishi meant is that for the first time since the war, his ultimate goal of a two-party system involving two big *moderate* parties, one conservative and the other progressive, might be within sight.

The new political group is headed by its founder, Suehiro Nishio. A veteran politician with square jaw, tight lips, and a small moustache, Nishio is convinced that the only way the socialists can win a parliamentary majority is to appeal to people from every class. Reflecting this view, his party's platform can hardly be distinguished from that of the British Labor Party. Democratic socialism, it says, is an ethical process of expanding civil liberties, established by the bourgeois revolution, to all sections of the population. It's aim is to create a welfare state based on

---

* Chairman Asanuma, a large, puffy-faced man with a gravel voice (he dubbed the voice of the old grandfather dog in the Japanese version of Walt Disney's *The Lady and the Tramp*), is an able but opportunistic politician who faithfully hues the Sohyo line.

parliamentary democracy, guaranteeing civil liberties to all. It declares that the party is "national," serving workers, peasants, small and medium businessmen, and other sectors of the population alike. The party, therefore, rejects nationalization of industries for the sake of nationalization and advocates planned economic order, placing public interest first.* Unlike the mother Socialist Party, it admits the need of a "balance of armed strength" as a basis for world peace, and approves a "minimum strength" for Japan. Refreshingly, the word "revolution," peaceful or otherwise, does not appear in the platform.

The road ahead is not likely to be a smooth one for Nishio's party. Though it is supported by *Zenro,* this union has not nearly the financial resources at its disposal that *Sohyo* can boast. Unless *Zenro* can make important inroads into *Sohyo*'s organization, the party will be severely handicapped. It cannot expect to receive much support from industry. Moreover, as a new party, it will have a harder time fighting tradition than the Socialist Party, which itself has suffered considerably from the fact that many people vote for the conservatives simply because they have always done so. Now, most of those who have been voting for the Socialist Party may feel obligated to continue their support of that group even if they find Nishio's party more to their liking. Also, leftists in Japan tend to lean toward theoretical Marxism rather than toward a mere welfare system, which lacks the idealistic flavor they are seeking to replace the tastelessness of postwar life.

In spite of these handicaps the new party may be the answer for discontented fringe groups in both the Socialist and Liberal-Democratic Parties. In any event, it might force the Socialist Party to brake its leftward tendency and perhaps eventually even forsake its close tie-up with *Sohyo.*

The government is, of course, assaulted as a "war-minded" and "American-dominated" clique, not only by domestic leftists, but by Japan's neighbors—North Korea, the Soviet Union, and Communist China —as well. North Korea is reaping important propaganda dividends for the communist cause in general by attracting to its shores some of the 600,000 Koreans who have been living in Japan. Japan agreed in December, 1959 to permit voluntary repatriation of Korean residents to North Korea, and only four months later more than 15,000 had departed—the first important migration from the Free to the Communist World. The figure, it is believed, may eventually exceed 50,000. This unique movement of

---

* Sohyo and the Socialist Party favor nationalization of most industries.

refugees is not likely to be disregarded by the uncommitted nations of Asia.

Yet it is not so much a question of political ideology as of traditional ill-feeling between Koreans and Japanese that is responsible for this migration. Korea, unlike most other areas of Asia, had been occupied long before World War II—since the Russo-Japanese War. The Koreans remember the Japanese not only for the cruelties they perpetrated, but for their effort to destroy Korean culture and replace it with their own. Conversely, most Japanese consider the Koreans as indolent, dishonest, inferior people, who, in the case of those living in Japan, are simply adding to an already explosive population problem. Thus, there were few dissents among the Japanese, including most right-wingers, when the Kishi government decided to permit Korean residents to go to North Korea in the face of frantic South Korean opposition.

One Korean who has chosen to remain in Japan is Kim Du-Jin, a husky, handsome scrap collector in Tokyo. Kim, a thirty-two-year-old bachelor, would like to marry and "raise many children." But even as a single man without family responsibilities, he can eke out little more than a marginal existence. He rejected the brand of "equality" promised by the Korean Reds only because he considers communism the worst of two evils. Kim, who is subjected to social and vocational discrimination not unlike that suffered by the Negro in the United States, earns $40 a month as an employee of a small Korean-owned metal scrap company. This is not much less than the average Japanese unskilled worker makes, but Kim does not receive the paternalistic fringe benefits that many Japanese get—no bonuses, free medical care, or housing allowances.

But even more important as far as he is concerned, no Japanese with his education would find his opportunities confined to scrap collecting. Kim has a degree in sociology from Tokyo's Waseda University, and had hoped to be a teacher, but Japanese schools, like most Japanese business firms, seldom hire Koreans. Most Korean schools, on the other hand, are communist-controlled, and the few that are not are unable to absorb all the Korean teachers who need jobs.

Kim lives in Shimoishihara Village, a shanty-town on the outskirts of Tokyo, together with about 1500 other Koreans, all of them anti-communist. Korean Reds from other parts of Tokyo "invaded" the area in daily waves of about fifty in December, 1959, calling at each house in an effort to intimidate the residents into going to North Korea. When Kim tried to stop one propaganda truck from entering the village, he was dragged into the vehicle and brutally beaten by seven communist thugs. He was finally rescued by police and hospitalized for a week.

Kim occupies one of four rooms in the crowded, Japanese-style home of Mrs. Chung Kuk-Tok and her seven children, aged six to twenty-five. Mrs. Chung, a widow, earns about $25 a month as a day laborer for the city, sweeping streets or helping push carts loaded with construction materials. A son, twenty-two, works as a truck driver's assistant, and a daughter, eighteen, has a job in a small workshop turning out camera parts. The eldest son, twenty-five, is unemployed.

Despite the hardships of life in Japan, Mrs. Chung, like Kim, has staunchly declined to go to North Korea. In holding to this decision, she has withstood the most strenuous efforts of her brother, a communist who has asked for repatriation, to persuade her to accompany him. It is difficult to determine why Mrs. Chung decided to remain in Japan. Perhaps she did not altogether trust her brother's promises and sensed that he wanted her to go because it would make things look better for him. Perhaps the difficulties and the risk involved in moving a large family made her stand firm. Mrs. Chung does not hate the Japanese the way many Koreans do. She remembers that when her husband died, many Japanese neighbors called to offer their condolences. Mrs. Chung and other Koreans also receive the same legal privileges as other aliens, and, in fact, enjoy certain advantages, such as the right to receive relief subsidies. The Chung family is granted eight dollars a month. But such official correctness can hardly placate Koreans like Kim, who must be satisfied with the career of a scrap collector.

Kim would like to return someday to his home in Oesong, South Korea, which he left in 1941 to pursue his studies in Japan. But, he explains, "I could not bear to lose 'face' before my family by returning as a failure." At the same time, Kim—and most other Koreans in Japan—had almost as little desire to live under the recently deposed regime of Syngman Rhee as under the communists. They are waiting to see if the new government does more for the "welfare of the people." Rhee, who, as a victim of Japanese torture, hates Japan more than do most Koreans, actually prevented repatriation of his countrymen to South Korea by demanding that Japan pay the Seoul government "compensation" in advance for the "ill-treatment" accorded them. Rhee, Kim feels, realized that the Japanese would not agree, but wanted an excuse for rejecting the return of the Koreans in order to avoid aggravating the serious unemployment problem already plaguing his country—a situation differing sharply from that in North Korea, which is underpopulated and in great need of labor.

Rhee also insisted that Japan should pay a bill of hundreds of millions of dollars to compensate for Korean funds that had been deposited in Japanese banks and never returned, for bonds held by Koreans that had never been redeemed, for wages owed Koreans that had never been paid, and for contracts concluded with Koreans that had never been honored. Japan replies that it will consider all legitimate claims, but that Japanese property in Korea had been transferred to the Koreans during the Occupation and compensated for many of these claims.

South Korea demands the return of all cultural property of Korean origin taken out of the country. Japan says it is sympathetic toward this claim, and would search museums and large collections for such items as part of a broad settlement, but that such an effort would have certain practical limitations, e.g. many things had been sold to the Americans during the Occupation.

The South Koreans insist on the return of a number of ships that had been registered by the Japanese in Korea. But Japan points to the "illegal" confiscation by the Koreans of Japanese fishing boats captured beyond the so-called Rhee Line.

The Rhee Line issue, is, in the view of most observers, the most unreasonable of all the Korean arguments. During the Korean War, the Americans established a boundary around South Korea, extending up to 190 miles from shore, beyond which Japanese fishermen were not allowed to go for the sake of their own safety. After the Korean conflict, South Korea arbitrarily established a similar barrier, claiming, in effect, sovereignty over a part of the open seas. About 5000 Japanese have been captured in the last several years for violating this Rhee Line, over two hundred of whom have been kept in prison or detention camps.

Relations between the two countries have improved slightly as the result of a recent agreement providing for the repatriation of these fishermen to Japan in exchange for the return of illegal Korean entrants held in a Japanese alien immigration center to South Korea. But while this accord, it is hoped, may lead to a settlement of other differences—especially now that Rhee has resigned—these differences, aggravated by the flow of Korean residents in Japan to North Korea, are causing American officials considerable concern. If an emergency erupted in the area, the present stalemate would hardly prove conducive to regional co-operation and unity.

But a far greater threat to Japanese and Free World interests than the complex Korean problem lies in the pressures being exerted on Japan by the Soviet Union and Communist China. Though Japan may not be the most important country in the Free World, nor Kishi the most important Free World figure, probably no other person has been more vitriolically attacked by Russia and China than this statesman. Yet Kishi's official attitude toward these countries, particularly Red China, has been more moderate than that expressed by many Western countries. This vicious and unrelenting hostility toward the Japanese government, which even the cold war "thaw" has not affected, is a revealing commentary on the significance that the communist world attaches to Japan, one of the most prized of all potential victims.

The Soviet and Chinese leaders, encouraged by the fact that there are so many leftists in Japan who are ready to foster their aims, say they are not interested in Japan going communist. They only want this country to adopt a neutralist policy and expel American troops. The two nations did all in their power to prevent adoption of the Mutual Security Treaty, using Kishi, the chief spirit behind the pact, as the focal point of their assault.

During the treaty ratification debate in the Diet, Russia grossly interfered in Japanese internal affairs, and cynically repudiated an international agreement, by warning Kishi that if the pact were ratified, Moscow would not return to Japan the islands of Shikotan and Habomai, as it had formally promised to do when a peace treaty between the two countries is finally concluded. One factor in this move was an attempt by Russia to make the issue of the two islands, which had previously been settled, a subject of renewed negotiation and thereby remove the pressure of Japanese demands for the return of the Russian-held Etorofu and Kunashiri islands. But Moscow almost certainly calculated as well that such a threat might intimidate the Diet into vetoing the treaty.

The Kremlin sometimes uses the carrot instead of the stick. It has repeatedly let it be known that if Japan were prepared to sign a "reasonable" peace treaty (providing, among other things, for Japan's permanent relinquishment of Etorofu and Kunashiri islands), and assume a "more friendly attitude" toward the communist bloc, all other pending problems would be solved. The Japanese could "gain untold riches" by helping Russia develop Siberia, and would win many fishery benefits in the northwest Pacific, which the two nations jointly exploit, a suggestion pointed up by Russia's refusal to permit Japan more than an 85,000-ton salmon quota in 1959, as compared to 110,000 tons in 1958, and 120,000 tons in 1957. To emphasize further the importance of Russo-Japanese friendship, the Soviets have dumped a considerable quantity of low-priced textiles on the Singapore market in direct competition with Japanese products.

One man, Nobusuke Kishi, says Russia, is largely responsible for the absence of "co-operative" relations.

Communist China has been even more brazen in its attacks on Kishi. An editorial in the *Peiping People's Daily,* official newspaper of the Chinese Communist Party, said:

"It is imperative that, in order to promote mutual, cultural and friendly exchange, the Chinese and Japanese peoples wage a determined struggle against the Kishi Government which has been maintaining a hostile attitude toward the Chinese people, trying to create 'two Chinas and obstructing the normalization of Sino-Japanese relations.' [The Japanese understand that] this struggle is being waged precisely to safeguard [their own] vital interests. . . . For the prevalence of this latent imperialist ambition of the Kishi Government will, first of all, spell a new catastrophe for the Japanese people. We know how to distinguish Japanese friend from foe. We also know how to deal with such evil-intentioned double-crossers as Kishi."

Kishi told me, "Communist China wishfully thinks that Japan is a very weak patient, and that it can, therefore, drive a wedge between this country and the United States. And in fact, this country is not completely healthy yet. But that is precisely the reason why the Security Treaty will help us. It is the best medicine we could take to rid ourselves of what weakness remains. When we are healthy enough, it will be possible to improve relations with Communist China. But our first effort must be to attain such a state of health."

Japanese relations with Peking have been virtually non-existent since May, 1958, when Communist China abruptly cut off trade with Japan, ostensibly because a hot-tempered Japanese youth tore down a Communist Chinese flag at a trade fair in Nagasaki. The Reds actually wanted to see how economic pressure might influence Japan's political policies. They hoped that in return for renewed trade with China, Japan, under pressure from the leftists, would get rid of Kishi and avoid solidifying its ties with the United States. Consistent with such concessions, Peking probably thought, Japan might be brought around to cutting its present ties with Formosa and establishing diplomatic relations with Communist China.

Before the severance of trade relations, Japan had maintained limited commercial ties with Peking, primarily through private channels. This trade effort begun in 1952 reached a peak in February 1957, shortly before Kishi came to power, when China appeared ready to purchase 200 million pounds of Japanese steel, and to conclude a fourth trade accord between the two countries. Kishi, on assuming power, confirmed, in stating his policies, that Japan would not recognize Peking, that no diplomatic privilege would be granted to a trade representation of the Communist Chinese Government to be set up in Tokyo under the new trade agreement, that due care should be exercised lest the establishment of the trade mission be interpreted as *de facto* recognition of the Peking regime, and that Japan would not permit the mission to hoist its flag. This was followed by Kishi's first trip to Southeast Asia, during which he embraced Chiang Kai-shek in Formosa.

After the Nagasaki flag incident, the time had come, Peking thought, to test the strength of the Kishi government, as well as popular Japanese sentiment toward Red China. Relations could not be re-established, it declared, until Japan discontinued its hostile attitude toward Communist China and disengaged itself from a "two Chinas" policy. Of course, it added, these conditions could only be met if Kishi were ousted.

Ironically, almost all Japanese, including Kishi, favor a renewal of trade relations with Peking. Not only do they feel that Japan needs all the trade it can get, but they harbor an emotional attachment to China, if not to its government, stronger than to any other nation in the world. Most, however, are not willing to pay a political price for Chinese trade and good-will. Thus, contrary to Peking's hopes, strong popular demand that the Tokyo government meet at least some Communist Chinese conditions has not materialized. In particular, small and medium businessmen who had previously exerted enormous pressure on the government to expand trade relations with China, no longer press so hard for such ties. One reason is that they have come to realize, as they did not before, that trade with China, in any event, could not even approach the amount of business they had once thought possible. Trade with that country in 1957, the peak year, amounted to only $145 million, or three per cent of Japan's total international commerce. The main trouble is the barter nature of this exchange. For while Red China needs many Japanese items, particularly steel and chemical products (largely fertilizer), Peking can provide little that Japan requires except moderate quantities of coal, iron ore, soybeans, and a few other products. Certainly Japan does not need Chinese manufactured goods. But aside from this economic factor, most Japanese are not prepared to tie trade to political concessions.

This is, however, hardly true of the leftists. Chairman Inejiro Asanuma of the Socialist Party, on a "good-will" mission to Peking in early 1959, not only condemned Kishi and approved Red Chinese conditions for a renewal of relations with Japan, but shocked the Japanese people and embarrassed his party by publicly stating that the United States is the "enemy of both Japan and Communist China."

Before Kishi finally quit, even some conservatives proposed, in effect, that Japan appease China with one small political concession—namely, Kishi's head. These ambitious men argued that Peking's attitude toward Japan would remain stiff as long as Kishi stayed in power. On the other hand, relations with Red China would improve, they claimed, if Kishi were replaced by a leader less directly associated with defiance of Peking. His resignation, they said, would permit the Chinese to switch tactics without losing "face." This argument gained considerable ground after a visit to Red China in late 1959 by Kenzo Matsumura, an anti-Kishi conservative leader. Matsumura returned to Japan "surprised" by the friendly reception accorded him by Red officials. The Chinese suggested that all that really stood between the two nations was the existence of the Kishi government.

If the desire for links with Red China is strong today when Japan is enjoying prosperity, it would be overwhelming if Japan were hit by a severe recession, which could result from heavy American restrictions on Japanese goods. The Japanese could be expected, quite understandably, to seek hungrily whatever crumbs of trade Communist China would hold out to it, even if this meant important political concessions such as a swing toward neutralism and related steps; e.g., abandonment of the "two Chinas" policy and recognition of the Peking regime. And being a totalitarian state, Red China could fit the economic prize to the circumstances, offering if necessary an extremely lucrative trade agreement that would not require Japan to import as much as it exported.

Still, trade between Japan and Red China, however intensely the Japanese may struggle in the future for every dollar of it, will always tend to be limited, for these two countries, when China is fully industrialized will have parallel economies. Peking may, in fact, be able to exert greater political pressure on Japan by using the much larger potential market of Southeast Asia as a bargaining lever. As the nations of this area, except for India, will never be heavily industrialized, they will inevitably become huge markets for imported manufactured products. Japanese trade with this region could eventually, therefore, develop into the biggest factor in Japan's economic well-being. However, the influence Red China would be able to exert in the determination of Japan's share of this market would be considerable.

Kishi said recently that "if the Chinese Communists are willing to engage Japan in an economic race of each developing its own country and waging fair trade competition abroad, Japan is not afraid to take them on at any time." But Kishi and other Japanese are fearful indeed on reading trade statistics for Southeast Asia. For though its own people may not have shoes, and certainly not sewing machines, Red China is today exporting these and many other items as well, to neighboring countries at prices that the Japanese could never meet, an indication of what havoc China, as a totalitarian state, may be able to create for Japan in the future.

Since early 1959, a notable slowdown in such exports has been observed, due mainly, it is believed, to the disruption of Red China's economy as a result of its great industrial and agricultural "leap forward," including the commune program. But there are signs that increasing quantities of Chinese products will soon begin to stream forth again. In any case, most economic experts are convinced that the Red Chinese trade campaign is by no means a token effort to impress Asia, but a genuine attempt to build up markets. In 1958, Peking's sales to Southeast Asia, totaled $450 million. This meant, subtracting imports, a favorable trade balance of $355 million. At first, competition from Red China was felt only in a few selected items such as sugar, cement, hogs, and textiles. But it has extended over a broad range of consumer items, ranging from synthetic camphor and edible oils to electric fans, flatirons, neon lighting tubes, and radio-controlled toys. Almost every world buyer, except the United States, is purchasing citronella oil from Chinese Hainan Island. An equally important hint of the future lies in the fact that Red China has begun to charter ships for Asian and European trade, charging freight rates much below those of Japan and other world shippers.

This pinch could grow into an economic stranglehold. Japan might very well find itself one day faced with the choice of losing many of its lifeline markets or reaching a political "accommodation" with Communist China. Many Japanese, should they be faced with a serious economic crisis, particularly as a result of short-sighted American policies, would be greatly impressed by the argument that a change in political attitude could mean a change in Red China's dumping and pricing habits. And therein lies one of the most serious long-range dangers confronting Japan's infant democracy.

CHAPTER XVIII

❦

THE FRAGILE FLOWERS

Does Japan practice true democracy today? Certainly in form. The Japanese people have a freely elected parliament and all the basic freedoms that the United States and other Western nations have. But as Kishi is the first to admit, the spirit and substance of democracy must still reach maturity. After his party's victory in the upper house elections of June, 1959, Kishi wrote in the newspaper, *Nihon Keizai Shimbun:*

"In the war, Japan sustained immeasurable damage to her land, human lives, and materials, and for a time even lost all spiritual support. From that state of despondency, we have reached the point where we now can support ourselves on democracy. Today, some ten-odd years after the war, the democracy that at the time was relatively unfamiliar to us, has at last spread its roots into Japan's soil. I feel that this democracy constitutes the spiritual foundation of the new Japan, and it is my intention to defend it, no matter what difficulties are encountered, and nurture it. This is the starting point of all my political activities. However, it will probably still take some time before this democracy will flower and bear fruit . . ."

The feudalistic tendency of the Japanese to follow established patterns of behavior rather than assert themselves as individuals is one reason why democracy is yet to flower and bear fruit. After their bitter experience with totalitarianism, they have turned to the alternative—democracy. But they are trying to build this new way of life, in large measure, on a foundation of decayed values. They are treating democracy as a new kind of ideological structure, hopelessly seeking their places within it. They do not completely understand that democracy denies such a structure as restrictive of individual liberty, that it actually represents freedom from systematization, with rules kept to a bare minimum. Kishi, who is himself in the process of learning the meaning of freedom, has advanced far enough to realize—no small achievement—that this concept cannot be simply imposed by fiat, but must be gradually fostered and encouraged, among the leaders and the people alike, as a broken limb just removed from a plaster cast must be massaged and exercised before it can be satisfactorily utilized.

Kishi's efforts to help his country grow and to grow with his country are not fully appreciated by the people, who, to begin with, were slightly wary of him because of his Imperialistic past. He is popular in some quarters, particularly in his native Yamaguchi and in most rural areas, but a sizable part of the urban population is rather cool toward him. This, however, is not overly significant in Japan, because it would be hard to name on the fingers of one hand prime ministers who have been popular. Prince Ito, who played a major role in lifting Japan, technically and industrially, into the modern era during the Meiji period, was disliked by the public. Tojo was considered, even in the days of Japanese victory, an incompetent politician and a vain man. Yoshida was regarded as smug and impolite, and as an American puppet, though now, several years after he was forced out of office, people are beginning to say that he did a pretty good job after all.

One reason for this widespread distrust of national authority is that the Japanese have never quite overcome their feudalistic provincial prejudices, which less than a century ago were expressed in perpetual inter-clan rivalry and conflict. A national leader is seldom fully accepted by people from other regions than his own, a problem, incidentally, that is closely allied with that of the factional divisions within the government.

In Kishi's case, moreover, many of his compatriots find him too embarrassingly pragmatic and rational, qualities that have never endeared leaders from Choshu, including men of the caliber of Prince Ito, to the generally sentimental Japanese people. They joke that the Premier lives up to his name, *kishi* meaning "river bank" in Japanese. He straddles both banks, they jest, though it is due in substantial degree to Kishi's tactical flexibility and sense of political realism that Japan is enjoying a very large measure of political stability today.

Further, while the natives of Choshu who know him well, and most people who meet Kishi personally, find him an engaging man with considerable warmth and charm—even some of his bitterest Socialist opponents privately admit that they feel a great fondness toward him as a person—the Prime Minister's personality often fails to project in the impersonal atmosphere of the meeting hall and television station. His critics complain that on the one hand, he smiles too much, a smile, they say, that is too impishly undignified for a man in his position. On the other hand, they think his serious expression is too much like a scowl, which suggests, they maintain, an unsympathetic heart.

In the past, whatever the people thought of their leaders, they obeyed them because they represented the Emperor. Since the war, with the Emperor reduced in status, the tendency to obey authority has been more of an inbred, instinctive nature. Most people, as Kazuo Hirohashi, the disgruntled college student, said, continue to vote for those they have voted for in the past, feeling a strange sense of obligation toward them, particularly if the candidate is running in his native province, as is usually the case. Thus the old and uniquely Japanese contradiction: the distrust of authority, yet the compulsion to maintain and obey it. Even in the privacy of the voting booth, which represents the political formalization of the severance of his bonds with the past, the Japanese citizen does not yet thoroughly comprehend the freedom he has been given.

Kishi, in trying to win the affection of his people, has faced not only the barrier of traditional attitudes, but of the Japanese press, which has criticized him unmercifully, and with very little justification. Such criticism might be understandable if it appeared in the opposition press. But most newspapers are conservatively inclined and support the Liberal-Democratic Party. Yet, however successful Kishi has been in carrying out its policies, the newspapers have always discovered some supposed flaw in his action, and then concentrated on this flaw, completely ignoring the positive aspects of his accomplishments.

Kishi has been condemned in the press even for such a minor thing as using the government-owned Chrysler that comes with his office rather than his own Japanese Toyopet Crown Deluxe when he goes for a weekend drive. When Kishi's secretary explained that the Prime Minister had used the American car on a particular trip because he feared the bad roads would ruin the Toyopet, the *Asahi Shimbun* scowled, "Hasn't this resulted in Mr. Kishi giving domestically-produced cars a bad name by intimating they cannot stand wear and tear?" Added the *Mainichi Shimbun*, "Just like rural theaters which show one Japanese film and one imported feature, it looks as though Mr. Kishi will use a

Japanese car for sunny days and a foreign one for rainy days. We hope this will not mean the much-publicized domestic car will become covered with dust in the garage."

When Kishi was quoted by a reporter in Honolulu, while on his way to Washington to sign the Security Treaty, as saying that the Japanese press is "unreliable," and that "I only read the sports pages," the press throughout Japan had a field day. "Could it be," asked the *Asahi Shimbun,* "that Mr. Kishi has become tired of Japan?" (Privately, many reporters admitted that Kishi's complaint was not altogether invalid.)

Probably the main reason for the extreme cynicism of the Japanese press is its distorted conviction that a free press must exercise its freedom by attacking, almost never praising, authority. It isn't the job of a democratic newspaper, the editors and publishers feel, to look at the good side of government. That smacks too much of the days when they were given handouts by the militarists and told to print them. The concept of editorial objectivity that is supposed to be the hallmark of a good newspaper in the West is simply not yet understood in Japan.

The press attacked Kishi with unprecedented bitterness when he pushed ratification of the new Security Treaty through the House of Representatives. The Premier had brought the pact up for an unexpected midnight vote, and, when the Socialists tried to prevent it from taking place by force, had called in five hundred policemen to remove them from the legislative chamber. Then, with only the majority Liberal-Democrats in attendance, the treaty was approved. There may be some weight behind the charge that Kishi ignored the spirit, if not the letter, of parliamentary rule with this maneuver, and perhaps unnecessarily generated the ill-feeling that led to mob violence.

Still, Kishi had permitted discussion of the pact for over two months, and every point had been gone over. The time had come, he felt, for a decision; either the leftist minority would be permitted to obstruct ratification indefinitely and thereby frustrate democratic processes, or the conservatives would use its legally held power to act. Kishi, not realizing that the issue could affect Eisenhower's visit, chose the latter course.

Kishi was taken to task by the newspapers with only slightly less enthusiasm in the autumn of 1958 when he tried to push a bill through the Diet that would strengthen the Police Duties Enforcement Law. But in this case, there was greater justification for criticism.

The revisions proposed in the controversial bill were of a moderate character. Under the present law, the Japanese police are among the most helpless in the world. Officers cannot make a person surrender a concealed weapon even when there is sufficient ground to suspect that he carries it for unlawful purposes. They can search an individual only after arrest. They cannot tamper with "human rights" (whether it is the "right" of a man on a subway to annoy the girl next to him, or the "right" of a drunkard to lie on the sidewalk) until the "life, person, or property" of somebody is clearly endangered. They cannot prevent an armed clash between two gangs until the moment when "a crime is about to be committed." Most important of all, they cannot break up mobs, even if violence appears inevitable, threatening democratic rule.

Although the police in most countries have the power to control such situations, the suggestion that the same power be given the Japanese police force drew gasps of horror from the people, who remembered only too well the wartime efficiency of the *Kempei Tai*. These fears were exhaustively exploited by the leftists, who saw the proposed new police measures as aimed primarily at preventing anti-government demonstrations. *Sohyo,* declaring that the police bill was "pregnant with political intrigue and horrifying schemes for suppression of the people," called a series of strikes and demonstrations. The Socialists threatened mass resignation from the Diet. Chairman Asanuma, then Secretary-General, was even heard exclaiming, "There is no other way to gain the reins of government but through violent revolution." Finally, when Kishi tried to get the Diet session extended to give the Liberal-Democrats time to push through the bill, the Socialists decided to use force to prevent such an extension. They blockaded the entrance to the Speaker's room, the Steering Committee room, and the House chamber, while another Socialist detachment occupied the rostrum area inside the chamber. But the Liberal-Democrats finally forced their way into the chamber, and the Vice-Speaker, gathering what remained of his dignity, declared the Diet session extended for thirty days.

Kishi eventually accepted a "compromise," agreeing to shelve the police bill for Socialist recognition of the validity of the extended session. But since the only purpose of the extension was to permit passage of the bill, Kishi in reality suffered a severe defeat and loss of "face." To no small extent, he was personally responsible. Sensing in advance that the bill would cause trouble, Kishi gave no prior notice in the Diet, or even to his own party, that he intended to introduce it, apparently hoping that it would be steam-rollered through the Diet before important opposition could develop. His party had no opportunity to explain the bill to the people and allay their fears before it was presented. Then, when many of his conservative colleagues, worried by this tactless handling of a delicate issue, tried to persuade Kishi to compromise or to withdraw the bill altogether, the Prime Minister, with the stubbornness of his Choshu ancestors, staunchly insisted that it be pushed through.

Democracy in Japan is handicapped by factors far more profound than clumsy and high-handed parliamentary procedure. One is the traditionally close relationship between government and business, which is openly permitted to help determine official economic policy. By Japanese standards, this relationship is considered a natural one. Industry contributes to the Liberal-Democratic Party political fund through a special collection organ called the Keizai Saiken Kondankai. It also makes private donations to the individual politicians, presumably for use in political campaigns. Without such support and influence behind him, it is difficult for a politician to attain any high public office or stay there. On the other hand, it is equally difficult for him to ignore *giri* to his benefactors.

Some politicians are more able to profit from such relationships than others. For example, Ichiro Kono, it is said, has a knack for extracting contributions from businessmen who don't even support him. According to Miss Kaji Onose, a political expert for the *Yomiuri Japan News,* Kono's trick is known as *wait a minute.* "If a private railway company," Miss Onose writes, "files a request with the government for a transportation fare hike, for example, he will invariably oppose it at the beginning. This opposition has nothing to do with his stand on the issue, but is meant as a hint that if the company wants Kono to drop his opposition, it should bring money to Kono. Whether or not this is true, Kono has opposed many such requests in the past and then later dropped his opposition for reasons of his own."

As for Kishi, no one has ever accused him of lacking business supporters. They can be divided, it is believed, into four main categories:

1. Businessmen whom he had known in pre-war days when he was in the Ministry of Commerce and Industry, such as Shinichi Kojima, president of the Yawata Iron Manufacturing Company, and Shinzo Okuda, president of the Ube Soda Company.

2. Foreign Minister Fujiyama and those connected with him, including Shigeo Mizuno, president of the Fuji Iron Manufacturing Company, Tadashi Adachi, president of the Radio Tokyo Company, Eiichiro Iwase, president of the Mitsukoshi Department Store, and Takeo Shoji, president of the Asahi Denka Kogyo Company.

3. Friends from his native Yamaguchi Prefecture, like Michisuke Sugi, president of the Osaka Chamber of Commerce and Industry and

JETRO, and Yoshihiko Sasaki, president of the Toho Rayon Company.

4. Classmates at the Tokyo First High School and Tokyo University, such as Kogoro Uemura, manager of the Keizai Saiken Kondankai, the industrial fund raising organization.

Other important business followers of Kishi include Yasutaro Niizeki, president of the Mitsui Trading Company, Katsujiro Takagaki, president of the Mitsubishi Shoji Company, Kensuke Matano, president of the Iino Shipping Company, Heigo Fujii, executive director of the Yawate Iron Manufacturing Company, Yoshinari Kawai, president of the Komatsu Works, and Gisuke Aikawa, Kishi's associate in pre-war Manchuria.

However, Professor Hirotatsu Fujiwara, a political and economic expert at Tokyo's Meiji University, wrote in the magazine *Chuo Koron* that "those who are supporting Kishi wholeheartedly seem surprisingly few. At the same time he apparently has the support of some financial circles because he is not mean about money." A poll conducted among 238 top business executives by the industrial journal *Nikkan Kogyo* to determine industry's choice for Prime Minister, gave Kishi only five votes, indicating that big business is not entirely satisfied that he has favored it to the "proper" extent.

Kishi's tax report offers no suggestion that he is a rich man. Paying $1555 in taxes, he reported his 1958 income as $6000—$3375 in salary as a member of the Diet, $1719 in personal allowances as the Prime Minister, and $906 from private business investments. He also drew funds, of course, for official purposes, including entertainment. But with the Socialists ready to spring on him at the least hint of corruption, Kishi cannot be too careful about the propriety of his financial dealings. The Socialists have accused him of engaging in questionable transactions a number of times, although their accusations have always been either disproved or unsubstantiated.

When Kishi was still Secretary-General of the Liberal-Democratic Party, they charged that he permitted the Fatherland Protection Youth Corps to extort $2800 from him following a brawl between Liberal-Democrats and members of this ultra-rightist group. A police investigation revealed no substance to the report.

During one of Kishi's trips to Southeast Asia in 1957, his political enemies pounced on a wire service report that he had spent $11,000 on jewels in Singapore, which, if true, meant that the Prime Minister had violated the Foreign Exchange Control Law. "Because of the question of political morality involved," shrilled a columnist in the *Asahi Shimbun,* "it could very well mean the fall of the Kishi Cabinet." As it turned out, Kishi had spent not $11,000, but $111, well within the amount allowed by law.

Early in 1959 Kishi was accused of building a villa in the resort town of Atami with means provided by companies that hoped to be awarded profitable government contracts. A Japanese trading company, Kino-shita Shotan, which was granted reparations contracts for nine of ten ships being given to Indonesia and twelve ships going to the Philippines, gave Kishi $28,000 to build the villa, the Socialists charged. They further maintained that it was no coincidence that the land on which the house was built had belonged to another trading firm, C. Itoh and Company, which had close business connections with the Grumman Aircraft Company, maker of the Super Tiger jet fighter. Kishi, it was pointed out, had purchased the land very cheaply at a time when the Japanese firm was plugging for the adoption of the Super Tiger as the new jet fighter for the Air Self-Defense Force. But the Socialists could not disprove Kishi's contention that he had built the villa with a bank loan. Moreover, the Super Tiger was rejected as the ASDF jet fighter.

Kishi (and most other male politicians) has been attacked (mostly by women politicians) on another score as well—for conducting what is known as *machiai* politics. *Machiai* literally means "house of assignation," and in the modern sense signifies "geisha house." When Prince Ito was Prime Minister during Kishi's childhood days, he wrote a poem, while lounging amidst his geisha girl friends:

When intoxicated, I use my beauty's knees for a pillow. Becoming sober, I control the power of the country.

Ito's poem has provided an inspiration for Japanese leaders that has survived shifts in political ideology, changes in social custom, and wars. Today, some of Japan's most important political and economic questions are still discussed while the delicate notes of the *samisen,* the sweet potency of sake and the shy smile of the geisha ease the way toward vital decisions. Kishi's Liberal-Democratic Party is estimated unofficially to spend up to six million dollars a year on such entertainment. This amount rises astronomically when parties thrown by various political factions and individual politicians are included.

Shocked by such figures, Miss Taki Fujita, president of the Japan Woman Voters' Federation and former delegate to the United Nations, recently declared that the practice of *machiai* politics is "outrageous" and a throwback to feudal times. The politicians are only looking, she maintained, for an alcoholic atmosphere to help them understand the hidden nuances in each other's character. Miss Fusae Ichikawa, a member of the House of Councilors, sharply criticized Kishi's frequent attendance at such parties and urged the Prime Minister to "take the initiative in a new life movement."

Kishi, who loves geisha parties, replied, "I don't think *machiai* politics are good. But as the Japanese are used to sitting on *tatami* rather than chairs, we can talk more smoothly in this way and can come to agreement much easier. The situation should be corrected in the future." Whereupon Kishi departed for his favorite geisha restaurant, the *Hasegawa,* or River in the Long Valley, in the exclusive entertainment district of Akasaka. Kishi is believed to have given considerable impetus to the rebuilding of Akasaka as Japan's "parliamentary row."

Machiai politics, with its emphasis on secrecy and back-room "deals," reflects one of the most important barriers to the growth of parliamentary democracy in Japan—factionalism. All Japanese political groups are afflicted by this disease, though the factionalism which exists in the Socialist Party is far more justified than that which plagues Kishi's Liberal-Democratic Party. The Socialists are divided mainly along ideological lines, with members joining groups that support their ideas. The conservatives are divided mostly on the basis of personalities. They do not differ greatly from each other, if at all, in their political thinking.

Kishi recently said:

"It is a matter of regret to me that there are many occasions when the outstanding abilities of the Japanese people go to waste because of their impetuosity. Perhaps I should say that factionalism in political parties is the worst example of such waste and a major difficulty on the path toward democracy."

Yet Kishi, though he may deplore factionalism, has mastered the political game of playing off various factions against each other, while making himself acceptable to all. Many conservative politicians have wanted to replace him during his several years in office, but he proved to have had enough general support, if lukewarm in some cases, to rule the party and the nation. Most may have an important influence in a few factions, but are intolerable to the members of most.

But if Kishi is a clever politician, he is not an unprincipled one. He will not hesitate to enter into complicated political alliances, or switch political allies and even policies of minor import when necessary, if such maneuvering will further an essential goal. But he will not modify this goal in the least degree, as his career so amply confirms, however much this rigidity might threaten his own interests. As Kishi himself explains his attitude toward politics, "The road to the mountain is obscured by many foothills. Some of these must be climbed, some must be gone around, and a good road must be built as the advance proceeds. In some places there will be shortcuts, but in general the going will be rough."

A good example of Kishi's political methods involved Ichiro Kono, also a clever politician, but one who sometimes tends to switch mountains rather than roads. Kishi was quite willing to accept Kono's support when he was struggling to become Prime Minister. At that time, his worst political enemy among the Liberal-Democratic leaders was Hayato Ikeda, an ardent follower of former Prime Minister Yoshida. Ikeda had not yet forgiven Kishi for the role he had played in ousting Yoshida from office, and on several occasions in the early days of Kishi's rule, such as during the police bill debate, he did his best to precipitate the Prime Minister's fall.

Meanwhile, Kono, suspecting that Kishi would not last long, tried to work his way into the post of party Secretary-General, from which he could easily swing into the premiership when Kishi resigned. Kishi appreciated Kono's help in getting him to the top, but had no intention of stepping down or of being replaced at an early date. And in any case, it was clear to him that Kono was by no means the kind of person to be charged with guarding Japan's vital interests. Therefore, he appointed Ikeda, a bitter opponent of Kono, as Minister of International Trade and Industry, knowing that this would force Kono to withdraw from his camp. Kono angrily did so, and Ikeda eventually became Premier.

Kishi can proudly bask in the knowledge that he led a government which, imperfect as it was, set its course along the path of democracy. Despite the shrillness of leftist tantrums and the echo of rightist drums, despite the confusion and uncertainty of the younger generation, despite the errors made by leaders just learning the essentials of democratic rule, Japan is likely to maintain a basically democratic course. True, the Japanese spirit is hungering for strong, idealistic nourishment, but until the people can stabilize their new way of life and develop fresh ideals, this spirit is adjustable enough to sustain itself on the remnants of tradition, and even on cold materialism.

A bad depression might prod the Japanese people to change course, and the possibility of a revolt engineered by a leftist minority cannot be dismissed. But barring such disasters, there does not appear to be much likelihood of an important switch in the foreseeable future. The attraction of ultra-rightism and militarism vanished in the horrifying glow of the atomic bomb. It probably could not be revived on a broad national scale. And while ultra-leftism represents a far greater threat, there are also powerful counter-forces resisting this extreme philosophy. One such force is the natural conservative tendency of the Japanese people. Many observers in Japan are seriously concerned lest Japan's traditional culture and way of life be completely replaced by foreign innovations. They fear the electric dishwasher will turn the Japanese into incurable materialists. They fear that foreign movies will spell the death of Kabuki. And they fear no less strongly that Marxist values will wipe out what remains of traditional family ties and supersede such spiritual pleasures as the tea ceremony and a walk in the garden.

But Japanese history points to a different result. Japan in the past imported Chinese culture, and later, many aspects of Western culture, on a vast scale. And in those periods, too, there was confusion, uncertainty, and concern that the character of Japan would be irrevocably altered. Instead of absorbing Japan, however, these foreign influences were absorbed by Japan, to be shaped, pruned, and fitted to meet Japanese requirements. Today, Japan may appear to be drowning in a sea of Western culture, including elements borrowed from both the free and the communist worlds. But in the years to come, there is likely to remain only a hard core residue of what was originally imported, appropriately modified in form and use.

The potential influence of both Marxism and of Western style democracy upon Japan is therefore likely to be limited. Democracy, however, will probably enjoy greater success, for being more flexible, it can more easily be adapted to Japanese tradition. Elements of Marxism may be fitted into the Japanese cultural scheme, but the basic ideology would probably not be accepted except perhaps under extraordinary pressures. It would be especially difficult making Marxism compatible with the principle of *giri*, which, even with its edge filed down, remains a potent social force in Japan today. A worker may favor the theory of eliminating capitalist "exploitation," but he still feels an intense sense of responsibility to his paternalistically inclined employer. A young man may urinate against the door of the Diet, but he probably would not marry a girl who did not have the approval of his parents. Youth is only one stage in the life of men, so that, as Kazuo Hirohashi, the student, pointed out, when schooldays are over, the adventure of radicalism usually dissolves in the bitter, yet soothing, solution of traditional Japanese life, though in many cases the effects of this adventure could prove dangerously durable.

At the same time, rising living standards have produced a materialistic attitude, consistent with Japan's "practical philosophy," that is likely to have an important stabilizing effect on the Japanese. Workers and farmers, suddenly in a position to buy new houses, television sets, washing machines, and other symbols of a wealth they had never dreamed could be theirs, find themselves with an exciting new purpose in life. The acquisition of material goods is far more exciting for the Japanese than it is for most Americans. A washing machine to an ex-tenant farmer's wife is a more precious thing than a new Buick, exchanged for last year's Chevrolet, is to her American counterpart. Needless to say, the attraction of leftism to the Japanese is weakened with the sale of every electric appliance. As one *Zengakuren* leader told me with splendid candor, "The main reason why we haven't the popular support we should have is that Kishi and his friends are bribing the people with all kinds of luxuries. For a television set or a refrigerator they are willing to remain capitalist slaves."

The question of Japan's future ideological orientation is really less pertinent at this time than that of its future foreign policy. For, with pacifism cutting across ideological lines, even some non-Marxists are wary of the Mutual Defense Treaty and Japan's commitments in the cold war. The United States must face the possibility that sooner or later a government will come to power that will tend toward neutralism. If this government should be led by the Socialist Party, neutralism could eventually lead to absorption of the nation into the communist bloc. If it should be directed by the new, more moderate Democratic Socialist Party, a "pro-Western" type of neutralism, perhaps similar to that of Sweden, might result. In either case, the United States would probably have to evacuate its bases in Japan, though the bitterly anti-communist Democratic Socialists, at least, would undoubtedly maintain other close ties with the West, and even a Socialist Party suddenly saddled with responsibility might see the wisdom of such ties.

Actually, no matter who is in power, Japan's economic relations with the United States are likely to constitute an important, if not a decisive, factor in determining the future Japanese attitude toward this country. As the Japanese proved after the defeats of Shimonoseki and World War II, they can be a realistic and flexible people. If close links with the United

States do not lead Japan toward prosperity and well-being, it is conceivable that the nation will switch to another path.

To keep them on the present path, the United States must help them make a success of their long-range economic plans, not, as in the case of many of America's underdeveloped friends, with monetary grants, but simply by promoting the expansion of the country's opportunities for export. We can, for example, invest more in such ventures as the Rourkela iron ore project in India, which will mean increased Japanese trade with that country. Nor should the United States ignore Kishi's proposals for more unified efforts to exploit Asian resources with Japanese know-how and American financing, which will become more feasible as Japan's neighbors learn to trust that once aggressive nation.

But America can play an even more direct role in bolstering Japan's economy. It can assure the nation a continuing and increasing American market for its products. Although Japan is already dependent on the United States for about one-third of its trade, this degree of dependency may increase in the near future and remain at a very high level at least until such time—and this will be many years away—as Southeast Asia develops a major consumers' market.

At present, despite recent Tokyo demonstrations, United States-Japan relations are good. But certain areas of friction exist, which, if they spread, could mean serious trouble. While American purchases from Japan are by no means meager, the Japanese have had to place "voluntary" export restrictions on a number of staple items in order to stave off efforts by American manufacturers to get the United States government to clap official quotas on these goods. Thus, Japan is restricting exports to the United States of cotton textiles, plywood, tuna, silk, umbrellas and umbrella frames, and stainless steel flatware. Voluntary quotas will also soon be placed on ready-made suits, and pressure is increasing in the United States for the limitation of transistor radios and other items.

The extent to which such restrictions can hurt industries producing these goods is mirrored in the fact that cotton textiles represent 40 per cent of Japan's exports, with most of this going to the United States, and that about 90 per cent of Japan's stainless steel flatware and 60 per cent of its transistor radios are sold to this country. The Japanese are worried. And they are not appreciative of the advice they receive from the United States government to refrain from "unfair" trade practices in disposing of many of their goods while this same government submits to the pressure of American "protectionist" businessmen to keep legitimately priced items out of the American market. Moreover, the Japanese point to the lack of ethics exhibited by some American businessmen in trying to give Japanese goods a bad reputation. They cite, for example, a case wherein American toy manufacturers spread a false rumor that the paint on Japanese toys was "poisonous," which severely hurt Japanese toy sales in the United States. They are particularly annoyed in view of the fact that, after Canada, Japan is America's best customer.

In contrast to America's relations with many European nations, there are few cultural or traditional ties between the Japanese and American peoples that could be depended upon to compensate for a deterioration of economic relations between the two countries. The Japanese, while absorbing many aspects of American culture, do not, in many cases, feel comfortable enjoying them in the company of Americans. Americans are rarely invited into Japanese homes, and even many clubs and bars will not permit them to enter. At the same time, any Japanese girl, however excellent her reputation, seriously risks soiling it by "dating" an American, or, for that matter, marrying him. Even prostitutes are expected to be discriminating in the dispensation of their favors. Those who serve Americans are often boycotted by the Japanese.

Some of the factors behind this aloofness may lend support to the conclusion that it is only a surface attitude. The Japanese are traditionally reluctant to violate the sanctity of the home by entertaining strangers, including fellow Japanese. Many also feel an odd sense of humility, even humiliation, about the simplicity of the traditional-style house, and do not wish to submit foreigners to such "discomforts" as the absence of chairs or a Western-type lavatory. They are as amazed as they are delighted when a Westerner expresses admiration for things Japanese, another strange contradiction in the character of the people, who only recently considered themselves the descendants of gods. Many proprietors of clubs and bars feel that the language problem and differences in customs will simply create friction if foreigners are welcomed. A Japanese guest at a club, for example, will sit with several hostesses simultaneously, as in a geisha house, and will not insult the waiter by asking for an itemized bill, while the American prefers one girl and a detailed account of the costs.

But the reserved Japanese attitude toward foreigners, and Americans in particular, reaches deeper than these explanations would indicate. The Japanese, in general, retain a friendly feeling toward Americans. But they are still too insulated in their own tight little world, held together by *giri* and traditional communal ties, to permit relaxed relations with people of such different racial and cultural origin. They do not know

how to cope with persons who are ignorant of the rules of Japanese society. Many Japanese, influenced by the G.I.'s who had occupied their
country, have the impression that most Americans lack refinement or
sensitivity. Japanese shops catering mainly to American soldiers and
tourists usually display only the gaudiest, most tasteless items in their
windows, such as cheap geisha dolls or a Westernized kimono with a
picture of Mount Fuji on the back. The arrival of a visiting American
symphony or art exhibit always surprises the Japanese, though, paradoxically, even the worst American cultural contributions inevitably
draw more people than can be accommodated.

Even more curiously, the Japanese are ready to borrow from the
American the externals of his strange culture (including the cheap cow-
boy films and rock-and-roll that he derides as representative of American cultural values) to be fitted into their own traditional ethos and way
of life. But that is quite different from inviting the American to explore
the intimacy of this way of life. The adoption by the Japanese of American customs, habits, mores, and morals by no means signifies, at least
up to now, anything resembling a spiritual communion between the
two peoples. And this lack of a deeper rapport would make it much
easier for Japan to break away from the United States if ever the economic conditions should arise that would favor such an eventuality.

The warm relations that today link the two nations are thus clearly
a matter of mutual self-interest, with little or no sentiment involved,
though the Japanese may feel a certain gratitude for the dignified way in
which the American conqueror treated them after the war. Kishi and
most of his people are no more pro-American than they are anti-Chinese.
They are simply pro-Japanese, and will shape their foreign policies accordingly—a fact that Americans, who often tend to take Japan for
granted, should not forget.

Still, there is no small possibility that one day Japan and the United
States will find common ground in tradition as well as in self-interest.
"The Japanese people can face the future with supreme confidence,"
Kishi recently stated. "For Japan, by treating its neighbors with a feeling
of love and respect, shall make the flowers of democracy bloom, and
thus shall it contribute to world peace. I say without any hesitation whatsoever that Japan shall live up to the expectations of the world."

BIBLIOGRAPHY

Benedict, Ruth, *The Chrysanthemum and the Sword,* Houghton, Mifflin, Boston, 1946

Bisson, Thomas Arthur, *Japan in China,* Macmillan, New York, 1938
　　Japan's War Economy, Macmillan, New York, 1945
　　Prospects for Democracy in Japan, Macmillan, New York, 1949

Borton, Hugh, *Japan's Modern Century,* Ronald, New York, 1955

Brines, Russell, *MacArthur's Japan,* Lippincott, Philadelphia, 1948

Brown, D. M., *Nationalism in Japan,* University of California Press, Berkeley, 1955

Cohen, J. B., *Japan's Economy in War and Reconstruction,* University of Minnesota Press, Minneapolis, 1949

Costello, William, *Democracy vs Feudalism in Post-War Japan,* Itagaki Shoten, Tokyo, 1948

Falk, Edwin Albert, *From Perry to Pearl Harbor,* Doubleday, Doran, Garden City, N.Y., 1943

Gayn, Mark J., *Japan Diary,* Sloane, New York, 1948

Gibney, Frank, *Five Gentlemen of Japan,* Farrar, Straus & Young, New York, 1953

Grew, Joseph Clark, *Ten Years in Japan,* Simon & Schuster, New York, 1944

Gubbins, J. H., *The Making of Modern Japan,* Seeley, Service, London, 1922

Hearn, Lafcadio, *Japan,* Macmillan, New York, 1917

Ike, Nobutaka, *Beginnings of Political Democracy in Japan,* Johns Hopkins Press, Baltimore, 1950

International Military Tribunal for the Far East, *Record,* Tokyo, 1946-48

Jones, Francis Clifford, *Japan's New Order in East Asia,* Oxford University Press, London, 1954
　　Manchuria Since 1931, Royal Institute of International Affairs, London, 1949

Kase, Toshikazu, *Journey to the Missouri,* Yale University Press, New Haven, 1950

Kelley, Frank R., and Ryan, Cornelius, *Star-Spangled Mikado,* McBride, New York, 1947

Kodama, Yoshio, *I Was Defeated,* Tuttle, Tokyo, 1951

Latourette, Kenneth Scott, *History of Japan,* Macmillan, New York, 1957

Matsuoka, Yosuke, *Building Up Manchuria,* The Herald of Asia, Tokyo, 1938

Murdoch, James, *History of Japan,* Paul, Trench, Trubner, London, 1925-26

Newman, Joseph, *Goodbye, Japan,* Fischer, New York, 1942

Reischauer, Edwin Oldfather, *Japan, Past and Present,* Knopf, New York, 1946

    The United States and Japan, Harvard University Press, Cambridge, 1957

Roth, Andrew, *Dilemma in Japan,* Little, Brown, Boston, 1945

Russell, Lord Edward, *The Knights of Bushido,* Cassell, London, 1958

Russell, Oland D., *The House of Mitsui,* Little, Brown, Boston, 1939

Sansom, Bailey, Sir George, *A History of Japan,* Stanford University Press, Palo Alto, 1958

Scalapino, R. A., *Democracy and the Party Movement in Pre-War Japan,* University of California Press, Berkeley, 1953

Shigemitsu, Mamoru, *Japan and Her Destiny; My Struggle for Peace,* Hutchinson, London, 1958

Togo, Shigenori, *The Cause of Japan,* Simon & Schuster, New York, 1956

Tolischus, Otto David, *Tokyo Record,* Reynal & Hitchcock, New York, 1943

Yanaga, Chitoshi, *Japan Since Perry,* McGraw-Hill, New York, 1949

INDEX

Abe, General Nobuyuki, 194, 197, 199-200
Abe, Shintaro, 10
Abe, Yoko (Mrs. Shintaro), 10, 110, 158, 233-234
Adenauer, Konrad, 272-273
Aikawa, Gisuke, 133-134, 137, 139, 142, 246, 276
Aishinkakura, Princess Eisei, 336
Akao, Bin, 347
Akihito, Crown Prince, 18, 20, 344, 349
Akimoto, Takeshi, 255, 258
All Japan Federation of Student Autonomy Councils (*Zengakuren*), 353-356, 358, 384
All Japan Trade Union Congress (*Zenro*), 362-364
Arima, Eiji, 258, 269
Asanuma, Inejiro, 370
Ashida, Hitoshi, 280
Ayabe, Kentaro, 258

Bagge, Widor, 205, 214
Bulganin, Nikolai, 293

Ching-wei, Wang, 147
Choshu clan, history of the, 32-39
Churchill, Winston, 179
Communist Party in Japan, founding of the, 103; postwar operations of, 259, 286, 349-352, 356-363

Dulles, John Foster, 288, 326

Eisenhower, Dwight D., 326, 327, 349, 353, 376

Farmers, postwar gains of Japanese, 307-312
Fillmore, Millard, 34
First World War, 87-88
Fujita, Miss Taki, 380
Fujiwara, Ginjiro, 184-186
Fujiwara, Hirotatsu, 379
Fujiyama, Aiichiro, 193-194, 199, 232, 256, 257, 265, 274, 315, 323-324, 347
Fuke, Toshikazu, 269

giri, definition of, 14-16; examples of, 32, 56, 58, 75, 105, 263, 275-276, 323, 356
Goering, Hermann, 229-230
Goto, Keita, 194
Great Reform (*Taika*), the, 26-27
Greater East Asia Co-Prosperity Sphere, 151-152, 157, 318-319
Grew, Joseph C., 263

Hagerty, James, 349
Halsey, Admiral William, 207
Hamada, Naotake, 269
Hamaguchi, Prime Minister, 113, 115
Hara, Takashi, 103

391

About the Author

Dan Kurzman has been a foreign correspondent for fifteen years. During that time, he has written or broadcast from almost every major country in Europe, the Middle East, Africa, and Asia.

His first assignment was as correspondent for the Paris Bureau of INS, and he later became Feature Editor of the Marshall Plan Information Division in Paris. From 1950 to 1952 he served as Middle East correspondent for NBC, covering such events as the assassination of Jordan's King Abdullah, the Iranian oil crisis, the Black Saturday anti-British riots in Cairo, the first nationalist riots in Tunis and the Arab-Israeli border disputes. In 1953 he made a year-long, village-to-village tour of North Africa, the Middle East, and Asia—from Casablanca to Tokyo. His articles appeared in several major newspapers and magazines.

In 1954 Mr. Kurzman returned to Tokyo as Far East Bureau Chief of the McGraw-Hill World News Service. In 1958 he visited Russia, entering that country by an unusual route—from Kabul, Afghanistan, across the Hindukush Mountains to Tashkent. Later in 1958 he went back to the Middle East to cover the landing of American Marines in Beirut, Lebanon, for the *Washington Post* and the American Broadcasting Company.

Early in 1959, Mr. Kurzman returned to the United States and began work on *Kishi and Japan*. He went back to Japan later in the year to complete the book and write a series of articles for the Scripps-Howard Newspaper Alliance.

Mr. Kurzman was born in San Francisco and graduated from the University of California. During the Second World War he learned Russian at the University of Pittsburgh under army supervision and served as a combat infantryman in General Patton's Third Army. After the war, he studied at the Sorbonne in Paris, where he received a diploma in French Civilization.